THE 101
MOST ASKED QUESTIONS
ABOUT
LAS VEGAS & CASINO GAMBLING

George Joseph

LAS VEGAS

ATIYEH PUBLISHING GROUP

FIRST EDITION 1996
SECOND EDITION 1999
THIRD EDITION 2001
FOURTH EDITION 2002

Cover photos: George Joseph
Cover, text design and production: Zee Designs (702) 795-7300 • www.zeedesigns.com
Printed in the United States of America

Library of Congress Cataloging-in-Publication Data

Joseph, George
    The 101 Most Asked Questions About Las Vegas & Casino Gambling / George Joseph.
        p.cm.

ISBN 0-9660017-0-2

HQ734.G727 1992
646.7'8—dc20
91-58370
CIP

Dedications

To my Dad, who taught me to look beneath the surface and ask the tough questions.

To my Mother, who used to beat us with a bamboo stick wrapped with barbed wire if we asked the wrong questions (just kidding, Ma).

To my wife, Candice, whose love is unquestioned.

Special dedication to the lovely LuAnn Jalet and the even lovelier Jim Jalet. Jim is my best friend and took absolutely no part in the writing, preparation or production of this book.

Contents

Introduction

I got the idea for this book after talking to casino employees on every level of the gambling business. A common thread seemed to exist when we spoke of casino customers and the questions they asked. Very simply, everyone wants to know everything about Las Vegas.

I travel extensively throughout the gaming world and many of the questions in this book came from airplane passengers I sat next to. If you told someone on an airplane that you were a plumber, they wouldn't say, "Great! I've always wanted to know how to sweat fit two pipes together." But when you say you're in the gambling business and live in Las Vegas, everyone wants to know everything about Las Vegas.

Some of the questions were absurd. "Do you live in Las Vegas?" "What time is the midnight show?" Most of the questions customers asked had to do with how to gamble at the table games and slots: "What are the best and worst bets?" "Can slot machines be set against you?" "What is the best way to play blackjack?" And so on. A lot of questions had to do with Las Vegas secrets: "Does the mob control gambling in Las Vegas?" "Do casinos cheat players?" "Is prostitution legal in Las Vegas?" "Do cheaters get beat up by casinos?"

Having lived in Las Vegas for 25 years, many of the questions seemed pretty silly. Thinking back, I have to admit, that I asked many of the same questions when I first moved to Las Vegas...even the dumb ones. So over the course of six to eight months, I compiled *The 101 Most Asked Questions About Las Vegas & Casino Gambling*. Because of my background in cheating at games and lecturing on game protection, I also included many of the mathematical proofs relating to gambling games, betting methods and slot machines.

This book offers a lot of information about gambling, Las Vegas and the casino business. This book offers some insight into the way Las Vegas was in the "old days." If nothing else, this book offers me $14.95.

Special thanks to...

Charlie Lombardo, V.P. Slot Operations, Bally's Las Vegas
John Avello, Race & Sports Book, Bally's Las Vegas
Vince Vitangeli, Surveillance Manager, Bally's Las Vegas
Eddie Brown, Surveillance Operator, Bally's Las Vegas
John O'Farrell, Surveillance Operator, Bally's Las Vegas
Kim Flowers, Dancer and Showgirl, Jubilee Show, Bally's
Jim Evans, Surveillance Operator & Friend
John Louis, Brother-in-law, Joe Louis's Son, Good Guy
Shonna "the woman in red" cover girl. Pretty, huh?!
Dennis Atiyeh, Cousin (Spheen) and Friend
Diane Palm, Asst. Company Manager Jubilee Show
John Thompson, "The Great Tomsoni"
John Thompson, Jr.
Vic Taucer, Owner, Casino Creations, Las Vegas
Doyle Davis, Owner, Capado Gaming, Las Vegas
Special thanks to...
Zee Marie and Max Moss at Zee Designs whose commitment to this project along with their exceptional artistic talent has propelled the third edition of this book light years ahead of the first.

About the Author

George Joseph began the study of magic and sleight of hand at the age of seven in Detroit, prompted by his father and other family members. At the age of thirteen, George met an old vaudeville magician (and ex-grifter) who began teaching him the methods of card and dice cheaters. After many years of ardent practice and self denial, and a few close calls with local police gambling raids, George moved to Las Vegas in the mid 1970's and embarked upon a career as an entertainer and in the casino business.

Over the years, he was the resident close-up magician at the Aladdin, Dunes and Tropicana Hotels and also sang in lounges around Las Vegas during the time when the Mob controlled many of the casinos. George offers some fascinating and interesting observations about those years.

Because of his background in gambling and cheating methods, George became very active in the surveillance of casino games. He is court qualified as the casino industry's leading expert in surveillance and casino cheating. He has testified and demonstrated cheating methods in many of the major casino cheating cases throughout the world. George regularly lectures and consults to police agencies and gaming regulators around the gaming world. George was until recently the Executive Director of Surveillance for the Paris and Bally casinos and now owns and operates Worldwide Casino Consulting.

George has been seen recently on several national television spots including Dateline NBC, *The Secrets of Las Vegas*, *Cheating Las Vegas*, *Cracking the Con* on The Learning Channel, *Watch Your Pockets on MSNBC*, Fox TV's America's Most Wanted and the A&E four-hour documentary on the history of Las Vegas named *The Gamble in the Desert* and *The House of Cards*.

$$\boxed{1}$$

What is the most money ever won or lost in a casino?

When I first moved to Las Vegas in the mid 1970's, the table limit at most Baccarat games in town was between $2,000.00 and $10,000 per hand. Considering that on average 72 hands are dealt from each shoe, a large sum could be won or lost very quickly. This was well before the Mexican peso was devalued, so many of the biggest customers in Las Vegas were from South America and/or Mexico. I watched an Argentine businessman lose six million dollars in one night of play. (To put it in perspective, I was waiting for my next paycheck so I could take down the sheets over my bedroom windows and put up blinds.) With the devaluation of the peso in the early 1980's, the customer base for big baccarat play shifted from the South Americans and Mexicans to the Asians.

Probably the craziest run of luck, both good and bad, occurred in the spring of 1996 at the Treasure Island Casino. As the story goes, a homeless guy cashes a $400.00 social security check at the casino. He begins playing $5.00 blackjack. This guy's play deviated from every known blackjack strategy and was so erratic and offbeat, outside experts were brought in to watch the game. The player himself was said to be very nasty and rude to the dealers, cocktail waitresses and the rest of the staff, but he kept winning. For the next week or so this guy "ran through the raindrops." He never got wet. The hand and story of a lifetime. In just about a week he was up over 1.5 million dollars off a $400.00 buy-in. This guy and his play became the gossip of the town. Every day we would call to find out how he stood. Well, you guessed it, he tried to "buck the tiger" too long and within the next couple of days lost all but $50,000.00

back to the casino. He blew the rest of his bankroll at the downtown casinos and reportedly died of a heart attack.

A Japanese businessman named Mizuno was reported to have lost over 30 million dollars to the Mirage Casino in Las Vegas. Mizuno also played heavily at the Tropicana Hotel and toked the dealers very well. The dealers at the Tropicana were so appreciative of Mizuno's generosity that they pitched in and bought him a golf cart. By comparison to the 1970's, there are almost 100 players on the books at the Mirage who can bet $100,000.00 per hand at the baccarat table.

High rollers today are known as *Whales*. A major whale of the 1960's and 1970's was Jay Sarno, the guy who founded Circus Circus and Caesar's Palace. Jay was said to have lost between 50 and 60 million dollars in his career. (Jay was in his 60's when he died, in bed with a girl in her 20's. Sounds like the biggest gamble of his life.)

There was a poker player who recently had the Horseshoe Casino in downtown Las Vegas beat for better than 15 million dollars over the course of several weeks. However, the biggest single win for one stay is attributed to an Australian gambler named Kerry Packard. He reportedly beat the MGM Grand Hotel for nearly 22 million dollars. Packard is also said to have toked back to the employees about one third of the entire win. He was giving cocktail waitresses a $5,000.00 chip each time they brought him a drink. (That's five thousand dollars for a free drink.) He also was betting up to $50,000.00 on one bet for the dealers.

To help understand how the gambling mind works, let me relate a true story which happened in the late 1970's. A shoeshine boy from a local sports book came to the Aladdin Hotel and bought in for $20.00 at a crap table. Well, when the smoke cleared the first time, this guy had run the $20.00 into $20,000.00 (the hand of a lifetime). The shoeshine boy, however, continued to press his luck and when the smoke cleared for the last time, he was broke. When he returned to work at the sports book the following morning, a friend asked how he had done the night before, he replied, "Oh, I lost 20 Bucks."

2

What is the most unusual thing you see in surveillance? (Why a woman shouldn't wear red in a casino.)

Most customers are aware that casinos have a surveillance department. This area is highly restricted and very few customers have ever seen the monitor room.

I suppose the most unusual occurrence that surveillance rooms encounter has nothing to do with gaming. I am surprised at the number of girls, who for no apparent reason, will pull up their tops or lower their dress or open the blouse to expose their breasts. It's not that I'm complaining, mind you, it's just interesting. Most surveillance departments will have a videotape of people having sex in the elevators or other more public areas.

It is also interesting to know that most hair pieces are made of polyester and or synthetic fibers that have no red fillers in them, and when viewed by a black and white camera, they are very noticeable. The hair line between the hair piece and the real hair is quite evident and the hair piece appears as a distinctly different shade of gray or black. Black suits or tuxedos may also look a little odd. If the sleeves and the coat came from different dye lots, there is a distinct difference in the black/gray tones seen by the camera. Surveillance operators joke that the guy must have bought the tuxedo from the Salvation Army. This is due to an unusual characteristic of a black and white surveillance camera and the way in which it processes the color red.

Red chips (or any red colored item) appear as an off white. The human eye sees between 400 and 700 nanometers of light, while the Infra-Red capability of a black and white camera sees up to about 1100 nanometers of light and can be set to see much higher. To the average surveillance operator, this information means very little until a woman walks into the casino wearing a flimsy red colored silk dress or top. In many cases, the camera doesn't see much of the color red and, in affect, you see through the dress. I'll leave the rest to your imagination.

In August of 1998, a news story ran on CNN. The reporter told of how a Sony camcorder equipped with infrared light capability for night vision was seeing through certain types of clothing. Calm down, come back! Before you go running to Circuit City, Sony has pulled the camcorder and adjusted the infrared level. It is available online . . . what a country!

One very unusual incident stands out in my mind. On November 21, 1980, the MGM Grand Hotel had a very tragic fire. More than 80 people died in that fire. I was Director of Surveillance at the Dunes Hotel at the time. The Dunes Hotel sat directly across the strip from the MGM. In the midst of the bellowing fire, smoke and confusion, I observed a man dressed only in his underwear walk across the street from the MGM to the Dunes. I thought the man was in shock and was disoriented by the fire. What he did next really shocked me. The guy walked up to a crap table at the Dunes, asked for and received a marker and began to shoot dice. He reckoned that, because he hadn't died in the fire, it must be his lucky day. (It was also reported that a pregnant woman kicked in a steel fire door during the fire and walked down 23 floors to safety.)

From the gaming side, it is interesting to see wives secretly pocketing some of their husbands' winnings or vice-versa.

This always reminds me of a Las Vegas joke. A woman approaches her husband at a crap table and asks for $10.00 to play the slots. The husband seems irritated and asks, "What happened to the $10.00 I gave you yesterday?" The woman replies, "I lost it." "You lost $10.00 playing the slots?" asks the husband. "Yes," snaps the woman, "but you've lost $1,500.00 shooting craps." "Yeah," barks the husband, "but I know how to gamble!"

3

Is prostitution legal in Las Vegas?

Although there are over thirty legal brothels in the state of Nevada, prostitution is not legal in Las Vegas. State law prohibits a brothel in any county with more than 400,000 inhabitants. Las Vegas is in Clark County which has a total population of over 1,116,177. Reno, Nevada, is in Washoe County and has a population greater than 400,000 so there are no brothels in Reno.

The closest brothels to Las Vegas are in Nye County about 60 miles or so away. About 12 miles outside of Reno is the famous Mustang Ranch, in Storey County. Actually, prostitution is a great business — you've got it, you sell it, you've still got it.

In the old days, prostitutes were very present on the Las Vegas Strip and in most hotels. It wasn't legal mind you, but for the most part, it was ignored. In many of the casinos, bartenders used to sell the bar stools to the working girls, charge them a nightly fee to work the bar and "reserve their seat" so to speak. With the growth of the town and because of the increased number of *trick rollers* (girls posing as prostitutes in order to rob money and/or jewelry from "Johns"), the street prostitute was run off by the local police.

(You might be able to predict the activity of trick rollers by the amount of Visine Eye Drops sold around town. Yes, I said Visine Eye Drops. Visine acts as a very strong purging laxative. Trick rollers have used Visine for years as a method to get "Johns" into the bathroom very quickly so they can go through the guys' pants and get away. Squirted into coffee or a drink the Visine cannot be tasted. The Visine gets the *red* out of your eyes and the *green* out of your pocket.

For your information, the working girls at any brothel in Nevada are subject to a police check and must have a work card issued by the police department. The girls must, by law, visit a health clinic on a regular basis to be tested for venereal disease and AIDS. Because of the concern over AIDS, it is now a law that every customer must use a condom.

There are shuttles and limo services from Las Vegas to the brothels in Nye county. The brothels even advertise in the local Yellow Pages. There are also advertisements in the Yellow Pages and in fliers being passed out by street vendors that hint at prostitution. Be wary of these false claims and sensational ads. They are not advertising legal prostitution in Las Vegas. The only legal brothels or prostitutes are outside of Las Vegas. For your information, the brothels do offer an *outcall* service. A customer can arrange to have a girl, or girls, leave the brothel on an hourly basis. Proper I.D. and precautions will be necessary and the price is agreed upon in advance.

Here is an interesting aside. There is a State law that prohibits the operation of a brothel within one thousand yards of a church or school. A few years ago, a small Nevada town measured the distance between the church and its brothel, the distance was less than the law legally allowed. The townsfolk voted, of course, to move the church.

The following cities and towns in Nevada have legal brothels:

Beatty	Fran's Star Ranch
Carson City	Kit Kat Ranch
	Kitty's Guest Ranch
	Moonlight Ranch
	Sagebrush Ranch
Battle Mountain	Calico Club
	Desert Club
	Sharon's Place
Elko	Inez's D & D
	Mona Lisa
	Mona's II
	P.J.'s Lucky Strike
	Sue's
Ely	Big 4
	Green Lantern
	Stardust
Fallon	Lazy B Guest Ranch
	Salt Wells Villa
Lida Junction	Cottontail Ranch
Mina	Billie's Day & Night
Reno	Mustang Ranch (Storey County)
	Old Bridge Ranch
Las Vegas	Cherry Patch Ranch
	Cherry Patch II (Nye County)
	Chicken Ranch
	Mabel's Whorehouse
	Shari's Ranch
Tonopah	Bobbie's Buckeye Bar
Wells	Donna's
	Hacienda
Winnemucca	My Place
	Penny's Cozy Corner
	Pussycat
	Simones De Paris
	Villa Joy

A player is walking through the casino and is approached by a working girl. The hooker tells the guy it will cost $100.00 for a date. "One hundred dollars?" questions the man. "I wouldn't pay more than $20.00." The two part company. A few hours later, the same guy is walking through the casino again, but this time with his wife. They pass the same hooker the guy had haggled with earlier. The hooker whispers to the guy, "See what you get for $20.00."

A guy walks into a brothel and says to the madam, "I want the worst sex in the place. If she's miserable, I want her." The madam asks, "Are you crazy sir?" "No," replies the guy. "Just homesick."

Are most gamblers superstitious?

Because the concepts of gambling and Lady Luck are so closely related, it is only natural that gambling and the absence of luck, or superstition, also are related. Some of the most common and interesting gamblers superstitions are:

- Fifty dollar bills are bad luck. In order to eliminate the bad luck you need to spit at the bill and/or tear a small piece of the corner off.
- The same holds true for the $2.00 bill.
- It is considered bad luck if, when throwing dice, they hit a customer's hand.
- When throwing dice, if one goes off the table, the superstition says that the next roll will be a loser. "One on the floor, seven out the door." (Seven out is a loser in dice.)
- It is considered good luck to shoot dice with a "virgin" dice shooter (a female who has never shot dice before).
- Left handed 21 dealers are bad luck.
- Left handed 21 dealers who have red hair are okay.
- Some slot players will only put coins in the machine in a certain order and then only use certain fingers to press the slot buttons.
- The number 13 is bad luck for most American gamblers, but the number 4 is bad luck to Asian gamblers.
- It is considered bad luck by Asian gamblers for dealers in baccarat to stand looking down on them. (Asians prefer baccarat dealers to be seated.)

- Some Asian gamblers consider table layouts with the color purple to be bad luck.
- Some dice shooters will preset the dice at a certain number so that it won't land on that number when the dice are thrown.
- Some gamblers feel it is unlucky for other players to clear their throat while gambling.
- It is an old superstition that you get really lucky just before you die. (The woman who owned the land on which the Edgewater Casino in Laughlin, Nevada, sits held out for years to get her price. As luck would have it, she got her price and the stipulation that she would live in a penthouse suite for the rest of her life. She died before the hotel opened.)
- An old poker superstition says, "Never play poker with anyone named after a city."

Superstitions about cutting cards are:

- Cut 'em deep and weep.
- Cut 'em thin and win.
- Deep is thin, just on the other end.
- If losing, some casino customers will get up, walk around their chair and sit down. (It's like starting over.)
- Some gambler's consider it bad luck if you stand over their left shoulder and watch them gamble.
- Blowing on dice is considered good luck. This practice comes from an old wives tale about breathing or blowing healthy or new breath on a wound.

There is an old gambling saying, "If you had a nickel for every gambler who wasn't superstitious, some day you might end up with a dime."

Are casinos superstitious?

Just as many gamblers are superstitious, it stands to reason that the gamblers who run casinos also have some less than scientific approaches to the games. Although the following list is not officially condoned by any gaming authority (just kidding), here are some common superstitions and practices.

- If a table is losing, remove the table paddle, turn it around and reinsert it.
- If a table is losing, remove the table paddle and replace it with a paddle from a game that is not losing.
- If a crap table is losing, exchange dice from a crap table that is not losing.
- If a table is losing, light a match, put it out and throw it under the table.
- If a table is losing, casino bosses have been known to hide a salt shaker in their hand and walk around the outside of the table sprinkling the salt.
- If a table is losing, casino bosses have been known to stand on one foot until the house begins to win.
- If a table is losing, casino bosses have been known to change their suit coat or other piece of clothing to try and change the table's luck.
- Losing dealers have been known to turn their apron around to try and turn the luck around.

On one occasion, in the mid 1970's when I was at the Aladdin Hotel, a customer won over $250,000.00 in about 45 minutes at a crap table. The next morning I followed members of the maintenance department as they, on orders from the casino manager, took the crap table outside and chopped it into pieces.

In 1970 people in Detroit bought the Aladdin Hotel/Casino from people in Chicago. Superstitious about almost everything, here's what the Detroit people did. Accountants on behalf of the Detroit people spent three days counting every penny in the joint right down to the last nickel in every slot machine. Instead of writing a check for the transfer of cash, the Detroit people insisted that every dollar of Chicago money be removed and replaced with Detroit money—even the nickels.

After the transfer of ownership was complete, 1,000 old employees were terminated and 900 new employees were hired from the Thunderbird to run the Aladdin . . . all in one day.

Each crap table was disassembled and the layouts replaced. It was common practice back then to use old newspaper, instead of foam, as a cushion underneath the crap layouts. The newspaper used underneath the crap layouts was, you guessed it, *The Detroit Free Press.*

Author's note: About twenty years ago I was Director of Surveillance for the Dunes Hotel. The casino was catering to a group of Asian high rollers. On one trip the Asian players brought along a priest, sort of a Shaman fella. Well the priest started doing a Feng Shui thing checking out the entire Hotel/ Casino, the guest rooms, the restaurants and finally the high limit Baccarat Pit. The priest stood for a moment over the Baccarat table and began meditating. He raised his hands and rotated them in a very elegant Ti Chi manner. Suddenly he stopped, repeated the ritual over the Baccarat table and again stopped suddenly and frowned. "There are bad vibrations coming from this spot," he proclaimed. He then Feng Shui'd the rest of the High Limit Room and announced that he had found an area where the vibrations were "ah, very good" and requested that the Baccarat table be moved to that exact spot. A little irreverant (and half a wse guy), I replied, "Let me get this straight. You want us to move the Baccarat Table from this spot, which has four surveillance cameras trained on it, to a spot over in the corner of the room with NO surveillance coverage. Well no offense, but say a prayer or burn some incense but the table stays where it is." Nice try "grasshopper"!

6

How can I tell if a table is "hot" or "cold"?

This is a difficult question to answer because of the number of variables involved. Here, however, is a method many players use. As you walk past a gaming table, take notice of the bankroll (the chips in front of the dealer). If the table bankroll is full up with chips, it might be an indication that the table is *cold* and the dealer has been winning the chips from the players who sit down at the table. Conversely, if the table bankroll is light (a lot of chips missing), it might be an indication that the customers have been beating the dealer and the table is *hot*. Some players have even been known to follow the security guards or chip runners who are bringing a *fill* from the cage to a game. If the fill is being made because players are winning, it might be an indication that the players are hot. Not a very scientific method, but one that some players use.

Another very simple method a lot of players use is to simply ask the dealer. During the course of a stay at a casino, you will meet and get a feeling for many of the dealers. Dealers are known to tell customers they like to stay away from their table when they feel the table is favoring the house. Again, not a fool proof method, but one that is used.

A method some dice shooters use to determine if a crap table is hot or cold is to listen for other players yelling on the games. When players are applauding and screaming, it is an indication that they are winning. Again, not always reliable, but a method some players use.

It is interesting to note that how the dealers are doing *toke* wise is a gross indicator of how the table is doing. In the old days, dealers use to place their tips in their shirt pockets. The dealer would then place those tips, along with all other dealers, in a large tip box usually housed in the podium in the center of the pit. Today, in most casinos, dealers place the tokes in a small clear box attached to the gaming table. On days when the dealers, as a whole, make big tips it usually means the customers are winning. When the toke rate is down, it may be an indication that the players are losing and the house is hot. Again, this is just a gross indicator, but customers have been known to search out tables where the clear toke box is full as a way of determining whether or not the table is hot or cold.

Old gambler's joke: I went to Vegas last week and lost all my money, my car, my house, my life savings and my jewelry. I lost everything except my good luck charm.

$$\boxed{7}$$

Does it make a difference which spot I sit in at a blackjack table?

Most serious blackjack players hate to see an inexperienced player seated at *third base* (the last players' hand at the dealer's extreme right). When a player hits a hand that is contrary to basic strategy (i.e., hits a 13 versus a dealer's 6, etc.), it is annoying to a basic strategy player. If the card the player at third base takes would have busted the dealer's hand, and the dealer makes a total that beats the table, it is especially annoying. It is not good practice to try and educate a player on the table in live play, particularly a stranger, as to the accepted basic strategy. Customers can and should be allowed to play their hand however they wish. Customers play hunches, have their own ideas or take advice from their friends. It is after all a customer's own money to wager as he/she sees fit and to play as they desire.

From a mathematical standpoint, how another player plays his or her hand and how they bet, does not really affect the statistical probability of the players around them. Basic strategy players are concerned with making decisions based on millions of hands of computer simulations... blackjack theory. A card counter is concerned with the plus and minus make up of the cards remaining to be played. Neither of these players, basic strategy or card counter, can know the next card out of the shoe. The decision by a third base player to take a card, when basic strategy dictates not to, may in fact help the other players and hurt the dealer's hand.

Keep in mind there is a big difference between knowing deck composition (the number of big cards vs. little cards) and knowing the order of the deck (the next card to be dealt).

A card counter using an advanced system involving a multi-parameter count and advanced plus and minus strategy decisions may want to be seated at third base. In order to make advanced plus or advanced minus strategy playing decisions, it is obvious that a certain number (plus or minus) must be reached. It is to the advantage of an advanced strategy player to see as many cards as possible before making an advanced strategy playing decision. Being seated at third base gives such a player the knowledge of more cards, which ultimately may indicate a play contrary to simple basic strategy, before he plays his hand.

If you are a casual player but like to see a lot of cards played before you act, then third base might be your spot. If you should find a player making decisions which bother you in some way, it might hurt your concentration and make your playing experience uncomfortable. If this is the case, then the prudent course of action is to simply change tables. Gaming should be fun.

Old gambler's saying: "It's not a crime to gamble illegally, but it is a sin the way some people do."

$$\boxed{8}$$

How do they mark playing cards?

Marking playing cards for casino play obviously implies cheating. There is no reason or any real mathematical advantage for the house to mark playing cards, unless they intend to selectively shuffle or deal seconds not off the top. In the old days this might be true but no longer, so the scam that is implied is a customer or group of customers attempting to cheat the house.

A corrupt casino employee may be involved but the cheating that happens is against the house not in the houses' favor. The marked card cheating takes two forms. Marking cards in some way during actual live play or obtaining casino cards in some way, marking them and reintroducing those cards to the game.

Marking cards in live play is attempted by several methods. Cheaters will bend cards to indicate their value. They may bend the cards along the edge to indicate high value cards and along the side to indicate medium value cards. With these two bends, called *waves* or *crimps* indicating cards of high and medium value, then cards with no bends would indicate low value cards. Card benders will put waves or crimps on just one side or edge of a playing card but will bend them in different directions or in different spots to indicate various values.

Some cheaters will glue a small piece of sandpaper to the underside of their finger. While handling the playing cards the cheater will attempt to scratch or sand a small amount of ink off the back or sides of the cards to indicate various values. This method of card marking is called *sanding* or *sand work* for obvious reasons.

Other cheaters will let their thumb nail grow and file it to a sharp edge. While handling playing cards the cheater will press his thumb nail into the edge of the playing card, creating a *nail nick*. Nail nicks on different areas on the edge of the cards will of course indicate various values.

Card markers will attempt to put various substances on the backs of playing cards to indicate various card values. A substance called *daub* is used to mark playing cards in play. Daub has the consistency and feel of women's lip rouge or eye shadow. The daub is made in different colors and shades for various colors of card backs. The daub is carried in a small container hidden in any number of places on the cheater's body. A very small amount of daub is lightly transferred to the tip of the cheater's finger. As the card cheat handles the playing cards, he will transfer a small amount of daub from his finger onto the back of the playing card. Obviously daub is placed in certain areas on the back of the cards to indicate high or low values. The daub appears as a slight discoloration or a faint shadow. Several other substances such as Vaseline, ashes, oils, soapstone and waxes have been used to mark playing cards in play.

In a very elaborate casino cheating scheme, playing cards are stolen from the casino or a casino employee is bribed to remove casino playing cards from the secured inventory. The playing cards are then marked by one of several methods. The marked playing cards are then reintroduced to play in order to cheat the casino.

One such method uses a special ink known as *cut out ink* or *block out ink* painted onto the back of the playing cards. The ink is used to alter the design of particular patterns or lines. The lines may be shortened or lengthened. The design may be extended or a small portion of it blocked out. Adding ink to the back of a playing card and blending it to avoid detection is not as easy as it sounds. The painting process may take several hours for just one deck of playing cards. The ink does not absorb through the finish of most playing cards, so acids need to be added to the ink to facilitate the marking process.

A card marking method known as *shade* or *shade work* is a very intricate cheating technique. A combination of chemical dyes, alcohol and acid is mixed to match the particular color of the back of playing cards to be marked. The chemical mixture sometimes known as *flash* or *juice* is painted or sprayed on the back of playing cards. The shade can be painted on particular areas of the card to slightly darken that area or design. A very small area or line on the back of a card can be masked off and the entire rest of the back painted. When the mask (a small piece of graphic's tape) is removed, the unpainted or unshaded area will appear lighter or shine brighter than the shaded areas. The shade is very, very light and the gradation of color between the shaded and unshaded areas is so slight that it may take several hours of practice to acquaint the human eye to those slight differences. One white line on the back of a playing card may be left unshaded so that the line then appears brighter than the rest.

In the old days, for private games like Gin, we would take the big cards out of a deck and bake them in the sun for a few hours. When the baked cards were returned to the deck, they would be slightly faded. We also used to mix the high cards from a pinochle deck with the low cards from a poker deck. Because the cards came from two different runs on the printing press, they may have slightly different shades right out of the box. (I could look at your gin hand and know if you were holding big cards or little cards. Now, of course, I realize how wrong that would be...ha ha ha.)

When I lecture to the gaming industry about the problem of marked cards, I tell casino executives not to be surprised when they find marked cards on their games. Every casino in the gaming industry, and every private game for that matter, has the same weakness where marked cards are concerned — human beings touch the cards. Someone is trusted to order and supply playing cards. A "trusted" person at the casino is given the responsibility to bring cards to and from the games. Another person is "trusted" to cancel the playing cards after the game. Somewhere along the chain, the integrity of card security is broken and cards are stolen and marked cards are returned to play. In order to illustrate this point, I relate a story from my old days.

I grew up in Detroit, and at one time there was a chain of drugstores that stayed open all night called Cunningham Drugs. There was a particular poker game that I wanted to beat. Obviously, if I brought playing cards to the game and marked cards were discovered, I would take the heat. The day before the big game I went to the Cunningham Drugstore and purchased half of all the Bee, Bicycle and Aviator playing cards on the shelf. (If I had purchased all of the playing cards in the store, they might have restocked the shelves with cards from storage. You'll understand why this is important as you read on.) I took the cards home, and using an exacto knife, removed the cellophane wrapping on the outside of the box, taking care to leave the Cunningham price tag in place. The wrapping was carefully slid off the box, leaving the cellophane string intact. The side of the box was opened with a razor blade, leaving the blue stamp on the top of the box glued in place. The playing cards were removed and marked. I used a marking technique that if discovered would look like the cards had been marked in play as opposed to painted or sprayed in private.

The now marked cards were put back in the box, the opened side was reglued and the cellophane wrapper was slid back over the sealed box. The cellophane wrapper was then carefully refolded as normal. I placed a cloth over the cellophane and pressed a hot iron lightly against the cloth. The hot iron sealed the cellophane. Now sealed in cellophane and protected by the glued stamp, the deck of cards were marked for the game of poker. In this case, maybe twenty to thirty decks were all marked and resealed in the original wrappings.

If I took these cards to the poker game myself, I would of course take the heat if they were discovered. Actually, why would anyone bring cards to another person's game? Instead, I took the playing cards back to the Cunningham Drugstore the next day. I went in and bought all of the remaining playing cards in the store. There were now no playing cards at all in the drugstore for about thirty seconds. My partner came in behind me, and like shoplifting in reverse, he restocked the shelves with the playing cards we had marked the night before. At this point every deck of playing cards in that Cunningham Drugstore was a marked deck. (Confused? Let me continue.)

We went to the game that night with no marked cards or any type of card marking chemicals on us. About 1:30 in the morning, my partner and I made some excuse to get angry over a losing hand. We took it out on the playing cards by tearing several of them in half. (Starting to get the idea?) Well, of course, we apologized for being a little drunk and a little stupid. To show how "really" sorry we were for ripping up their playing cards I threw cash on the table and said, "I apologize. Send someone to buy pizza and beer on me. And you know what? I ain't won a hand in this place all night. Buy some new cards to change my luck." Well, where could they send anyone at 1:30 a.m. in Detroit? Cunningham Drugs, of course, almost 12 miles away from the game. About forty-five minutes later, one of the guys came back to the game with pizza, beer and playing cards with Cunningham price tags on them. It was better than most sex! I knew we were in.

Author's Note: Some years ago Warren Beatty starred in a movie entitled Kaleidoscope. He secretly altered the printer's engraving plates at a playing card company. Marked cards were unknowingly being supplied to casinos in Monte Carlo. He gambled and made a fortune. Just a movie—right? Wrong! In April of 1999 an employee in a playing card company in South Africa was caught doing the exact same thing.

Two cheaters talking to one another: "Did you hear that Wayne got arrested last night for having a bad memory?" "Yeah, he forgot to wipe the daub off his fingers!"

$$\boxed{9}$$

Should I ever split Tens?

Anytime you are playing blackjack and are dealt a pair, (two cards of matching values), you are allowed to split the pair and make two separate hands. You must place a bet exactly equal to your original bet on the split or second hand. The basic rule of good blackjack play says, "Always split aces and eights." — a pair of aces or a pair of eights, not one of each. All tens, jacks, queens and kings are valued as 10. Therefore, any two cards valued as 10 are considered a pair. The standard rules for basic strategy pair splitting are illustrated in the following chart.

PAIR	DEALER'S UP CARD									
	A	10	9	8	7	6	5	4	3	2
A—A	SP	SP	SP	SP	SP	SP	SP	SP	SP	SP
2—2	H	H	H	H	SP	SP	SP	SP	H	H
3—3	H	H	H	H	SP	SP	SP	SP	H	H
4—4	H	H	H	H	H	H	H	H	H	H
5—5	H	H	DB	DB	DB	DB	DB	DB	DB	DB
6—6	H	H	H	H	H	SP	SP	SP	SP	H
7—7	H	H	H	H	SP	SP	SP	SP	SP	SP
8—8	SP	SP	SP	SP	SP	SP	SP	SP	SP	SP
9—9	ST	ST	SP	SP	ST	SP	SP	SP	SP	SP
10—10	ST	ST	ST	ST	ST	ST	ST	ST	ST	ST

ST = STAND • SP = SPLIT • DB = DOUBLE DOWN • H = HIT

For the most part, cards valued as 10's are never split. The average winning total for a blackjack hand is 18.5. For this reason, it is sometimes to a player's advantage to split a pair of nines. (There are some advanced card count strategies which call for splitting tens, but for the most part, it is not a smart play.) This total was arrived at after several hundred million hands of blackjack were simulated by computer programs.

Should I hit a 16 against a dealer's 7?

The question of how to best play blackjack will be covered in detail in Question ☐7☐; however, we will examine here the proposition of 16 vs. a dealer's 7.

A hand of 16 in blackjack is a very weak total for either the player or the dealer. The reason a 16 is so weak for the player is that in order to win the bet the dealer must *bust* (go over 21). There cannot be a tie hand because the dealer must draw until he reaches at least 17. A total of 16 is also weak because of the number of one card draws that can bust the hand (take it over 21.) Any single card of 6, 7, 8 , 9, 10 or face card will bust the hand. The 16 is a weak total for the player, so whether or not you hit the 16 or stand on the 16, you will lose more hands to the dealer than you will win. By hitting the 16, you will, however, lose less hands than by standing.

To prove this proposition a computer simulation was run using a program called "Blackjack Master" (copyright ©1986–1992 ELITE). The program runs and simulates the game of blackjack with any rules or strategy you care to enter. The following strategy table shows the player's total across the top and the dealer's up card along the side. The player's total of 16 has been highlighted and the decision to HIT the 16 against a dealer's 7 is also highlighted.

STRATEGY TABLE

Dealer's Up Card   PLAYERS TOTAL

	6	5	1	1	1	1	1	1	1	1	A	A	A	A	A	A	A	A	A	A	2	3	4	5	6	7	8	9	X
	2	3	9	0	1	2	3	4	5	6	2	3	4	5	6	7	8	9	X	A	2	3	4	5	6	7	8	9	X
A	H	H	H	H	H	H	H	H	H	H	H	H	H	H	H	H	S	S	-	T	H	H	H	H	H	H	T	S	S
2	H	H	H	D	D	H	S	S	S	S	H	H	H	H	H	S	S	S	-	T	H	H	H	D	H	T	T	T	S
3	H	H	D	D	D	H	S	S	S	S	H	H	H	H	D	D	S	S	-	T	H	H	H	D	T	T	T	T	S
4	H	H	D	D	D	S	S	S	S	S	H	H	D	D	D	D	S	S	-	T	T	T	H	D	T	T	T	T	S
5	D	D	D	D	D	S	S	S	S	S	D	D	D	D	D	D	S	S	-	T	T	T	D	D	T	T	T	T	S
6	D	D	D	D	D	S	S	S	S	S	D	D	D	D	D	D	S	S	-	T	T	T	H	D	T	T	T	T	S
7	H	H	D	D	D	H	H	H	H	H	H	H	H	H	H	S	S	S	-	T	T	T	H	D	H	T	T	S	S
8	H	H	H	D	D	H	H	H	H	H	H	H	H	H	H	S	S	S	-	T	H	H	H	D	H	H	T	T	S
9	H	H	H	D	D	H	H	H	H	H	H	H	H	H	H	H	S	S	-	T	H	H	H	D	H	H	T	T	S
X	H	H	H	H	D	H	H	H	H	H	H	H	H	H	H	H	S	S	-	T	H	H	H	H	H	H	T	S	S

The program allows for up to a million hands of blackjack to be simulated. In addition, the player's first and/or second cards and the dealer's up card can be designated as any card from ace through 10. The following illustration shows the setup menu and the net results for 100,000 hands of blackjack where the player's first card is a 10 and the second card is a 6 (16 total) and the dealer's up card is a 7. (Remember the strategy table is set such that the player will hit the 16 vs. the 7.)

Blackjack Master Simulation

A. Set Number of Hands   [100000]
B. Clear statistics
C. Fix player total   [ ]
D. Fix first player card   [X]
E. Fix second player card   [6]
F. Fix dealer up card   [7]
G. Begin/continue simulation
H. Display statistics by hand type
I. Display statistics by adjusted count
J. Display card deal statistics
K. Print statistics
L. Write statistics to disk
M. Simulation log file   [OFF]
X. Return to first menu

Select:

Hands:	100000
Shuffles:	14840
Wins:	28560
Loses:	65330
Net Chips:	-36770.0
Expected return:	-0.3672

Dealer Up Card	Times Occurred	Hands Won	Hands Lost	Net Chips
A	0	0	0	0.0
2	0	0	0	0.0
3	0	0	0	0.0
4	0	0	0	0.0
5	0	0	0	0.0
6	0	0	0	0.0
7	100000	28560	65330	-36770.0
8	0	0	0	0.0
9	0	0	0	0.0
X	0	0	0	0.0

The net result over 100,000 hands (betting $1.00 each) was a loss of 36,777 chips or $36,770.00.

Another simulation was run changing only the proposition that the player would Stand on 16 vs. a 7. The strategy table below illustrates the change highlighting the player decision to stand on 16 vs. the dealer 7.

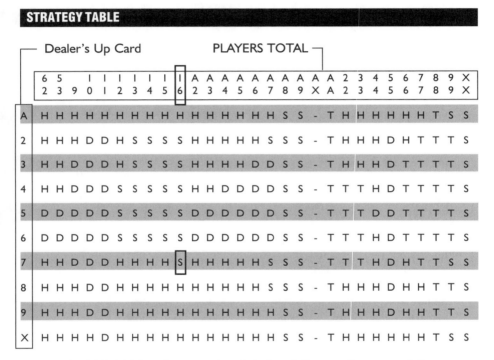

Again 100,000 hands were simulated and the results are as follows:

Blackjack Master Simulation

A. Set Number of Hands   [100000]
B. Clear statistics
C. Fix player total   [ ]
D. Fix first player card   [X]
E. Fix second player card   [6]
F. Fix dealer up card   [7]
G. Begin/continue simulation
H. Display statistics by hand type
I. Display statistics by adjusted count
J. Display card deal statistics
K. Print statistics
L. Write statistics to disk
M. Simulation log file   [OFF]
X. Return to first menu

Select:

Hands: 100000
Shuffles: 14670
Wins: 25440
Loses: 74560
Net Chips: -49120.0
Expected return: -0.4907

Dealer Up Card	Times Occurred	Hands Won	Hands Lost	Net Chips
A	0	0	0	0.0
2	0	0	0	0.0
3	0	0	0	0.0
4	0	0	0	0.0
5	0	0	0	0.0
6	0	0	0	0.0
7	100000	25440	74560	-49120.0
8	0	0	0	0.0
9	0	0	0	0.0
X	0	0	0	0.0

The results show a loss of 49,120 chips or $49,120.00 when standing on 16 vs a 7. By way of comparison then:

Stand on 16 vs. 7	–49,120
Hit 16 vs. 7	–36,770
Difference	12,350

The simulations clearly indicate that a hand of 16 vs. a 7 is very weak. However, the simulations also indicate that hitting the 16 vs. the 7 is far more advantageous to a player because it produces far less losses.

A friend of mine told me he just took up blackjack. He said, "One day I win, the next day I lose." I told him, "Play every other day."

What are the odds in blackjack?

There have been scores of books written and several computer studies run to quantify the house or player's mathematical advantage for the game of blackjack. Simulations allow for each individual sub-set of cards to be analyzed, every conceivable rule change to be examined, any number of decks to be used, the effects of card removal from the decks to be gauged, betting systems and card count and shuffle strategies to be entered and tested....but the examinations of this question must always begin with the basic premise that the house's inherent advantage arises from the simple fact that the *house hits last!*

Consider a blackjack game with seven customers and the dealer (eight hands total). Let us assume that the first six players bust (go over a count of 21), and the dealer takes their money in turn as they bust. Let us further assume that the seventh or last player stands and that the dealer *breaks*. The dealer will, of course, pay that last player. The first six players and the dealer all busted (which some argue is really a tie), but because the players busted first, their wager is lost.

The basic mathematical advantage that the house enjoys because of this simple rule is approximately 6.97%. A rate of win of 6.97% for the house would cause the players to lose at such a rapid pace that the game would soon be considered a carnival activity and would not be at all popular with customers or profitable for casinos. In order to create a more level playing field for the game of 21, the house makes rule changes to give back some of the advantage to the player. This is done by the number and types of rule changes that the casino offers. In addition, a player following basic strategy can also reduce the house's starting advantage.

The single biggest advantage the house gives to the player is paying 3 to 2 on blackjacks. This payoff returns approximately 2.33% to the customer. For your information, a player should be dealt a blackjack about 4.5% of the time or once every 21 hands. The single strongest thing that a player can do to reduce the house's advantage is to hit and stand according to basic strategy. Basic strategy, which includes proper pair splitting, doubling down and hitting soft hands, returns over 4% to the player. It is, of course, academic that basic strategy must be played perfectly all the time to make the full mathematical gains.

You could probably win a bet if you asked most blackjack players the average total you need to win a hand. The answer is 18.3. This means you could sit with a total of 18 the entire night and lose money. The table below shows the odds of a dealer busing with various up cards.

Probability of Dealer Busting with Various Up-Cards

				Dealer's Up Card					
2	3	4	5	6	7	8	9	10	Ace
35%	38%	40%	43%	42%	26%	24%	23%	21%	11%

For your information the next table shows the effects of rule changes for the game of blackjack.

Gambler's joke: "I love to play twenty one. Unfortunately my lucky number is 22."

House's Starting Advantage Over Basic Strategy Player

One Deck\	0.00%
Two Decks	-0.32%
Four Decks	-0.47%
Six Decks	-0.52%
Eight Decks	-0.58%

RULE CHANGE	1DK	2DK	4DK	6DK	8DK
DEALER HITS SOFT 17	-0.19	-0.20	-0.21	-0.22	-0.22
DOUBLE AFTER SPLIT PAIRS	+0.13	+0.13	+0.12	+0.12	+0.12
RESPLIT ACES	+0.03	+0.05	+0.07	+0.07	+0.08
DRAWING TO SPLIT ACE	+0.14	+0.14	+0.14	+0.14	+0.14
DOUBLE ON 3 OR MORE CARDS	+0.24	+0.23	+0.22	+0.22	+0.22
LATE SURRENDER	+0.03	+0.04	+0.07	+0.08	+0.08
EARLY SURRENDER	+0.62	+0.62	+0.63	+0.63	+0.63
6 CARDS UNDER WINS	+0.10	+0.13	+0.15	+0.16	+0.16
DOUBLE ON 10 AND 11 ONLY	-0.26	-0.22	-0.19	-0.18	-0.17
DOUBLE 9, 10 OR 11 ONLY	-0.13	-0.11	-0.10	-0.09	-0.09
SPLIT ACES ONLY	-0.21	-0.23	-0.24	-0.24	-0.25
NO SPLIT ACES	-0.16	-0.17	-0.18	-0.18	-0.18
NO RESPLIT OF PAIRS	-0.02	-0.03	-0.03	-0.04	-0.04
NO HOLE CARD DEALT	-0.11	-0.11	-0.11	-0.11	-0.11
DEALER WINS ALL TIES	-9.00	-9.00	-9.00	-9.00	-9.00
BASEBALL BAT	+100%	+100%	+100%	+100%	+100%

What does first and third base mean?

The first hand (betting spot) to the dealer's left is called *first base*. The last hand (betting spot) to the dealer's right is called *third base*. These positions have nothing to do with a baseball diamond in the light that they are actually backwards from the baseball base path direction as we know it. First and third base are the same for all 21-type tables regardless of the number of player spots or betting circles.

On a crap table, the stickman is called the *pole*, the dealer on the right of the boxman is called the *second base dealer*. The dealer on the left of the boxman is called the *third base dealer*.

What does it mean in a blackjack game when a dealer calls for insurance?

When looking at a standard 21 layout, you will see a line that reads "Insurance Pays 2 to 1." When the dealer has an ace up, he/she will ask if anyone wants insurance. The dealer asks for an insurance bet before peeking to see his down card. Taking insurance means that you are betting the dealer has a blackjack (an ace up with a ten in the hole). As a player, you can make an insurance wager for up to half of your original bet. If the dealer does not have a blackjack, you lose the insurance bet and continue to play on the original bet. If the dealer does have a blackjack, then you lose the original bet but win the insurance bet.

Assuming a $10.00 original bet, you could place a $5.00 insurance bet. If the dealer has a blackjack you would lose the $10.00 original bet but you would win the $5.00 insurance bet and be paid $10.00 — you break even.

For the most part, an insurance bet is a *sucker bet*. When the dealer has an ace up, there are only four cards that will give him/her a blackjack: 10, jack, queen or king. There are nine cards that will not make blackjack: ace, 2, 3, 4, 5, 6, 7, 8, 9. The odds are 9 to 4 that the dealer will not have a blackjack. In addition, it is foolish to insure a bet with a weak total. If you are holding a count of between 12 and 16, you have a weak hand because of the high probability of busting.

There are certain card count indexes used to estimate the times when insurance is a stronger bet. Obviously it would be more to your advantage to take insurance when there are a lot more 10 value cards (10, J, Q, K,) left in the deck. Some players will always insure a blackjack, ensuring them of even money.

From a mathematical standpoint it's foolish to insure a blackjack unless you are counting cards. There are 13 possible cards underneath the dealer's Ace. Let's assume a $10.00 bet. If you took insurance every time, you would win $10 times 13 (every possible down card) which equals $130.00. (See question 13 on Even Money.) If you never insured a blackjack, you would *push* with the dealer 4 out of the 13 times—Ten, Jack, Queen or King in the hole means dealer has blackjack. You would win 9 times—Ace, 2, 3, 4, 5, 6, 7, 8 or 9 in the hole and be paid $15.00 for your blackjack 9 times which equals $135.00. Even though it's a close call, you are better off not insuring a blackjack unless you are a card counter.

Most gamblers see any form of insurance as a sucker bet. Life Insurance is a bet with the insurance company that you'll die young.

1 4

What is a paint, a stiff, and to be pat?

Because of the amount and colors of ink on face cards (jacks, queens and kings) and because face cards were actually hand painted in medieval times, they have been nicknamed *paints*.

A *stiff* is a hand that can be broken (go over 21) by taking only one card. Any total of between 12 and 16 is a stiff. One card could take the total over 21 and bust the hand. This does not include *soft hands*. A soft hand is any total involving an ace (counted as 1 or 11) which cannot possibly go over 21 by drawing one card. A 5 & ace is a soft 16. No one card drawn to this hand will take it over 21. A 10 & 6 is a hard 16 because one card could take this total over 21. A soft hand can turn into a hard hand. A 5 & ace is soft 16, however drawing a 10 to this hand makes the soft 16 a hard 16.

To be *pat* simply means to have a hard total of 17 or better and it means you don't want another card. To say, "I'm pat" is like saying, "I'm good." The term came from the practice of patting the table when you don't want to draw another card.

A guy has a dream one night in which he hears the voice of God. God tells him, "Go to Las Vegas and play Blackjack." As his day progresses, the voice gets louder and more intense. "Go to Las Vegas and play Blackjack!" The guy hops a plane and heads for Vegas. He begins to play black jack and the voice tells him when to hit, stand or double down. The guy plays the entire weekend and amasses a small fortune. He grabs a taxi and starts for the airport. Again, he hears the voice of God, "Go back and shoot dice." He bellies-up to the first crap table he sees. The voice says, "Bet 11." He places all of his winnings on one roll of the dice on the number 11. The dice roll and the dealer calls, "Seven out — loser." The voice says, "DAMN!"

What is card counting?

Most players have a misconception regarding what actually happens during card counting. You do not need to memorize the entire deck and remember each card played. Very simply, card counting keeps track of big cards versus little cards. To understand how card counting works, you must first understand the house's basic advantage in the game of blackjack. It is very simple. Are you ready? Here it is: THE HOUSE HITS LAST. That's it. You bust first.

Consider a 21 game with seven players. Let's suppose that the first six players bust (go over 21). The dealer takes their money. Let's also suppose that the seventh player stands and that the dealer then acts on the house's hand and busts. Well, the dealer pays the seventh player, but wasn't it really a tie with the first six? The players busted and so did the house, but the dealer took the players money because they busted first. This simple fact gives the house a whopping 6.97% starting mathematical advantage over the player. A 6.97% rate of win is greater than any game except the Big 6 and a 5 number bet in Roulette.

In order to make the game more fair (and keep customers playing), the house concedes certain rule changes. Paying 3 to 2 on a blackjack (called *time-and-a-half* by dealers) reduces the house's edge by 2.33%. Allowing double downs, splitting of pairs, double after a split and the various other rule changes reduces the house's starting advantage to a level where playing basic strategy and card counting can actually give the player an advantage over the house. See Question 11.

Blackjack is the only game where the mathematical advantage flows back and forth between the house and the players. Card counting allows a player to recognize the advantage and bet accordingly. The house plays by a fixed set of rules. The dealer must hit 16 or less and must stand on 17 or greater. Because of these fixed rules for the house (and because the dealer hits last), counting the relationship of high cards to low cards helps the player.

When there are more big cards than small cards left to be played, the player has the advantage. The dealer must make a count of between 17 and 21. The big cards put the dealer's total over 21 more often. When there are more small cards by ratio than big cards, the house has the advantage because the small cards help the dealer make a hand between 17 and 21 more often.

Most people think you need to remember every card played. There is a fundamental difference between counting and remembering. Suppose I gave you a handful of coins of various denominations and asked you to count them. You could easily arrive at a total sum. However, if I asked you to now tell me how many coins of each denomination you counted, you probably couldn't remember. Keeping track of a running total is easy. Having to remember each denomination that got you to the total is difficult and unnecessary. The total is the thing.

Card counting runs a ratio of big cards to little cards and recognizes when the ratio is tilted one way or the other. This ratio is kept by assigning a plus or minus number to each card value. The simple plus/minus numbers for each card value are as follows:

2, 3, 4, 5, 6	+1 (PLUS)
7, 8, 9	0
10, J, Q, K, ACE	–1 (MINUS)

As each card is seen, the card counter simply adds or subtracts plus or minus one.

For instance, let's suppose that your first two cards are a 6 & 4 and the dealer's up card is a 3, the simple running count is a + 3 — you added +1 for each small card. Suppose you draw a 10 as your next card — the count is now +2 because you subtracted one (-1) from the +3. When the dealer turns over his down card, you add or subtract that to the running count, and so on as each card is seen. The simple running count tells you if the ratio of big cards to small cards is out of line. The higher the Plus Count, the more the ratio of big cards to little cards is out of line (better for the player). The higher the Minus Count, the more little cards (better for the house). Understand that the Plus/Minus Count cannot tell you what cards you are going to receive. With a high Plus Count, you and the dealer have the same chance of achieving the same total but the big cards help you more than the dealer.

The ace, for example, is the most powerful card in the game. The ace does not, however, impact both the dealer and player's hand equally. When the dealer receives a blackjack, he takes the player's money. When the player receives a blackjack, he gets paid 3 to 2. When a player is dealt two aces, it is to his advantage to split them and double his wager on two strong cards. The house obviously does not share that same advantage. For this reason, most good card counters will keep a separate side count of the aces played. If the remaining cards are lopsided with aces, the card counter will bet more. The dealer and card counter have an equal chance of getting an ace but the ace translates into money for the player.

When the count is plus, it is to the player's advantage to double down more often and take insurance. (The Plus Count means big cards are coming and big cards are what you want when doubling.) In advanced card counting, a player will stand more often on weak hands (i.e., 16 vs. 10) because he knows big cards are coming. When the count is minus it is not to the player's advantage to take insurance because the Minus Count indicates more small cards and one of them is more than likely the down card. On a Minus Count it is also not to the player's advantage to double as often.

A very important factor in the Plus/Minus Count is the number of decks in play. The greater number of decks, the higher or lower the Plus/Minus Count must be in order to add or subtract money from your bets. In theory, a card counter will lose more hands than he wins—approximately 48% losses, 43% wins and 9% ties. However, the Plus/Minus Count allows the card counter to win more big bets and lose the smaller amounts.

The simple Plus/Minus Count necessary to move bets up or down for the various number of decks is as follows:

1 deck	+2 to –2
2 decks	+3 to –3
4 decks	+6 to –6
6 decks	+9 to –9
8 decks	+12 to –12

The running count always starts at zero (0) after a shuffle so the wager is flat. (Any count in-between the plus or minus numbers listed above indicates a flat bet.) Very simply, you begin with a flat bet. Let's assume a $10.00 flat bet on a six deck game. As long as the running count stays between +9 or -9, the bet stays flat. If the running count were to hit +9—which simply means 9 extra big cards—or greater, then the bet would be increased to a plus bet...$20.00. If the running count were to drop to -9—9 extra small cards—or lower, then the bet would drop to a minus bet...$5.00. Simply stated, Flat Counts = flat bets, Plus Counts = plus bets and Minus Counts = minus bets.

Advanced card counters take the entire process one step further. A running count of +9 is much stronger with two decks left to be played than it is with five decks remaining in the shoe. The reason for this is obvious. The +9 with two decks left to be played is concentrated in approximately 104 cards. The same count of +9 with five decks remaining means the +9 is spread out over approximately 260 cards. For this reason, the running count is converted to the *true count*. The running count is divided by the number of half decks left to be played. With five decks remaining to be played, there are ten half decks, therefore, the true count is as follows: $9 \div 10 = .9$ True Count is .9

With two decks left to be played, there are four half decks remaining so the true count is as follows: $9 \div 4 = 2.25$ True Count is 2.25

The true count with two decks remaining is much stronger than with five decks.

There are several good books available on the subject of card counting. Remember that card counting uses the relative value of the cards already seen to predict the relative strength of the remaining cards.

It would take an entire book to do justice to the theory and practices of card counting, so let me list a few of the best books available.

THE THEORY OF BLACKJACK
PETER GRIFFIN

MILLION DOLLAR BLACKJACK
KEN USTON

BASIC BLACKJACK
STANFORD WONG

PROFESSIONAL BLACKJACK
STANFORD WONG

THE WORLD'S GREATEST BLACKJACK BOOK
LANCE HUMBLE & CARL COOPER

FUNDAMENTALS OF BLACKJACK
CARLSON R. CHAMBLISS & THOMAS C. ROGINSKI

Available through:
GAMBLER'S BOOK CLUB
630 S. 11TH STREET
LAS VEGAS, NEVADA 89101
702-382-7555

GAMBLER'S BOOK STORE
4001 S. VIRGINIA STREET, #8
RENO, NV 89501
775-825-7778

GAMBLER'S GENERAL STORE
500 SOUTH MAIN STREET
LAS VEGAS, NV 89101
702-382-9903

Author's Note: Some players have used small, custom-built card count computers hidden on their bodies to keep track of the cards. Oversized cowboy boots are outfitted with micro-switches above and below the toes. Using a binary input system (1, 2, 4, 8), all of the cards played are entered into the computer with up or down pressure applied by the toes. There are wires running from the computer to small, round electro-pads strapped to the players' thighs (or wherever—oooh!). A coded series of vibrations tells the player when to hit, stand, double down, etc. and when to bet big or small. Very clever, but very illegal. There are laws on the books in every gaming jurisdiction that outlaw the use of any device to "predict the future outcome of a gaming event." (See Question #59)

Now, from the sublime to the ridiculous. A couple of years ago the Ontario Provincial Police asked me to examine the play of a customer in a Canadian casino. This guy had attached three small golf score clickers to a leather watchband around his wrist. After every round of cards dealt he would move his hands under the table and click away. "Nice try, Captain Obvious!"

What is even money on insurance when I have a blackjack?

An insurance bet pays 2 to 1. This is a bet that is called for when the dealer has an ace up. You are betting that the dealer will have a 10-value card in the hole and, therefore, has a blackjack.

When you have a blackjack, you are paid 3 to 2 unless the dealer also has a blackjack, in which case the hand is a tie. Suppose you had a $10.00 bet and you insured the blackjack with a $5.00 insurance bet. If the dealer has a blackjack, you tie the blackjack bet and win $10.00 on the insurance bet. You're up $10.00. If the dealer does not have the blackjack, you lose $5.00 on the insurance bet but win the blackjack bet and are paid $15.00. $15.00 minus the $5.00 you lost on the insurance bet means you win $10.00 or *even money*.

In Nevada casinos, the dealers can pay even money on a player's blackjack before checking under their ace. In Atlantic City, the dealers are not allowed to offer even money so the player who desires even money must go through the process of putting up the insurance bet and waiting until the dealer's hand is checked.

As we discussed in a previous question, most gamblers think of insurance as a *sucker bet*.

One friend of mine told me he thought he got a great deal on fire and theft insurance. However, when reading the policy, it seems that he is only covered if he's robbed after someone sets him on fire.

What is the best way to play blackjack?

For the casual player who wants to improve his play without memorizing a lot of charts and learning to count cards, there are several simple rules to follow.

1.   Always play as if the dealer has a 10-in-the-hole.
2.   Always split aces and eights.
3.   Double down with 11 against all dealer up cards except an ace.
4.   Double down with 10 against all dealer up cards except a 10 or ace.
5.   Never take insurance.
6.   If you have a total of twelve and the dealer's up card is a 2 or 3, draw one card.

Point number one above is a simple rule which governs most 21 decisions. As a player, you know one of the dealer's two cards...the up card. For this example we'll say the up card is a 7. Assuming that the dealer has a 10-value card in the hole, his count would be 17. As a player holding a count of 16 or less, you should draw a card because standing creates more losses than hitting. If the dealer's up card is 2, 3, 4, 5, 6 and we assume a 10-value card in the hole, then we know that the dealer must draw a card. So as a player you would stand on 12 or more, let the dealer draw and take the chance of busting. Stating this rule another way:

1.   If the dealer's up card is 7 or better, then you hit 16 or less.
2.   If the dealer's up card is 6 or less, then you stand on 12 or more.

Point number two says, "Always split aces and eights." An ace is the single strongest card in the game of blackjack. The ace is counted as either 1 or 11. Together they make a count of 12. Splitting aces is a very strong move because you double your wager with a very strong card in each hand, even if you can only draw one card to each ace. A pair of eights makes a weak count of 16. By splitting the eights, you are taking the chance of improving both hands.

Points number three and four above say to double a 10 or 11 against a dealer's weak up card, but not to risk doubling your bet against a dealer's strong card.

Point number five simply says that insurance is a *sucker bet*. With an ace as the dealer's up card, the odds are 9 to 4 (or about 2.25 to one) that he will not have a blackjack. The insurance bet is, therefore, a bad bet unless you are a card counter doing a side count for insurance.

Point number six states that if you have a total of twelve and the dealer has a 2 or 3 showing, you should assume the dealer's total is twelve or thirteen respectively. Your count of twelve is not as bad as it seems. There are more cards that will help the hand than hurt the hand. This is the same for the dealer's hand—assuming he has a total of 12 or 13. The dealer has a very good chance of making a hand, so percentage wise you're better off drawing one card with a 12 or 13 against a dealer's 2.

Expanding these simple rules above, we arrive at *basic strategy*. The basic strategy for blackjack was developed over several years and proven by many independent computer simulations of the game. In addition, all possible player totals were analyzed against all possible dealer up cards. This vast body of work produced the accepted basic strategy for any number of decks and rule changes, along with the advanced strategies and betting patterns for even the most infrequent plays and conditions. It is far more difficult to memorize basic strategy for all conditions than to learn card counting. However, for the player who has the time and interest, the following is a basic strategy for any number of decks.

BASIC STRATEGY (No Double After Split)

Dealer's Up Card

Player's Total	2	3	4	5	6	7	8	9	10	Ace
A-A	SP	SP	SP	SP	SP	SP	SP	SP	SP	SP
10-10	S	S	S	S	S	S	S	S	S	S
9-9	SP	SP	SP	SP	SP	S	SP	SP	S	S
8-8	SP	SP	SP	SP	SP	SP	SP	SP	SP	SP
7-7	SP	SP	SP	SP	SP	SP	H	H	H	H
6-6	H	SP	SP	SP	SP	H	H	H	H	H
5-5	DB	DB	DB	DB	DB	DB	DB	DB	H	H
4-4	H	H	H	H	H	H	H	H	H	H
3-3	H	H	SP	SP	SP	SP	H	H	H	H
2-2	H	H	SP	SP	SP	SP	H	H	H	H
SOFT 21	S	S	S	S	S	S	S	S	S	S
SOFT 20	S	S	S	S	S	S	S	S	S	S
SOFT 19	S	S	S	S	S	S	S	S	S	S
SOFT 18	S	DBS	DBS	DBS	DBS	S	S	H	H	H
SOFT 17	H	DB	DB	DB	DB	H	H	H	H	H
SOFT 16	H	H	DB	DB	DB	H	H	H	H	H
SOFT 15	H	H	DB	DB	DB	H	H	H	H	H
SOFT 14	H	H	H	DB	DB	H	H	H	H	H
SOFT 13	H	H	H	H	DB	H	H	H	H	H
HARD 21	S	S	S	S	S	S	S	S	S	S
HARD 20	S	S	S	S	S	S	S	S	S	S
HARD 19	S	S	S	S	S	S	S	S	S	S
HARD 18	S	S	S	S	S	S	S	S	S	S
HARD 17	S	S	S	S	S	S	S	S	S	S
HARD 16	S	S	S	S	S	H	H	SRH	SRH	SRH
HARD 15	S	S	S	S	S	H	H	H	SRH	H
HARD 14	S	S	S	S	S	H	H	H	H	H
HARD 13	S	S	S	S	S	H	H	H	H	H
	2	3	4	5	6	7	8	9	10	Ace
HARD 12	H	H	S	S	S	H	H	H	H	H
11	DB	DB	DB	DB	DB	DB	DB	DB	DB	H
10	DB	DB	DB	DB	DB	DB	DB	DB	H	H
9	H	DB	DB	DB	DB	H	H	H	H	H
8	H	H	H	H	H	H	H	H	H	H
7	H	H	H	H	H	H	H	H	H	H
6	H	H	H	H	H	H	H	H	H	H
5	H	H	H	H	H	H	H	H	H	H

S = STAND   H = HIT   SP = SPLIT
DB = DOUBLE; IF YOU CANNOT DOUBLE THEN HIT
DBS = DOUBLE; IF YOU CANNOT DOUBLE THEN STAND
SRH = SURRENDER; IF YOU CANNOT SURRENDER THEN HIT

If you are allowed to Double Down after a Split, then substitute the following pair splitting rules.

BASIC STRATEGY (Double After Split Allowed)										

	Dealer's Up Card									
Player's Total	2	3	4	5	6	7	8	9	10	Ace
A-A	SP	SP	SP	SP	SP	SP	SP	SP	SP	SP
10-10	S	S	S	S	S	S	S	S	S	S
9-9	SP	SP	SP	SP	SP	S	SP	SP	S	S
8-8	SP	SP	SP	SP	SP	SP	SP	SP	SP	SP
7-7	SP	SP	SP	SP	SP	SP	H	H	H	H
6-6	SP	SP	SP	SP	SP	H	H	H	H	H
5-5	DB	DB	DB	DB	DB	DB	DB	DB	H	H
4-4	H	H	H	SP	SP	H	H	H	H	H
3-3	SP	SP	SP	SP	SP	SP	H	H	H	H
2-2	SP	SP	SP	SP	SP	SP	H	H	H	H

You'll notice that when doubling after a split is allowed, you will split more often.

Learning basic strategy is nothing more than memorization of the tables above. For the advanced or professional player, several book and computer programs are available through Gamblers Book Club in Las Vegas.

Note: Bill Cosby tells of a sure fire method of winning at blackjack. While on the table, you fake a heart attack. You then fall on top of the table with your face in the bankroll and swallow as many chips as you can.

What is the difference between 21 and blackjack?

A blackjack is a two-card hand totaling 21. A blackjack must be a 10-value card and an ace dealt on the first two cards. If a player splits aces and draws a 10-value card to each ace, he has a total of 21 on both hands but neither one is a blackjack. The 21's were achieved with the third and fourth cards dealt to that player.

A blackjack in most casinos pays 3 to 2. For a $10.00 bet, you win $15.00. A 21 pays even money.

The game of blackjack was at one time called "Twenty-One". In the old days, if a dealer approached a casino boss for a job and referred to himself as a blackjack dealer, he would be told, "Hit the road. We don't want clerks who deal blackjack; we want 21 dealers."

For your information, a blackjack should be dealt about 4.5% of the time. The mathematical proof is as follows:

$$\frac{(4 * 16 * 2)}{(52 * 51)} = \frac{128}{2652} = 0.048265 \text{ or } 4.83\%$$

The number 4 represents the number of aces in a deck. The number 16 represents the number of tens, jacks, queens and kings. The number 2 implies that the ace or ten-value card could be dealt as the first or second card. The number 52 is the number of cards in a deck and the number 51 is the number of cards remaining after the first card is dealt. For you Virgos out there (*knit pickers*), the following formula indicates the probability of having an *untied blackjack* (the player has a blackjack and the dealer does not or vice versa).

$$\frac{(4 * 16 * 2)}{(52 * 51)} = \frac{1 - (3 * 15 * 2)}{(50 * 49)} = 0.04649 \text{ or } 4.65\%$$

The number 4 represents the number of aces in a deck. The number 16 represents the number of tens, jacks, queens and kings. The number 2 implies that the ace or ten value card could be dealt as the first or second card. The number 52 is the number of cards in a deck and the number 51 is the number of cards remaining after the first card is dealt. The second parentheses indicates that the dealer will not simultaneously have a blackjack. The odds being 1 minus the probability of the first. The number 3 indicates the number of aces which would be remaining if the first hand received one. The number 15 indicates the number of ten value cards remaining if the first hand received one. Again the number 2 implies that the cards could be in either order. The numbers 50 and 49 represent the third and fourth cards dealt.

For you non-mathematicians, it's just as easy to remember that the name of the game is Twenty-One and you should get a blackjack once every 21 hands.

A Las Vegas comedian told a joke about the old days when they first began to hire black dealers: A very timid little customer was playing 21 on a table with a very muscular black dealer. The player got an ace and jack but was afraid to say blackjack. When the dealer asked, What do you have?, the scared little guy said, "Gin."

What is Double Exposure Blackjack?

In the late 1970's, a different form of blackjack was introduced by the Vegas World Casino in Las Vegas. The game is played on a standard 21 table, but with several rule changes and restrictions. Both dealer's cards are dealt face up. You know the dealer's two card total before you draw or stand on your hand. *Double Exposure*, also called *Nude 21*, *No Guess blackjack* and a variety of other names, sounds too good to be true...and it is. The following rule changes are in place, but are not advertised.

1.   The dealer takes all pushes (tie hands)

2.   A player's blackjack pays only even money (not 3 to 2)

The house taking all ties means that you will be faced with the possibility of having 20 and having to draw to that 20 because the dealer also has 20. In some cases, there are restrictions allowing double downs on 10 or 11 only. No double exposure game allows double downs after a split. Restricting double downs to 10 or 11 only gives the house an additional advantage of almost 1.5%. If the dealer hits soft 17, they gain another 0.3% advantage.

If you are going to play the Double Exposure Blackjack game, then look for the dealer to stand on soft 17 and doubling allowed on any two cards.

The following is a basic strategy for double exposure with doubling allowed on any two cards and the dealer standing on soft 17.

Blackjack players joke: They don't lie about the rules of the game. They just rearranged the truth in their favor.

DOUBLE EXPOSURE BLACKJACK

Player's Total	Dealer's Total													
	7	8	9	10	11	12	13	14	15	16	17	18	19	20
A-A	SP	SP	SP	SP	H	SP	SP	SP	SP	SP	H	H	H	H
10-10	S	S	S	S	S	S	SP	SP	SP	SP	S	S	S	H
9-9	S	SP	S	S	S	SP	SP	SP	SP	SP	S	SP	H	H
8-8	SP	SP	S	S	S	SP	SP	SP	SP	SP	SP	H	H	H
7-7	H	H	H	H	H	SP	SP	SP	SP	SP	SP	H	H	H
6-6	H	H	H	H	H	SP	SP	SP	SP	SP	SP	H	H	H
5-5	D	D	H	H	H	D	D	D	D	D	H	H	H	H
4-4	H	H	H	H	H	D	D	D	D	D	H	H	H	H
3-3	H	H	H	H	H	D	D	D	D	D	SP	H	H	H
2-2	H	H	H	H	H	D	D	D	D	D	SP	H	H	H
5	H	H	H	H	H	H	H	D	D	D	H	H	H	H
6	H	H	H	H	H	H	H	D	D	D	H	H	H	H
7	H	H	H	H	H	H	H	D	D	D	H	H	H	H
8	H	H	H	H	H	D	D	D	D	D	H	H	H	H
9	H	H	H	H	H	D	D	D	D	D	H	H	H	H
10	D	D	H	H	H	D	D	D	D	D	H	H	H	H
11	D	D	D	H	H	D	D	D	D	D	H	H	H	H
HARD 12	H	H	H	H	H	S	S	S	S	S	H	H	H	H
HARD 13	H	H	H	H	H	S	S	S	S	S	H	H	H	H
HARD 14	H	H	H	H	S	S	S	S	S	S	H	H	H	H
HARD 15	H	H	H	S	S	S	S	S	S	S	H	H	H	H
HARD 16	H	S	S	S	S	S	S	S	S	S	H	H	H	H
HARD 17	S	S	S	S	S	S	S	S	S	S	H	H	H	H
HARD 18	S	S	S	S	S	S	S	S	S	S	S	H	H	H
HARD 19	S	S	S	S	S	S	S	S	S	S	S	S	H	H
HARD 20	S	S	S	S	S	S	S	S	S	S	S	S	S	H
HARD 21	S	S	S	S	S	S	S	S	S	S	S	S	S	S
SOFT 13	H	H	H	H	H	D	D	D	D	D	H	H	H	H
SOFT 14	H	H	H	H	H	D	D	D	D	D	H	H	H	H
SOFT 15	H	H	H	H	H	D	D	D	D	D	H	H	H	H
SOFT 16	H	H	H	H	H	D	D	D	D	D	H	H	H	H
SOFT 17	H	H	H	H	H	D	D	D	D	D	H	H	H	H
SOFT 18	S	H	H	H	H	DS	D	D	D	D	S	H	H	H
SOFT 19	S	S	S	S	S	DS	DS	DS	DS	DS	S	S	H	H
SOFT 20	S	S	S	S	S	S	DS	DS	DS	DS	S	S	S	H
SOFT 21	S	S	S	S	S	S	S	S	S	S	S	S	S	S

Which is better...single deck or six decks?

To the professional blackjack player, a single deck game with liberal rules is the optimum game to play. The plus/minus ratio of big cards to small cards changes radically even from one hand to the next. Playing perfect basic strategy, the house and the player are about dead even at the beginning of play. Some mathematicians give the basic strategy player about 0.02% edge over the house to start. Really profitable single deck 21 games are becoming very rare as the casino operators restrict the rules of the game. Dealers hitting soft 17, restricting double downs to 9, 10 & 11, not allowing soft doubles and not allowing a double down after a split, all favor the house over the player. In a single deck game, a very small change in the ratio of big cards to little cards is necessary to increase or decrease the betting range. The rule changes, however, more than make up for the favorable count systems.

Most six deck or eight deck games offer much more favorable rules for the customer. The drastic changes in the ratio of big cards to little cards does not happen as often. Most of the time the betting count is in the flat range. In order to make the six or eight deck game profitable, it is necessary to stay much longer and ride out the long flat counts.

For the casual player, it really boils down to a matter of choice. Most six and eight deck games are dealt face up so it is much easier to count because you have more time to see all the cards. Single and double deck games are normally dealt from the hand and the players are allowed to touch the cards. The hand–held games offer more of a mystique if that is your preference.

Blackjack players joke: "I played 21 for 12 hours yesterday and didn't get hit with a blackjack until I went home."

Why are some discard racks made of red plastic?

In the old days, and in many casinos today, the plastic discard racks were made of clear plastic. On the single deck games, no discard racks were on the tables. Used cards were placed on the bottom of the deck in the dealer's hand underneath the cut card.

There is a particular method of marking cards known as *Luminous Readers*. A green or violet ink or pencil is used to mark the backs of red playing cards. The ink is painted on so lightly that the human eye cannot read it against the red background of the playing card. By wearing red tinted sun glasses or deep red contact lenses, the cheater can read the marks. The red glass or lens eliminates or cancels out the red card and you see what is left...the green or violet ink. Anyone with dark brown eyes could wear the deep red contact lenses. A person with blue or green eyes would look pretty silly wearing deep red contacts. A clear contact lens with a deep red center is used by cheaters with blue or green eyes. Cheaters may also wear a lightly tinted pair of sun glasses to help mask the red contacts. A color surveillance camera with a red filter in front of the lens will see the mark as well.

There is also a luminous daub which is used to mark cards in live play. Cheaters have been known to coat a dollar bill with the luminous daub and transfer a small amount of daub to their fingertip and then onto the back of a red playing card in live play. The resulting smudges are read by the same types of red glasses or contact lenses.

The red plastic of the discard rack acts as a filter and the floorperson standing behind the game can look through the red discard rack and check for this type of luminous reader.

Why can't I touch my bet once I place it in the circle?

Once a bet has been placed in the circle or betting area you are not allowed to touch the chips or money. The casino is concerned with cheating attempts by customers known as *capping* or *pinching*. Capping is a term meaning to secretly add chips or money to a wager. Obviously, this capping or *pressing a bet* is attempted once the player knows he/she has a winning hand and before the dealer pays the bet. A cheater may attempt to cap a bet even if he has a good hand and the dealer's cards have not yet been turned up. Some cheating methods involve using playing cards as a cover to add chips. Players have also been known to use items such as a cigarette pack or eyeglass case to help conceal their attempts to press or cap a bet.

Some cheaters will place a stack of $5.00 chips in the betting circle and angle the chips slightly towards the dealer. This is an attempt to block the dealer's view of the bottom chip. If the cheater gets a good hand he will slide a higher value chip ($25.00 or $100.00) underneath the angled stack of $5.00 chips. Dealers are trained to *case* the layout before each go-round looking for high denomination chips and straightening sloppy or angled bets.

Pinching a bet is just the opposite of capping. Trying to remove chips or money from a losing bet before it has been taken by the dealer is pinching. Again, some cheaters will use cards or other items to help mask their pinching attempts. You'll notice that the dealers will always insist that the larger denomination chips be on the bottom of a bet; $25.00 chips on the bottom, $5.00 chips on top of the $25's, and so on. This helps keep all bets and payoffs standard and makes it a little more difficult for a cheater to cap or pinch the larger denomination chips. Most dealers do not like to see what is called a *barber pole bet*. This is a bet with mixed colors in the stack. Instead of all the red chips on top of all the green chips, a barber pole has red and green mixed. This makes paying the bet more difficult as the stack must be broken down in order to pay a winner. Dealers would much rather pay color for color.

Two blackjack players talking: "I played real lucky last night." "How's that?" "I forgot my wallet at home."

Why don't dealers look under 10-value cards and aces anymore?

In the old days in Las Vegas, dealers *peeked* at the down card when they had a 10-value or ace card up. The dealer peeks to determine if he has a blackjack. If the dealer lifts the hole card too high while peeking, someone standing behind the dealer or seated across and behind the dealer can read the hole card. In the trade, this is known as *spooking*. The person reading the hole card would, of course, be working with a player on that dealer's game and would signal the value of the down card. (There was a depiction of spooking in the movie *Casino*. In the movie, the player spooking the game from behind was using an electronic device to signal his partner on the game. This device is known as a *thumper*.)

A more recent version of the same scam involves the use of a miniature hidden camera, a transmitter and receiving devices. A group of cheaters out of Minnesota concealed a battery powered zoom camera and transmitter inside a woman's purse. The woman would carry the purse over her shoulder and sit at a game across the pit "kitty-corner" from the target game. The woman stayed in contact with the receiver by means of a small electronic device concealed in her ear known as a *German bean*. The person controlling the receiver would direct the woman to aim the purse left or right, up or down, until he had a view of the hole card from behind. He could then zoom the camera in on the peeking action and read the hole card. The cheaters didn't reckon on the ability of the black and white surveillance cameras in the casino to see light wavelengths far beyond those of the human eye. The surveillance cameras saw a beam of red light emitting from the purse and the scam was uncovered.

A very old time method for the same scam involved a person on the game concealing a hand held mirror. The mirror is set at an angle which gives the cheater a periscope-like view of the table surface. By looking down into his hand (where the mirror was hidden), the cheater could pick up the value of the hole card as the dealer placed it under the up card.

When dealers bend the cards during the peeking process they create what are called *natural warps*. (The term *warps* simply means bent cards). Because the 10-value card or ace is face up when the peek happens, and most down cards will not be 10-value cards or aces, the big cards are bent in one direction and most other cards in the opposite. A person playing the warps would look at the way in which the up card rested on the down card. By virtue of the warps, a player had a good idea of the value of the dealer's hole card.

It is also possible for a dealer himself to signal the value of the hole card after peeking. For your information, the signal can at times be unintentional. It was common knowledge around the casino industry that if a dealer had a 10-value card up and peeked and then peeked again, he had a 4 in the hole. This is because the top of the 4 at first glance looks like the top of the A on an ace. If the dealer had an ace up and peeked twice, the down card was usually a 9. The top of the 9 was confused with the top of the Q on a queen.

The casinos were also concerned that dealers were unintentionally giving up the hole card after the peek by means of a *tell*. Some dealers would not look you in the face if they had your hand beat. Other dealers might pat the table differently or be more aggressive in the way they asked you to hit or stand...unconsciously telling you that you should hit or stand. Just like players in a poker game who do not have poker faces, 21 dealers had tells which gave away their down card. Players who played a dealer's tells watched for subtle differences in the dealer's body language when the down card was big or little.

Understand that no matter how a player gets knowledge of the down card, his play must be altered to accommodate that knowledge. His pattern of play (hitting and standing decisions) will alert the casino boss that something is not right. The player never guesses wrong and plays like a mind reader.

There are now several types of mechanical peeking devices which let the dealer check for a blackjack without lifting the hole card or knowing its' value. In some cases this will mean that the playing cards are printed differently. The aces may be printed with an "A" in all four corners and the rest of the indexes off center. The differences in printing are made to accommodate the various peeking devices.

Depending on which mathematician you believe, a player picking up the dealer's hole card 100% of the time has between a 5% and 9% edge over the house.

Blackjack player's joke: "Blackjack actually brought my family closer together. I lost all my money and we had to move into a one-room apartment."

2 4

Why shouldn't I play blackjack with the same rules as the dealer?

At first thought, this playing strategy seems to be a viable method. The dealer must draw on 16 or less and will stand on 17 or greater. Since both the dealer and the player have an equal chance of receiving the same first two cards, and thereafter achieving the same final total, it would seem to make sense that *miming* the dealer (called *mirror play*) would at least be a dead even proposition. The major flaw in this system is soon evident. When a player's hand busts (goes over 21), you lose immediately. The dealer acts upon his hand after you bust. The player must act on his/her hand first and, therefore, takes the chance of breaking first. This simple fact gives the player, playing a mirror strategy, a disadvantage of well over 5%.

There is also a blackjack strategy known as "No Break" play. The strategy says you stand on any count of 12 or more. You never hit a possible breaking hand. This is the very macho attitude of "I'm not gonna give up anything. If you want my money, come and get it!" Be assured that if you play the "No Break" strategy the casino will send a plane not only for you and your money, but for all your relatives who play the same way. You are giving up well over 5.0%.

You are far better off to learn basic strategy, money management and/or card counting if you are a serious 21 player.

A guy loses a fortune playing blackjack. At four o'clock in the morning, he asks a blackjack dealer on break in the restroom, "What's the secret?" The dealer replies, "It's Saturday night, four o'clock in the morning, I'm working, we're standing in a toilet and you're asking ME for the secret?"

Will card counting work for other casino card games like baccarat and poker?

The casino game of baccarat has its origin in the French game Chemin de Fer. In the old Chemin de Fer games, players could, when holding a two card total of 5 ask for a third card or not. In the baccarat games offered in casinos today (including mini-baccarat), the rules are fixed. The players betting either side have no decision in the cards being dealt. When the cards show a certain total, a third will be dealt regardless of any bets or players. Listed below are the rules for baccarat. You do not need to know the rules in order to play the game because the rules never change.

BACCARAT RULES

PLAYER HAVING

1-2-3-4-5-10	DRAWS A CARD UNLESS THE BANKER HAS A NATURAL
6-7	STANDS
8-9	TURNS CARDS OVER - NATURAL

BANKER HAVING	DRAWS WHEN PLAYER'S 3RD CARD IS	DOES NOT DRAW WHEN PLAYER'S 3RD CARD IS
3	1-2-3-4-5-6-7-9-10	8
4	2-3-4-5-6-7	1-8-9-10
5	4-5-6-7	1-2-3-8-9-10
6	6-7	1-2-3-4-5-8-9-10
7	STANDS	
8-9	TURNS CARDS OVER	

FACE CARDS AND TENS DO NOT COUNT
BANKER DOES NOT DRAW WHEN THE PLAYER HAS A NATURAL

When two or three cards total over ten, the first digit is dropped, i.e. a $9 + 6 = 15$, the total is 5.

There was at one time a side bet in baccarat for *naturals*; an 8 or 9 on the first two cards. This bet is no longer offered. There was a card count method to help determine mathematical advantage for this natural bet, but it is now academic as the bet no longer exists. For the game of baccarat itself, there is no card count method that will work to determine the winning side. I wrote a Baccarat card count computer program based on the work of Peter Griffin and Ed Thrope. The count program does in fact determine which side has the mathematical advantage. A significant usable advantage arises so rarely, about one in 500 hands, that you may as well just flip a coin.

For casino games like poker, there is no card count method such as a Plus/Minus Count. However, keeping track of cards that have been played is a common technique to help determine the odds of drawing a particular hand or the odds against an opponent having a better hand. Some cheaters have been known to lay back very low in their chair at a poker table, in an attempt to see cards being dealt in the air. Another technique, known as a *peek store*, involves a third party standing or hiding behind players to signal their cards to an accomplice. A couple of friends of mine once built a peek store into false kitchen cabinets at one of their homes. One cheat would actually be hidden in the false kitchen cabinets and look over the shoulder of the *mark*. He would then signal the value of the mark's cards to his partner. The scene in the James Bond movie *Goldfinger* is an example of an electronic peek store, but a peek store none the less. If you remember, a girl in a hotel room was using high-powered binoculars to peek at the playing cards of Goldfinger's opponents. She would then transmit the information to Goldfinger, who had what gamblers call a

German bean in his ear. This was also the same type of electronic arrangement that was used to cheat several celebrities playing gin rummy in Palm Springs at the Friars' Club.

Old Gambler's Joke: "I'll bet you a hundred bucks at 6 to 5 on a reverse parlay that I can stop gambling anytime I want."

2 6

What is the difference between baccarat and Chemin De Fer?

Chemin De Fer was the forerunner of the game we know as baccarat. Chemin De Fer was first introduced in France in the 15th century. Many of the French terms have survived to the present day. The chips were called cheques, dealers were called croupiers and the dealing shoe was called sabot (French word for shoe). The word sabotage arose from the practice of French factory workers throwing wooden shoes into the machinery to disable them. The game is also known as Punter/Banco in casinos in South Africa.

There is a tremendous amount of pomp and circumstance surrounding the game of Chemin De Fer, also called Shimmy or Baccara-en-Banque. The croupier uses a palette to handle the cards and cheques. A very elaborate shuffle-up process happens to start the game and to continue from one shoe to another. Beautiful women known as *shills* are hired to sit at the game to attract male customers and give an impression of glamour.

In Chemin De Fer, when the first two cards for the player's side total 5, the player has the option of drawing a third card or not. In baccarat there is no time when a player, on the bank or player's side, ever has an option or makes a decision about drawing cards. In baccarat the cards play themselves.

The main difference between the two games is that in Chemin De Fer, the customers wager against one another. In baccarat, all players bet against the house. Chemin De Fer is a banking game for the casino. The casino takes a commission of the winning bets, usually 5%. The customer with the shoe is known as the *banker* and places the first wager. The next customer to his right, known as the *fader*, has the option of accepting any or all of the wager placed by the banker. If that player does not accept all of the banker's wager, then the remaining amount can be accepted by the next player to the right and so on. The problem with Chemin De Fer in most casinos is that unless players are willing to wager against one another, there is no game.

Some casinos have reduced the bank side commission to 4% vig. This is a marketing attempt to stimulate play by attracting customers to a more favorable game. There is also a game known as Dragon Baccarat where no vig is taken. The house's advantage is derived when a tie hand occurs. On a tie hand, the house takes 25% of any wager on the bank side. Tie bets will, of course, win. From a mathematical standpoint the 25% exacted on the bank side when tie hands happen is almost exactly the same as taking 5% vig on all bank side wins.

A high roller walks out of the casino one night and sees a very dejected man standing in the taxicab line crying. "What's the problem?" asks the higher roller.

"My wife and I have been married 22 years. She's the love of my life. I just got off the phone and the doctor says she has a very rare blood disorder that needs immediate surgery and extensive medical care." The man continues, "I don't know where I'm going to get the money."

Touched by the story of woe, but still a little suspicious, the high roller asks, "How do I know that if I give you the money for your wife's operation you won't go back in the casino and gamble it all away?"

"Oh," replies the guy, "I *have* gambling money!"

How do dice dealers know which bets belong to who on a crap table?

The game of craps is a little more difficult to learn than the other casino games. Each player can place over a dozen different bets all working at the same time. On a crap table you will notice a set of numbers across the top and in front of each dealer.

The numbers 4 – 5 – 6 – 8 – 9 –10 are each in their own box.

Bets placed inside the numbered box are *come bets* for that particular point. Bets placed on the line of the numbered box are *place bets*. If you are standing next to the stickman and make a place bet, the dealer will put your chips on the line corresponding to your position on the table. Let's assume a place bet on the point 6 and that you are standing next to the stickman. The dealer will place your chips in the position marked ① above. If you are standing next to the base dealer, your bet would be placed in the position marked ⑥ above. If you are standing at the corner of the table midway between the stickman and the base dealer your bets are placed in the position marked ③ above.

In the center of the table are the *prop bets*; short for propositions. The stickman uses the same clocklike arrangement to place your prop bets in relationship to where you are standing at the table.

In private (illegal) games where a gambler books all the bets and players bet paper money, the arrangement is slightly different. As each bet is accepted it is turned sideways—*criss-crossed*—from the next and stacked one on top of the other in a pile. If the booker wins he simply picks up all the money. If the players win, the booker works backwards and un-crosses each amount and pays each bet in the reverse order from the way they were placed.

Old gamblers joke: "No one could be as loaded as the dice in this joint."

$$\boxed{2}\boxed{8}$$

How do they load dice?

One of the steps in the process of manufacturing dice is to drill the cubes (made of cellulose acetate) on all six sides. The drilled holes are filled with paint, actually a catalytic resin which makes a permanent bond with the cellulose acetate, to make the six numbers. The normal depth of the drill for standard spots is 1/20,000th of an inch. Dice cheaters will drill further into the cube on certain sides and add tiny wafer like slugs of gold, platinum or tungsten. The extra weight will have a tendency to cause the die to come to rest with the weight on the bottom. The weight is put on the opposite side of the number the cheater wishes to favor. (To load a die to throw a three 3, the weight is put on the 4 side.)

In white or opaque dice, the drilled spots can be made much deeper and a less expensive load of lead can be used. In transparent casino dice, the spots cannot be drilled as deeply, usually three to four thousands of an inch, because the spots begin to look very thick. The loaded spots and the fair spots are filled with paint. Some cheaters have been known to drill all the fair spots to the same depth as the loaded spots and fill the fair spots with paint only. This is an attempt to make all the spots appear the same depth. However the spots still appear deeper or thicker than normal.

A very sophisticated dice cheating scam is attempted with the use of *magnetic* loads. Instead of a weighted load the dice spots are loaded with tiny cobalt magnets. Wafer-like slugs of Neodymium or Samarium cobalt magnets are used. In one illegal gambling joint back east, the police removed a 2500 pound electromagnet from the floor underneath a crap table. Magnetic dice have surfaced in casinos in Nevada and throughout the gaming industry. In the game of Pai Gow Tiles, cheaters have been known to glue a tin plate to the underside of the table. The magnet can then be attached to the tin and removed easily. A very memorable incident involving magnetic dice occurred several years ago in Las Vegas. Some very ingenious cheaters built a 300 pound electromagnet into the seat of a standard wheelchair. The guy in the wheelchair could turn the "juice" on and off. It is not uncommon to see players in a wheelchair playing craps. In order not to block the aisle way, the wheelchair customer is usually placed near the dealer towards the inside of the pit. This is the perfect spot at which to operate the electromagnetic wheelchair. On this occasion however, the electromagnet malfunctioned and the battery power to the magnet overheated and began to burn the legs and butt of the guy in the chair. Instead of falling on the floor and pretending the wheelchair batteries had burned him, the guy had a miraculous recovery and got up and ran out of the casino.

A few years back I invented a dice stick to protect casinos from magnetic loads. A small neodymium cobalt magnet is imbedded in the front of the stick. Magnetic dice will quickly be discovered as they will adhere to this dice stick.

There are several tests which indicate the presence of loaded dice. The *spin* or *pivot test* is the easiest. Holding a cube between the thumb and index finger at diagonal points the cube is spun. A fair cube will spin smoothly and stop spinning in a very natural fashion. A loaded cube because of the extra weight will actually spin back at the end of the spin or make a small but sudden move forward at the end. A fair cube set into a tumbler filled with water will float down with the same number always pointing up. If you set the cube in the water with a 6 pointing up, the 6 will remain facing up as the cube floats down. If the cube is loaded, the weight turns to the bottom and the loaded number appears on top. It is also possible to burn the cube and pick the slugs out of the ashes. In the old days, dice were produced using cellulose nitrate. This was a very unstable material, to the point that if dice were left on the shelf for more than six months they would begin to shrink or change shape. If you were foolish enough to burn the old cellulose nitrate dice (Nitrate . . . Nitro . . . Boom), it would fill the room with clouds of black nasty-smelling smoke. (Ask me how I know.) Drilling or scratching away the paint will also expose the loads.

Under normal drilling and filling conditions the weight of the catalytic resin added to make the spots exactly matches the weight of the cellulose acetate removed so that the cubes always remain perfectly balanced. The illustration above shows the wafer slugs being added to the spots.

Authors' Note: To show you how bad some people's luck is, my brother Larry, who is also a magician, once switched *phoney dice* into a crap game and won a handful of counterfeit money.

What are free odds in craps and how much should I take?

When you begin a crap game, there is no point to shoot for. The first roll is called the *come out roll*. On that first roll if you throw 7 or 11 you win...2, 3, or 12 you lose. Any other number 4, 5, 6, 8, 9, 10 becomes your point. You must now make the point before you roll a 7.

There are 36 possible combinations that can be thrown with two dice. They are:

NUMBER	COMBINATIONS	# OF WAYS
2	1-1	1
3	1-2, 2-1	2
4	1-3, 3-1, 2-2	3
5	1-4, 4-1, 2-3, 3-2	4
6	1-5, 5-1, 2-4, 4-2, 3-3	5
7	1-6, 6-1, 2-5, 5-2, 3-4, 4-3	6
8	2-6, 6-2, 3-5, 5-3, 4-4	5
9	3-6, 6-3, 4-5, 5-4	4
10	4-6, 6-4, 5-5	3
11	5-6, 6-5	2
12	6-6	1

Once you establish a point, it is easy to determine the odds against making the point. Let's assume the point 4. You must roll a 4 to win...if you roll 7 you lose. The chart above shows there are three ways to make a 4, but six ways to roll a 7. The odds therefore are 6 to 3 against your making the point 4. The odds 6 to 3 reduces down to 2 to one. So the *true odds* of making the point 4 are 2 to one.

When you place a pass line bet and establish a point, the casino will pay you even money for that bet. The casino also allows you to back up the pass line bet with an odds bet also called *betting behind the number*. This odds bet is paid at the correct true odds for the point on the pass line. The true odds, also called *free odds*, for each number are as follows:

POINTS		TRUE ODDS
4 or 10	pays	2 to 1
5 or 9	pays	3 to 2
6 or 8	pays	6 to 5

So let's consider the point 4 with a $10.00 pass line bet. The term *single odds* means that the casino allows you to bet one times the amount of your pass line bet. In this case you have $10.00 on the line, so you can back it up with up to $10.00 behind. If you win the bet, you will be paid $10.00 for the pass line and $20.00 (2 to 1) for the odds bet. The term *double odds* means that you are allowed to bet two times the amount of your pass line wager. In this example with a $10.00 pass line bet, you could bet $20.00 behind the line. The amount of odds bets allowed by a casino does not affect the payoff for the pass line. With double odds you will be paid $10.00 for the pass line bet and $40.00 for the odds bet.

At first glance it may appear that odds bets are very profitable. However, it is my opinion that odds bets are nothing more then a marketing issue. Anytime you pay a bet at true odds, there is no profit for either side. Let me demonstrate in the following chart. As each example shows, there is no real advantage, mathematically speaking, for taking more odds. You lose the same $30.00 dollars based on the pass line wager only. The odds are paid at the correct mathematical probability, so it's just like paying 50/50 on the flip of a coin.

There is one intangible in the odds bets question. If the dice are passing, you would want to bet as much as your bankroll and personal preference will allow. You will be risking more at one time in order to try and win more. So taking full odds will cause you to win or lose much faster.

The point is 4 and we'll assume no odds bet.

You will lose		6X	$10.00 x 6 = $60.00 loss
You will win		3X	$10.00 x 3 = $30.00 win
Your net loss is			$60.00 - $30.00 = $30.00 net loss

SINGLE ODDS

The point is 4, $10.00 pass line, $10.00 odds

You will lose	$20.00	6X	$120.00 loss
You will win	$10.00 pass line and $20.00 odds bet		
		3X.	$30.00 x 3 = $90.00 win
Your net loss is			$120.00 - $90.00 = $30.00 net loss

DOUBLE ODDS

The point is 4, $10.00 pass line, $20.00 odds

You will lose	$30.00	6X.	$180.00 loss
You will win	$10.00 pass line and $40.00 odds bet		
		3X	$50.00 x 3 = $150.00 win
Your net loss is			$180.00 - $150.00 = $30.00 net loss

TRIPLE ODDS

The point is 4, $10.00 pass line., $30.00 odds

You will lose	$40.00	6X	$240.00 loss
You will win	$10.00 pass line and $60.00 odds bet		
		3X	$70.00 x 3 = $210.00 win
Your net loss is			$240.00 - $210.00 = $30.00 net loss

5X FREE ODDS

The point is 4, $10.00 pass line., $50.00 odds

You will lose	$60.00	6X	$360.00 loss
You will win	$10.00 pass line and $100.00 odds bet		
		3X	$110.00 x 3 = $330.00 win
Your net loss is			$360.00 - $330.00 = $30.00 net loss

10X FREE ODDS

The point is 4, $10.00 pass line., $100.00 odds

You will lose.	$110.00	6X	$660.00 loss
You will win	$10.00 pass line $200.00 odds bet		
		3X	$210.00 x 3 = $630.00 win
Your net loss is			$660.00 - $630.00 = $30.00 net loss

Old gambler's joke: How drunk was he? He was so drunk he gambled for two hours and was 'dead even' before someone finally told him he was playing a change machine.

What are the worst bets on a crap table?

As a general rule of thumb, stay away from anything big on a crap table. The *field* is a sucker bet as are the *prop bets*. The "Don't Pass" line is very small...this is the best bet on the table.

The field bet has as much as an 11% edge against the player.

The prop bets have between 11% & 17% edge against the player.

The hardway bets have between 9% & 22% edge against the player.

The Big 6 & 8 have over 9% edge against the player.

Old crap shooter's joke: A guy gets arrested for running a dice game and goes before a judge who has never tried a gambling case. The judge, trying to be wise, says to the gambler, "Here's how it's going to work. You roll the dice and whatever number comes up is the number of days you spend in my jail." The gambler being a 'wise-guy' switches the two white dice for two white sugar cubes. The courtroom laughs, but the judge laughs last. "Well, my boy," says the judge. "I guess you stay in my jail until the spots come back on these dice."

What are the odds in craps?

When you lose a bet in craps, or in most casino games, you lose exactly what you should lose...the amount you had wagered. When you win a bet is when you really lose. This sounds funny, but when you win you are not paid the full amount mathematically speaking. The difference between the mathematically correct payoff and the actual payoff is the house's advantage or rate of win. The casino has to have a built-in house advantage in order to make a profit and stay open.

Rather than presenting a long mathematical proof for each of the crap table bets, I will briefly describe a simple formula to determine house advantage. You determine what the bet should pay based on the mathematical probability and then compare that to what the casino actually pays. The formula is as follows:

> Subtract what you actually take down from the correct mathematical payoff then divide the difference by what you should have taken down.

Let's assume a place bet on the point 10. The true mathematical probability for this bet is 2 to 1 against. (There are six ways to lose by rolling a 7 and only three ways to win by rolling a 10. Therefore 6 to 3 reduces to 2 to one). Suppose you place the 10 for $5.00. If the bet loses, you lose $5.00. When the bet wins you should be paid 2 to one; $10.00 for the $5.00 place bet. You are actually paid at 9 to 5; $9.00 for the $5.00 place bet. So the formula is:

You should take down	$15.00	$5.00 + $10.00
You actually take down	$14.00	$5.00 + $9.00
The difference is	$1.00	

Divide $1.00 by what you should have taken down (1.00 ./. 15.00 = 0.0666 or 6.666%). The house advantage on the place bet 10 is 6.666%

The following tables list the house advantage for the various dice table bets. Note the difference between the payoffs when it reads **to 1** or **for 1**. Some crap layouts read **30 to 1** while others read **30 for 1**. 30 to 1 gives you 31 chips while 30 for 1 gives you 30 chips. You make one extra unit on the to 1 payoffs.

CASINO ADVANTAGE ON CRAP TABLE

BET			HOUSE ADVANTAGE
PASS LINE	(WIN)		1.414%
COME BETS			1.414%
DON'T PASS	(LOSE)	BAR 6-6 OR 1-1	1.402%
DON'T COME	(LOSE)	BAR 6-6 OR 1-1	1.402%
DON'T PASS	(LOSE)	BAR 1-2	4.385%
DON'T COME	(LOSE)	BAR 1-2	4.385%
PLACE BETS	(WIN)		
POINT 4 or 10	PAYS 9 to 5		6.666%
POINT 5 or 9	PAYS 7 to 5		4.000%
POINT 6 or 8	PAYS 7 to 6		1.515%
BUY BETS TO WIN	(5% VIG)		
POINT 4 or 10	PAYS 2 to 1		4.761%
POINT 5 or 9	PAYS 3 to 2		4.761%
POINT 6 or 8	PAYS 6 to 5		4.761%
BUY BETS TO LOSE	(5% VIG)		
POINT 4 or 10	PAYS 1 to 2		2.439%
POINT 5 or 9	PAYS 2 to 3		3.225%
POINT 6 or 8	PAYS 5 to 6		4.000%
FIELD BETS			
FIELD		2, 3, 4, 9, 10, 11, 12	11.111%
FIELD		2, 3, 4, 9, 10, 11, 12	
		(Pay Double On 2 & 12)	5.263%

BIG 6 or 8	PAYS 1 to 1	.... 9.090%

PASS LINE WITH SINGLE ODDS	.... 0.848%
PASS LINE WITH DOUBLE ODDS	.... 0.606%

DON'T PASS LAYING SINGLE ODDS	.... 0.832%
DON'T PASS LAYING DOUBLE ODDS	.... 0.591%

HARDWAY BETS

POINT		HOUSE ADVANTAGE
4 or 10	PAYS 7 to 1	.... 11.111%
4 or 10	PAYS 7 for 1	.... 22.222%
6 or 8	PAYS 9 to 1	.... 9.090%
6 or 8	PAYS 9 for 1	.... 18.181%

PROPOSITION BETS

BET		HOUSE ADVANTAGE
DOUBLE 1-1 or 6-6	PAYS 30 to 1	.... 13.888%
DOUBLE 1-1 or 6-6	PAYS 30 for 1	.... 16.666%
ELEVEN 6-5	PAYS 15 to 1	.... 11.111%
ELEVEN 6-5	PAYS 15 for 1	.... 16.666%
THREE 2-1	PAYS 15 to 1	.... 11.111%
THREE 2-1	PAYS 15 for 1	.... 16.666%
ANY SEVEN	PAYS 4 to 1	.... 16.666%
ANY SEVEN	PAYS 5 for 1	.... 16.666%
ANY CRAPS (2,3,12)	PAYS 7 to 1	.... 11.111%
ANY CRAPS (2,3,12)	PAYS 8 for 1	.... 11.111%
HOP BET (Any combination called for such as 5 - 2 on the next roll)		
	PAYS 15 for 1	.... 16.666%

Old Street Joke: A wise guy is trying to outwit God and asks, "Hey God, what is a million years like to you?" God answers, "A million years to me is as a second." The wise guy continues, "Hey God, what is a million dollars like to you?" God answers, "A million dollars to me is as a penny." The wise guy quips, "Hey God, could you give me a penny?" And God replies, "Sure, just wait a second."

Author's Note: Don't try to hustle the Big Guy. God knows everyone's hole card.

What is a boxman looking for when he picks up dice?

When one or both dice are thrown off the table, or in some way leave sight of the boxman, he/she needs to examine them to make sure they have not been switched.

The casinos have several methods of marking their dice for quick identification. Each casino uses their own logo and lettering type. Each die is also stamped with a two, three or four digit number which changes from day-to-day and from manufacturer-to-manufacturer. The numbers may be of different fonts and colors, as are the logo's. In addition, some dice companies stamp a letter or number on the backside of one of the spots. This mark can only be seen by looking through the transparent cube from the opposite side. (If the letter or number is stamped on the backside of the center spot of the three, then to read it you must look through the cube from the four side. Note: the opposite sides of a pair of dice always add up to seven (i.e., 6 opposite 1, 5 opposite 2, 3 opposite 4.) Some casino operators will also scribe a number or initials onto the dice in a different spot for each shift or game. A dice manufacturer can also produce dice with a *glow spot*. One of the white spots is treated with an ultraviolet chemical which glows under a black light.

If a dice shooter is being unusually rough with the dice, such as banging them on the table, hitting the mirror constantly or rubbing them on the felt, the boxman may also be looking for chipped corners or rounded edges.

Here are some interesting and colorful terms that dealers and players use when dice go off a game or when calling for a certain number.

Too tall to call .... Means the dice go off the game

No good, in the wood .... Means a die in the rail

Hippity hop, over the top .... Means dice off the game

One on the floor, seven at the door .... Means one or both dice go off the table and the next roll will be a "Seven Out" loser

No number, in the lumber .... Means dice in the rail

Too high to classify .... Means dice off the game

Fever five .... Point 5

Little Joe, Little Joe from Kokomo .... Point 4

Little Joe from South Boston .... The point 4

Snake-Eyes .... 2 • an ace on each cube

Bull's Eyes .... 2 • an ace on each cube

Postholes .... 2 • an ace on each cube

Boxcars .... 12 • a six on each cube

Highnoon .... 12 • a six on each cube

Midnight .... 12 • a six on each cube

Dirty Dozen .... 12 • a six on each cube

Big Red .... 7 • any seven

Bugle .... A horn bet • 2, 3, 11, 12

Cocked Eyes .... 3 • an ace and deuce

E.T. .... 11 and 12

On the Turn .... A hop bet • the next roll

"It plays where it lays." .... A winning bet the player forgets to pick up and is treated as a new bet by the dealer.

"Nothing to do. I'm bringing 'em through." .... When no bets have to be paid and the stickman gives the dice right back to the shooter.

What shot Jessie James? A forty-five. .... Point 9 • a four on one cube and a five on the other

Two Texas wallflowers .... a 5 on each cube

Two Kansas sunflowers .... A hard 10

Two California sunflowers .... A hard 10

Big Dick from Boston .... a "hard" 10

Eight skate & donate .... a losing bet on the point 8

How do ducks go to the water, two by two .... Hard 4...a 2 on each cube

Lay $150 against the 5, but I ain't got a penny ...... Laying against a number means you are betting the number will lose. The dealer puts a *lay button* on top of the bet. In the old days they used a penny instead of a lay button.

Little Nina from Pasadena	The point 9
Eighter from Decatur	The point 8
2 Picture Frames	A hard 8
2 Buck Sergeants	A hard 6
2 Trees	A hard 6
Can't read'er, in the cider	In the Rail
Ellaveene the dancing queen	The number 11
Cinco-Dos, Adios	5 & 2 - loser seven 5, 2, seven out, good-bye
Donny & Marie	A pair of squares, two 4's, a 4 on each cube
If ya snooze ya lose	Forget to make a bet
If ya sleep ya weep	Forget to pick up a bet (A "Sleeper" is a winning bet that a player forgets to pick up or walks away from. If the player doesn't come back or the bet loses the bet is *locked-up* for the house or dealers.)
How tall is your sister, 5'6"?	The number 11 (I guess you could ask, "How tall is my brother, 6'5"? Same number, 11.)
Tension Totty, all ass and no body	The point 10
Sister Hicks from the sticks	The point 6
They're upside down, just turn'em around	The number you want is on the bottom.
Can't tell 'er, in the cellar	The dice go under the table

Special Thanks to Eddie Brown, John O'Farrell and Vic Taucer for help with the above terms.

Old gamblers' joke: "His luck is so bad if he tried to whip butter, the butter would win."

What is a horn bet and a horn high bet?

A *horn bet* is a one roll, four part bet. You are wagering that one of the following four numbers will be rolled on the next roll of the dice (i.e., 2, 3, 11, 12). If you made a $20.00 horn bet, you would in effect be betting $5.00 each on the 2, 3, 11, 12.

A *horn high bet* is a one-roll five-part bet. You are wagering on the same four numbers as in the horn bet but with an extra bet (the fifth part) on one of the numbers you call. A $20.00 horn high aces would be a $4.00 bet on the 3, 11, & 12 and an $8.00 bet on the 2. A $20.00 horn high 11 would be a $4.00 bet on the 2, 3 & 12 and an $8.00 bet on the 11. You are free to call the high bet on any one of the four numbers.

If any other number besides the horn bets are rolled, you lose all the horn bets. If one of the horn numbers is rolled you win the bet on the number rolled, but you lose the other three bets. In this case, the dealer will pay you for the horn bet winning number and take enough out of your winnings to leave you up again for the next roll. You can of course ask to be taken down for the horn bet before the next roll.

For your information, a C & E bet is a two-part bet. Half of the money is bet on craps (2, 3, 12), and the other half on 11. This is also a one roll bet. You will win or lose the bet on the next roll of the dice.

A *whirl bet* is a horn bet with any 7 added. A *hop bet* is a one roll bet. You are calling for a specific number with an exact combination. A "6 - 3" on the hop means you must roll 6 - 3 on the next roll of the dice. A hop bet pays the same as an eleven.

Losers' saying: "I hope this joint has more luck with my money than I did."

What is the Big 6 & 8 and why don't some crap tables have the bet?

The *Big 6 & 8* is an even money bet. If you wager on the Big 6 you are betting that any 6 will show up before any 7 is rolled. The Big 8 is a bet that any 8 will be rolled before any 7 shows. The bet is really a sucker bet. If you were to wager $6.00 on the Big 8 and the 8 showed, you would be paid $6.00. If you took the same $6.00 and made a place bet on the 8 and the 8 showed, you would receive $7.00 for your $6.00 bet. Betting the Big 6 or 8 is the same proposition as a place bet on the 6 or 8; you win if your number 6 or 8 shows and you lose if the dice roll 7.

The Big 6 or 8 has over 9% edge against the player. A place bet on the 6 or 8 has 1.515% against you. You are far better off to place the 6 or 8 than to bet the Big 6 or 8. Keep in mind that you can take down any place bet or the Big 6 or 8 at anytime you chose. By gaming statute in some areas, the Big 6 & 8 have been eliminated from crap layouts. Many casino operators have removed the Big 6 & 8 because it does not get much play and it takes up a lot of space on the layout.

Las Vegas, a place where you can get tanned and faded at the same time.

Why does a hardway 6 or 8 pay more than a hardway 4 or 10?

Of the 36 possible combinations that can be made with a pair of dice, there is only one way to make a hard 6 (a 3 on each die). The same holds true for the hard 8 (a 4 on each die). The same holds true for the hard 4 (a 2 on each cube) and the hard 10 (a 5 on each cube). There is only one way in the 36 possible combinations to roll each of the hard ways. The difference in the payoffs arises from the fact that there are more ways to lose a hard way 6 or 8. You will lose the hard way bet if a 7 is thrown or if the number is rolled *easy* (not a pair). The winning and losing combinations for the hard ways is as follows:

HARD WAY	WIN	LOSE	
4	2-2, 1 WAY	ANY 7	6 WAYS
		ANY OTHER 4	
		3-1 or 1-3	2 WAYS
	WIN 1 WAY		LOSE 8 WAYS
10	5-5, 1 WAY	ANY 7	6 WAYS
		ANY OTHER 10	
		6-4 or 4-6	2 WAYS
	WIN, 1 WAY		LOSE 8 WAYS
6	3-3, 1 WAY	ANY 7	6 WAYS
		ANY OTHER 6	
		1-5 or 5-1	
		2-4 or 4-2	4 WAYS
	WIN 1 WAY		LOSE 10 WAYS
8	4-4, 1 WAY	ANY 7	6 WAYS
		ANY OTHER 8	
		2-6 or 6-2	
		3-5 or 5-3	4 WAYS
	WIN 1 WAY		LOSE 10 WAYS

As you can see, there are more ways to lose a hardway bet on 6 or 8 then on a hardway 4 or 10, therefore the increase in payoff. The hard 6 or 8 pays 9 for 1 or 9 to 1 while the hard 4 or 10 pays 7 for 1 or 7 to 1.

Old Gambler's Joke: "If you give up gambling, alcohol and drugs you really may not live any longer, but it sure as Hell will feel longer."

Why is craps not popular in many areas?

There are two reasons why craps or dice games are not popular or legal in some areas of the country. One reason is political and the other is religious.

In England, in centuries past, dice games were outlawed by the King when he found his Royal Guardsmen playing backgammon while on duty. In order to correct this problem, the King outlawed all dice games. This law, along with many others, was adopted as a matter of course by most countries in the Empire.

It is interesting that in many states dice games are not legal but card games are. Dice games had their origin in African and Arab countries. Crude dice were formed from animal and human bones and were used to predict the future and for gambling games. Actually, the ankle bone of sheep were perfectly suited for making dice. The sheep's ankle or huckle is a square, four-sided bone called an *Astragal*.

Many religious denominations have an aversion to dice games because of references in the Bible. Roman soldiers were said to have *cast lots* for the robe of Jesus at the foot of the cross. Other references to casting lots or bones are associated with the devil and dark forces.

(Luckily for us Catholics, there was no mention of ping pong balls in the bible...so "Bingo.")

Can a player track where the ball is going to land in a roulette wheel?

The answer to the above question is yes and no. The most important element in this equation is the type of roulette wheel being considered. The older wheels had several weaknesses inherent to their design. The *wells* were much deeper and the *frets* on either side of the *wells* were a high curved assembly. The center cone of the wheel was very high by comparison to the newer wheels. These elements combined to make wheel tracking much more profitable. There was an old axiom that the ball would never move more than four or five numbers away from the first number it landed in. The ball did not have as much action on the older wheels. Therefore, it was easier to attempt tracking. The tracker was not trying to predict a number but rather trying to track a section of the wheel. The tracking was an estimation of the speed of the ball as it slowed in the wheel track. The tracker was also looking for a dealer who spun the wheel at a predictable speed. Once the tracker could clock the number of revolutions left in the spin, he would attempt to gauge the section of the wheel most likely for the ball to fall in.

The wheel head is actually designed so that continuous numbers on the layout are opposite each other on the wheel head. You'll notice that except for the numbers near the "0" and "00" the arrangement is "odd-odd" "even-even." This system of numbering is meant to thwart wheel trackers and systems players. If you record the 38 numbers on a wheel head starting clockwise from the zero, and then divide that list into two 19 numbered halves, you would see the following:

0-28-9-26-30-11-7-20-32-17-5-22-34-15-3-24-36-13-1
00-27-10-25-29-12-8-19-31-18-6-21-33-16-4-23-35-14-2

Notice how the numbers are opposite one another, i.e. 0/00, 28/27, 9/10, etc.

A computer-assisted wheel track is possible when considering that both the speed of the wheel and the speed of the ball can be determined to a very accurate degree. By taking two strobe lighted photos of the ball spinning in the track, the speed of the wheel going in one direction and the ball slowing down going in the other direction can be determined to predict the fall off point of the ball. The fall off point, however, cannot indicate what will happen when the ball hits the bumpers (called canoes). The new wheels with the shallow wells and flat frets create a lot more action with the ball. The shallow cone allows the ball to cross over the wheel head.

Simply stating a very complex question: The older wheels are much more susceptible to wheel tracking. The newer type wheels are next to impossible to profitably track.

I did some consulting for the Philippine Government in casinos after Ferdinand Marcos was ousted. Roulette dealers ring a bell for players to make their bets. Once all bets have been placed the dealer rings the bell a second time before spinning the ball announcing, "No more bets." Players cannot bet while the ball is spinning. Nobody moves—nobody gets hurt. This procedure eliminates wheel tracking and past posting.

Old Danny Thomas joke: A guy is out jogging around a lake when he sees a guy in the water drowning. The jogger swims to the drowning guy and drags him kicking and fighting to the edge of the shore. Laying exhausted, the jogger sees that the guy is choking so he jumps on the guys stomach and starts pumping his chest. Water gushes from the guys mouth and the more he pumps the more water gushes. Finally an old Irish cop walks up and says, "What is that you're doing me boy?" "What do you mean what am I doing? I'm saving this guy's life. I'm pumping the water out of his lungs." "Well, my son," replies the cop, "You're gonna drain the lake if you don't get his ass out of the water!"

Can the dealer make the ball land in any number they want on a roulette wheel?

If you asked a good roulette dealer the above question, they would honestly answer, "No." There are just too many variables. The newer wheels with shallow wells and flat frets make number placement almost impossible. If you asked the same dealer could he/she place the ball in a ten number section more often than probability dictates, you might find dealers saying they could. The ball should land in a ten number section about 25% of the time. Hitting a section of the wheel is still a very difficult proposition. Dealers may get the impression that because they can out guess the drop off point for the ball on occasion, that this means they can hit a section. There is a real difference between hitting the same drop off quadrant point in a fixed wheel head and then having the ball land in a fixed ten number section of a moving wheel. The reason some roulette dealers think they can consistently hit a moving section in a wheel is that they occasionally try and do. In most cases, however, the dealer is falling in and out of luck.

A more interesting proposition concerning a roulette wheel revolves around (no pun intended) the ability to miss a ten number section. The casino has a mathematical advantage of 5.263%. The correct odds on a 38 number wheel is 37 to 1. If you bet one check straight up on a number, you should win 37 checks and take down 38. That would be a dead even proposition. The casinos, however, pay 35 to 1 and you take down 36 checks. The house holds back two checks. Two checks out of 38 can be expressed fractionally as 2/38ths. 2/38ths = 1/19th = 1 ÷ 19 =

0.0526315789 or 5.263% . If a dealer could consistently miss a ten number section leaving about 3/4ths of the wheel to hit, he/she would in effect change a 38 number wheel into a 28 number wheel. The dealer would be working in concert with an outside agent who would, of course, stay away from the section the dealer was attempting to miss and only bet the other 28 numbers. A dead even proposition on a 28 number wheel would be 27 to 1, however, the casino pays 35 to 1. The cheater takes down 36 checks when in fact they should be taking down 28 checks. The eight check difference is profit and is a positive expectation for this proposition. Assuming that the dealer can miss the ten numbers 100% of the time, the net advantage is 8 ÷ 28 = 0.2857142857 or 28.57% . This is, by the way, a very great assumption.

Roulette joke: "I don't know if the roulette wheel is *fixed,* but the table says *tilt!*"

How do they cheat in roulette?

There are several methods by which players and/or dealers attempt to cheat at roulette. The cheating that occurs in roulette, as in the vast majority of casino games, is an attempt by players alone or in concert with a dealer to take money from the house. Anything from moving bets from a loser to a winner, adding checks to a winning number, mis-marking the number and switching bets have been tried. Probably the most bold cheating attempt is a dealer intentionally mis-marking the number. A confederate approaches the roulette game and places a bet on one red number and one black number. Whichever color hits, black or red, the dealer puts the marker down on his agents' number. Obviously, this is not attempted when the table is packed with players. Some dealers or outside cheaters have been known to try and move a losing bet to a winner.

Basically, it is a simple game to protect because: "Nothing happens until the ball lands." The most common cheating attempt made at a roulette table is what is called *past posting*. The term *past post* originally came from horse racing. It meant to place a bet after post time. (You already know the winning horse or the horse in the lead.) To past post on a roulette table means to make a bet after the ball has landed and the winning number is established.

Usually there are three members in a past post team. (NOTE: each player at a Roulette table is given different color chips to identify one customer and his bets from all others. The roulette chips are not the same kind of chip used in the rest of the casino.) One member near the top of the layout, close to the wheelhead, will secretly pass a stack of his color chips to his confederate at the bottom of the layout, furthest from the dealer. The third member of the team will engage the floorperson in conversation to distract or lure them away from the game. The two cheaters on the game are waiting for the ball to land in a number from the center of the table down (the bottom half of the layout). When this happens the player near the top of the layout will openly attempt to place a late bet or move an existing bet. The dealer sees this activity and removes the late bet and the player argues with the dealer. This distraction at the top of the layout is cover for the cheater at the bottom of the layout to place the other cheater's chips on the winning number.

The cheaters are hoping that because the dealer is arguing with the player near the top of the layout, and sees his hands and knows the color of his chips, that he will assume the stack of chips must have been there already. The cheater at the bottom of the board will often place a big stack of the other cheaters chips on the winning number with a small amount of his color chips on top. If the dealer should happen to see his hand come out and place a bet, the cheater will remove only his small amount of chips leaving the larger stack of his confederate's chips on the winning number.

The reason cheating at roulette is attempted so often is the larger payoffs — 35 to 1 on a single number.

A very bold cheating attempt at roulette (and blackjack for that matter) involves placing a legitimate bet on the layout. Let's suppose a $1,000.00 wager on the outside bet 19 trough 36. If the ball lands on any number between 19 and 36, the cheater wins on the square. If the bet loses, the cheater simply grabs the $1,000.00 and runs. Not very clever, but it gets the job done.

Some cheaters will attempt a variation of the above theme. They will wrap several one hundred dollar bills with a single and place this pack of bills folded onto the layout just before the ball lands. They will also have a similar sized pack of one dollar bills folded, ready and secretly hidden on their person. If the bet wins, they leave it alone and are paid. The dealer picks up the folded bills and opens the one dollar bill to reveal several hundred dollars inside. If the bet loses, the cheater picks up the folded pack of one hundred dollar bills (covered by a single dollar bill) and switches the entire pack for the folded pack of singles. The dealer never saw the hundred dollar bills inside the first pack, and when switched, the dealer opens the second pack to reveal a stack of singles. (Dealers are now taught to unfold any folded money before accepting it as a bet.)

In the old days, the cheaters used to try and stop the ball in the track and drop it straight down into a number or section. This was attempted a couple of different ways. Using a needle fine drill bit attached to a battery-powered drill, cheaters would drill through the wooden side of a roulette wheel right into the wheel track. When the cheaters were ready to steal, one member of the crew would stand near the wheel and insert a lady's hatpin into the drill hole. As the roulette ball was slowing, the pin would be pushed all the way through the hole into the wheel track and would stop the ball and drop it straight into a number or section with little or no action on the ball.

In an overseas casino, a female player got the dealer used to her purse being on the layout a little too close to the roulette wheel. Inside the purse was actually a spring steel apparatus which, when triggered, would shoot a small metal finger out of the purse over the top of the wheel head and into the track stopping the ball. The metal piece would, of course, quickly retract into the purse.

Cheaters have been known to try and coat half of the wheel with a sticky substance hoping that the ball will land and stay on the sticky side more often than the non-sticky side. Using what looked like a nasal spray or perfume bottle, the cheater would walk past the roulette table and spray half of the wheel with this sticky substance. Casinos finally put plastic shields up around the wheel head to stop such attempts.

Old hustlers' saying: "You can fool some of the people some of the time, and you can fool some of the people some of the time, and if you can fool some of the people some of the time, that's enough to make a decent living."

What is the difference between a double zero wheel and a single zero wheel?

The double zero wheel has 38 numbers, 1 to 36 and two house numbers — zero (0) and double zero (00). Customers can, of course, bet on the house numbers. The double zero, 38 number wheel, is called the American wheel. For your information, adding every other number on an American wheel totals 37 with the exception of the two numbers next to the zero (0) and double zero (00) which total 37 but are right next to one another. The sum total of the numbers 1 through 36 is 666 (not a good omen if you believe in the devil). The house pays 35 to 1 on a single number bet. The correct odds on a 38 number wheel are 37 to 1. The house holds back two units on the payoff. The house advantage is therefore 2 out of 38 or expressed in percentages 5.26% (2 ÷ 38 = 0.05263). The house has the same advantage on every bet on the layout odd/even, red/black, split bets (means two numbers) with the exception of the 5 number bet (0, 00, 1, 2, 3). The house enjoys a 7.368% on the 5 number bet.

The single zero wheel was 37 numbers, 1 to 36 and one house number — zero (0). The single zero wheel is called the European wheel. The house pays 35 to 1 on a single number bet. The correct odds on a 37 number wheel are 36 to 1. The house holds back one unit on the payoff. The house advantage is, therefore, 1 out of 37 or expressed in percentages 2.70% (1 ÷ 37 = 0.02702).

The double zero wheel has almost twice the house advantage over the player as the single zero wheel.

Old gamblers' joke: "His luck is so bad he once bet on a horse who lost a photo finish to the old man who shovels crap off the track."

The roulette layout is also known as *Baize*.

Double zero wheel with American table layout.

Single zero wheel with French table layout.

$$\boxed{4}\boxed{1}$$

Why do they spin the ball one way and the wheel the other?

The action of the ball bouncing in the wheel is created when a small object going in one direction (the ball) hits a large object going in the opposite direction (the wheel). If both the ball and the wheel were spinning in the same direction, there would be almost no action when the ball falls out of the track into the wheel.

There are, of course, several other factors which affect the randomness and action of the ball. The term coefficient of restitution is a fancy term which only means how much does the ball bounce. Such things as the angle of the ball track, the number and placement of the ball stoppers, the depth of the wells, the swoop of the center cone, the angle and design of the frets on either side of the wells all affect the action of the ball. Couple the above considerations with the size and weight of the roulette ball and the type of material the ball is made of. Add to the mix the balance of the wheel head, the balance of the table, the balance of the bowl and you now have a complete look at the coefficient of restitution.

In addition, rumor has it that a wheel can more easily be tracked by the player or dealer when the ball and wheel spin in the same direction.

In some casinos you might see the dealer spin the wheel and the ball in opposite directions and change directions every other spin.

Here's a true story about the early days of Atlantic City gambling. A player stood behind a roulette table and very intensely watched the ball spin. The guy had no money on the layout. The ball landed in a number (let's say 17), and the guy disgustingly threw the roulette dealer a $25.00 chip saying, "Darn, I was betting on #22." Understand the guy had never asked for or put the bet down before the ball landed. He then just simply walked away. The dealer was not sure how to handle the situation and asked the floorman for help. Together they decided to *lock up* the $25.00 chip as if it had been a bet. Well, you guessed it, about 20 minutes later the same guy returned, stood behind the game, did not call for or place a bet, but this time when the ball landed he threw in a $25.00 chip and yelled, "I won, I won!" The dealer and floorman, of course, did not pay the bet. The customer appealed to the Division of Gaming Enforcement on property in every casino in Atlantic City. When he explained that the same floorman and dealer had taken his money on a "mind bet," the DGE made the casino pay the guy $875.00...not a bad little scam.

A guy walks past a young kid who has a lemonade stand. A sign above the stand reads, "Lemonade $3,000.00 a glass." The guy jokes, "Isn't $3,000.00 a little steep for a glass of lemonade?" The young boy replies, "Yeah, but at this price I only have to sell one glass!"

4 2

Are those credit cards that people use in slot machines?

In the strict sense of the word, the plastic cards you see players insert in slot machines are credit cards. They are not, however, a credit card like Visa or MasterCard. Most every casino in the industry has a player tracking and rating system. The MVP card (Most Valuable Player) is issued by the casino to identify a player's activity as they gamble. A combination of time played and "coins-in" create a rating of your play. The rating may also entitle the customer to: credit towards gifts, cash back, hotel rooms, food comps, shows, or qualify them for other casino slot promotions.

Most casinos have a slot promotion booth at which you can check the status of your account. Inserting your MVP slot card in a reading device shows the current activity and total points or credit towards your account. Many casino corporations will allow customers to use the same slot card account from one casino in their chain to the next, even from state to state.

Slot joke: A woman is standing behind a stranger watching him play the slot machines. As the player pulls the handle, his hand slips and he hits the woman in her breast with his elbow. Embarrassed, the man attempts to be charming, "If your heart is as soft as your bosom," says the man, "I know you will find it in your heart to forgive me." The woman replies, "If the rest of you is as hard as your elbow, I'm staying in room 215."

Can a slot machine be "hot" or "cold"?

This is one of the questions most frequently asked by tourists in Las Vegas. Theoretically, the simple answer is: "No, the payoffs are based on a random selection criteria." As we all know, however, perception is reality. At times it seems that certain machines pay more than others or the same machine pays off in cycles...*hot* and *cold*. Slot machine operations by and large, hold the same percentage as they did in the past. Several considerations need to be noted in order to understand the hot and cold perception. (Keep in mind that slot machines may be set to hold a particular percentage for the house, but the machine is still governed by a pay cycle.)

In years past in Las Vegas and the entire gaming industry, the pay cycle of slot machines was much different. Slot machine manufacturers were hindered by the limitations of a mechanical slot apparatus. The pay cycle was limited by the number of symbols that could be placed on any one reel and by the number of cuts that could be fitted on a star payoff wheel inside the machine. (Imagine a wheel similar to the round blade of a carpenter's power saw. On this star wheel, also known as payout disc, were various depths of cuts or indexes. The deeper the cut, the more the machine would pay. There was a star wheel (payoff wheel) for each reel on the machine.) The payoff cycle is determined by the number and types of symbols on each reel and the number of reels on the machine.

In the old days, the average slot machine had 20 or 25 symbols on each of three reels and a similar number of stops on the star payoff wheel inside the machine. Let's suppose you need three 7's in order to win the big jackpot. One 7 on each of the three reels needs to line up on the pay line.

Let's also assume three 20 symbol reels with one 7 on each reel. The odds of all three 7's appearing at once are as follows:

20 x 20 x 20 = 8,000

The odds of three 7's hitting is 8,000 to 1. The casino may have paid only 500 or 1000 for the jackpot. On a 25 symbol three-reel machine the odds are as follows:

25 x 25 x 25 = 15,625

Add a fourth reel with only one 7, and the odds become:

25 x 25 x 25 x 25 = 390,625

If a machine had two 7's on one of the reels the odds were as follows (assuming 20 symbols with three reels):

20 ÷ 2 x 20 x 20 = 4,000

This formula indicates two chances for a 7 on the first reel.

What the payoff schedule (or pay cycle) also indicates is that all payoffs should happen during the cycle. The average pay cycle of the old slot machines was between 8,000 and 15,625. Less money was paid more often and achieved the same hold percentage.

The slot machines in today's Las Vegas, and the entire gaming industry, have an average pay cycle of 262,000. (There are some newer slot machines with pay cycles approaching 16 million). The increase in the pay cycle is due to the electronic operation of the slot machines. More symbols can be utilized and there is no limitation due to a fixed number of stops on a mechanical starwheel. The payoffs and stops are randomly arrived at by one or more random number generators. Because of the random number generations, and the greater pay cycle produced, slot machine manufacturers can utilize a greater variety of symbols (this is known as *mapping*). Double payoff symbols, wild symbols, jokers and various other multiplying payoffs are now possible. In effect, what this means is that the machines will pay off larger amounts, but less often. The pay cycle becomes very volatile and the machine is perceived to be hot or cold.

Keep in mind that the casino is holding the same average percentage, or paying back the same average amount to the customers as they were in the past. It is just the hit frequency and excitement that has changed.

In fairness to the question, there is another point to be mentioned. If a casino advertises a payback of 97% or 98% you must look very closely at how it is worded. If the ad reads "Average Payback 98%," it means the average for all machines in that bank will be 98%. If the ad or sign reads "Up to 98% Payback," it means only one machine has to be set at 98%. Obviously, the casino doesn't tell you which machine it is. By law, casinos cannot advertise a payoff which is not possible.

Helpful hint: On the top of a slot machine is a light pole known as a candle. The candle lights up and/or flashes to alert slot personnel if you need change or assistance. The candle also alerts security and surveillance for various security codes—legal vs. illegal entries. The candles are color coded for different machine amounts: blue candles indicate $1.00 machines, yellow candles indicate 25 cent machines, orange candles are used on 50 cent machines and 5 cent machines have red candles.

Slot joke: A drunk walks up to a slot machine and puts a quarter in. As luck would have it, three 7's show up on the payline. The drunk stands back and cries, "Oh my God...I weigh 777 pounds!"

Author's Note: Stephan Coleman, a good friend and Director of Loss Prevention at the Ritz Carlton, San Juan tells me he once saw a female slot player with a bizarre superstition. The lady would dangle a small canvas bag by the purse strings over a slot machine. Inside the bag was a stone, a bone and a piece of metal. If the "magic bag" began to rotate clockwise she would play the machine counter clockwise and "bad voodoo," she would move on. (I don't know . . . it's worth a try.)

Can slot machines be set against you?

This was also one of the most frequently asked questions I heard when preparing this book. Unfortunately, the answer to this question is, "Yes, they can." From a practical standpoint, however, there is no credible reason why a licensed casino would ever set slot machines to cheat customers. I will explain this in more detail as we discuss this question, but first let me describe the most common methods (old and new) of setting a machine against a customer.

As I described in the previous question on hot and cold machines, there was in mechanical slot machines, a star wheel, also known as payout disc, which determined the amount the machine would pay. The star wheel resembles the blade of a standard carpenter's power saw, but with much wider and deeper cuts. In the old days, some unscrupulous slot operators would block the opening on the starwheel of the index that paid the big jackpot. All of the necessary symbols were present on the slot machine reels, but the reel could not stop on the star wheel in the index necessary to pay the jackpot.

Nevada State law says that all jackpots advertised must be capable of being hit and paid. The intentional blockage of a star wheel is, of course, a violation of State law and can result in heavy fines, terminations and/or the loss of the gaming license for the casino and/or its employees. This particular method went the way of the mechanical slot machine and is no longer a real consideration.

Keep in mind, also, that the State of Nevada Division of Gaming Enforcement or the Audit Division of the Gaming Board can, and do, inspect slot machines on a regular but random basis. Something as blatant as a metal guard over a star wheel payoff index was very easy to spot and is very strong evidence. An old mechanical slot machine could not possibly wear out that way. The metal blocker was an absolute indication of intent to cheat players.

Some oldtime slot operators had devised methods whereby the slot machine hopper would not pay the entire amount of a medium to large payoff. Suppose a slot machine payoff was to be 25 coins. The machine was rigged to pay between 20 and 23 coins — a short payoff. If the customer was diligent enough (as my mother would be) to count each payoff and complain (as my mother would), they would simply be paid the extra coins. The excuse would be that the machine had malfunctioned and would be repaired as soon as possible, and "Thank you for bringing this problem to our attention." If the customer did not count the payoff or complain (as my father wouldn't), the slot operator made an extra profit on each player by short paying.

One very old method which could still be used today involves the change girl or slot booth attendant. The method is known as *short rolling* a customer. The change person or slot booth attendant would secretly open a roll of dollar tokens. They would remove one coin from the roll and then carefully rewrap the rest to look like a full roll. For each roll sold, the attendant would pocket one dollar. If a customer complained (as my mother would), she was given a dollar with the excuse that the coin rolling machine in the count room must have made a mistake.

It was also common knowledge that dollar coin token racks could be used to steal from the customers or the house. Brand new wooden racks were sometimes so tight that only 19 tokens, instead of 20, would make the tube look full. An unscrupulous coin cage employee would short the house by *short stacking* the bank and pocketing one coin from each tight rack tube. Conversely, the same unscrupulous cage employee would find a worn out wooden rack where he could force 21 coins, instead of 20, into a tube. In this case, when cashing out, the player would be shorted $1.00 on each packed tube. With the use of high speed coin sorters and counters and coin count displays, the rack thefts have all but disappeared.(For your information, surveillance or outside companies will routinely check the buy-ins and cash-outs of slot employees to keep them honest.)

The newer slot machines are no longer mechanical. The electronic slot machines in today's casinos are controlled by random number generators and EPROMS. The source code and a master EPROM chip must be approved for use by the Electronic Services Division of the Nevada Gaming Control Board. The master EPROM is used as a comparator by which any similar slot machine EPROM can be tested. One local Las Vegas slot machine company was accused of tampering with the EPROMS of video draw poker machines in local bars. The allegation was that the company had altered the EPROM program to prevent certain cards from being dealt once the machine had paid out over a particular amount. The royal flush jackpot could not be hit if all five coins were played. This incident only affected local bars and local establishments and did not affect any casino. This company has since been fined and put out of business.

It is important to understand that casinos have no need or desire to cheat customers. Today's casinos are not the old sawdust joints of early Nevada where taking from a customer went right into the pocket of the owner or boss. In today's casinos, the owners and/or bosses are not allowed by law to count the money. Today's casino owner is, for the most part, a publicly held and traded corporation. Even a hint of scandal could be disastrous to the management, stock, and gaming license of a casino, and, in fact, jeopardize the corporation's interests in the other gaming areas of the country or the world.

Slot players' joke: "My luck has been really bad lately. Last night I put a quarter in a parking meter and lost my car."

How do customers try to cheat the slot machines?

The vast majority of cheating that happens in a casino takes place in the slot machine areas. This cheating is, for the most part, attempted by outside agents against the house. Unlike table games, casino surveillance of slot areas is not as rigid. Casinos have a dealer on each table game, a floorperson, pit boss to backup the dealer, a shift boss, the casino manager and surveillance. It is obviously not possible or practical to post an employee on each slot machine. The cheaters are aware of this and, consequently, they go after slot machines more often.

In fairness to casino slot operations, many hotels have installed slot control systems. Programs such as Bally's SDS System connect every slot machine in the casino to a master computer. Anytime the door of a slot machine is opened a print out is generated. A legal door opening, when an authorized employee is entering the slot machine, shows up differently from an illegal entry. The SDS and other systems like it, can be equipped with a camera alarm interface. When an illegal entry is made, the alarm will interface with the camera and move it to that location.

Cheating at slots takes many forms from the simple to the high-tech. One method known as *stringing or yo-yoing* is simply attaching one end of a string to a coin and the other end to a paper clip. The coin on the string is inserted in the slot machine, and the paper clip clips onto the outside of the coin entry preventing the coin from falling into the hopper. The string has been cut to the proper length to allow the coin to come to rest on the coin acceptor switch. By simply lifting the string up and down, the cheater is attempting to trigger the machine and register several coins in without any coins actually dropping. In order to combat the *stringer*, most slot machines are outfitted with tiny razor blades along the coin entry path. The idea is that when the stringer pulls the coin back, the razor blade cuts the string. When the cheaters began waxing the string and using metal strings, the casinos countered with more cutters—a game of "cat and mouse."

Another very common cheating method attempted in the slots is *slugging*. Slugging involves the use of counterfeit coins or tokens. In the old days, with the mechanical slot machines, there were several kinds of slugs that would be accepted in a slot machine. Foreign coins, washers, the metal pop-out circles from electrical outlet boxes, lead fishing sinkers melted down and molded, and tokens from children's arcades have all been used as slugs. Today, slot machines are electronic and have an electronic coin comparator. One of the casinos tokens, or a coin of the realm, is placed in the comparator. When a customer puts another coin in the machine, the comparator compares the metal alloy content, the diameter and weight before it allows the coin to pass.   There are a few clever cheats who have gone to the trouble of minting counterfeit tokens and attempt to match the exact alloy content of the casino tokens.

A common problem in casino protection of slot machines is key control. A cheater with access to slot machine keys can be very dangerous. In the old days, a cheater would make any excuse to have a slot floorperson or mechanic open the slot machine. If the floorperson were to leave the slot machine key in the lock while looking in the machine, the cheat would remove the key and make a wax impression.

There was also a very clever method of opening a slot machine without having the key. A cheater would find a slot machine in an area away from view. He would then spray hair spray or some other gummy substance into the lock. On the pretext that the machine had not paid correctly or had taken a coin without registering, the cheater would call the floorperson to the machine. The floorperson would, of course, unlock the machine, the key would remain in the lock and freeze the tumblers in place.

(We're talking about the ace-type tubular lock as opposed to a pin-type tumbler lock). When the floorperson removed the key, the latch would close but not lock. The cheater could then open the machine and either steal from the hopper or set the reels for a jackpot.

In most cases, slot cheaters will attempt to corrupt an inside person and simply buy the slot machine keys. Because slot personnel have to sign out keys for progressive slots, cheaters have been known to outfit a van with key duplicating equipment so the key will be off property as little as possible. It is now a State regulation, and just plain common sense, that all progressive jackpot machines must be recorded on videotape on a continuous basis.

A relatively new slot cheating attempt is known as *surfing*. Cheaters will attach a piece of clear Mylar tape to a $20.00 or $100.00 bill. The cheat approaches a slot machine or change machine and inserts the bill while, of course, keeping hold of the Mylar tape. The cheater may have previously prepared the bill by spreading a thin layer of baby powder on both sides. Just as the machine begins to register and accept the bill, the cheat will pull the bill back out. When timed properly, the slot machine registers the amount of the bill and the cheater still has the bill to use, again. (In an interesting aside to this method, it seems that the first cheaters to use this method saw it on a TV episode of *MacGyver*. There is also a similar, but not exact, method shown in a *Terminator* movie. The slot machine manufacturers have since adjusted the bill acceptors to prevent surfing.

Most electronic slot machines have a light optic reader which counts the number of coins being paid out. A clever piece of apparatus known as a *light device* has recently plagued the gaming industry. Imagine a thin piece of coat hanger wire about six to seven inches long. At one end of the wire is a small battery pack and a ceramic magnet. At the other end of the wire is a mini-mag light bulb and a small plastic deflector, which looks like a large clear guitar pick. The light device is inserted into the machine through the same opening as the coins pay out. The mini-mag light on the light device is positioned directly in front of the slot machine's optic reader light. When the mini-mag light is turned on, it in effect blinds the optic reader. Coins will now pass by the optic reader, be deflected by the light device "guitar pick," and never be counted. The net result is that a 20 coin credit may deliver as many as 200 coins. The slot manufacturers have now moved the optic reader to a position that better protects it. There are similar devices known as *monkey paws* and *kickstands* which hold open the latch on the coin hopper thereby dumping the coins without being counted.

A very *Mission Impossible*-like slot cheating scam involves the video draw poker machines. The EPROM chip from a video poker machine is deprogrammed and the source code and logic is known. One cheater plays on a video poker game while the other is in a hotel room nearby. The two cheaters are in communication via wireless transmitters and receivers. The cheater at the machine calls out the five cards dealt in order. Let's suppose the five cards are: JH, 5D, 3C, JS, 9S. The cheater in the hotel room has the EPROM video program running on his computer. The two cheaters are getting the two programs (the one in the machine and the one in the hotel) to sync up with one another. He instructs the cheater at the poker machine to hold positions one and four, the two jacks. As the program sequences through the remaining 47 possible draw cards, the cheater in the hotel rooms says, "Position two...wait, wait, wait...draw." He is waiting for another jack to show up in the second position. The same procedure is followed for position number three. The cheaters now have four jacks. The cheaters could, in some cases, be reading the cards behind the dealt cards. (Some video poker machine programs in the past called for ten cards to be dealt. Five cards you see and five cards behind those; in essence "back to back") The cheaters program could also be searching forward to determine when the Royal Flush would hit.

To combat this very clever cheating scam, slot manufacturers have installed three or more random number generators from which the hit cards can be drawn. The cheaters can't know which generator is in use or in what order the cards will be drawn. In addition, the random cards are not drawn until the draw button is pressed.

Attacking the EPROM of a slot machine has been attempted in various ways. One very clever method involved reprogramming the EPROM of a video draw poker machine. The player played until he was dealt five unmatched cards on the first deal. Normally under these conditions, the player would draw all five cards or hold only the jacks or better. The cheater, however, would hold all five cards and be paid as though a full house had been drawn. The EPROM program had been altered to pay a full house amount when five unmatched cards were held.

Here's a very clever and intriguing slot cheating method from the past. Mechanical slot machines were outfitted with two micro switches. The micro switch was housed in a small plastic covering approximately 3/4" x 1/2" x 1/2". The clever cheat had removed the microswitch components and replaced them with a miniature radio receiver. By one of two methods, the cheat had his microswitches installed in slot machines. Posing as a slot machine parts supplier, the cheater sold his microswitches to the casinos at a big savings. The other method was to simply pay off a slot mechanic working for the casino to install the gaffed microswitches. A player would approach the machine which had the gaffed microswitch. This cheater would play until he legitimately had a payoff, let's suppose 20 coins. This cheater would collect the 20 coins and walk away, leaving the winning symbols in line on the payline. Here's the clever part. Another player would approach the machine holding a fat cigar between his fingers. In point of fact, the cigar was a phoney. Inside the hollowed out cigar covering was a miniature radio transmitter. When the customer touched the cigar to the metal side of the machine, it would turn on the transmitter.

The receiver in the gaffed microswitch would cause the machine to pay another twenty coins. If, after the payoff, the machine was touched once more, it would again pay twenty coins. The scam was eventually uncovered when one of the members went to jail on an unrelated charge. He "ratted out" the scam in exchange for his freedom.

Old Arabic saying: "Three people can keep a secret if you kill two of them."

How does Megabucks work?

In many of the Las Vegas and Nevada casinos you will see a bank of progressive slot machines known as Megabucks. Megabucks is a multi-property linked progressive. The link is made via telephone lines between all subscribing casinos in the state. In this regard, the link is an intrastate arrangement. The Megabucks you might see in Atlantic City, Mississippi, or any other gaming area has nothing to do with the Megabucks in Nevada. The Megabucks progressive meter you watch increase in one casino, is affected by all Megabucks slot machines in all casinos in the state.

A company called IGT invented the multi-property link-up idea. IGT shares in the bulk of the profits from the Megabucks slots. Each casino, of course, has a smaller share.

You shouldn't confuse Megabucks with any other progressive jackpot slot machines you see. Megabucks is the only progressive payoff that links up several casinos in the same jackpot. The other progressive machines are only in house. The idea is similar to the Power Ball State Lottery which links up twenty different states as opposed to the individual state lotteries which represent only that one state.

There are casino table games such as Caribbean Stud Poker and Let It Ride Poker that now have progressive meters on them. Caribbean Stud is the only game which has a slot-like coin drop that directly affects the metered amount. Each casino, however, is independent of the others as far as the progressive amount is concerned.

Originally when the Megabucks jackpot was hit, the progressive meter was reset to one million dollars. The jackpot is paid by IGT and not the casinos. IGT buys an annuity in the name of the winning customer. The jackpot amount is paid out over 25 years. (Originally, the annuity was for 20 years but moved to 25 years when the meter reset was moved up.) The Megabucks meter reset moved from one million to three million and now to five million dollars after a jackpot win.

For your information, the odds of hitting the Megabucks jackpot (remember, you must play $3.00 each pull) is about 50 million to 1. Up to November of 1998 the biggest Megabucks jackpot was just under 12 million dollars. The customer invested $9.00 (pulled the handle 3 times). On November 15, 1998, a Las Vegas woman playing at the Palace Station won the largest Megabucks jackpot ever of $27,582,539. The lucky lady will receive $1,104,895.06 per year for 25 years.

Update: Mega-Bucks began in 1986 and has produced over 60 jackpots. On January 26, 2000 a woman in her early twenties invested $27.00 in a Mega-Bucks machine at the Desert Inn Casino. This young woman won the biggest Mega-Bucks jackpot in history—$34,955,489.56. She claims she will split the winnings, $1,398,219.58 per year for 25 years, with her boyfriend. Lucky girl . . . even luckier guy!

Author's Note: There's an old proverb that says lightning doesn't strike twice. In October of 1998, one month before she hit Megabucks, the same Las Vegas woman won $683,000 on the IGT Wheel of Fortune slots. So much for old proverbs in the gambling business.

A drunk walks up to a bank of vending machines in the airport in Las Vegas. He starts putting money into each machine. Soon he has all his pockets filled and both arms loaded down with items, yet he continues to put more coins in. A passerby asks the drunk, "Hey buddy, don't you think you should quit?" "Why?" replies the drunk, "While I'm still winning?"

What is rhythm play?

Rhythm play has nothing to do with the old Catholic birth control method. (Sorry Ma.)

In the old mechanical slot machines, there was a timing device known as a *clock* or *fan* (imagine a small four blade fan). The clock would begin to spin when the handle was pulled. As the clock slowed, each slot reel would index and stop. Rhythm play was an attempt to outguess the clock and determine the position of the reels for the next spin.

Since slot machines no longer have a mechanical clock, rhythm play is obsolete.

Question: What do you call a man who practices the old birth control method of "rhythm?" Answer: Daddy.

Special thanks to my dear friend, John Thompson, *The Great Tomsoni*, for the above joke. I lifted the joke from John's Polish Mind Reading act.

Old bookmaker's joke: An old street gambler was getting ready to take his first trip on an airplane. A little afraid, he decides to check out all the angles and visits the local bookmaker. "What are the odds of someone on an airplane having a bomb?" asks the gambler. The bookmaker thinks for a second and replies, "About a million to one." The old gambler snaps, "That ain't good enough." "What are the odds of two bombs being on an airplane?" The bookmaker thinks again and replies, "About 50 million to one." "Well," says the old gambler, "that's a whole lot better." So now the old gambler flies, but he always carries one bomb with him."

What percentage does the house have on slot machines?

Here is another very commonly asked question regarding slot machines. (You might wish to refer to Question [4][3] regarding payoff cycles and hot and cold machines).

On average the casino slot operations are holding about the same percentage they always have. There are a few variables such as slot machine mix (nickels vs. quarters vs. dollars) and slot machine types (video poker vs. coin multipliers vs. progressives). But, by and large, here are the average hold percentages for the Las Vegas Strip, Downtown Casinos and Local Bars:

Average Payback by Area & Machine — Gaming Control Board Figures					
	.05	.25	$1.00	$5.00	Mega-Bucks
L.V. Strip	90.39%	92.95%	94.99%	95.86%	89.05%
Downtown	92.18%	95.06%	95.43%	95.97%	89.34%
Boulder Hwy	93.45%	96.21%	96.69%	97.26%	89.97%
N. Las Vegas	93.61%	96.72%	97.40%	N/A	89.19%

Local bars and other such local slot outlets have almost exclusively Video Draw Poker machines. The Las Vegas Strip and Downtown casinos, of course, produce tens of millions of dollars more revenue.

The only way to beat the slot machines in a casino is with a hammer...a really big hammer.

What is the best video poker machine to play?

Video Draw Poker is most popular in Las Vegas and particularly in the local bars and establishments.   The average hold percentage in most bars is 2% for the house and a 98% return to the player. This hold percentage varies dependent upon the payoff schedule and the level of skill of the player. Take notice of the payoff amounts for the *Flush* and the *Full House*. A Flush is five cards of the same suit in any order. Five cards of the same suit and in consecutive order is a Straight Flush. A Full House is three of one kind and two of another. Look at the payoff amount for a single coin for the Flush. The payoff should be five or six coins. The payoff for the Full House will be seven, eight or nine coins for one coin bet. The payoff configurations are designated by the payoffs for the Flush and the Full House. The payoff schedule could be a 5 to 7 (five coins for a Flush and seven coins for a Full House.) The payoffs can vary by machine types or from location to location. The other two common payoffs are a 5 to 8 (five coins for a Flush and eight coins for a Full House) and a 6 to 9 (six coins for a Flush and nine coins for a Full House).

If all payoff amounts for the other hands are the same, then the Flush and Full House payoffs determine the strength of the entire payback. Following are the standard payoff amounts for most common Video Draw Poker machines:

	1	2	3	4	5
Royal Flush	250	500	750	1000	4000
Straight Flush	50	100	150	200	250
4 of a Kind	25	50	75	100	125
Full House	*				
Flush	*				
Straight	4	8	12	16	20
3 of a Kind	3	6	9	12	15
2 Pairs	2	4	6	8	10
Jacks or Better	1	2	3	4	5

All things being equal, if the payoff amounts for the rest of the hands are as above, then the best Video Draw Poker machine to play is the 6 to 9.

*Could be any one of the following combinations:

	1	2	3	4	5
Full House	7	14	21	28	35
Flush	5	10	15	20	25
Full House	8	16	24	32	40
Flush	5	10	15	28	25
Full House	9	18	27	36	45
Flush	6	12	18	24	30

Author's Note: Here's a hot tip. Most quarter progressive video poker jackpots hit between $1,300.00 and $1,400.00. A quarter video poker machine with a jackpot over $2,200.00 actually has an advantage for the player. A royal flush happens on average once every 40,200 hands.

Video poker is the biggest thing to hit Las Vegas locals since Las Vegas started. You can't swing a "dead cat" in Las Vegas without hitting a video poker machine.

Which makes more money...the slots or the table games?

In the old days of Las Vegas, the table games made considerable more than the slot machines. At the time, slots were thought to be "just for the women." When I first moved to Las Vegas, in the mid 1970's, slots and table game revenue were about 40/60. With the emergence of the electronic slot machine and the increase in game types they provide, slot revenue is now about 50% vs. 50% for table games.

In Atlantic City the ratio is approximately 70% slot machine revenue and 30% table games. In many other states the slots produce up to 90% of the casino's revenue.

The nickel slot machine was, in the old days, the staple of the slot revenue. Today the nickel slot machine is being phased out in Las Vegas (However, they are still found in all major casinos). The nickel slot machine has a much greater house advantage than the quarter or dollar slots. The average nickel slot holds about 15% for the house and returns 85% to the customer.

For your information, quarter slots and dollar slots make about the same amount of money for a casino. There are, however, four times as many quarter slots as dollars.

Slot players' saying: "I have enough money to gamble with. I wish I had enough money for food."

Will a magnet move the reels on a slot machine?

In the past, slot machine operators produced machines with steel reels (or other ferrous material) which would, in fact, be attracted to a magnet. What cheaters would attempt to do was stop the internal slot machine clock and move the reels to a jackpot. When the handle of a mechanical slot machine is pulled, the clock or fan begins to spin. The thief would drill the side of the machine on which the clock was located. The drill used to penetrate the side of the machine was very ingenious. Imagine a battery operated drill with a head the size of a dentist's drill. Using another person as a blocker, the slot cheat would drill the machine in just a few seconds in the precise spot necessary.

The next step was also quite interesting. In order to cover up the drill hole (which was about the diameter of a standard paper clip), the cheat would fill the hole with a dab of chocolate from a candy bar. The sides of most slot machines are about the same color as a chocolate bar. The drilled slot machine would stay in use as normal until the cheaters were ready. Finally, another slot cheat would approach the slot machine along with a blocker. Using a piece of piano wire or spring steel, the cheat would push through the drill hole and attempt to stop the clock. If successful, the slot machine reels would now be *free wheeling*. A powerful magnet (sometimes concealed in a pack of cigarettes) would be placed up against the window of the slot machine. The reels could then be maneuvered into place and a jackpot set.

The first attempt by slot machine manufacturers to overcome the magnet was a failure. The companies began producing slot machines with reels that were made of nonferrous material. The problem was that the spokes on which the reels spun were still made of steel. The machine manufacturers finally changed all of the components to non-ferrous materials.

Slot cheats were, and sill are, very clever at their craft. The casino slot operations personnel and slot technicians are also pretty clever. In order to combat drilling attempts, casinos installed armor plates on the sides of the slot machines. A very clever counter measure was the installation of a thin piece of glass—sort of on a flap-type arrangement. As the cheater inserted the drill bit, the glass flap would move slightly causing the drill bit to buckle and break. Also the drill bit might break the glass leaving additional evidence.

Slot players' joke: "If this joint gets hit with a nuclear bomb, I'm gonna hide under this slot machine. It's never been hit yet!"

5 2

Do players play against the house in Poker?

In a private game, the deal goes from player to player and you are betting against each other. Each player may call the game...dealer's choice.

In a casino poker room, you play against other players but not against the house or dealer. The dealer will rotate the position from which he begins dealing by moving clockwise from player to player. The house only deals the game and takes a *rake* from each pot.

There are times when you are playing against a player paid by the house to play. This player is known as a *shill*. In most cases, shills are given one stack of chips by the poker room to start play. From that point on the shill plays with his/her own money. In some casinos the dealers will shill other poker games on their breaks. A casino poker room who uses shills will allow so much per day to bankroll shills.

Be wary of any poker game where you don't know the other players. It was common knowledge in Las Vegas that in certain poker rooms the local players were waiting for tourists to get in the games. The locals would then *double team* the inexperienced tourists. (Refer to the Question 5 6 on the most common cheating methods in poker.) Through a series of signals and *board talk*, the locals would exchange information about their own cards and the possible value of the tourists cards. One tip-off may be that a couple of players are raising the pot with no real strength showing in their cards. They are working with each other to drive you out of the game. The beauty of this type of cheating is that there are no sleight of hand moves and the cheaters always have a simple *out*...they were just speculating on a bad hand and just didn't draw the cards...logical story.

Let me relate a story from my past to illustrate that most hustlers have a logical way out of a jam. A couple of years back, a television pilot was shot here in Las Vegas called *Nasty Boys*. They used my hands to perform the sleight of hand cheating moves, and also this story from my youth:

> "One time in a poker game back home, I was holding–out
> (*palming*) a pair of kings. Well, somebody at the game decided
> to count down the deck. Of course, they counted 50 cards
> instead of 52. Great concern fell over the table at this point.
> If I waited long enough, they would of course get to me. I
> could have dropped the cards on the floor but, again, it was a
> pair of kings, and underneath my chair it still would not
> have looked good for me. ("Oh my, look at the pair of kings
> on the floor under my chair. I wonder how they got there?")
> I needed to take control of the situation, as bad as it was. As
> soon as the guy who counted the cards placed them on the
> table, I grabbed the deck, added the two kings back on top,
> and said, "Let me count those cards." The question is, "How
> many cards did I count?" Most people say, "Of course you
> counted 52." Wrong. Hello! If I counted 52 cards, the entire
> table would know that I had added the missing cards to the
> deck. I finished counting the cards, and even though there
> were now 52 cards, I slammed the deck down on the table
> and yelled, "50 cards! You rotten bastards!" By this time, the
> guys running the game had come to the table to see what the
> trouble was. Well, the next poor bastard who pick up the
> deck counted, you guessed it, 52 cards. He took all the heat.
> I tried to put the guys running the game on the defensive,
> and cover myself by changing the order of the count. I said,
> "What the F@#% is going on here? I counted 50 cards, this
> guy counted 50 cards, and now all of a sudden there's 52 (I

made it sound like I counted first.) I can't fade this
B@#%S@#%, I'm getting out of here!"

Sometimes I wonder if the poor guy who picked up the cards after me realized it was me who added the pair of kings. Sometimes I wonder, but not very often.

Author's Note: On November 22, 1998 one of the all time great poker players and a world class money gin player, Stu Unger, died. Stu was nicknamed "The Kid" or "Stuey the Kid." Stu Unger won the $1,000,000 prize of the World Series of Poker at the Horseshoe Casino in 1980, 1981 and 1997. Unger was a brilliant player and a real force in the world of high stakes poker. Stu and his family were close with my wife and her family, so just a personal note to say, "So long Kid."

Old street joke: A mob boss and a wise guy are in a poker showdown. They raise and reraise each other until money covers the table. At the end, the wise guy cracks, "Beat this! I got a full house, aces over kings. What have you got?" The mob boss says, "I got a pair of duces and a switch blade." Says the wise guy, "Damn, you're lucky!"

How do you play Pai Gow Poker?

Pai Gow Poker is dealt with a standard 52 card deck and one joker. Each player is dealt seven cards. The object of the game is to make two poker hands. One of the two hands is made up of five cards (called the *high hand*), the other is the two card hand (called the *low hand*). The five card hand must be better then the two card hand. For instance, let's assume that in the seven cards there are two pairs — a pair of 10's and a pair of 9's. You can play both pairs in the high hand if you wish or you can split the pairs. You cannot, however, put the pair of 10's in the low hand because your high hand must be better than the low hand.

The joker is counted as either an ace, or to complete a flush, or to complete a straight. The joker is not a universal wild card.

You will see the dealer shake a dice cup with three dice in it. The total of the three dice will tell the dealer which spot (counting himself) will receive the first set of cards. The dealer is spot number one and will receive the first set of cards if the dice total 8 or 15. The spot to the dealer's extreme right is number two and the extreme left is number seven. If the dice total more than 7 you simply subtract 7 from the total. For example, if the dice total 11 then the player in spot four gets the first set of cards. If the three dice total is 15 or greater, you subtract 14 from the total to determine the first hand.

Most Pai Gow Poker tables are now using an automatic shuffler that deals cards and uses a random number generator to decide who gets the first set of cards.

In order to win a Pai Gow Poker hand, you must beat the dealer by winning both the high and low hands. To lose, you must lose both hands. Winning one hand and losing one hand is a tie.

Also the bank has one additional advantage—the bank wins all exactly matching hands. Suppose the player and the bank both have an Ace/Queen (or whatever) in the low hand. Even though the card values match, the bank would win the low hand. The bank would also need to win the high hand to win the bet. In some California card rooms and private games, the joker is used as a universal wild card. It would be to your advantage to bank the game because of the additional tie hands created by the universal joker. In order to play the game well, you need to learn when to split up the two pair, full house and four-of-a-kind hands. If you have trouble deciding how to play the cards, the dealer will help you set the hand according to the house rules known as *house way*.

When you win a hand, the house will pay you even money minus a 5% commission i.e., $95.00 on a $100.00 bet. On every other hand, the house will offer the *bank* to a player on the game. If you accept the bank, you are then playing against the house and banking against all other players on the game (You will need a good sized bankroll to bank the game). The house will still take a 5% vig on the winning bets. If the player does not want the bank, it reverts back to the house.

Approximately 42.5% of the hands in a Pai Gow Poker game are tie bets, so a player can last a long time on a relatively small bankroll.

Old gambler's joke: A guy comes running into a bar and says to the bartender, "Hurry! Set up 10 shots of your best scotch whiskey down the center of the bar, each one exactly four inches apart." A little intrigued the bartender complies. The guy starts at one end of the bar and slams down each drink one after the other until all 10 shots are gone. The bartender is stunned and says, "Man, you're gonna die if you keep drinking like that." The guy replies, "Yeah, well you'd drink like this too if you had what I have." The bartender asks, "What do you have?" The guy answers, "Seventy-five cents."

What are the odds of being dealt a good hand in poker?

The probability for a five card poker hand begins with the proposition 52 cards taken 5 at a time. Expressed mathematically, that is (52/5)! The math looks like this:

$$\frac{52 * 51 * 50 * 49 * 48}{5 * 4 * 3 * 2 * 1} = 2,598,960$$

There are 2,598,960 possible five card hands that can be dealt in a five card game. This means that the odds of being dealt a Royal Flush in spades, (10, J, Q, K, A) is one in 2,598,960. Understand that this also means the odds of being dealt *any* called for five card hand is the same — one in 2,598,960. Being dealt the 5D, 6C, AS, 10H, 9H in the first five cards is the same as the Royal Flush in spades. Given that there are four different suits that the Royal Flush could be made in, the correct odds for any Royal Flush in the first five cards is:

$$\frac{2,598,960}{4} = 649,740 \text{ to one}$$

Similar calculations can be made for each of the other hand types. Take, for instance, the odds of being dealt a flush (five cards of the same suit, not in order). There are 13 cards in each suit. You need five of the 13 cards in the first five dealt to make a flush. The math looks like this:

$$\frac{13 * 12 * 11 * 10 * 9}{5 * 4 * 3 * 2 * 1} = 1287 \text{ x 4 suits} = 5148$$

The number above, however, includes all Flushes, Royal Flushes and Straight Flushes as well.

You must now subtract the number of Royal and Straight Flushes to determine the accurate count for a standard flush.

5148	
– 4	Royal Flushes
– 36	Straight Flushes
5108	Flushes

The following chart shows the odds of being dealt the different ranked hands in the first five cards.

HAND TYPE	NUMBER OF WAYS IN FIRST FIVE CARDS	ODDS IN FIRST FIVE CARDS
ROYAL FLUSH	4	649,740.00
STRAIGHT FLUSH	36	72,193.33
FOUR-OF-A-KIND	624	4,165.00
FULL HOUSE	3,744	694.16
FLUSH	5,108	508.80
STRAIGHT	10,200	254.80
THREE-OF-A-KIND	54,912	47.32
TWO PAIRS	123,552	21.03
ONE PAIR	1,098,240	2.36
NO PAIR	1,302,540	1.99

The above chart shows the odds of being dealt a Royal Flush are one in 649,740. The odds of being dealt one pair is about dead even and the odds of no pair is just about the same. As you can also see, there are more hands with no pairs than for all other hands combined.

These charts are very relevant when analyzing the game of Caribbean Stud Poker.

The breakdown for *no pair* hands is as follows:

ACE HIGH	502,860
KING HIGH	335,580
QUEEN HIGH	213,180
JACK HIGH	127,500
TEN HIGH	70,380
NINE HIGH	34,680
EIGHT HIGH	14,280
SEVEN HIGH	4,080
TOTAL NO PAIR HANDS	1,302,540

FIRST FIVE CARDS - ONE JOKER WILD

HAND TYPE	NUMBER OF WAYS IN FIRST FIVE CARDS	ODDS IN FIRST FIVE CARDS
ROYAL FLUSH NO JOKER	4	649,740.00
FIVE-OF-A-KIND	13	220,745.00
ROYAL FLUSH WITH JOKER	24	119,570.20
STRAIGHT FLUSH	216	13,285.50
FOUR-OF-A-KIND	3,120	919.70
FULL HOUSE	6,552	437.90
FLUSH	7,768	369.30
STRAIGHT	20,532	139.70
THREE-OF-A-KIND	137,280	20.90
TWO PAIRS	123,552	23.20
ONE PAIR	1,268,088	2.26
NO PAIR	1,302,540	2.20
TOTAL HANDS	2,869,685	

The above chart shows the breakdown of hands with a joker wild. The joker is used as an ace or to make a Straight or Flush.

Two poker players talking: "I can't play in the game tonight. I had the money put away, but my wife blew it on the rent."

What is the "dead man's hand" in poker?

This particular poker hand has a very colorful history. If you have ever visited the historic town of Deadwood, South Dakota, you will see Saloon #10 advertised as a tourist attraction. It was in Saloon #10 that Wild Bill Hickcock was shot in the back of the head. Wild Bill is buried in that town on Boot Hill next to Calamity Jane and Deadwood Dick.

On August 2, 1876, in Saloon #10, Wild Bill Hickcock was playing poker when he was shot by Jack McCall. The hand that Wild Bill was holding at the time of his death has become known as the *dead man's hand*. Four of the cards were known for sure to be a pair of black aces and a pair of black eights. There seems to be a discrepancy over the fifth card. Some say the fifth card was a red queen, others say the 9 of diamonds. Whatever the fifth card was, a two-pair hand of black aces and black eights is the dead man's hand.

An interesting observation in Deadwood is that many store owners and casino operators claim to be Saloon #10. The actual site of the real Saloon #10 was destroyed by fire many years ago. One enterprising operator even displays a chair with a bullet hole through the back. This bullet hole implies Hickcock was shot in the back, when in fact he was shot in the head.

Here's a piece of poker trivia: What are the three face cards in profile? Jack of hearts, jack of spades, king of diamonds (the one-eyed jacks and the one-eyed king).

What is the most common cheating method in poker?

This is a very interesting question. If you were to ask two cheating experts for the most common cheating method in poker, you'll probably get three opinions. Well, here are two of mine. One poker cheating method involves sleight-of-hand manipulation of the cards and the other does not involve sleight-of-hand at all.

The non sleight of hand method I am referring to is *team play* also known as *double teaming*. A group of two or three players are in league with one another. Anytime one of the players has a good hand, he secretly signals the other members of the team. This is known as giving the *office*. The term office really means to *tip us off* or *off us* or *give us the off*. The team now attempts to drive the *pot* up by raising and re-raising the other legitimate players. Even a good player with a fair hand may not want to risk his bankroll by fading all of the raises.

In addition, the team members give each other information as to the probability of making certain hands. Knowing the value of the cards, the other team members hold allows me to determine the chances of the non-team members drawing to or making certain poker hands. Again an *office* is used. Certain code words or hand signals are used by the cheaters to tell each other the card values they hold. When playing against inexperienced players, cheaters may also use another form of the *office*. One team member folds his hand and then simply leans over to see the cards being held by the squares. In many so called "friendly" poker games, it is not uncommon to see players looking at each others cards once one of them has folded. The cheater folds, you let him look at your cards, and he signals your hand to his partners. The term *playing it close to the vest* means a person is not giving up information. It is a poker term which means holding your cards near to yourself so as not to expose them to view. Many inexperienced poker players hold their cards *away from the vest* exposing them to view.

In my opinion, the most common (and easiest to accomplish) sleight-of-hand cheating method is *bottom retention*. Bottom retention is also referred to as *location play*. Simply stated, a known group of cards is kept on the bottom of the deck during the shuffle. This is a very simple sleight of hand technique to master. During the riffle shuffle the cards are just not mixed on the bottom. It is also possible to perform *top retention*, however, it is much more noticeable that you are not mixing the top cards. It is much easier to retain cards on the bottom of the deck. During an overhand shuffle, cards are drawn from the middle of the deck to begin the shuffle, thereby leaving the bottom cards in place. It is also very easy during an overhand shuffle to shuffle the bottom cards to the top of the deck and then simply shuffle them right back to the bottom. During a running strip cut (also known as *sidlings* or *stripping*), the bottom cards are stripped to the top and can easily be run right back down to the bottom. With this known order of cards in place (either bottom or top), the final cut before dealing puts the stack into or out of play.

In a private game, the dealer may be using the information himself or be in league with partners on the game. If the known cards are on the bottom and the dealer makes a deep cut, he will, in affect, bring those cards to the top. These cards will then be the first cards dealt and become the down cards in a stud game or known cards in each players hand in a draw game. The confederate working with the dealer also knows the order of the cards controlled on the bottom and simply waits to see which of the cards he himself receives. By simply counting forward and/or backwards from his own hand, he can determine the known cards in each other player's hand. The cut after the shuffle (and just before dealing) can also put the known cards out of play. A thin cut (not too deep into the deck) will leave the known cards near the bottom and thereby eliminate them from the next round of play. Knowing what cards cannot come into play is very strong as well. By cutting to the middle of the deck, the cheater knows the bottom cards will be dealt in the second or third round of a stud game or will be the draw cards in a draw poker game. It is also possible to attempt to steer the known cards (by virtue of the cut) to land in the *flop* for board games such as Hold 'Em or Criss Cross.

You might run into magicians or pseudo-gambling experts who will disagree with my opinion. They may attempt to impress you with clever sleight of hand moves and complicated card maneuvers; however, most of them never cheated in a game...I did.

A poker cheat says to a square who just won the big pot, "You couldn't possibly have won that hand. I know exactly what cards I dealt you."

5 7

Are "free drinks" really free?

The obvious answer to the above question is no. The casinos give free drinks to those customers who are gambling at the table games or playing the slots. You are paying for the drinks by wagering in the casino. Although some customers will try to give the impression of playing in order to obtain free drinks, they are the exception not the rule.

In Atlantic City the cocktail servers say, "Coffee, tea, soda." They are not allowed to solicit alcohol. You can of course ask for a drink. In many Indian casinos no alcoholic beverages are allowed at all.

The only person who might really get free drinks is the bum who walks through the slot machine areas looking for drinks that other customers have left. In the industry this is known as *looking for seconds*. According to my wife, it's "yuck!"

Alcoholic's jokes: "Things got so bad that for a while there I was living on nothing but food and water!"

How drunk was he? He was so drunk he walked into the bathroom, unbuttoned his vest, pulled out his tie and peed in his pants.

Are the odds better in downtown Las Vegas or on the Strip?

There is no single answer to this question. Depending on the type of game you play, the odds could be better in either location.

The crap table layout has traditionally offered better odds in Downtown Las Vegas. The difference in the proposition bets and the hardway bets are shown in the table below.

BET	DOWNTOWN	STRIP
DOUBLE SIXES		
DOUBLE ACES	30 to 1	30 for 1
ELEVEN 6-5		
THREE 1-2	15 to 1	15 for 1
SEVEN HOPPING		
(3 - 4) (6 - 1)		
(5 - 2)	15 to 1	15 for 1
HARD 4 (2 - 2)		
HARD 10 (5 - 5)	7 to 1	7 for 1
HARD 6 (3 - 3)		
HARD 8 (4 - 4)	9 to 1	9 for 1
FIELD BET		
2,3,4,9,10,11,12	TRIPLE ON 2 OR 12	DOUBLE ON 2 OR 12

Some of the Las Vegas Strip casinos are paying the downtown odds. The difference in the above payoffs is one unit. A $1.00 bet on a hardway 8 pays 9 to 1 on a downtown layout. You take down $10.00; the $9.00 that you win plus the $1.00 you bet.   The same bet on a standard Strip layout pays 9 for 1. You take down $9.00; you receive $9.00 for your $1.00 bet.

The difference in layouts is a marketing issue meant to attract customers to the better payoffs.

The Las Vegas Strip casinos have traditionally offered a better single deck 21 game for the customer than the Downtown Las Vegas casinos. The following rules given by the Strip casinos were much more advantageous to the player:

- Dealer stands on soft 17
- Double down on any two cards
- Double down on soft hands
- Double down after a split
- Surrender

Many of the Downtown and Northern Nevada casinos hit soft 17, restricting double downs to 10 or 11 only with no soft double downs and no double after a split. All of these rules are to the advantage of the house. (Refer to Question 11 on blackjack odds for the exact percentage of advantage or disadvantage for the above rules.)

In all fairness to the question, many of the Las Vegas Strip and Downtown casinos have changed rules so that the strong distinction between the two is not as strict as it once was. For the serious 21 player, it is wise to search out the casinos with the best rules.

Author's note: Las Vegas is really a very civic and ecologically minded place. You'll notice signs in the airport, "Keep Las Vegas green...bring money."

Are there laws against cheating in casinos?

The State of Nevada and the Nevada Gaming Control Board and Gaming Commission have enacted several laws specifically designed to regulate, define and prosecute cheating in Nevada casinos. The following are excerpts from Chapter 465 of the Nevada Statutes: Crimes And Liabilities Concerning Gaming.

465.015 Definitions. As used in this chapter.

1. "Cheat" means to alter the elements of chance, method of selection or criteria which determine:
   a. The result of a game;
   b. The amount or frequency of payment in a game;
   c. The value of a wagering instrument approved by the State Gaming Control Board for use in connection with a cashless wagering system.

465.070 Fraudulent acts. It is unlawful for any person:

1. To alter or misrepresent the outcome of a game or other event on which wagers have been made after the outcome is made sure but before it is revealed to the players.
2. To place, increase or decrease a bet or to determine the course of play after acquiring knowledge, not available to all players, of the outcome of the game or any event that affects the outcome of the game or which is the subject of the bet or to aid anyone in acquiring such knowledge for the purpose of placing, increasing or decreasing a bet or determining the course of play contingent upon that event or outcome.

3. To claim, collect or take, or attempt to claim, collect or take, money or anything of value in or from a gambling game, with the intent to defraud, without having made a wager contingent thereon, or to claim, collect or take an amount greater than the amount won.

4. Knowingly to entice or induce another to go to a place where a gambling game is being conducted or operated in violation of the provisions of this chapter, with the intent that the other person play or participate in that gambling game.

5. To place or increase a bet after acquiring knowledge of the outcome of the game or other event which is the subject of the bet, including past-posting and pressing bets.

6. To reduce the amount wagered or cancel the bet after acquiring knowledge of the outcome of the game or other event which is the subject of the bet, including pinching bets.

7. To manipulate, with the intent to cheat, any component of a gaming device in a manner contrary to the designed and normal operational purpose for the component, including, but not limited to, varying the pull of the handle of a slot machine, with knowledge that the manipulation affects the outcome of the game or with knowledge of any event that affects the outcome of the game.

465.075 Use of a device for calculating probabilities. It is unlawful for any person at a licensed gaming establishment to use, or possess with the intent to use, any device to assist:

1. In projecting the outcome of the game;

2. In keeping track of the cards played;

3. In analyzing the probability of the occurrence of an event related to gaming; or

4. In analyzing the strategy for playing or betting to be used in the game; except as permitted by the commission.

465.080 Use of counterfeit, unapproved or unlawful wagering instruments; possession of certain unlawful devices, equipment, products or materials.

1. It is unlawful for any licensee, employee or other person to use counterfeit chips or other counterfeit wagering instruments in a gambling business.

2. It is unlawful for any person, in playing or using any gambling game designed to be played with, receive or be operated by chips, tokens or other wagering instrument approved by the State Gaming Control Board or by lawful coin of the United States of America.

    (This section goes on to describe the various elements necessary to manufacture or fabricate *slugs* or counterfeit tokens. This also includes the tools and materials necessary to make slugs or tokens.)

465.083 Cheating. It is unlawful for any person, whether he is an owner or employee or a player in an establishment, to cheat at any gambling game.

465.085 Unlawful manufacture, sale distribution, marking, altering or modification of equipment and devices associated with gaming; unlawful instruction.

1. It is unlawful to manufacture, sell or distribute any cards, chips, dice, game or device which is intended to be used to violate any provision of this chapter.

    (This section describes the use of such things as marked cards, loaded or gaffed dice and any device, such as mirrors, electronic equipment and so on used to cheat at gaming. This section also covers teaching or instructing any person in the methods of cheating or stealing from casinos with the knowledge that

that person will in fact use the information or training to cheat or steal from a casino.)

465.088 Penalties for violation of NRS 465.070 to 465.085, inclusive.

1. Any person who violates any provision of NRS 465.070 to 465.085, inclusive, shall be punished:

    a. For the first offense, by imprisonment in the State prison for not less than one year nor more than ten years, or by a fine of not more than $10,000, or by both fine and imprisonment.

    b. For a second or subsequent violation of any of these provisions, by imprisonment in the State prison for not less than one year nor more than ten years, and may be further punished by a fine of not more than $10,000. The court shall not suspend a sentence of imprisonment imposed pursuant to this paragraph, or grant probation.

Author's note: It's always interesting to listen to the excuses defendants will come up with in court. One time I heard a drug addict tell the judge, "I don't do cocaine, your Honor, I just like the way it smells."

Can dealers gamble in the casino where they work?

Most casinos do not allow dealers to gamble on table games in their own casinos. A 21 dealer, or other table game employee such as a floorman or pit boss may be allowed to gamble at the slot machines, keno, bingo or the Race & Sports Book, but not at the table games.

There are a few very foolish casino operators who allow dealers to play table games at their own casino. The temptation is too great for other dealers, on the game, to help a friend or fellow dealer. One minute you're the employee the next a customer. One minute you're dealing to the boss or vice versa.

In the early days of Atlantic City, casino employees could not gamble at any game or slot machine in any casinos in Atlantic City. That law has since been amended and casino employees can gamble at casinos other than their own in Atlantic City.

Dealer's joke: "I gave up gambling, women and alcohol about five years ago. It was the longest 20 minutes of my life."

Can I use chips from one casino at another casino?

In the old days, it was very common for casinos to accept *foreign* chips. The security departments would, on a regular basis, make foreign chip runs to the other casinos in town and redeem the chips for cash. The sheer size of the town now and the much greater number of casinos has restricted the use of foreign chips. As a courtesy to some customers, casinos will still change foreign chips. If you are attempting to cash-in a large quantity of foreign chips, the cage may call the casino from which the chips came to make sure there is not a *hold* on the chips. Casinos will regularly inform each other when, for whatever reason, chips are suspect.

Most casinos throughout the gaming industry use a standard color scheme for various denominations of chips: $5.00 chips are red, $25.00 chips are green, and $100.00 chips are black. The chips vary from casino to casino by the insert in the center of the chip and the markings along the edge of the chips called *snake bites*. In the past, casinos used actual silver dollars, called *dealing silver*. When the Eisenhower dollar replaced the silver dollar, dealers referred to it as *dealing iron*. One casino in the past was foolish enough to change the color scheme. They produced a $1.00 chip which was black. It didn't take long for cheaters to buy $1.00 chips at that casino and pass them at other casinos in town by slipping a black $1.00 chip into a stack of black $100.00 chips. The Gaming Control Board quickly made the casino pull those $1.00 chips.

A standard casino chip is 39mm in diameter. Many casinos have gone to an oversized chip for their $1,000.00, $5,000.00 and larger denominations. Dealers refer to handling the bigger chips as *dealing cookies*.

The $1.00 gaming token used in slot machines may or may not be accepted by slot machines from one casino to the next. The tokens are manufactured with a particular alloy and the coin comparator at one casino may be set differently at another. High security slot tokens are now being produced which have a distinct resonating frequency and unique concentric ridges. The coin comparator not only matches the frequency but checks the weight, speed and direction of the token as it enters the slot machine. By Federal Law the slot machine tokens cannot be used or be capable of use in any other department except in the casino.

The practice of accepting foreign chips has been legislated against in most other gaming areas of the country.

In Las Vegas, money isn't everything and if you stay long enough, it's nothing.

$$\boxed{6}\,\boxed{2}$$

Do casinos cheat customers?

This is an interesting question because in the real old days of Nevada the answer was, "Yes, in some places." It was not uncommon for certain casinos to have a person known as a *mechanic* who could manipulate the cards and cheat the players. This was usually accomplished by sleight-of-hand techniques such as *peeking* (secretly looking at the top card of a hand held deck) and then dealing *seconds*. Dealing seconds simply means to deal the second card of the deck instead of the first card. After peeking, the dealer would determine if the card would help his own hand or hurt the player's, and then decide whether or not to hold this card back. Other unscrupulous casino operators were known to remove big cards (10s, face cards & aces) from a six deck shoe and replace them with small cards. Because the house hits last and must make a count of between 17 and 21, the extra little cards help the dealer's hand fall into that window of 17 to 21. Extra big cards would hurt the dealers chances of making a hand so a few of the big cards were removed. Removing aces really hurts a player because it reduces the number of blackjacks, soft double downs (a soft hand is a hand with an ace in it), and splitting ace pairs. All of these hands directly impact a player's money. When the house has blackjack, they win even money. When a player has blackjack, they win 3 to 2. Doubling down and splitting aces also allows a player to maximize their winnings by increasing the amount bet at the right times.

Again, in the real old days of Nevada, some slot machine operators would *rig* machines to restrict payoffs. The old mechanical slot machines had a star wheel which controlled the payoff amounts. The star wheel looks sort of like the round blade of a circular saw but with varying depths on the teeth. The deeper the cut or depth of the tooth, the more the machine would pay. By blocking access to the deeper teeth the slot machine was restricted from paying a big jackpot. (Note: Almost all slot machines produced today are electronic and do not have the old star wheels.)

In the old days, cheating players at the crap table usually involved *flatted* dice. Today's casino dice are perfect cubes made to 1/10,000th of an inch alignment. Flatted dice are just what the name implies: dice that are flat, or bigger, on certain opposite sides. The most common combination of flatted dice (also called *mis-shapes* or *shapes*), is the six-ace flat. The six side and ace side are opposite one another. These two sides are cut slightly larger then the other four sides. The laws of physics says that the cube will land on the side with the greater surface area more often than probability dictates. (Each side should have an equal chance of one-in-six of landing facing up.)

It is also very common for cheaters to *bevel* (slightly round) the other four sides that are not flatted. The bevel has a tendency to help the dice roll off the beveled sides onto the flatted sides. The six-ace flat combination favors double sixes (boxcars), double aces (snake eyes), and sevens...they are called Mis-out dice. Given that the vast majority of craps players are *right* bettors, the *mis-out dice* weigh heavily against the player and in favor of the house. (The old saying is, "If you bet the *don't side*, you live on the outside.") Casinos that used flatted dice were known as *flat stores* because you couldn't get a *square game*. Flatted dice are made with as little as 3/1000th of an inch advantage to as much as 40/1000th of an inch edge.

Another method of cheating at dice is mis-spotted dice. The opposite sides of a fair cube will always add up to seven. If you're holding a cube and looking at the 3, then the 4 will be on the other side. The 6 is opposite the 1 and the 5 is opposite the 2. Mis-spotted dice, known as *Tops* or *T's*, do not have all of the numbers on the dice — they have doubles. Suppose a cheater eliminated the 2 and had the die made with an extra 5. Instead of a 2 opposite the 5, you would have a 5 opposite another 5. Tops are based on the premise that you cannot see more than three sides of a cube from one vantage point. A double five would, of course, favor the higher numbers and because the 2 is eliminated, there is a disadvantage on the smaller numbers.

A very bold set of Tops eliminates three of the six numbers and doubles the remaining three. These are known as *three way tops*. Three way tops are very powerful but are also very dangerous to use because if someone picks up the dice, it is quickly obvious that they are doubles and all the numbers are not there. When I was a kid we called three way tops "door pops" because it was best to use them next to a *door* in case you had to *pop* outside and run.

A tops combination known as *snowballs* favors high numbers and pairs. The dice are double 4's, double 5's and double 6's. This set of dice is called snowballs because of the increased number of white spots. There are 42 spots on a standard pair of dice. The snowballs have 60 spots.

Back in the 70's I invented a mirrored table game paddle to help casinos protect against tops. The handle of the paddle is a long triangular shaped piece of mylar mirror. When the stickman puts the dice in the center of the table (in front of the paddle), anyone at the game can see both sides of the dice.

When I first moved to Las Vegas, I met and became close friends with a very famous magician, John Thompson. John does a comedy magic act and calls himself the *World's Greatest Polish Magician*. John has consummate knowledge of all forms of magic. He has been, and is, a mentor to many magicians around the world. What most magicians do not know is the amount of knowledge John possesses regarding gambling games and cheating methods. John works with his wife Pamela Hayes and they are billed as *The Great Tomsoni & Company*. Pamela is a wonderful actress and really is the heart of the comedy characters. Pam is not, however, a gambler.

Back in the 70's, Pam was trying to teach me to play backgammon. We played backstage between shows. It never occurred to her that I might already know the game. We played for an imaginary $1.00 per game which, of course, increases dramatically with the use of the doubling cube. I would offer and accept the most terrible doubles driving our imaginary bets way up. Pam would patiently and politely explain how foolish my play was especially in light of the board position and the doubling cube. I, of course, thanked her and played my own way in spite of her wise advise. I always won and Pam owed me an imaginary fortune. She would comment to John on how bad my play was and how foolish it was to offer and accept those doubles. What Pam did not know was that I was switching in snowballs at the end game which gave me an overwhelming advantage. John, of course, spotted my move early on, but true to the code of the hustler, he said nothing. This went on for months before I let Pam in on my little secret. I love you Pamela, but don't take up hustling for a living!

Ask the same question about today's casinos and the answer is, "No, casinos do not cheat customers." There are many reasons why this is true. Some of the old time casino operators started off as gambling cheats. In addition, many of the early casinos did not have a big or stable bankroll so they tilted the games in their favor.

With the emergence of the Nevada Gaming Control Board, and the investigative and enforcement powers it has over Nevada casinos and casino employees, cheating of customers has all but vanished into the story books. The Nevada Gaming Control Board and Gaming Commission have mandated the installation of closed circuit TV surveillance systems in all casino operations and can on demand review and inspect any video tape or paperwork relevant to the casino operation. Casino operators and employees are subjected to an intense personal background investigation and can lose their license or work permit for any improprieties.

Most casinos are operated today by large corporations. There is no vested interest in cheating customers. A casino operation could lose a multimillion dollar a year license if cheating were uncovered. This would also impact the corporation's gaming operations in any other gaming area of the country. The publicity alone would destroy the credibility of the corporation with their stock holders, to whom they are accountable. Ask yourself, "Would the CEO of a major corporation risk giving authority to a dealer to cheat customers?" The dealer (the bottom rung of the ladder) would have a tremendous hammer over the head of the corporation. In addition, the surveillance team would have to be in on the cheating in order *not* to uncover the scam and not to notify the Gaming Commission. (By State law, any cheating activity must be reported to the Enforcement Division of the Nevada Gaming Control Board. This means, at times, that casinos are self reporting (shooting themselves in the foot) by reporting and recording gaming activity.

The cheating that happens in today's casinos takes one of three forms. A casino employee stealing from the house (for himself), an outside cheater or group of cheaters stealing from the house, or a casino employee and an outside agent stealing from the casino.

Author's note: Las Vegas in recent years has become the Magic capitol of the country. There are magicians and magic acts of all types in several of the showrooms around town. The magicians use lions, tigers and panthers in their acts, but there is one cat they cannot use...Las Vegas won't let in the *CHEETAHS*. Get it? *CHEETAHS*!

Do casinos get many counterfeit chips?

What most people do not realize is that casinos count every chip in the casino three times a day. At the end of each shift, the outgoing and incoming pit bosses count down each table bankroll. On most tables, the large denomination chips are not even brought to the games until high rollers show up. The point is that there are only a fixed number of chips in each denomination in each casino. There is only a limited amount of space in which to house the chips. Regardless of the amount of cash that the casinos handle in a day, there will always be a fixed number of chips. This is not to say that a small amount of counterfeit chips cannot be passed, but at a certain point, the overage will be discovered. In addition, most counterfeiters do not want to leave a trail of their exploits. Keep in mind that there are surveillance cameras everywhere. If a customer comes to a table with a large amount of chips, the dealer must inform the floorperson, and they in turn alert the camera room.

The same type of policy holds true when a person approaches the casino cage. The first question which might be asked of an unknown customer with large denomination chips is: "Are you paying off a marker?" If the answer is, "No," then the next question is, "Where did you win these chips?" The counterfeiter may answer, "The Dice Pit." The cage cashier will call the pit to verify. If the pit doesn't recognize the person at the cage, the chips can be held until the Gaming Board has been notified. Given that most casino cage windows are covered with surveillance cameras all the time, it is relatively easy to identify any patron at the cage, even for several days before. Adding phony paper money to a fluctuating bankroll may not show up very soon. However, adding additional inventory to a fixed number that is counted so often usually shows up very quickly.

Even attempting to cash in found or stolen high denomination chips is not an easy matter. After the heavyweight fight in which Mike Tyson bit the ear of Evander Holyfield, a near riot broke out at the MGM Grand casino. Gaming tables were turned over and chips fell everywhere. A patron picked up and pocketed a $25,000.00 chip. When he attempted to redeem the chip for cash he was simply asked, "Where did you get this chip?" The customer foolishly claimed he won the chip gambling. Anytime chips of that high a value are in play, the pit keeps a record and surveillance would have the play on video tape. A review of the video tapes of that night's riot clearly showed the customer picking up something off the floor near the high limit games. "Nice try pal!"

In addition to the above considerations, many casinos are going to high security chip inserts which are difficult to copy. There are also high security chips that have an electronic insert similar to the ones that beep in a department store when you walk out. Most casinos have a back up set of chips in each denomination which can quickly be exchanged if the integrity of the current set is in question.

Old street joke: "I heard Jimmy made big money in counterfeiting." "Yeah, he's in prison...it was a quarter-of-an-inch too big!"

Do cheaters get beat up by casinos?

"Yes, they do. We know where you live. Just kidding!"

In the old days of Las Vegas and Nevada, it would not be uncommon for a casino thief to have to deal with a couple of very large security guards on the way out the door. Remember who they were stealing from...the mob or a private owner. Cheaters also had a different code in the old days. It wasn't so much the idea of being caught that bothered them, it was the idea that they were stupid enough to get caught. In other words, my move or technique was not perfect. It was also not uncommon in the old days for casino cheats to approach a shift boss and ask, "How much do you want to make tonight?" The cheaters and the boss would agree on a percentage and the boss would turn his back. If the crew was caught, the boss made a big deal about throwing them out of the joint. "And don't ever let me catch you in here again." The boss and cheaters would then meet later to cut up the stolen money.

Today's Las Vegas casinos are more concerned that cheaters will make false claims. It has happened that cheats will allege to have been manhandled by security guards on the way to the security office, in hopes of a profitable civil law suit. In most casinos, surveillance and audio monitoring of the security holding room are now mandated by State law. These rooms are recorded and controlled by monitors outside of the security office.

One very famous story that most Las Vegans have heard goes like this. A casino owner in downtown Las Vegas got a call from a friend in jail. The owner sent a security guard to the jail and bailed the kid out. The casino owner gave the kid some pocket money and put him to work on a 21 game. A couple of weeks later, the owner discovered the kid stealing from the game. As the story goes, security guards handcuffed the kid to an overhead pipe in a basement room and took turns beating the hell out of him. This went on for a couple of days until the owner's mother put an end to it.

Another story is told about a cheater who is caught stealing from a casino and is handcuffed with his hands behind his back. The casino owner arrives and orders a security guard to beat the crap out of the cheater. The guard begins to remove the handcuffs and is chided by the casino owner, "I didn't tell you to fight him. I told you to beat the shit out of him."

In the old days, if you chose to steal from casinos, then having to deal with the big security guards was considered just the price of doing business. It wasn't legal, but it was just. Today you have to deal with State Gaming Enforcement and corporate attorneys. Personally, most cheats liked the old days better.

Author's note: It is common knowledge that a great many of Las Vegas' secrets are buried in "holes in the desert." This is affectionately known to street guys as taking a "dirt nap." A Vegas secret of another sort was uncovered in September of 1998. Long time Las Vegas casino executive and member of the Binion family, Ted Binion, was found dead in his home. A few days later three guys were arrested in the desert as they dug up a large vault allegedly belonging to Ted Binion. The vault was so big they needed heavy digging equipment to remove the ground around it. Inside was nearly 16 million dollars worth of pure silver bars. Each bar was 14" x 6" x 5". On May 19, 2000, Teddy's girlfriend and an associate were convicted of the first degree murder of Ted Binion.

Question: What do you call a corporate attorney with an I.Q. of 50? Answer: Your Honor.

Do the casino workers live in Las Vegas?

As silly a question as this sounds, it is the most frequent question dealers told me they get asked by customers. Apparently tourists think that casino employees live in Southern California and commute to Las Vegas by plane or bus to come to work everyday. A special thanks to the Las Vegas Chamber of Commerce for the following facts.

For better than two decades, Las Vegas has been the fastest growing city in the United States. Approximately 5,000 to 6,000 people a month relocate to Las Vegas as permanent residents. The word Las Vegas is Spanish and means "The Meadows." The city was founded in 1905, but the real growth began in 1931 when the state passed legislation to legalize gambling. The city of Las Vegas covers a little more then 82 square miles and is one of five cities in Clark County. There are 424,171 people in the city of Las Vegas proper. The population of the Las Vegas Valley is 1,155,771 and there are 1,205,177 people living in Clark County. Clark County is the population center for the state with only about 500,000 people inhabiting the entire rest of Nevada.

Las Vegas is home to more than 500 churches and synagogues with better than 63 faiths represented. Las Vegas has more churches per capita than any city in the country. Las Vegas is the 11th largest school district in the country with 219 primary and secondary schools. Las Vegas schools rank in the top 10 percentile of the nation. There are 23 libraries, 37 golf courses and 200 tennis courts. Not only is Las Vegas the "Gaming Capitol of the World," but the more than 50 wedding chapels make Las Vegas the "Wedding Capital of America." (In 1997 there were 108,310 marriages performed in Las Vegas wedding chapels.)

A special thanks to Kevin Janison, KLAS TV8 Meteorologist and self proclaimed "King of the Civilized World" for the following facts. The hottest day on record in Las Vegas history was July 24, 1942 when the temperature at McCarran International Airport reached 117 degrees. The coldest temperature recorded in the Las Vegas Valley was 8 degrees which occurred twice, January 25, 1937 and January 13, 1963. The average yearly temperature is 66.3 degrees, with 4.19 inches of rain annually and an average humidity year round of 29%.

A couple of other silly questions that customers and tourists have asked.

- What time is the midnight show?
- Do they serve food at the dinner show?
- How much is the $3.95 buffet?
- So you live in the hotel?
  (In the old days some customers actually thought the dealers and casino staff lived on property in the hotel.)

Las Vegas is the only place you'll ever ask a hotel or casino worker on a Tuesday, "How are you doing?" and receive the answer, "It's my Friday." This means that the next two days are that person's days off.

Old Vegas joke: A high roller at the Las Vegas airport approaches the ticket counter of a major airline. "I'm traveling to Detroit and I have three pieces of luggage to check. I want you to send one of my bags to Chicago, one of my bags to New York and the last one to Portland, Oregon." The clerk was somewhat bewildered and replied, "Sir, we can't do that." "Why not?" snapped the high roller. "You did it when I flew out here."

Do dealers keep their own tips?

Today, in Las Vegas casinos, all dealers share equally in all tips (called *tokes* or *zooks*). Some casinos will segregate dealers by games. The 21 dealers and roulette dealers share in the 21 table's tips and crap dealers share just in the crap table tips. In the past, crap dealers would share tips on a crew for crew basis. The four man crap crew would split all the tips that table received amongst themselves. This is still the case in a few casinos, but not nearly as many as in the past.

In recent years, the IRS has cracked down on dealers and any employee whose income is derived in most part from tips. Cocktail waitresses are charged a flat amount per drink served as a basis for income tax debt. In most casinos a list is kept by the cage, at the direction of the IRS, showing the average daily toke amounts for dealers to be assessed withholding tax. In many cases, dealers will receive the toke amounts in check form with the tax already withheld. (In the old days, dealers received a toke envelope everyday containing their share of the previous days tips.)

From time to time, a few foolhardy casinos allowed dealers to keep their own tips table for table. This is a disaster waiting to happen. A player who is winning will place a wager for the dealer along side his own. In order for the dealer to receive the toke, the customer must win the bet. There is just too much incentive for a dealer to help a customer win or outright cheat to win.

Dealer's joke: Question: "What do you call 100 IRS agents handcuffed together at the bottom of the lake?" Answer: "A good start."

Question: "What do you call 100 IRS agents buried up to their necks in sand?" Answer: "Not enough sand."

6 7

Does organized crime control casino gambling in Las Vegas?

Organized crime built Las Vegas from the early days and was involved in a few casinos until the mid 1980's. Contrary to the Hollywood version, Benjamin "Bugsy" Siegel did not invent Las Vegas. Siegel bought into the Flamingo Hotel project about midway through the construction. A Los Angeles restaurant owner named Billy Wilkerson was the real inventor of the Flamingo. After a failed opening in 1946, and Bugsy's murder, Wilkerson was "squeezed" out.

Organized crime figures began to realize that the same types of illegal activities they were involved in around the country were, in fact, legal in Nevada. (In 1931, the state of Nevada had passed legislation to legalize gambling.) The potential for great profits brought several casino operators to the state. The casinos drew upon the only gambling talent available, illegal gamblers and bookmakers from around the country to staff and operate the games. Given that the illegal operations were (and are) run by organized crime, it only stands to reason that many early operators and employees were also affiliated with organized crime.

In my opinion, it is the illegal bookmakers from around the country who created and built Las Vegas. Bookmakers were ideal for the task because they knew the gamblers in their area. More importantly, bookmakers know who pays and who doesn't pay gambling debts and how to collect on delinquent accounts. Illegal gamblers such as Meyer Lansky, Frank Costello, Moe Sedway, Ross Miller, Gus Greenbaum and "Ice Pick" Willie Alderman were involved in many casinos in the early years such as the Riviera, Sands, Flamingo, Desert Inn and Thunderbird. Because of their background in illegal gambling, many of the early operators preferred to stay out of the limelight and allow a *front man* to be the licensed owner. The Desert Inn was originally known as Wilbur Clark's Desert Inn. In fact, the casino was owned by a one-time bootlegger and bookmaker from Cleveland, Moe Dalitz, and his partners Sam Tucker and Morris Kleinman.

One talent that organized crime as a whole has mastered is the ability to maximize profits in a business while not always showing the revenue to the proper authorities (a polite way of describing the *skim*). Most banks and lending institutions at the time were reluctant to invest in a casino in the middle of the Mojave desert. In order to finance a new casino venture, it was necessary to deal with such entities as the Teamsters Union (pension funds). It is also a gimmie that organized crime and its associates were involved in the Teamsters Union.

Question: How many teamsters does it take to change a light bulb? Answer: Seven... you got a problem with 'dat?

The real growth of Las Vegas under the mob's influence began in 1957. In that year, Alan Dorfman (son of an Al Capone gunman, Red Dorfman), began securing loans from the Western States Pension Fund of the Teamsters Union for casino ventures in Las Vegas. Through the next two decades many hotel/casino projects such as Caesars Palace, Circus Circus, The Stardust, The Fremont, The Dunes and the Aladdin were funded by Teamsters Union loans. Frank Sinatra, at one time, owned the Cal-Neva Casino in Lake Tahoe. Sinatra was forced to sell the resort by the Gaming Board because of his alleged involvement with Chicago mob boss Sam Giancanna. I got to meet Frank Sinatra on a few occasions. We actually hit it off right from the start. We quickly got to be on a nickname basis with one another. I used to call him "Mister Sinatra, Sir" and he used to call me, "Get the fuck out of my way." In 1973, Allan Glick secured a 67 million-dollar loan from the Teamsters Union to purchase the Stardust, Fremont,

Sahara and Marina Hotels. In 1977 the Aladdin Hotel, owned and run by Lebanese and Jewish partners from Detroit and St. Louis, was given a 37 million dollar loan to complete a major expansion. The final chapter of the mob's involvement in Las Vegas began in 1968 when billionaire Howard Hughes purchased the Sands, Frontier, Desert Inn, Silver Slipper, Castaways and the Landmark casinos. The Frontier Hotel at the time had mob influence tracing to St. Louis and Detroit, as did the Aladdin Hotel/Casino and Edgewater Casino. The Sands, Dunes and Desert Inn were also known to be mob connected. Hughes paid far more for the properties than anyone thought they were worth. The mob guys took the money and ran.

An interesting aside about the casino business at the time was that everyone knew who really controlled what casinos. You were identified as being *connected with* or *belonging to* a particular city or mob. When I first moved to Las Vegas from Detroit, my sponsor introduced me around and from that point on people would say, "He's okay, he's with 'The Little Guy'." For years I called guys at other hotels around Las Vegas and asked for information, received comps to shows and dinners, and returned the same favors without ever once meeting them face-to-face. Everybody on the inside just knew who you were with and your word of honor was "gold". If your friends or relatives came to town, they were okay because you were okay because the guy you were with was okay. An otherwise average guy could come to Las Vegas and get special treatment because he knew a guy who knew a guy. In these connected joints, the junket reps and casino hosts were also connected and okayed by illegal gambling forces (the mob) in cities all across the country.

With the scrutiny of the union loans by several different federal and state investigators and regulators, the involvement of organized crime in the casino industry was uncovered. With the emergence and strengthening of the Nevada Gaming Control Board, coupled with the Federal government, the handwriting was on the wall for organized crime in Las Vegas. Several major prosecutions and indictments in cities such as Detroit,

Chicago, Cleveland, St. Louis, Kansas City, Milwaukee, New York and in California closed the book on what was, if nothing else, a very colorful and intriguing chapter in Las Vegas history.

If you asked most of us who survived the 70's in Las Vegas, we'd say things were better back then. Actually, from a selfish standpoint it was a better time for many reasons. There was only Las Vegas—no Atlantic City, Indian or State sactioned gaming. The town was much smaller, a couple of hundred thousand people as opposed to the million and a half today. For the most part we only brought in gamblers. These guys didn't pay for anything in the casino or hotel, airfare, rooms, food, beverage, shows, gourmet meals—nothing. The government was not yet requiring the CTR cash reporting, and so there was always a steady stream of street guys and street money. Gamblers and street guys (especially when they weren't paying) toked everybody, actually they *over* toked everybody. Casino and hotel workers did not as yet have the I.R.S. as partners closely taxing their tips. Dealers got their tips in cash once a day. The local bars, small casinos and dance clubs were major party hangouts.

The strict cash reporting regulations dried up most of the regular street guys. The explosion of legal gaming throughout the country spread the high rollers very thin and toke earners now have Uncle Sam in their pocket.

A lot of wise guys think the old timers who built Las Vegas would turn over in their graves if they saw the Eiffel Tower or a roller coaster on the strip. I think they would tip their hats to the next generation of Las Vegas entrepreneurs and say, "God bless ya! you found a way to survive and bring people here."

Another reason a lot of Las Vegans liked the old days better is, "HELLO," we were all 25 or 30 years younger. Now it takes all night to do what you used to do all night. You know you're getting older when the only time you feel like making love twice, is just before you make love once.

I understand the Mob and the Gay Liberation Front have made an alliance. Now the "kiss of death" includes dinner and dancing.

172 The 101 Most Asked Questions

How does keno work?

The game keno has its roots in the Orient. Keno is basically a lottery game drawn every five to ten minutes. Traditionally, the game begins with 80 ping pong balls in some sort of cage. By either means of a hand crank or a system of air blowers, 20 of the 80 balls will be delivered to two plexiglass tubes known as *goose necks*. The more modern version of the same game has the 20 numbers drawn by a random number generator in a computer.

As a player, you mark a keno ticket. You can choose between one and 15 numbers. A payoff schedule tells you the amount won if your numbers are drawn in that game. When choosing a one or two number ticket, the single number or both numbers must be drawn for you to win. On the higher number tickets, you do not need to have all numbers drawn to win. On a three number ticket you will be paid if two out of the three, or all, numbers are drawn. The following chart titled **Keno Payout Schedule** shows a typical payoff schedule for a keno game.

Most serious keno players do not like the random number generator draw because it seems that you, as a customer, pick a certain amount of numbers, the keno writer enters those numbers into the computer, and then the computer tells you who wins. Many players feel that the ping pong balls and air blowers offer the semblance of a much fairer game. The argument against the computer is, "I tell the computer my numbers and it just doesn't pick them."

The simplest odds to figure on the keno game are the odds for betting on one number. If you bet on one number and it is drawn, you will receive $3.00 (3 for 1). Considering that 20 numbers out of 80 are drawn, the correct odds are 4 for 1 (you should receive $4.00). The math for one number is very straight ahead.

If you bet $1.00 on all eighty numbers for one game of keno the results would be as follows:

One game.: 80 numbers X 1.00 ea	= $80.00 invested
Draw 20 numbers you win all 20	
20 wins at $3.00 each	= $60.00 win
Net loss	= $20.00 (loser)

Mathematical advantage for the House:
$20.00 \div 80.00 = 0.25 = 25\%$ House Advantage

In order to figure out the odds for two through 15 numbers, the math becomes much more difficult. Take, for example, a five number ticket. The first question is, "How many five number combinations are possible with 80 numbers?" The math looks like this:

$$\frac{80 * 79 * 78 * 77 * 76}{5 * 4 * 3 * 2 * 1} = 24{,}040{,}016 \text{ Ways}$$

Therefore, if you played $1.00 on every possible five number combination of 80 numbers, it would cost you $24,040,016.00.

Next you need to determine the winning combinations. The total number of ways 20 numbers can be taken five at a time. The math looks like this:

$$\frac{20 * 19 * 18 * 17 * 16}{5 * 4 * 3 * 2 * 1} = 15{,}504$$

Therefore, out of the 24,040,016 total combinations, you would win five out of five a total of 15,504 times at a payoff of $550.00 each or $8,527,200.00.

Next, you need to determine the winnings when four out of the five numbers hit. The math looks like this:

$$\frac{20 * 19 * 18 * 17}{4 * 3 * 2 * 1} \quad X \quad \frac{60}{1} = 290,700$$

This formula takes into account 20 numbers drawn where four of the five hit. The 60 divided by one account for the fifth number being any one of the 60 remaining undrawn numbers. Therefore, you would win four out of five, a total of 290,700 times at a payoff of $20.00 each or $5,814,000.00.

Finally, you must determine the total number of three out of five winning combinations. The math is as follows:

$$\frac{20 * 19 * 18}{3 * 2 * 1} \quad X \quad \frac{60 * 59}{2 * 1} = 2,017,800$$

This formula takes into account 20 numbers drawn where three out of five hit. The 60 times 59 divided by 2 times 1 accounts for the fourth and fifth numbers being any one of the 60 remaining undrawn numbers. Therefore, you would win three out of five a total of 2,017,800 times at a payoff of $1.00 each or $2,017,800.00.

Now compare the total amount won to the total amount invested.

Total Invested		$24,040,016.00
Win 5 of 5	15,504 x $550.00	$8,527,200.00
Win 4 of 5	290,700 x $20.00	$5,814,000.00
Win 3 of 5	2,017,800 x $1.00	$2,017,800.00
Total Win =		$16,359,000.00
Total Investment		$24,040,016.00
Total Win All Hits		$16,359,000.00
(Subtract Wins from Loses)		
Total Loss to Player		($7,681,016.00)

House Advantage = 7,681,016 ÷ 24,040,016 = 0.31951
House Advantage on a five spot ticket is 31.95%

Unfortunately, the odds for keno do not get much better than this. It is, however, one of the only games where you can invest as little as $1.00 and win $25,000.00.

KENO PAYOUT SCHEDULE (Bet $1.00)

MARK 1 SPOT
HIT 1 NUMBER..........................$3.00

MARK 2 SPOTS
HIT 2 NUMBERS......................$12.00

MARK 3 SPOTS
HIT 3 NUMBERS......................$42.00
HIT 2 NUMBERS............................1.00

MARK 4 SPOTS
HIT 4 NUMBERS....................$120.00
HIT 3 NUMBERS............................2.50
HIT 2 NUMBERS............................1.00

MARK 5 SPOTS
HIT 5 NUMBERS....................$550.00
HIT 4 NUMBERS..........................20.00
HIT 3 NUMBERS............................1.00

MARK 6 SPOTS
HIT 6 NUMBERS.................$1,750.00
HIT 5 NUMBERS..........................80.00
HIT 4 NUMBERS............................3.00
HIT 3 NUMBERS............................1.00

MARK 7 SPOTS
HIT 7 NUMBERS.................$5,000.00
HIT 6 NUMBERS........................300.00
HIT 5 NUMBERS..........................21.00
HIT 4 NUMBERS............................3.00

MARK 8 SPOTS
HIT 8 NUMBERS...............$20,000.00
HIT 7 NUMBERS.....................1,500.00
HIT 6 NUMBERS..........................88.00
HIT 5 NUMBERS............................8.00

MARK 9 SPOTS

HIT 9 NUMBERS $20,000.00
HIT 8 NUMBERS 3,950.00
HIT 7 NUMBERS 300.00
HIT 6 NUMBERS 40.00
HIT 5 NUMBERS 4.00

MARK 10 SPOTS

HIT 10 NUMBERS $22,500.00
HIT 9 NUMBERS 20,000.00
HIT 8 NUMBERS 3,950.00
HIT 7 NUMBERS 300.00
HIT 6 NUMBERS 40.00
HIT 5 NUMBERS 4.00

MARK 11 SPOTS

HIT 11 NUMBERS $25,000.00
HIT 10 NUMBERS 15,000.00
HIT 9 NUMBERS 2,000.00
HIT 8 NUMBERS 380.00
HIT 7 NUMBERS 80.00
HIT 6 NUMBERS 8.00

MARK 12 SPOTS

HIT 12 NUMBERS $25,000.00
HIT 11 NUMBERS 10,000.00
HIT 10 NUMBERS 2,400.00
HIT 9 NUMBERS 740.00
HIT 8 NUMBERS 250.00
HIT 7 NUMBERS 30.00
HIT 6 NUMBERS 4.00

MARK 13 SPOTS

HIT 13 NUMBERS $25,000.00
HIT 12 NUMBERS 20,000.00
HIT 11 NUMBERS 8,000.00
HIT 10 NUMBERS 4,000.00
HIT 9 NUMBERS 750.00
HIT 8 NUMBERS 88.00
HIT 7 NUMBERS 16.00

MARK 14 SPOTS	
HIT 14 NUMBERS	$25,000.00
HIT 13 NUMBERS	25,000.00
HIT 12 NUMBERS	16,000.00
HIT 11 NUMBERS	3,500.00
HIT 10 NUMBERS	1,000.00
HIT 9 NUMBERS	320.00
HIT 8 NUMBERS	50.00
HIT 7 NUMBERS	10.00
MARK 15 SPOTS	
HIT 15 NUMBERS	$25,000.00
HIT 14 NUMBERS	25,000.00
HIT 13 NUMBERS	25,000.00
HIT 12 NUMBERS	8,000.00
HIT 11 NUMBERS	2,500.00
HIT 10 NUMBERS	400.00
HIT 9 NUMBERS	144.00
HIT 8 NUMBERS	30.00
HIT 7 NUMBERS	6.00

Keep in mind that when you play three or more numbers on a keno ticket, you do not need all the numbers to hit in order to win. In the early 1970's, my sister Carmelita and her husband Jim were in Vegas on their honeymoon. They threw away a keno ticket with 9 out of 10 ($20,000.00) because they thought they needed all ten.

In the old days, a keno ticket had to be cashed before the next game began. If you didn't get to the window in time, it was your bad luck. (If you snooze you lose!) Today, you can buy tickets for up to 1,000 games in advance. If you play 20 games or less, you have up to five days to collect. If you play more than 20 games, you have up to one year to collect on a winning ticket.

Bill Cosby explains Keno this way: "We'll, make the game real simple. Instead of 80 numbers, we'll just use two. Give me a dollar. What was your number? One...wrong...wanna play again?"

How does the casino figure out how much it wins?

Anytime during the gaming activity of a casino that a gaming table runs short of chips, a *fill* of chips is brought from the casino cage to that game. A copy of the *fill slip* transaction is dropped in the table drop box affixed to each game. At those times, when a table game has too many chips in the bankroll, a *credit* transaction occurs. Chips are taken off the game and a copy of the *credit slip* is dropped in the table drop box. When a player takes credit from the casino, they sign a *marker*. (A player may also sign a marker against *front money* they have deposited in the casino cage). A copy of all marker issues is dropped in the table drop box along with copies of *marker buy-backs* where a player redeems a marker. Cash buy-ins that happen at a gaming table are also dropped in the table drop box.

Three times a day (once at the end of each eight hour shift), the table bankroll is counted for each game. A copy of this chip inventory is dropped in the table drop box. Shortly thereafter, the drop box for each game is *dropped* and a new empty box, to hold the cash and paperwork transactions for the next shift, is locked onto the table in its place.

All of the table drop boxes are taken to and stored in a room known as the *soft count* room. (Soft count because there is paper money and paperwork counted as opposed to coins or tokens which are counted in the *hard count* room.) Once a day the *count team* counts the cash and reconciles the paperwork (credits against fills, marker issues against marker buy-backs, opening against closing table chip inventory). This produces a win or loss figure for each table. (Markers bought back at the cage are also debited against the table from which they were issued.) The total win or loss from each table game then makes up the casino win/loss for the entire day.

Coins and/or tokens from the slot machines are taken to and counted in the hard count room. The coin drop has to be adjusted for the jackpots paid by hand (jackpots over a certain amount cannot be paid by the machine) and fills to the machine. The paperwork from these slot transactions adjusts the slot drop to determine the slot win.

In the old days, it went like this: "One for the house, one for Vito. Two for the house, one-two for Vito. Three for the house, one-two-three for Vito."

How many casinos are there in Las Vegas?

There were 1,290 gaming licenses in Clark County in 1998. This accounts for licenses in major casinos as well as those to operate slot machines in local bars, grocery stores, car washes, restaurants and convenience stores. There are some 176,628 slot machines in Clark County, 4,379 live table games and 429 poker and pan games. These machines and gambling tables produced a revenue for 1998 of over 6.5 billion dollars. There are 80 major hotel/casinos in and around the Las Vegas valley with 105,357 guest rooms, and an additional 61 small casinos making a total of 141. The 196 motels in Clark County have a total of 20,207 guest rooms. The casino hotel and gaming industry employ approximately 166,047 workers.

As of this writing, there are plans for three more local casinos and one more strip casino.

Actually Las Vegas is a very religious place. You can walk through any casino in town and see people of all races and creeds at the crap tables looking to the heavens and saying, "Please, God, please, God."

Las Vegas Trivia: Question: "What is the only casino in Las Vegas whose free standing sign is on the opposite side of the street?" Answer: "The Railroad Pass Casino."

(As you drive to the Railroad Pass Casino, you are driving up a mountain road. The casino is set back off the road and would be out of sight as you approach.)

Special thanks to Lou DeGregorio at D.P. Stud for this piece of trivia.

Is betting a horse in a Race & Sports Book the same as betting at the track?

The answer to this question depends on whether or not the race book subscribes to the pari-mutuel pool organization. As you know, at a race track when you place a wager on a horse or dog, a certain percentage of every bet is set aside for the track. At most tracks this is between 14% and 17% and known as the *take off*. The rest of the money wagered on a particular race is then placed in a pari-mutuel pool. The percentage of money in the pari-mutuel pool bet on each horse or dog in the race (after the track's percentage) then determines the odds for that horse or dog when the race begins. It is a common gambler's claim to say that he/she *beat the track*. However, the only ones who get beat are the other bettors. You aren't betting against the track, the track gets its end up front before the race is even run.

If the race book belongs to the pari-mutuel organization, then betting at the race book is the same as betting at the track. Your wager is in effect wired to the track before the race and is included in the race pari-mutuel pool. Your wager can, and does, affect the odds at the start of the race. Your wager is affected by all other wagers in the pari-mutuel pool at the track itself and any other race book or OTB (Off Track Betting) parlor.

Many race books do not subscribe to the pari-mutuel organization for dog tracks. The reason being that the dog race handles are much smaller for each race.

If a race book does not bet into the pari-mutuel pool, it will normally limit its exposure by limiting the amount that can be bet on a race. This protects the race book from a wire scam where a person at the track bets a horse at one number and a person at a race book lays off at better odds.

Horse bettor's joke:

A guy wakes up at 5:55 a.m. one morning and takes the numbers as an omen. He gets in a taxicab, #555. He goes to the track and bets $555.00 to win on the fifth horse in the fifth race, and sure enough, the horse came in fifth.

What is a point spread in a Race & Sports Book and what is the money line?

I remember growing up in Detroit and sitting with my brothers at my father's feet as he imparted these words of sage and wisdom, "It's not whether you win or lose, my sons, it's the point spread!"

When two teams meet in a sporting event, one team is usually considered more powerful than the other. A team's strength is measured by a number of different factors. Such things as past performance against opponents, player injuries and home and away field performances are used to establish the *favorite* (the strongest team) and the *underdog* (the weaker team). For betting purposes only, a point spread is established. The point spread is an estimate prepared by a *handicapper* as to the number of points the underdog would need for the teams to be equal. (You could also look at it as the amount of points by which the stronger team is favored over the weaker team.) The point spread does not, in any way, play a part in the actual score of the sporting event. As a bettor, you are getting or laying points for betting purposes only. Take the following example. The San Francisco 49ers are established as 10.5 point favorites over the Detroit Lions. The board would look something like this:

SAN FRANCISCO	-10.5
Detroit Lions	42

The –10.5 next to San Francisco means that they are favored to win by 10.5 points. The capital letters usually mean this is the home team.(Some sports books will always place the home team on top.) The number 42 is the betting number for the total points scored in the game by both teams. This is called the *over/under*. You can bet the total points scored in the game will be over 42 or under 42. Suppose that you bet San Francisco and *laid* 10.5 points. For purposes of the bet, San Francisco would have to win the game by more than 10.5 points. (Since teams cannot score a half point, San Francisco would have to win by 11 or more points for you to win your bet.) Let's assume the final score was:

San Francisco   24
Detroit Lions   20

Even though San Francisco actually won the game, they did not cover the point spread, and therefore, you would lose your bet. Had you bet Detroit, even though they lost the actual game, you would win the bet because for betting purposes Detroit was getting 10.5 points. Had you bet the *over* on the over/under bet, you would have won because the total points scored was 44, more than the over/under number posted. If the total score had added up to exactly 42, the over or under bet would be a tie.

When you make a *straight bet* (one proposition such as the 49ers to win by 10.5), you must *lay* $110.00 to win $100.00. This is called the *juice*. If you win the bet, you will take down $210.00 (the $110.00 you bet plus the $100.00 you won). The sports book has a mathematical advantage as follows:

$10.00 ÷ $220.00 = 0.0454545 or 4.54%

You could make a two part bet, called a *parlay*. (San Francisco -10.5 and over 42). A two bet proposition means both parts have to win. If the parlay wins, you are paid 13 to 5. ($13.00 for every $5.00 bet). What you take down is $18.00, the $13.00 you won plus the $5.00 you bet. What you should actually take down is $20.00. If you bet $5.00 on the first proposition and win, you would take down $10.00 (the $5.00 you bet plus the $5.00 you won). If you parlayed the $10.00 on to the next bet and won, you would take down $20.00. The house advantage on a two bet parlay is as follows:

$2.00 ÷ $20.00 = 0.10000 or 10.0%

Some sports books have gone to paying 13.5 to 5 on a two part parlay. You would take down $18.50 on a $5.00 two part parlay. The house advantage changes to the following:

$1.50 ÷ $20.00 = 0.07500 or 7.50%

If you were to bet a three team (or three part) parlay, you would be paid at a rate of 6 to 1. On a $5.00 bet, you would take down $35.00, the $5.00 you bet plus the $30.00 you win, ($5.00 x 6 to 1). You should have taken down $40.00. A $5.00 bet wins $5.00 on the first bet of the parlay, the $10.00 bet wins $10.00 on the second part of the parlay, and the third bet, $20.00, wins $20.00 and you should take down $40.00. The sports book's mathematical advantage on a three team parlay is as follows:

$5.00 ÷ $40.00 = 0.12500 or 12.50%

The other method of handicapping a game and betting is the *money line*. There is no point spread given for the money line. In our example, San Francisco and Detroit would be playing even–up for purposes of betting. The sports book still considers San Francisco to be the favorite and Detroit to be the *dog*, but they attempt to even–up the betting proposition by adjusting the money. The board might look like this:

SAN FRANCISCO 49ers	-500
Detroit Lions	+400

What this money line means is that if you want to win $100.00 on San Francisco, you must *lay* $500.00. (You bet $500.00 to win $100.00.) On the other side, called the *come back* price, the Detroit Lions are +$400.00. If you bet $100.00 on Detroit (and they win the game outright), you win $400.00, plus the $100.00 you bet. The correlation between the money line and the point spread is usually pretty standard. On a point spread of 10.5, the money line on the favorite is somewhere between –400 and –500. The comeback price is somewhere between +300 and +400. With a point spread of 7, the money line on the favorite is between –300 and –400, and on the dog, the come back price is between +200 and +300.

The sports books are not usually in the business of gambling, but rather in the business of booking. In order to encourage customers to bet on the favorite or the dog, the book will adjust the point spread or money line. Suppose that a great deal of money was being wagered on San Francisco and not so much on Detroit. In order to equalize the amounts on both sides, the sports book might raise the point spread from –10.5 to –11.0. Moving the line in this direction makes the bet on San Francisco a little less attractive, and at the same time, attempts to stimulate wagering on Detroit. The book might move the money line to –550 on San Francisco and +450 on Detroit, again an attempt to stimulate wagering on Detroit. Conversely, if the amount wagered is lopsided in Detroit's favor, the book might lower the point spread to –10. This makes the Detroit bet a little less attractive and encourages betting on San Francisco.

Old bookmaker's joke: And God said to Moses, "Moses come forth." And Moses came fifth, and it cost God two hundred and fifty bucks.

Is there a difference in Indian casinos?

In 1988, the Federal Government passed the National Indian Gaming Act. This legislation in affect gave Indian Nations within the United States the sanction to make pacts with individual states in which they are located. The pact, depending on the state, can allow for any type of gambling on Indian reservations, from slot machines to pull tabs, bingo, poker and/or table games. For the most part, if there are charitable organizations in the state who run Millionaire Parties to raise funds and operate all the standard table games (21, craps, roulette, Big 6), then the Indian casinos can run the same types of games. In some states, dice games are outlawed as a matter of law. In those states, an Indian casino cannot operate crap tables. In California, for instance, Indian casinos are not allowed to have slot machines. They cannot operate table games they book themselves. So in California Indian casinos you will have poker (where the house takes a rake of the pot) and other casino card games where players actually buy the deal for an entire shoe and pay a commission to the house. In effect, the other players are betting against the one player who bought the shoe.

Some non-Indian casino operators feel that the Indian casinos have an unfair business advantage. Indian casinos are not subject to Federal and State taxes as are non-Indian casinos in the country.

Note: On March 7, 2000, California voters overwhelmingly approved Proposition 1 which allows Las Vegas-style card games and slot machines in Indian Casinos.

A guy working in an Indian casino goes to a medicine man for help. Says the man, "Sometimes I dream I'm a wigwam, then I dream I'm a teepee. Wigwam, teepee, wigwam, teepee...can you help me?" The medicine man replies, "It's simple, you're too tense."

$$\boxed{7}\boxed{4}$$

On what amount do I have to pay income tax on winnings in a casino?

This is not a trick question, because the answer is you must pay income tax on all winnings you make in a casino. You are allowed by law to deduct your gambling losses up to the amount of your winnings but you had better be ready to substantiate your losses in some real way. Whether or not you choose to list a casino win as undeclared income on your income tax return is, of course, your business. The Internal Revenue Service, however, does not, for some reason, accept the excuse "I forgot."

In a casino, if you win more than $1,200.00 in a slot jackpot, on a bingo game or keno ticket you will be asked for identification and will receive a W4 tax form. (W4 tax forms are issued to record undeclared income.) In some cases, for very large jackpots, the IRS insists that the casino withhold a percentage of the payoff immediately for tax purposes (up to 34%). Understand that the casinos are only following the Federal law for which they can be punished if they do not comply. Some casinos and local slot routes have set the royal flush jackpot amount at $1,199.00. This amount helps speed up the payoff process and eliminates a lot of paperwork as no tax form has to be filled out.

Some slot customers have been known to record in a diary a record of their wins and losses as proof to the IRS of the amount actually subject to income tax. Other customers will use canceled checks to casinos, cash withdrawals from ATM machines at casinos, and marker buy-back stubs as another method of recording their losses.

Old street gambler's joke: I don't gamble illegally anymore, I just give the money directly to the cops.

What are the odds of winning a coverall at bingo?

Many Las Vegas casinos still offer bingo games in their establishments. Bingo is a very popular gambling game in Indian casinos and in churches and charitable organizations around the country. (For many years, growing up as a Maronite Catholic, I thought "bingo" was the name of a revered Saint or pious monk...just kidding, mom.)

A cage or container of some sort houses 75 ping pong balls. The balls are numbered in accordance with the bingo card each customer receives at the beginning of play. The letters B I N G O are printed across the top of the bingo card. In vertical rows below each letter are five numbers from each of 15 numerical sets. Under the letter "B" (the first column) are five numbers anywhere from 1 to 15. Under the letter "I" (the second column) are five numbers anywhere from 16 to 30. Under the letter "N" (the third column), are five numbers anywhere from 31 to 45. In the center of the "N" column (the center of the board) is a *free* square or *coverall* square. Every player is given that square as a free spot. Under the letter "G" (the fourth column) are five numbers anywhere from 46 to 60. Under the "O" (fifth and last column) are five numbers anywhere from 61 to 75. (Some casinos offer an 80 numbered card, known as Racehorse Keno. The five rows are then divided in sets of 20 numbers instead of 15.)   The ping pong balls are marked with a letter and a number to identify the row in which they might be found. To play the game, one ball at a time is drawn and the letter and number on the ball is announced. A player with that particular letter and number then covers over that spot on their bingo card. In order to win a coverall game, each of the spots on the card must be called.

The first step in determining the odds to win a coverall bingo game (covering all 24 numbers...remember the free spot) is to find the total number of ways that 75 numbers can be arranged on a 24 number bingo card. The math looks like this:

$$\frac{(75)!}{24} = 75 \text{ numbers taken 24 at a time}$$

$$\frac{75 * 74 * 73 * 72 * 71 * 70 * 69 * 68 * 67 * 66 * 65 * 64}{24 * 23 * 22 * 21 * 20 * 19 * 18 * 17 * 16 * 15 * 14 * 13}$$

$$\frac{* 63 * 62 * 61 * 60 * 59 * 58 * 57 * 56 * 55 * 54 * 53 * 52}{* 12 * 11 * 10 * 9 * 8 * 7 * 6 * 5 * 4 * 3 * 2 * 1}$$

$$= \quad 25,778,699,578,994,555,700$$

Next, you need to determine the number of ways that the 50 drawn balls can be arranged 24 at a time. The math is the same (just smaller):

$$\frac{(50)!}{24} \quad \text{The number of ways 50 balls can be drawn in groups of 24 at a time}$$

$$\frac{50 * 49 * 48 * 47 * 46 * 45 * 44 * 43 * 42 * 41 * 40 * 39}{24 * 23 * 22 * 21 * 20 * 19 * 18 * 17 * 16 * 15 * 14 * 13}$$

$$\frac{* 38 * 37 * 36 * 35 * 34 * 33 * 32 * 31 * 30 * 29 * 28 * 27}{* 12 * 11 * 10 * 9 * 8 * 7 * 6 * 5 * 4 * 3 * 2 * 1}$$

$$= \quad 121,548,660,036,300$$

The last step is to divide the number of ways 75 balls can be taken 24 at a time by the number of ways 50 balls can be taken in groups of 24. The math looks like this:

$$\frac{25,778,699,578,994,555,700}{121,548,660,036,300} = 212,085$$

The odds therefore of covering all 24 numbers in a 75 ball bingo game, with 50 numbers drawn, is 212,085 to 1.

It might be of interest to know the number of bingo cards that can be printed without any two cards being the same. The math is a little more complicated. There are 15 possible numbers in each of five lettered rows. One of the rows has only four spots, the "N" row has the free spot dead center on the card. The math looks like this.

B   I   N   G   O
(15)! * (15)   * (15)! * (15)! * (15)!
5   5   4   5   5
=   111,007,923,832,370,565 different bingo cards

Gambler's joke: The problem with winning a jackpot in bingo is it takes so long to put the money back in the slot machines.

7	6

What does 86'd mean?

The term 86'd means to be thrown out or asked to leave the premises and not come back. Some oldtimers tell me that the term comes from the saloon days. Good whiskey is over 90 Proof. When a customer became too drunk to know the difference, they "86'd" him, meaning to give him the cheaper 86 proof whiskey. Others say the term "86" came from the address of a Speak Easy in the Roraring Twenties. As it relates to the gaming industry, it is meant to describe the Trespass Act (Nevada Revised Statute 207.200).

The NRS 207.200 reads in part:

Trespass on land, in building of another after warning;

1. Any person who, under circumstances not amounting to a burglary:

    a. Goes upon the land or into any building of another with intent to vex or annoy the owner or occupant thereof, or to commit any unlawful act; or

    b. Willfully goes or remains upon any land or in any building after having been warned by the owner or occupant thereof not to trespass, is guilty of a misdemeanor.

The trespass act is read in the following form to such persons as panhandlers, drunks, prostitutes, known cheaters and disorderly patrons (usually read by a security officer):

"As a duly appointed representative of the owner of this property, I hereby warn you that you are trespassing upon this property as defined by the Nevada Revised Statute 207.200. If you do not leave these premises immediately, you will be subject to arrest for a misdemeanor. Your subsequent return to the premises after being duly warned not to return will subject you to immediate arrest for trespassing."

The 86'd person is then asked to sign the above statement in the presence of the security officer.

Security once 86'd a midget from the casino for sticking his nose in other player's business. (Bad joke!)

What does color change mean?

It is the responsibility of a casino floorperson to keep track of all chips on the games he/she is responsible for. In order to facilitate this record keeping, the dealer is asked to convert the chips of customers leaving the games from the lower denominations to higher denomination chips. Rather than having a customer walk away from the game with 20 $25.00 chips, the dealer will call out *color change*. After an acknowledgment from the floorperson, the dealer will bring in the 20 $25.00 chips and give the customer five $100.00 chips or one $500.00 chip.

This color change also is a courtesy to the player so they will not have to walk around with a handful of chips. Players with too many chips to carry are also more likely to go to the casino cage and redeem the chips for cash. The casino would rather that you carry a smaller number of chips around with you so that you are more inclined to buy-in on another game. Also, a color change helps keep the casino bankroll filled with the lower denomination chips and, therefore, necessitates fewer chip fills from the cage.

Old gambler's saying: "He's as unlucky as a pickpocket at a nudist camp."

What does rake or vig mean?

The term *rake* usually applies to poker type games. The house takes or *cuts* from the pot a certain amount per hand or per hour as their profit. The amount of the rake should be posted for all players to see. When an overzealous poker dealer takes too much from the pot, he/she may be *padding* the rack (the bankroll), so that he/she may be stealing from the players. If the dealer is instructed by the poker operator to rake more than the posted amount, it is known as a *snatch* game.

The term *vig* is short for vigorish. This term applies to any percentage held back by the house on a bet. In the game of baccarat, a 5% vig (also called *commission, juice* or *cut*) is paid by the customer on any winning bank side bet. In craps, a 5% vig is paid by the customer when buying a number. Pai Gow Poker has a similar 5% vig exacted against winning bets. The vig is a built-in profit and the term originally meant to win with *vigor* because the vig is always taken.

The FBI defines a game as gambling when:

1. A charge, such as an admission charge, is made at the door.
2. There is an inherent mathematical advantage for one side over the other.
3. A *vig* or *rake* is taken.

Old Mob joke: Question: What does FBI stand for?

Answer: Forever Bothering Italians

$$\boxed{7}\boxed{9}$$

What game has the best odds for the player?

The only game where the customer ever has a mathematical advantage over the house is 21 (blackjack). The advantage in the game of blackjack floats back and forth between the house and the players. A basic strategy player reduces the house's starting advantage because of his perfect computerlike play. A card counter simply identifies the times when the house or player has the advantage or when the game is even up. (Please refer to the questions on card counting and basic strategy.) At the times the player has the advantage, the card counter places bigger bets. When the house has the advantage, obviously, the card counter places smaller wagers. The house has about one half of one percent starting advantage over the basic strategy player. The card counter can gain more than 2.0% advantage by betting at the proper plus and minus counts. A card counter can accurately identify those times when the mathematical advantage is in his favor. Keep in mind that at the same time the non–counter has exactly the same advantage, you just don't know it. This explains those apparent runs of "luck" when the dealer breaks a lot or the bad runs when you can't seem to win a hand.

The Pass Line bet of the crap table has a mathematical advantage for the house (against the player) of 1.414%. The Don't Pass Line has an advantage of 1.402% for the house and against the player. Some will argue that taking the odds will reduce the house advantage. On paper this sounds logical because mathematically the house's rate of win is reduced. For single odds, the house has 0.848% rate of win on the Pass Line and 0.832% on the Don't Pass. With double odds, the house's rate of win is

0.606% on the Pass Line and 0.591% on the Don't Pass. Keep in mind, however, that you are now risking more money by taking the odds to win or lose the same amount. (See Question [2][9] on free odds.) I am not talking about a lucky streak where you win and get out, or a losing streak where you can't seem to win a bet, but on the normal flow of the game. All the odds do is decrease the percentage rate at which the house wins a larger bet or the rate at which you win or lose.

Baccarat and/or mini-baccarat have a rate of win for the house of approximately 1.34% on the player side and about 1.21% on the bank side. Any game that has around a 1% house edge is, of course, a good game for a player.

Games that have a big payoff amount like Caribbean Stud Poker and Let It Ride have a little more advantage for the house because the house has to fund the big jackpot amount.

The best bet for a player to make is what is called a "mind bet." You stand behind the game, watch the action, and attempt to predict the winner. You never bet any real money, you only bet in your mind. Last week a friend of mine lost his mind three times.

What game has the worst odds for the player?

Roulette has a very high rate of win for the casino. Every bet, one number, two numbers, three numbers, four numbers, six numbers, red/black, odd/even, the columns, 12 numbers or 18 numbers all have 5.5/19ths% house advantage. The five number bet (0, 00, 1, 2, 3), known as a *basket bet*, has a 7.7/19ths% advantage against the player.

Far more disastrous is the Big 6, also known as the Wheel of Fortune or Money Wheel. The standard Big 6 wheel has 56 slots in between which the leather flap, called a *flapper*, can come to rest. The typical Big 6 wheel is divided as follows:

```
24 ............................................ #  I's
16 ............................................ #  2's
 8 ............................................ #  5's
 4 ............................................ #  10's
 2 ............................................ #  20's
 1 ............................................ #  40
 1 ............................................ Jackpot Pays 40
56   Total Numbers
```

If you wager $1.00 on the number one you win $1.00. You take down $2.00 — the one you've bet and the one you've won. To determine the house advantage, you need to find the amount you should actually take down. If all 24 number ones hit, you would take down $48.00 — the $24.00 you've bet and the $24.00 you've won. For this to be a dead even proposition, you should have taken down $56.00. The difference between what you should have taken down ($56.00), and what you actually take down ($48.00), is $8.00. To find the house advantage in percentage form, the math looks like this:

$$8.00 \div 56.00 = 0.14286 \text{ or } 14.286\%$$

For the number one to be a dead even bet, there would need to be 28 number one's.

The odds for the rest of the numbers on the Big 6 are not any better. They are as follows:

> \# 2........... 14.286% House Advantage
> \# 5........... 14.286% House Advantage
> \# 10 .... 21.429% House Advantage
> \# 20 .... 25.000% House Advantage
> \# 40 .... 26.786% House Advantage

I suppose it's all in the way you look at it. (Is the glass half filled or half empty?) There are countless stories of players who defy the odds and win a fortune. This kind of luck is known as *running between the raindrops*.

Old gambler's joke: A friend of mine went to Las Vegas in a $25,000.00 car and came home in a $150,000.00 bus.

8 1

What happens if the dealer makes a mistake?

We bury them in a dirt grave in the desert and then we fire them for "no call, no show."

Seriously speaking, mistakes are a part of any job. If a mistake arises over a payoff, the dealer has several options. He/she can simply correct the payment if it is possible to figure out. If not, the dealer calls the floorperson to try and correct the mistake. If the amount of the payoff is substantial, the last resort would be to call the "eye in the sky" to determine if the game was on videotape. If the game is on tape, a review of the play would decide the issue. If a player is dissatisfied with the decision of the casino manager, they may appeal this ruling to the Enforcement Division of the Nevada Gaming Control Board. Enforcement agents will review the video tape of the play and inform the customer and casino of their decision. Most casinos are reluctant to show patrons video tape of any play. Teams of cheaters have been known to make false claims in a casino for small amounts and dispute a payoff or rule. A member of the cheating team will demand to see the video tape. This is an attempt by the cheater to see the kind of surveillance coverage that the casino has on a particular game.

You can always recognize the "break-in" 21 dealers. They have their shoes and socks off and their zippers down in case they have to count to twenty-one (Bad joke.)

What is a chip hustler?

A chip hustler is a person who attempts to steal, con or ingratiate a customer out of their money or chips. Under the guise of helping a player learn to play a table game, a chip hustler will *palm* (secretly hide chips in his hand) some of the player's chips and then go to his pocket with the chips (called *going south* or *rat hole*). Even if the chip hustler doesn't steal a player's chips directly, he will expect to receive a part of the winnings (called *being pieced off* or *getting his end*).

Some chip hustlers will make up an elaborate story for a potential *mark*. The hustler will brag of his ability to read dealers or tell of watching games to determine *hot* or *cold* dealers. Hustlers have been known to tell players that they have a network of dealers who call in when their tables are going bad. "Of course," says the chip hustler, "we'll have to piece off the dealer too." In reality, there are no dealers calling. The chip hustler is just taking a chance on gambling with the player's money. The hustler has nothing to lose and shares part of the winnings. The *piece off* for the dealer goes into the hustler's pocket.

Some hustlers will steal chips from a customer at the crap tables. When a player reaches down to place a bet or collect a winner, the chip hustler will reach right underneath that player's arm and steal chips out of the rail. (When you reach down onto a crap table, you must lean forward and, in essence, your own shoulder and arm block your site of the rail underneath your arm.) This type of chip hustler is known as a *rail thief* or *rail bird*.

Chip hustle also happens in the slot machines. A hustler will tell a mark that a slot floorman or slot mechanic is turning him on to hot machines. The story is that the slot tech or floorman sees a computer list every day of all the machines in the casino and knows which ones are overdue to pay. "The inside guy," says the hustler, "also knows which machines the casino has set *loose* and which are *tight*." If asked why he doesn't play the slot machines himself (or the table games), the hustler tells the mark that he has been winning too often at this casino and is *too hot* to play himself. All of this, of course, is nonsense (short for "B#@%S#@%").

Hustling players is not restricted to casinos, but is actually quite common at race tracks. A race horse *tout* will approach several different bettors and claim to have *inside information*. The hustler touts a different horse to each bettor in the same race. After the race, the hustler returns to the bettor with the winning horse and expects a piece of the winnings.

Female chip hustlers will try and get next to a player and become very friendly and flirtatious. Dressed for the part, the chip hustler will ask a potential mark how to place bets and pretend not to know the game. "I'm going to make the same bets you do," says the hustler. However, the girl doesn't have enough money to place all the bets and hints that the *mark* should place bets for her because she is bringing him luck. Some girls will even hint about sexual favors or a date after the game in order to hustle a "mark" for chips or bets.

Chip hustling is closely related to an old grifter's con known as the *pigeon drop*. (The *pigeon* in this case is the person being scammed.) While preparing this book, I was contacted by the Nevada Gaming Control Board Enforcement Division to review tapes of a suspected chip hustle. A wealthy older woman was convinced by a couple of hustlers that they had hooked up with a network of Las Vegas dealers who were stealing high value chips from casinos all over town. Because the chips were of high value, "it would look suspicious," said the hustlers, "for the average customer to attempt to cash them in at a cage." The hustlers needed some wealthy person to cash the chips. The pigeon was told that the stolen chips could be bought for half price. (This is known as *telling the tale*.) These guys convinced this woman to come up with $100,000.00 in cash to supposedly buy $200,000.00 worth of stolen casino chips. The woman came up with the $100,000.00 in cash and brought it in paper bags to the casino where she met the two hustlers. She gave the money to one of the hustlers who was going to *buy* the stolen chips. (What comes next is known as the *blow off*.)

The hustler returns with the paper bags filled with what the woman now believes is $200,000.00 worth of stolen casino chips. When he was within earshot of the woman and the other hustler, he was approached by two men announcing themselves as hotel security agents. They took hold of his arms and marched him away. The hustler with the woman hurried her away in the opposite direction so that she wouldn't get *pinched* as well ("Just looking out for you."). The two so-called security agents were, of course, members of the scam. The hustler drove the woman to another casino and promptly disappeared.

Most pigeon drops work because the pigeon is convinced he/she is involved in an illegal venture of some kind. After the blow off, the pigeon is faced with the prospect of admitting to the cops that not only were they stupid and greedy, but in fact were involved in a scam. This woman would have to admit to the cops that she was willing to buy stolen merchandise. Most pigeons never go to the authorities. (This one did and the case is under investigation.)

If you are approached or bothered by a chip hustler, the safest thing to do is to notify the nearest floorperson or hotel security. The hustler will be read the trespass law and 86'd from the property or arrested. Casinos do not want customers bothered by chip hustlers or thieves.

Definition of a chip hustler: A pickpocket who lets you use your own hand.

What is a comp and how do I get them?

The term *comp* is short for complimentary or compliments of the house. In other words, you don't pay. In most casinos comps can be given for such things as drinks at the table games (or slot machines), drinks at the casino bars, food in the coffee shop and/or buffets, gourmet restaurants, lounge shows, main showroom shows, rooms or suites in the hotel, golf course fees, airfare tickets and even purchases in the arcade shops.

Casino executives have the authority to write comps, called the *power of the pen*, for any or all of the above services or items depending on their level in the company. A floorman may have the authority to comp food in the coffee shop or buffet but not in a gourmet restaurant. This doesn't mean that a floorman cannot go to an executive with a higher comp authority and put a player or friend into a show or restaurant. In order to receive a comp, certain criteria must usually be met by a player. Again, this is not to say that casino executives won't comp a friend or relative, but for the most part comps must be justified.

The criteria is centered around the amount of time a customer plays a game or slot machine and the average bet made during that time. The win or lose can also play a part in the rating of a customer. When you begin play at a table, it will not be long before a floorperson asks your name and asks if you would like to have your play rated. The approach may differ from casino to casino but basically the house wants floorpeople to rate players. If you choose to be rated you will receive a plastic card (called an MVP or rating card). You can present this card anytime you begin playing a table game or can insert the card in a slot machine card reader. The card identifies you and your play is then rated. The card can also be presented at the Race & Sports Book to have those bets credited to your account.

In order to qualify for such things as airline tickets or direct purchases from hotel shops, you would have to be a very big player. These types of comps are costing the hotel substantial money so your play must warrant the expenditure.

Comps are written off by the hotel as a business expense, but the casino executive must justify the comp to his/her boss and/or the comp committee.

It is wise to have all of your casino play rated because it is cumulative. You may bet a smaller amount than the next player, but qualify for a comp because you play longer or play several different games. Some hotels have a more liberal comp policy than others. The only way to know the comp policy is to play at the casino or ask an executive or another player.

Showroom maitre d' joke: "Would the person who lost the wallet with $1,000.00 in it please form a single line to the right."

What is a marker?

Many customers apply for credit with a casino in much the same fashion as for any other form of credit. An application, along with bank information, is filled out and processed by the casino's credit department. Casinos all around Las Vegas share a common credit reporting bureau known as Central Credit. Central Credit has records dating back several years on all subscribing casinos. The amounts owed, and any derogatory information, is available to the casino credit department.

When a player has established credit with the casino, he can play against his credit line by signing a *marker*. A marker is, simply speaking, an I.O.U. between the player and the casino. The marker itself looks like a blank bank check. In the old days, the marker was hand written by a floorman. The marker contains the game number, the amount taken, the player's signature and the initials of the floorman and dealer. The marker consists of three parts. The top copy is the original which contains the actual signature of the player. There is an issue copy which is removed after the marker is complete with all signatures and initials. The issue copy is dropped in the table game drop box. The marker is then used as part of the overall handle for that game to determine the win or loss for that shift. The last copy is a marker redemption slip. If a player buys back the marker (returns to the table an amount of chips equal to the amount signed for on the marker), the marker buy slip is filled in and dropped in the drop box as verification that the marker was paid backed. The original top copy of the marker is returned to the player as his receipt that the marker was bought back. Most players will tear up the marker right at the table as soon as the original is returned to them.

With the advent of the computer age, most markers are now generated by a computer printer. The advantages are obvious. A computer record is maintained of all marker issues and payments. A marker accounting can be generated at anytime to determine the amount of markers issued in the entire casino and the amount outstanding.

Markers are made to resemble a personal check. In cases where a customer refuses to pay his markers, casinos have been known to attempt to run the markers through the player's bank for payment.

Most casinos are very cautious when issuing credit. Many players will attempt to obtain an interest free loan from the casino. A player will take out several thousand dollars worth of markers. He will not play any significant amount and will not buy back the markers before returning home. The player has redeemed the chips for cash at the casino cage and will go home owing the amount of his markers but with a pocket full of the casino's money.

The player will eventually pay back the markers owed, but this may take three to six months. During that time, the customer has used the casino's money without paying any interest.

In the old days, most states in this country did not consider a gambling marker a legal debt. In order to collect a bad debt, casinos were forced to employ such personages as "Three Finger Louie" and "Vito the Axe." (It was Vito who gave Louie his nickname.) With the nationwide explosion of legal casino gambling and because of new legislation, casino debts are now a legal debt, subject to criminal and civil prosecution in many states.

An old time gambler's expression for someone playing with markers is, "on the finger". This term refers to the practice of simply raising a finger to ask for or approve a marker. They say, "the guy's on the finger for 5 dimes" means $5,000.00.

Old gambler's puzzle: How much is two plus two minus two plus two? Most people will say the answer is zero. The answer is four. Think of it this way 2+2-2+2. Solution: 2+2=4-2=2+2=4. (Special thanks to Richard Willemin, a good friend, for the above puzzle.)

8 5

What is a wheel crank?

Many new hires (called *break-ins*) in the gaming industry will be asked to go pick up a *wheel crank* from another pit or casino executive. The break-in is told that the roulette wheels are slowing down and the wheel crank is needed as quickly as possible to maintain the wheelhead speed and alignment. Sending someone for a wheel crank in a gambling house is akin to sending an apprentice carpenter for a *board stretcher* or asking a plumber's helper for a *left-handed monkey wrench*. The point is there is no such thing as a wheel crank.

Typically the casino boss will wait for a very cocky new dealer or employee. The other casino bosses will take delight in ping-ponging the new person from pit to pit, to the maintenance office and/or any other department they can think of. One casino recently sent a break-in in a cab to another casino to pick up a wheel crank. The casino boss called a friend at the next casino and when the break-in showed up, he was given a stick with a bolt screwed to it. Upon his return to his casino, the boss informed him of how stupid he was. "You brought back a clockwise wheel crank. You know we needed a counter-clockwise crank."

Question: "Can you wear a turtle neck sweater with a henway?" "What's a henway?" Answer: "About 3 or 4 pounds, like a chicken."

What is a toke and when should I toke?

A tip in the gaming industry is called a *toke*. This term is obviously short for token, as in "a token of my gratitude" or "a token of my appreciation." Dealers, bartenders, valet car attendants, cocktail servers, waiters and waitresses, keno runners and bellmen survive in large part on the tips or tokes given to them by casino and hotel customers.

The question of when you should toke is simple. Toke when you feel you have received good service. At a gaming table when dealers are friendly and/or remind you of a particular bet, they are giving you service. Most dealers are pulling for the customers to do well. The more a customer wins, the more likely he/she will be to leave a toke or place a bet for the dealers. Most dealers are paid between $25.00 and $45.00 a day by the casino. This amount is not a very good wage by any means, so dealers rely very heavily on the toke rate. If a dealer is rude or indifferent to you as a customer, then, of course, they are not giving you service. In some casinos where dice dealers are cutting tokes crew for crew (splitting tips four ways with the other dice dealers on that game), a problem known as *hustling* occurs. Hustling a customer means to ask or constantly remind a player to place bets for the dealers. The hustle can be *soft*, being courteous and jokingly asking for a bet. On the other hand a *hard* hustler will continually press a player and even be rude to customers. Most casinos have gone to a system where all dealers share in all tokes. This eliminates the incentive for strong or hard hustling. When dealers are splitting tokes crew for crew, then each member of the crew gets 25% of each toke for that table for that shift (25% is a strong incentive). Cutting man for man throughout the casino means splitting that toke with as many as 300 dealers; about 0.03% (not much incentive). In either case, casinos frown on dealers being rude or pushy with customers. If a dealer is rude or otherwise offensive to you, the casino would appreciate you letting an executive know about it.

In most gambling situations, it is appropriate to toke when you are winning...if you feel like it. After all, it is your money. In other areas such as food and beverage, you should tip as you normally would. Fifteen percent is not a bad toke. In a case where you are being comped, you might want to tip a little better. Here's a tip for you about a comped check. Some food servers or bartenders have been known to pad a comped check. They will add another customer's order to your comped check or push you to go for the most expensive bottle of wine. Most customers who are comped will not even look at or question the amount of the bill (they aren't paying anyway). By increasing your bill, the waiter or bartender is hoping for a bigger toke on the bigger amount.

Growing up in Detroit, I frequented many of the local pool halls. Almost every regular had a nickname. "The Detroiter," "Cornbread Red," "Ray the Rat" — a lot of guys called me "Fingers." There was a guy with the nickname "Johnny No Pockets." You might think because it was a pool hall that Johnny couldn't make a ball in the pocket of a pool table. The real reason he got the nickname was because when it came time to pay a check or leave a toke, he couldn't find his pocket to reach for the cash. We would take delight in mimicking Johnny by pretending to reach for imaginary pockets. There was also a guy nicknamed "Red" because he once read a book. A friend of mine, Frank Rinella, the Marketing Director for Fitzgeralds' Casino in Las Vegas, tells me he grew up with a cheap guy nicknamed "Crime" because "Crime Doesn't Pay." Thanks Frank.

What is Pai Gow Dominoes?

Pai Gow Dominos is an Asian gambling game played mainly by Asian customers. The Pai Gow dominoes resemble the standard dominos we are familiar with in the Western World, but that is where the similarities end.

In order to understand or play Pai Gow dominoes, the book says you need to be "Chinese and 500 years old." I'm not sure of the Chinese part, but the 500-year-old part makes sense.

The game of Pai Gow uses a set of 32 Chinese dominoes, sometimes called *tiles*. The object of the game is to set the four dominoes dealt to each player and the dealer, into two separate hands, a high hand and a low hand according to the ranking combinations (see the chart). In order to win, the player must win both the high and low hands. (The house will collect a 5% commission on all winning hands.) In order to lose, the player must lose both the high and low hands. If the player wins one hand and loses the other, the bet is a *push*. (The players hands are compared to the dealer's hand in order to determine the winning or losing hands.) The game is started by rolling three dice. The total of the dice determines which spot will receive the first set of four tiles. The remaining hands are then dealt in a counter clockwise direction from the first hand. A unique feature about Pai Gow is that each player has an option of being the banker. The house will always bank the first hand. After the first hand, the bank will be offered in turn (counter clockwise) to each player. If a player refuses, the bank will pass back to the house.

All dominoes have a combination ranking and an individual ranking. The rankings are based on symbolism and not their numerical value. (See the chart.) The rankings 1 through 16 are pairs, called "Bo." (The highest possible pair, 1-2 & 2-4 is called "Gee Joon" or "Supreme.") The rankings 17 through 20 are called "Wongs" and "Gongs." If any of the 20 combinations cannot be played, the player will then try to get two separate hands as close to 9 as possible. This will be done by totaling the spots on two dominoes; for example, a 3-1 and 1-1 = 6.) If the dealer and player have the same value hand, the hand with the single highest ranking tile will win. If the player and the banker have the same exact hand, the banker wins. The four rules listed below account for about 80% of all Pai Gow hands and should be played in order.

1. Play pairs (do not overlook unmatched pairs)
2. Play 6-6 (Teen) or 1-1 (Day) with any 7-8-9
3. Play two small tiles that equal 7-8-9
4. Play the biggest tile with the smallest tile. Try to make the low hand as high as possible.

The dealer or floorperson in any Pai Gow tile game will help you set your hands if you ask. (Remember the 500 year old rule...tough game.)

The Pai Gow tile hand formulation is shown on the next two pages.

Author's note: If you can figure out this next little puzzle, then you'll have no trouble with Pai Gow Tiles (or nuclear fission).

Three guys rent a hotel room for $30.00. Each guy throws in $10.00. When they get to the room they don't feel it's worth $30.00 so they ask for a discount. The manager gives the bellman $5.00 to return to the men. The bellman figures he can't split $5.00 evenly between 3 guys so he gets five singles. The bellman gives each guy back one dollar and keeps the remaining two dollars for himself.

Now here's the question: If each guy originally put up $10.00 and each guy got back $1.00 from the bellman, then each guy spent $9.00—right? Well, 9.00 x 3 = $27.00 and the bellman has $2.00. $27.00 + 2.00 = $29.00. "So what happened to the other dollar? Think about it then forget about it. It'll drive you crazy!

Special thanks to Albert Einstein for the above puzzle. This is his theory of the "lost dollar."

PAI GOW TILE HAND FORMULATION: RANKING COMBINATIONS

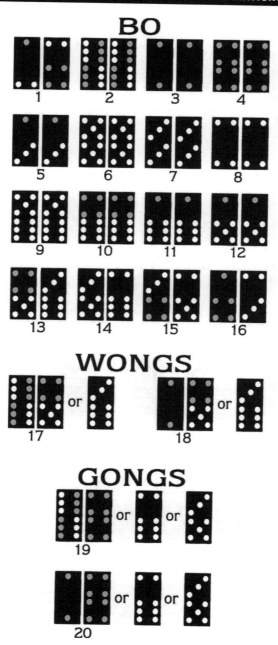

PAI GOW TILE HAND FORMULATION: INDIVIDUAL RANKINGS

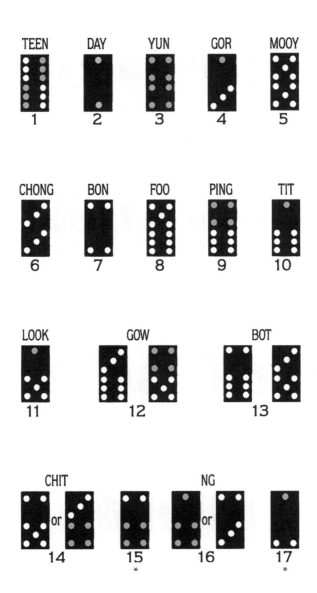

*These two dominoes are wild and are interchangeable. The 3 can be used as a 6, and the 6 can be used as a 3. Together this combination makes the highest ranking pair called "GEE JOON."

What is the biggest bet ever made in a casino?

There are a few of the major casinos in Las Vegas who will regularly allow customers to bet $100,000.00 to $200,000.00 per hand on a baccarat game. Considering that the average baccarat shoe (with eight decks) will generate about 72 hands per shoe, we are talking serious money.

The biggest single bet, however, seems to be attributed to a player at the Horseshoe Casino in downtown Las Vegas. The Horseshoe Casino is owned by the Binion family. The Binions are one of the last great old time gambling families and casino operators. The Horseshoe has a policy that has made them world famous in the gaming industry. You can bet any amount you want at the Horseshoe as long as it's your first bet. In other words, you can set your own limit. If you have the bankroll and intestinal fortitude (in Arabic we say "Bidots Ou Jamul" or "the testicles of a camel") and wish to wager a half a million dollars a hand, you can, as long as you bet the half a million on your first bet.

As the story goes, a player from Texas came to the Horseshoe. This particular player owed his creditors about one million dollars. He had liquidated his assets and had almost enough cash to settle his debts. Settling with all of his creditors would leave him essentially broke and with no prospects of earning the style of living to which he had become accustomed. So early one morning, this guy walks up to a crap table at Binion's carrying a small suitcase. In the suitcase was $777,000.00. The guy asked to make a *don't bet* on the crap table for the full amount. (A don't bet means you are betting the shooter will lose, either crap out or seven out.) The casino floorman called Jack Binion who came down and examined the dice. The bet was accepted. A female customer was shooting the dice on the *come out roll* (the first roll). If the woman had rolled a 7 or 11, she would win and the big bettor would lose. (There are six ways to throw a 7 and three ways to roll an 11...nine ways to lose on the don't side on the come out roll.) If the woman had rolled a 2 or 3 (craps), she would have lost and the big bettor would have won. (There is one way to throw a 2 and two ways to throw a 3...three ways to win on the don't side on the come out roll.) Had she thrown a 12 (one way), she would have lost her bet on the pass line and the big bettor would have pushed the bet on the don't side (tie bet). The first roll of the dice was a 5. No winner or loser, but the number 5 becomes the *point*. This means that in order for the woman to win, she must make the point i.e., roll a 5 again before rolling a 7. If she rolls the 7 before she makes the point 5, she would *seven out* and the $777,000.00 don't bet would win.   The next roll of the dice was a 9...no decision. The third roll was a 7 (seven out). The don't bettor won $777,000.00 on one bet.

As the story goes, the customer now had over one and a half million dollars. He did not, however, pay off his creditors but instead came back a few weeks later and blew the entire amount. He then went to his hotel room and committed suicide (a permanent solution to a temporary problem).

There is also a story about a *long distance* bet attributed to the Horseshoe Casino when Benny Binion was alive. Four high rollers who were poker buddies of Benny called the Horseshoe one night from Texas. They each pledged $250,000.00 for a one million dollar bet on a crap table. Benny approved the bet and held the phone receiver up so the guys in Texas could hear the stickman call the roll of the dice. The bet lost, and true to their code of honor, the four gamblers paid Binion.

An old time gambler once told me, "I went through a fortune on alcohol, gambling and women...the rest I blew."

What is the Black Book and who gets in?

What has become known as the *Black Book* is in reality the State of Nevada's *List of Excluded Persons*. First instituted in 1960, the Black Book became part of the Nevada Gaming Control Act in 1967. The law was enacted to protect the gaming industry by "avoiding any potentially significant criminal or corruptive taint and thus maintaining public confidence and trust in the gaming industry." Persons included on the list are first nominated for inclusion by the Nevada Gaming Board or the Las Vegas Metropolitan Police Department. Once nominated, a candidate has the right to a hearing to discuss and/or defend himself against inclusion. Once included in the Black Book, a person has the right to legally appeal their entry. Upon death, your name is removed from the Black Book.

Since 1960, there have been 38 people entered in the Black Book. By far, the majority are alleged organized crime members or associates. Recently, several slot cheaters have been nominated and entered. The criteria for entry into the Black Book includes the following:

1. A prior felony conviction or conviction of a crime involving moral turpitude.
2. Violation or conspiracy to violate gaming laws.
3. A notorious or unsavory reputation which would adversely affect public confidence and trust that the gaming industry is free from criminal and corruptive elements.
4. Previous exclusion from licensed gaming activities of other states.

A person included in the Black Book is prohibited from entering a licensed gaming establishment under penalty of arrest. A licensed gaming establishment has the obligation to exclude and notify the Gaming Board of any Black Book member found on their premises.

Most Black Book challenges have been defeated by higher courts because the gaming industry is considered a *privileged* business. You do not have a *right* to conduct a gambling business; it is a privilege granted by the State. Since casinos are private property, you do not have a right to enter and the regulating body has the authority to exclude.

There are some casinos who agree and some who disagree with those entries in the Black Book. Many cheaters convicted of gaming crimes are not included in the Black Book.

Because of my background, I'm often asked who was the greatest cheater I ever knew. In my mind, there is a distinct difference between cheating and hustling. There are strong-arm guys who will put a gun to your head and steal a lot of money. A hustler, on the other hand, makes you think everything is okay. Let me tell you the story of the best hustler I ever knew:

My Grandmother was an old Arab woman who spoke very guttural Arabic and broken English. She never attended a day of school and could not read or write. The Arabic word for Grandmother is "Sito." Sito was the matriarch of our family. She had eight children who produced 33 grandchildren, and at last count, nearly 100 great grandchildren. Let me tell you how big my family is. I have a pretty young cousin, Sandra Joseph, who sings the lead in the Phantom of the Opera on Broadway. When Sandi came through Detroit, my brother Wayne purchased a block of 413 tickets for one night. Our family reunions are now held in a small baseball field. ("Sandra, is anybody bothering you?"—private joke)

Sito lived with my family for almost 40 years. We always gambled at my house. After dinner or whenever family visited, we pulled out the cards or dice. Sito loved to play any gambling game but especially Gin. The thing was, she cheated! She would hold her cards in one hand and her rosary in the other. When she would finish dealing, she always looked at the bottom card. Well, it was my grandmother, so I gave her the bottom card. When I would catch her with points (knock early), her tactics would change. Suppose she had 50 points against her, she would mumble something in Arabic and announce, "30." If I challenged her count, she would look at the cards and then look at her rosary and say, "Una un Sullee," which means, "I'm praying." Well, what do I do now? Argue with God? The woman is praying and some of the prayers are for me. So, being a wise guy, I thought this was her hustle. She could always blame her cheating or mistakes on the rosary. On the other hand, if Sito caught or suspected me of cheating she would say, "Roouh Huff Thesuck Ou Hiht" ("Go scratch you fanny on the wall") or "Hut Eeduck Be Thesuck Ou Shoufut" ("Put your finger up your butt and whistle.").

Sito died at the age of 95 on the same day of the month she was born, February 12th, a very unusual occurrence for a very unusual and special woman. Sito always took delight in her family. If she heard my cousin Alex and I sing, or saw my cousin Chuck or brother Larry score a touchdown, or saw any of us accomplish the simple tasks of growing up she would say, "Yut Berni Toulou." It's a very endearing Arabic saying which doesn't translate very well. Literally it means, "Bury me the length of my grave." From the heart it means, "I'm so proud, bury me before they bury you." As is our custom, we had a "mercy dinner" after the funeral service. We all began recounting Sito stories. The time she accidentally dropped Kibbee (an Arabic dish made of raw beef) into clean dish water. She rinsed off the Kibbee and didn't tell us until after dinner. My brother Wayne, who called her "Sito Baby," told of her "asbestos hands." Sito could reach into a hot oven as she baked Arabic bread and turn the bread over by hand or stir boiling water with her finger to check the temperature without burning herself. Sito always blessed the car (she called "machine") before you drove off. My mother recounted the time when she left Sito to be examined for eyeglasses. The young doctor determined a prescription and asked if Sito could read a newspaper. Sito replied she couldn't and the doctor changed the prescription again and again for the next 45 minutes with Sito telling him each time that she could not read the newspaper. My mother finally took pity on the college graduate telling him that Sito was just having fun with him because she couldn't read in the first place. Sito just laughed.

We could never be to Sito what she was to us. When your mother wasn't home, Sito was your mother. She was your best friend. If you needed love, she gave you love. If you were hungry, she cooked for you. If you needed sympathy, she cried for you. If you were sick, she nursed you to health. When you needed her to jump in front of your father to prevent the ass-kicking you probably deserved, she did that too. She was your parent and best friend without the value judgement. Her value was love.

When I told the story of how Sito used the rosary beads as her way out of cheating, my father began to laugh. I asked him what he was laughing at. "You...you used to cheat in the games and now you're a big shot who runs around the country showing other big shots how the cheating happens. Did you know that for 30 years your grandmother was counting cards on those beads?" Sito had apparently developed the Arabic version of a Chinese abacus. I'm still not certain of her exact method but for over 30 years, the woman hustled me right to her grave. Victoria Safi Joseph (Sito) was always a source of love and pride for me and my entire family. So I say to Sito "Yut Berni Toulou. Your memory will last longer than mine."

I used to include this story in my game protection seminars to illustrate the point that anyone can be hustled under the right conditions. The "Sito" story sounded to some like "B.S." So I took the story out. A couple of years back, a group of shuffle trackers was arrested in Windsor, Canada. I was asked by the Canadian government to write an expert witness opinion relating to their methods. One method the group used to account for the cards they tracked was beads sewn into the bra straps of the female members of the team. As particular cards were played the girls would slide a bead from the bra strap and drop it into a sack at the end of the slide. I put the Sito story back into the lecture.

What is the CTR requirement?

In 1970, the United States Congress passed into law the Bank Secrecy Act. Originally the law only affected financial institutions and cash transactions occurring there.

The letters CTR stand for Currency Transaction Report. The Federal Government requires all casinos to complete a CTR on any customer who transacts or buy-ins more than $10,000.00 in a 24-hour period. Keep in mind this is not the casinos idea, but rather a requirement of the Federal Government. In 1986, 1988 and again in 1990, Congress enacted the Anti-Drug Abuse Act which further defined the penalties for failure to comply with or evade the CTR requirement. The law attempts to control the flow of illegal drug and gambling money. The CTR reporting requirement is also known in the gaming industry in Nevada as Reg 6. This refers to the State regulations 6A.030 through 6A.070.

The Reg 6 statutes go on to describe the types of transactions covered by the CTR. They include markers at the cage or table games, cash buy-ins at the cage or games, and chip buys at the cage. The CTR requirement also covers checks cashed at the cage.

Drug dealers have been known to try and *launder* drug money by coming to casinos and putting large sums of money in the cage as front money. A day or two later, the drug dealer takes the front money down and in affect washes the money. Many casinos have made a practice of holding front money on a suspicious customer to see if he in fact plays against the front money. If the customer does not play in earnest against the front money, the casino will return the exact same money, bill for bill, to the customer.

Several casinos have been fined by the Federal Government for not disclosing or accurately recording the money transactions of their customers.

Gamblers joke: If you're a petty thief, you will be charged and put into prison. The really good thieves are put into the Federal Government.

What is the "eye in the sky"?

In the old days of Las Vegas, when a casino boss or owner suspected a dealer or player of cheating, they would send a *shill* to the game to pose as a player. The shill would watch the dealer and customers for any number of cheating moves. The dealers, however, soon became aware of the owner's shills making their presence on a game a deterrent, but it did not stop the cheating.

The next step in the evolution of the *eye in the sky* was the installation of one way mirrors above the table games. Above the one way mirrors in the ceiling was a system of catwalks to allow surveillance personnel access to a view over each game. Equipped with a pair of binoculars, and in some cases a lunch pail, a surveillance observer would camp out over a suspected dealer or player. Some casino catwalks were outfitted with a series of periscope-like viewing devices spread throughout the casino. These devices were very cumbersome to use as well as very tiring on the eyes, take my word for it.

In many cases, in the old days, a surveillance observer would take an 8mm home movie camera along to film the game or activity. The movie cameras were soon replaced by the bulky first generation home video cameras. In many casinos, dealers were aware that an observer was above their game because a very fine mist of dust would float down through the lights. The fine particles of dust were very subtle, but there were times when the observer's presence over a game was not so subtle. On more than one occasion, a surveillance observer has fallen through the one way mirror or ceiling. In some cases only a leg was exposed. In one very memorable incident, the observer fell through the glass and landed face down on a crap table. As you might have guessed, some customer placed a $5.00 bet on the guy's ass. (No kidding!)

Although the catwalks and one-way mirrors are still in use in many casinos, they have been replaced by the next generation of eye in the sky technology — the closed-circuit TV surveillance systems. As you walk through a casino, you will notice a series of plastic bubbles in the ceiling. Housed inside the bubble is a pan/tilt/zoom camera, called a PTZ. The cameras may be in color or black and white. The motorized controlled camera can pan at variable speeds from one degree per second to as fast as 180 degrees per second. The tilt function allows the camera to look straight down or to move to any viewing angle from one to 180 degrees. Most surveillance cameras are equipped with a zoom lens with a 6 to 1 or 10 to 1 zoom ratio. The entire surveillance system is controlled by a microprocessor that allows a surveillance observer to operate and view any camera in the system.

It is now a requirement of the Nevada Gaming Control Board Enforcement Division that every casino must have an operational surveillance system. The system must have the capability to videotape record any camera in the system. Gaming Control Board agents have full access, at anytime, to the surveillance monitoring room and must on demand, be given any video tape they request.

Most surveillance systems have a mixture of PTZ and fixed cameras. Many of the larger casinos have well over 500 cameras in their surveillance system.

Casinos differ in the number of games they can record at any one time. At the Bally and Hilton properties, we record virtually every table game and cash handling function 24 hours a day. Most casinos will save video tapes on a seven day rotation, although by law, certain areas must be maintained for 30 days.

The casinos are prohibited by law from recording audio in public areas or on table games (violation of the Federal wire tape law). At one time in the early 1980's while I was at the Dunes Hotel, we installed exposed microphones on the Crap tables. Well, dealers began tapping the microphone with the dice stick and spitting at it. Some customers auditioned for the *lounge show* by singing into the microphones. (Needless to say, the microphones did not last long.) Casinos do, however, audio tape record the hard count and soft count rooms. Employees in these areas are aware of the microphones. The function of the audio is to verify cash amounts.

Most surveillance systems are equipped with alarm modes or pre-set functions. If an alarm is tripped, a camera will automatically move to that area and begin recording.

As technology advances, so do surveillance systems. Many casinos are moving to digital cameras with zoom ratios over 100 to 1. Digital recorders will allow taped information to be stored on an almost indefinite basis.

Casino security and surveillance departments are also experimenting with various facial recognition technologies. A hardcopy picture or video image of a person's face is scanned into a computer program. The computer creates a *mask* or *mathematic grid* of the captured image. The program stores those measurements and facial relationships that are distinct to that individual's face and are least likely to change due to aging, weight gain or loss, or disguise. The computer can then search through a stored database of known and suspected cheaters to help quickly identify an individual.

At one time, most surveillance departments had a police mentality; they only wanted to apprehend or arrest. Many surveillance departments have now turned to a prevention and backup mode.

A few years back, I sang in the lounges around Las Vegas. The entertainment director at the Maxim Hotel was a great guy named Frank Fink. Frank made a joke about surveillance. "We don't have the eye in the sky above the games, we have mirrors on the floor. We don't know if you're cheating, but we know where your ass is at all times."

9 2

What is the Griffin Book?

The Griffin Book is a "Who's Who" of casino cheaters and their associates. The Griffin Detective Agency began operations in the 1960's. It was founded by former Las Vegas Police Officer Bob Griffin. Casinos throughout Las Vegas, and now throughout the world, subscribe to the monthly service. The Griffin book contains several hundred pages of pictures and mugshots of known and suspected casino cheaters. The Griffin books are the sole property of the Griffin Detective Agency and are leased to each casino property on a monthly basis. The books are updated on a monthly basis throughout the gaming industry.

Along with the pictures, information such as height, weight, hair and eye color and so on is listed. All known aliases for each person are given. Also a brief description of the cheating method or methods used by the person is described. Each entry includes a list of known associates.

The pictures in the Griffin Book come from a couple of different sources. One source is the Las Vegas Police Department. Each person who works in a casino or hotel in Las Vegas must be on record with the Sheriff's office. A work permit, known as a Sheriff's Card, is issued to every gaming and non-gaming employee. (Employees must carry their work card with them at all times while on property. If, for any reason criminal or otherwise, Metro Police or the Gaming Control Board should pull your work card, you cannot work.) Each casino/hotel employee is photographed, finger printed and entered into Metro's computer to search for criminal history, wants and warrants.

The other source of pictures and information for the Griffin Agency is the casinos themselves. When an employee or outside person is apprehended for cheating at gaming, there are usually several video tapes and still photographs of the play. In addition to the monthly Griffin book updates, the Griffin Agency distributes flyers on a regular basis. The flyers alert the gaming industry to the particular cheaters who are currently active in the casinos.

The Griffin book should not be confused with the State of Nevada's List of Excluded Persons, known as the Black Book. Individuals in the Black Book are prohibited by law from entering a casino.

Many cheaters are in the Griffin Book because they have been *ratted* out by other cheaters. The old code of *omerta* (silence) is not adhered to by a lot of the new young thieves.

Old Arabic saying: "Is ah myit ehkey." When you're dead, then you can talk.

Was the movie Showgirls a realistic depiction of Las Vegas showgirls?

The movie *Showgirls* wasn't a realistic depiction of anything, much less Las Vegas showgirls. The idea that a girl could come from the streets, with little or no formal dance training, do a two-minute audition and go to work in a Las Vegas show that evening is ridiculous and insulting.

Las Vegas showgirls are, first and foremost, trained dancers. This means years of classical, ballet and/or jazz classes. Even the topless showgirls who walk in the big headdresses have some dance and poise training in their background.

There are auditions for Las Vegas shows known as *cattle calls*, where anyone can tryout. However, you might simply be asked to do a dance step such as an Assemblé, Piqué, Pirouette or Chaine Turn. Most people can't even pronounce these terms much less do one. Diane Palm, the assistant company manager for Bally's Jubilee show (and a good person in her own right), tells me, at this point, they will lose about half of the hopefuls at the audition after one ballet pass. An untrained dancer would have no way of passing an audition and making it into a Las Vegas show in one day. Dance club dancers may well be beautiful and able to do the current dance steps in club settings, but this in no way qualifies them to perform in a Las Vegas show. Even experienced trained dancers must go through several weeks of rehearsals and coaching before being allowed in a live performance.

The movie shows children in a backstage dressing room. This would never be allowed in a Vegas show. Male dancers and casino executives were seen in the girl's dressing room. This would never be allowed; I know, I've tried (just kidding, honey). Also, people were shown smoking backstage which is not allowed.

The typical Las Vegas showgirl is signed to a contract between three months and one year. A showgirl could receive a weight notice, meaning that she has put on too much weight and has a specific amount of time to reduce. A girl could also receive a weight notice for being too thin and would have to add weight — what a burden! Show people have much the same working conditions with management as most workers. They can receive warning notices for being late and/or performance mistakes and face the same disciplinary consequences as any other casino employee.

Girls in a Las Vegas show are in one of three general categories, dancers, acrobats (smaller very athletic girls) and showgirls (tall, very statuesque). Showgirls wear the large head dresses and feathered costumes. The elaborate costumes were conspicuously absent from the movie.

The movie attempts to imply that the two different worlds of showgirls and strippers in some way are akin to one another. There is a tremendous difference between the mentality that allows for lap dancing and stripping on cocktail tables or in private rooms and the pursuit of a dancer in a Las Vegas show. I'm not making a value judgement of the two lifestyles, I'm just pointing out that the two worlds are worlds apart.

Kim, the showgirl, was so "busty" that when she fell down it took four men to carry her off stage...two abreast.

Author's Note: Diane Palm used to conduct backstage tours open to the public. It is really amazing to see the shear size of the stage, overhead flies and understage mechanical apparatus that is necessary to produce a show the magnitude of Jubilee. Diane remarked she gets asked some pretty silly questions by the tourists. The oddest question seems to be, "Does the hotel pay for showgirls to have their teeth whitened?"

9 4

What is the greatest amount of money ever stolen from a casino?

For purposes of this question, we are not going to speculate as to the amount of money skimmed from casinos in the old days when the mob and private owners had free run of the count rooms.

I have been personally involved in the investigations of several casino scams where over three million dollars was stolen. One of the scams occurred in Bophuthatswanna, South Africa, in the Sun City Casino. A group of about 10-12 individuals were involved, both from the inside and as players. The method used to steal was a clever, but old time device, known as a *chip cup*. Imagine a hollow tube which was painted and designed to look like a stack of small denomination chips. The chip cup is made slightly larger than a standard 39 millimeter casino chip. Because the cup is larger than standard chips, it can easily slide over a stack of four standard casino chips. (The casino chips are hidden inside the hollowed cup.) A standard casino chip of small value is glued to the top of this hollowed tube. The chip cup is made of aluminum, spring steel or brass and is painted and scored to look like a stack of five $1.00 or $5,00 chips. In Sun City the chip cup was painted to resemble a stack of five $10.00 chips (dollars there are called rands).

The beauty of the chip cup is that a player brings the cup into play and also takes it out again. The dealer and player are obviously working together in this scam. In Las Vegas, or casinos in the U.S., the chip cup scam is normally attempted on a crap table. This is because the dealers stack chips straight up in front of them on a crap table, as opposed to laying them down in a table rack, as in a 21 game. (Chips stacked straight up in front of a dealer makes it much easier for the chip cup to be placed over the chips.) In South Africa, in the mid 1980's, craps was not at all popular in casinos. Casino craps is an American game. The big money game in Sun City is baccarat, called Punter-Banco. In this game, unlike the Las Vegas baccarat games, chips are stacked straight up in front of the dealers.

The scam works like this. The player/cheater (known as an *agent* or *A*) sits next to the dealer who is standing. The agent places the hollowed empty chip cup on the layout as a bet. It looks, to all intents, like a $50.00 bet (50 rand); a stack of five $10.00 chips. (There are also bettors wagering $100.00 (rand) chips on the game.) If the bet wins, the dealer/cheater simply pays the bet as he would any legitimate bet, by stacking five $10.00 chips next to the chip cup.

What the cheaters really want is for the bet to lose; that's how the cheaters really win. When the bet loses, the dealer/cheater picks up the empty chip cup, and in the process of picking up losing $100.00 chips, he secretly slips the chip cup over four one hundred dollar chips. (There are now four $100.00 chips hidden inside the chip cup.) As the dealer begins to put the chips away, he makes sure the chip cup remains on top of the stack of $10.00 chips. The player/cheater then simply buys the loaded chip cup back from the dealer/cheater. The agent throws in $50.00 cash. The cash is dropped and the dealer/cheater hands the loaded chip cup back to the agent as change. The cheaters have netted $350.00. (The loaded chip cup cost $50.00 to buy, but it had $400.00 inside.)

The real strength of the transaction with the chip cup is that the house has just won big bets from the players. Afterwards, a relatively small amount ($50.00) is exchanged as a cash buy-in by a dealer and customer. One key element in the success of the chip cup scam at Sun City was the inside pit boss (called inspectors in Sun City). The inspector was key to this scam because he controlled the dealer's schedule. This particular pit boss designated which games the dealers would go to on arrival to start work, and which games they would go to on return from breaks. In effect, this one inspector could send his crew of three cheating dealers all to one game. The inspector chose Punter-Banco games where the house was winning. This practice helped to disguise the activity as the bosses and surveillance were watching the Punter-Banco games where the house was losing. In addition, the floorman on the game was also in on the scam, and could alert the team if a non-member boss were to approach the table.

One other key element in the chip cup scam was a cage employee. This senior cage cashier allowed the agents to cash out considerable sums of money without question. At the time, South Africa had a very strict currency transaction policy. Large cash outs should have been recorded and/or brought to the attention of upper management. In the end, it was the currency transactions outside the casino which proved to be the downfall of the scam and its members. (Large amounts of cash were being wired from a house in Rustenberg, a town right outside Sun City, to England.)

Over the course of several months, the team was estimated to have removed between 2.5 and 3.5 million dollars from the Punter-Banco tables. I personally polygraphed about fifty employees to determine the extent of the scam for insurance purposes. The casino received a settlement from Lloyd's of London of better than two million dollars. The exact amount of the insurance settlement was not disclosed. A formula of historic win versus the deflated win for those months was used to determine the amount of the insurance claim.

Sun City is operated in the Black homeland of Bophuthatswanna. The government of the homeland shares in 50% of the profits of the casinos in it's jurisdiction. Stealing from the casino then, is also stealing from the Chief/King/President; all the same guy. When facing criminal charges in a foreign country, with long prison terms attached, it became easy and expedient for the prosecution to plead out the team members. (Consider also that the judge was the President's relative.) All but one of the team members was British. The one lone American was out of the country at the time of the arrests. The British male members involved in the scam pled guilty in return for the female members' deportation. Each male member received six years of hard labor in a South African prison. A key element in the prosecution of this scam was the meticulous notebook and records kept of payoff amounts to each team member. These records included the casino cage cash-out amounts for each night.

In point of fact, the Sun City casino was very lucky to have prosecuted the guilty and more than very lucky to receive an insurance settlement. Not so for two casinos in Atlantic City, who were cheated out of three million dollars in two nights of play.

When I was Director of Surveillance at the Dunes Hotel, I was contacted by the New Jersey Department of Criminal Justice to review several video tapes of suspect baccarat play. The play happened over a two night period at two different Atlantic City casinos. A group of between six and eight Asian customers were playing on the High Limit Baccarat tables. The players were betting up to $10,000.00 per hand (times six to eight players makes $60,000.00 to $80,000.00 per hand).

The first unusual activity I noticed on the video tape was the particular manner in which one of the players held the baccarat dealing shoe. (A baccarat shoe is much longer than a standard 21 shoe and may be a little more ornate.) Most baccarat players position the shoe in front of them to either the left or right side of their body. The shoe is normally pointed towards the left or right, depending on whether the player is left or right handed. This particular player had positioned the shoe in the center of his body and pointed directly straight ahead.

Secondly, the player had placed his right forearm on the table directly along side of the shoe in such a position that his right wrist was right along side and under the right front lip of the shoe cover. The player was also wearing a highly polished bracelet on his right wrist.

Thirdly, the player had two distinct methods of dealing cards from the shoe with his left hand. One dealing method was to simply draw the card from the shoe with all four fingers of the left hand touching. The second method was one in which the fingers of the left hand separated. The index and middle fingers remained fixed at the top opening of the window in the shoe. The ring and little fingers spread open to draw out the card.

I noted a fourth unusual activity by the player seated next to this customer. When a player loses the shoe (the bank side loses), the shoe passes to the next player to the right. That player has the option of dealing the shoe or passing to the next player. The shoe was continually being passed around the table right back to the unusual dealer. The player just to the left of the unusual dealer was grabbing the shoe and violently shaking it in one forward and backward motion. He would then pass the shoe to the unusual dealer. Pretty confused so far? Now let me explain what was really happening:

The player to the left of the unusual dealer was violently shaking the shoe for two good reasons. He was attempting to "jog" the cards in the shoe to a more distinct angle and secondly he was breaking the cards free of the underside lip in the inside front of the shoe. The lip inside the shoe is placed there to prevent a card from sliding or being pushed back into view when looking through the lid. The combination of breaking the cards free of the lip and shaking them into a more acute angle allowed the unusual dealer to peek through the clear lid of the shoe and see the value of the first card.

The peek was accomplished in one of three different methods. If the first card caught the inside lip of the shoe, a light press on the cards with the left fingers through the opening of the shoe would cause the first card to be bent and exposed in the upper right corner on the inside of the shoe. Secondly, if the first card was slid up just slightly past the inside lip, it would be exposed in the same spot, just not bent. Lastly, and very cleverly, the peek was accomplished by means of a *shiner* (any mirrored device or item which will reflect). A shiner could be a mirror hidden in a cigarette pack, or a shiny cigarette lighter or a piece of jewelry. Using a shiner is called *playing the lights*. In this case the shiner was the highly polished bracelet the player was wearing on his right wrist. The right wrist never moved from its position on the right side of the shoe. If the first card was pushed back too far, it would curl over the top of the other cards in the shoe. If this happened, the cheater could look down into the shiny bracelet and see a reflection of the first card.

Suffice to say that to this point I have only described the methods by which this team was able to secretly view the value of the first card in the shoe. To understand this scam it is only important to know that the value of the first card was being seen before it was being dealt.

The odd positioning of the shoe, in front and straight ahead of the player, allowed him to peek at the first card in one of the manners described above. The two different methods of drawing the card from the shoe come into importance next.

The first card being dealt in any baccarat hand goes to the player. Knowledge of the first card would tell you whether or not to bet on the player's side. If the first card was a 6, 7, 8, 9, the mathematical advantage is on the player's side over the bank. Any other card, ace, 2, 3, 4, 5 or 10, favors the bank side over the player's. A direct correlation of big bets and the first card is an indication that the first card is known in some way (peeking or marked cards). When players are betting heavily on the player's side, and the first card out of the shoe is 6, 7, 8, 9, and conversely when the same players are betting heavily on the bank side, and the first card dealt to the player's side is a weak card, (Ace, 2, 3, 4, 5 or 10) the first card becomes suspect. (In order to prove the exact mathematical percentage of advantage, I wrote a computer program to run the game of baccarat. The program simulates a standard baccarat game and rules. The program could be altered to designate the value of the first card. The results of the computer simulation are as follows:

FIRST CARD DEALT	ADVANTAGE		
ACE	BANK SIDE	9.63%	
TWO	BANK SIDE	8.68%	
THREE	BANK SIDE	7.61%	
FOUR	BANK SIDE	5.50%	
FIVE	BANK SIDE	3.28%	
SIX	PLAYER SIDE	2.24%	
SEVEN	PLAYER SIDE	10.12%	
EIGHT	PLAYER SIDE	22.87%	
NINE	PLAYER SIDE	27.16%	
10 & FACE CARDS	BANK SIDE	10.77%	

The vig will alter these percentages from a betting standpoint, but the above percentages are theoretical simulations of the game.

So if the value of the first card is known, you would expect to see the players jumping back and forth between the player and bank sides depending on the first card. This, however, was not the case with this group of Asians. As a group, they always wagered on the bank side. (Remember, I said the two dealing methods was important?) Well, here it is — the unusual dealer was able to hold back the top card and deal the second. If the first card was a strong card, it was held back (not dealt to the player's hand) and given as the first card to the bank side. If the first card was a weak card, it was, of course, dealt to the player's side.

An interesting footnote. Only two of the players on the game made any real money — the unusual dealer and the shoe jogger. These two players put up all the money and hired the other players to bet with their bankroll. In fact, the other players were waiters from a Chinese restaurant in New York. The two big players turned out to be members of an Asian crime family, known as Triad. I testified before a grand jury in New Jersey and duplicated live and on video tape the exact methods of this scam. The grand jury returned an indictment but the players had returned to Hong

Kong. This scam netted $1,400,000.00 at one casino on one night and $1,600,000.00 at another casino the following night.

Old street joke: If you give a criminal enough rope, he'll tie you up, steal your stuff and beat the crap out of you.

Author's Note: During the writing of the second edition of this book, I was involved in the investigation of a very high tech casino cheating scam. We apprehended a player with a hidden digital camera up his sleeve. By use of a microwave transmitter also concealed on his body, he was sending high speed pictures of the playing cards as they were shuffled or dealt. A guy hidden in a small truck outside in the parking lot, about 500 yards away, aimed a 42" microwave dish through the casino, hit this guy in the back and recorded the video coming out of his sleeve at the table. He would then playback the video at super slow motion and wire information back to the player on the game who would make large bets knowing in advance what cards would be dealt or what the dealer's cards were. I estimated this crew has stolen several million dollars from casinos around the gaming world. Because this case is still in litigation I cannot comment any further.

What is the most common crime in a casino?

Several questions in this book recount many of the cheating methods attempted in casinos at the gaming tables. By far the most common crime reported in a casino does not occur at the table games, but rather at the slot machines. The crime is coin bucket thefts and/or purse snatching. The criminals usually target the elderly or anyone they think cannot chase them. The cheaters vary in age, gender and race, but the method is basically the same. A mark is picked by the team. The cheaters are looking for a slot player who has a bucket filled with coins and is keeping the bucket rested between or next to the slot machine they are playing.

Let's suppose you are playing a slot machine and have your coin bucket next to your machine on your left side. A member of the cheater's team will walk by you and drop coins on your right side. (This is known as *salting*.) He/she will point to the coins and inform you that you must have dropped coins while playing. This person continues on past you to your right. A second member approaches from your left side as you reach down (to your right) to pick up the coins you think you dropped. When you bend down, your sight is blocked and the second cheater simply reaches in and takes the bucket. Some teams employ a third person to whom the stolen bucket is passed. Some cheaters have been seen by surveillance dumping the bucket of coins into a fanny pack and continuing to simply walk away.

Another version of this same theft goes like this. A pretty girl will sit next to a male slot player. She may engage him in friendly conversation, but at some point while they are talking, she will drop coins on the floor between them. As the male player gallantly reaches down to help the lady in distress, the second cheater approaches from the opposite side and snatches the coin bucket. The cheater who actually snatches the coin bucket may be seated at a slot machine in the next row over. Most slot machines are placed in rows back to back. As the mark reaches down to retrieve coins on the floor, the cheater simply reaches in between the machines from the next row over. Most casino slot departments have installed plastic or wooden panels between the machines to prevent this type of theft. Thieves have become wise to the panels and, from time to time, find a casino where the panels can be lifted or slid up out of the way and allow them to reach from one row to the next. Most casinos have now bolted or glued the slot panels in place.

Purse snatchers will work in about the same way with one major difference. Being caught with another person's purse is pretty damning evidence. A thief with a coin bucket can always try and claim it is his; the coins have no I.D. on the them. It's tough to explain having a purse with another person's identification. The purse snatcher will almost always have a person to pass off the stolen purse to.

The money and credit cards are quickly lifted and the purse is discarded as soon as possible. Some inexperienced purse snatchers will have a female not carrying a purse steal a customers purse or will pass to a female with no purse. That female will then simply walk out of the casino as if the stolen purse were hers, which is still very dangerous because of the identification in the purse. Most seasoned purse snatchers will dump the purse as quickly as they can.

The best protection against being victimized by coin bucket thieves or purse snatchers is to keep your bucket or purse in front of you or on your lap. If you are approached by anyone trying to distract your attention, remember to pick up your bucket or purse first before picking up the coins on the floor.

My nephew, Sean Young, is a surveillance agent at a major Las Vegas casino (and an aspiring writer). Sean tells me he likes to see it when the bad guys get their due. On one occasion Sean recalls a strong, young kid stealing a coin bucket from a little old lady. The thief turned to run away and ran right smack into a cement post. As this "tough guy" spun off the post he continued to run and slammed into a bank of slot machines bouncing him on his ass. He knocked himself silly and was still having trouble counting to three when security snatched him up. Good work God!

Pickpockets also fall into the same category as purse snatchers or bucket thieves. However, pickpockets are the elite of the group. A pickpocket needs far more talent and guts to dip into another person's pocket and remove their valuables. The bravest of all pickpockets is the one working alone, called *Single-O*. The tip off to surveillance and/or security is a person carrying his coat draped over his forearm. The second tip off is the same person eyeballing customers. This person is more interested in watching other people's pockets than in the activity around him. The Single-O pickpocket (also known as *The Dip*, *Mechanic*, *Wire* or *Whiz*), uses the coat as a blocker or feeler. When standing next to a mark, the coat brushes up against the intended victim. The victim feels the coat, which is not threatening. (A mark would be offended or uneasy if feeling another person's arm, but not a coat.) The pickpocket reaches (dips) into the marks pocket with the index and middle fingers of the hand draped by the coat.

Watching a good pickpocket at work is really a thing of beauty. (More for the person watching than the person being picked.) We recently apprehended a pickpocket who had dipped into the pockets of five customers (three back pockets and two front pockets). Not one customer knew he had been picked.

An old time and often bloody method of picking a rear pocket is to cut the back pocket with a razor blade. The pickpocket makes two cuts, one vertical and one horizontal, on the pocket of the intended victim. The wallet simply falls out into the waiting hand of the pickpocket. Several marks have been razor cut by this method when the pickpocket cuts too deeply.

Pickpocket teams work a little differently. A typical scenario is as follows: The mark is riding up an elevator. Behind him is the *mechanic*, while in front of him is a *stall* or *bumper*. At the top of the elevator, the stall drops coins or some other item. The stall will time the drop so that the mark will bump into him as he reaches down to pick up the dropped items. As the mark bumps into the stall, the mechanic dips into the marks back pocket, taking his wallet. The mechanic walks away and passes the wallet to a shill working with the team. The stall is apologizing to the mark for being in the way and for the apparent accidental contact.

Pickpockets will also go after a woman's purse hanging from a shoulder strap in much the same fashion. A stall distracts the woman while another team member simply opens the purse, still hanging on the mark's shoulder. It is wise for women who carry a purse on a shoulder strap to keep the purse flap towards their body as protection. Teams will scope out a potential mark by following him/her from the casino cage, change booth or ATM machines. By watching a person at these locations, the team knows where the mark keeps their cash. It is also interesting to watch from surveillance the number of times a player will touch his money in his pocket, even from outside the pants. This is known as a *tell*. You are telling me, by your actions, where your money is.

I'm reminded of the joke told about pickpockets. A player at a crap table finds another man's hand in his pocket. When asked what he's doing, the pickpocket answers, "Just making change." When asked, "Why didn't you ask me for change?" The pickpocket replies, "I don't talk to strangers."

96

Are there any gambling systems that really work?

When considering the dozens of gambling systems being written up, advertised and sold for all casino games, you should ask yourself the following questions: "Why aren't these guys playing the systems and becoming rich?" "Why am I so lucky that these guys are sharing this system with me?" "Why would these guys let the casinos know about their secrets?" (Starting to get the picture?)

There really is only one system that has been proven to work consistently, and that is playing basic strategy and card counting in blackjack. The only game where the mathematical advantage floats back and forth between the house and the player is 21. Playing basic strategy reduces the house's starting advantage over the player to an almost dead even proposition. Card counting allows the player to identify the times and situations when the player or house has the advantage. When the house has the advantage, the player bets less and when the player has the advantage the card counter bets more. Basic strategy play with card counting methods and betting patterns have been proven to be effective in several computer simulations with a body of work to support it that spans better than 30 years. (See Questions 1 5 and 1 7 on card counting and basic strategy.)

Rather than calling the dozens of other systems a system, I would rather call them a method. Let's examine a couple of well known betting methods.

The *Martingale Method* is the most basic of betting methods and has been around for hundreds of years. Very simply, the method is to double up when you lose. If your first bet is $5.00 and you lose, your next bet will be $10.00. If you lose the $10.00 bet, your next bet is $20.00, and so on. A typical progression of the Martingale method is as follows:

BET 1	2	3	4	5	6	7	8	9
$ 5	10	20	40	80	160	320	640	1,280

The Martingale method of betting attempts to win the amount of the first bet in the progression, in this case $5.00. If you were to lose eight bets in a row, your next bet would have to be #9 ($1,280.00). Understand that you are now betting $1,280.00 in order to win $5.00. The real problem with a Martingale betting method is that you will run into the house's table limit. If the house had no limit, the Martingale method would become a system that could not fail as long as you had an unlimited bankroll. The progression would continue as follows:

BET ... 10	11	12	13	14	15
$ 2,560	5,120	10,240	20,480	40,960	81,920

After fourteen losses in a row, you would need to bet $81,920.00 in order to win $5.00. Keep in mind that you have already lost the total of each of the 14 bets you placed before the 15th ($81,915.00 plus the 15th bet of $81,920.00, so far you need a bankroll of $163,835.00 to win $5.00).

The point is that this Martingale progression has to stop at the house limit. At a casino with a $2,000.00 limit you could not place the 10th bet of $2,560.00. You would have already lost the total of the previous nine bets ($2,555.00), and not yet won $5.00. If you began the progression again (as the method says), you would need to win 511 bets in order to recoup your $2,555.00 loss.

There is also a method known as the *Grand Martingale*. This method calls for you to double up when you lose and add to the next bet. A typical Grand Martingale progression might look like this:

BET 2	3	4	5	6	7	8
$ 15	40	100	250	600	1,500	4,000

The problem with the Grand Martingale is obvious; it takes you to the table maximum much faster.

There are several betting methods which have as their core a *Cancellation Method* in the progression. Let us assume that you have a progression as follows:

BET 1	2	3	4
$ 10	20	30	40

In most cancellation type methods, your bet is equal to the sum of the two outside uncancelled numbers (in this case 10 + 40, or a $50.00 bet). If you lose the bet, you cancel the two outside numbers, add the amount of the loss to the end of the progression and place the next bet. The progression now looks like this:

BET 1	2	3	4	5
$ .... (10)	20	30	(40)	50

The next bet is the sum of the two outside uncancelled numbers, so 20 + 50 = 70. The next bet is $70.00. If the $70.00 bet is lost, then the two numbers used to arrive at the $70.00 bet are cancelled and the 70 is placed at the end of the progression as follows:

BET 1	2	3	4	5	6
$ .... (10)	(20)	30	(40)	(50)	70

The next bet is the sum of the two outside uncancelled numbers, in this case, 30 + 70 = 100 (a $100.00 bet). The lure of these types of betting methods is, that a player who becomes proficient at completing the mathematics of the progression thinks that he has in some way affected the outcome of the activity. It takes a certain amount of intuitive process to remember and correctly administrate the progression, but in the game of blackjack, for instance, your betting progression may have you risking a very large portion of your bankroll at a time when the house has the overwhelming mathematical advantage. The simple fact that you have trained and are capable of crossing out two numbers and adding two others together to make a betting total may make you a wonderful fourth grade student, but not a gambling expert.

Understand one important element of gambling. The cards, dice and roulette balls do not have a memory — they don't know what total or number they last achieved. (In all my discussions with cards and dice and roulette balls, they tell me they don't even particularly care — just kidding.) Just because the roulette ball landed in a black number the last three spins, does not mean the ball knows it should even things out by landing in a red number. The odds that the ball will land in a red number after three black numbers in a row are still the same 18 out of 38. From a purely mathematical standpoint, there is a great difference in betting that three numbers in a row will be black. This is one bet dependent on three independent trials. The odds would be 18/38 x 18/38 x 18/38. The fourth spin is an independent bet dependent on one independent trial...18/38.

There are several betting methods that seem to make sense to a player strictly because they propose to cover every possibility. The following is one example of a betting method proposed for craps:

The *Treadmill Method* is a very foolish betting method which calls for the player to place the numbers 5, 6 and 8, and to bet the *field* as well. With this method, all of the numbers are covered, with the exception of the 7. To most players this sounds like an overwhelming advantage in their favor. You have the 2, 3, 4, 5, 6, 8, 9, 10, 11, 12 covered. Let me explain the fallacy. The method says to place the five for $10.00 and the 6 and 8 for $12.00 each and to bet $7.00 in the field. If you win the place bet on the 5, 6, or 8 you win $14.00. (The place bet on the number 5 pays 7 for 5 or $14.00 on the $10.00 bet. The place bets on the 6 and 8 pays 7 for 6 or $14.00 on the $12.00 bet.) The field bet of $7.00, pays even money on the 3, 4, 9, 10, 11 and double on the 2 or 12. So let's simply add up all the wins and losses for each bet.

(Remember, there are 36 possible combinations that can be thrown with two dice.)

Number Thrown	Amount Bet	Number of Times Thrown	Amount Won	Amount Lost
2	7.00	1 (Double)	14.00	0.00
3	7.00	2 (2x7)	14.00	0.00
4	7.00	3 (3x7)	21.00	0.00
5	10.00	4 (4x12)	48.00	(4x7) 28.00 *
6	12.00	5 (5x12)	60.00	(5x7) 35.00 *
7	0	6	0	(6x41) 246.00 **
8	12.00	5 (5x12)	60.00	(5x7) 35.00 *
9	7.00	4 (4x7)	28.00	0
10	7.00	3 (3x7)	21.00	0
11	7.00	2 (2x7)	14.00	0
12	7.00	1 (Double)	14.00	0
TOTALS			294.00	344.00

*   When you win the place bet, you lose the field bet.

** When the 7 is thrown you lose the field bet of $7.00 and the three place bets totaling $34.00, a total of $41.00 lost each of the six times a 7 is rolled.

The above chart shows a net loss with this betting method of $50.00 ($344.00 – $294.00 = $50.00). The mathematical disadvantage to any player using this method is as follows:

$50.00 \div 344.00 = 0.145348$ or 14.53% against

This ridiculous betting method gives the house a 14.53% rate of win against the customer foolish enough to use it.

There are several betting methods for all of the casino games. They have elaborate and imposing sounding names such as: Hedge Type System, Counteraction System, Labouchere, The Reverse Labouchere, The Martingale, The Grand Martingale, The Reverse Martingale, The Split Martingale, The D'Alenbert, The 2-5 System, The Treadmill and so on and so on with dozens more. There is one old gambling saying which goes like this, "Systems players die broke."

Author's note: There is one system which I know of that has been reported to work with significant success. As you exit the airplane in Las Vegas, you make a sharp turn to the left and walk directly into the jet engine.

Additional author's note: Talk about foolish gambling methods . . . how about internet casinos? Let me see if I have this straight. Basically, you begin by sending a total stranger somewhere in cyberspace a chunk of your cash. Next you dial up a casino *in-the-blind* and play against a dealer on the telephone (via modem) who you can't see. Finally, someone else you don't know shows you a computer generated picture of the cards he says you have and the cards he says he has and then tells you whether or not you lost your money. Is that about it "Mo Mo"? I got your *mouse* RIGHT HERE!

Thankfully the federal government has ruled internet casinos illegal because the Pentium processors sure haven't made anyone "street-wise."

Why do dealers clap their hands before leaving a table?

You will notice dealers clapping their hands as they leave a table to go on break or leave for the day. The casino's working commodity is money, in the form of chips on the games. There is no way to conduct a standard inventory as you would in any other business. This is due to the fact that there is an element of luck involved in the gaming industry. Dealers watch the players, floormen watch the dealers and the players, the pit bosses watch the floormen, dealers and players and the eye in the sky watches everyone. Anytime a casino employee handles chips or money, he must clear his/her hands before touching his/her body or leaving the game. The dealers must clear their hands for the eye. This means that the dealer should turn his/her hands over to show them palm up and clap them to prove there are no chips hidden in his/her hand. This procedure is followed whenever a dealer touches their body i.e., adjusting his apron, putting his hand to his mouth to cough or sneeze. Dealers have been known to put chips in their mouth, called *chip monking*. (One boxman I knew at the Aladdin Hotel would chip monk and swallow the chip if he were approached. He would go home and drink a half pint of mineral oil in order to retrieve the check, disgusting but profitable).

You will also notice that a dealer will never take chips or money from a customer's hand directly. The dealer will insist you drop the chips or money on the layout, they will then pick the chips or money up off the layout. This procedure is in place to prevent what are known as *hand off* moves. (The dealer secretly palms several high value chips and in the act of taking a chip or small bill from a player, quickly passes the high value chips from his hand to the customer's hand.)

Dealers have been known to use a secret pocket known as a *sub* (short for submarine, meaning underneath) to help steal chips. The sub is worn underneath the pants and is designed such that when the dealer sucks in his/her stomach the pocket opens allowing chips to be dropped in. A couple of opposing pieces of spring steel are used to make a sub, even hacksaw blades have been used.

A few years back, a dealer was using a shirt sub. (In the past, dealers used to put tokes in their outside shirt pocket. On each break the dealers would go to the pit podium and empty their shirt pockets and place all tokes in a large toke box housed there.) This particular dealer had a tailor design a double pocket with a cloth slide. The double pocket allowed the dealer to pull one pocket inside out to prove the pocket was empty. The slide went from the pocket, down the front of the shirt into a pair of pantyhose the dealer was wearing. The pantyhose prevented the chips from falling on the floor and also allowed this dealer to explore the feminine side of his being. All in all a pretty clever arrangement. An executive from the same casino happened into the tailor's shop one day. The tailor and casino boss began talking casinos and when the executive asked to have a shirt made, the dealer was *ratted out*. The tailor asked if the boss wanted the same special shirt he had made for the dealer at the casino.

Employees have also been known to hide chips under a large watch band or watch face.

Recently, an employee in the hard count room of a major casino was apprehended for stealing $5.00 tokens. He had designed slides built into his pants that unloaded the tokens into false bottoms in oversized shoes. Sounds like *Mission Impossible*.

A dealer starts betting with an illegal bookmaker. He bets every football game, college and pro, and can't win a bet. He owes the bookmaker a fortune. The bookmaker says, "How about baseball?" So the dealer bets every baseball game and can't win a bet. He owes the bookmaker two fortunes. The bookmaker suggests, "How about basketball?" So the dealer bets every basketball game, college and pro, and still doesn't pick a winner. He now owes the bookmaker two fortunes, his house and his car. So the bookmaker says, "How about hockey?" "Hockey," says the dealer, "what in the hell do I know about hockey?"

9 8

Was the Robert DeNiro movie, Casino accurate and who were they really talking about?

As close as possible, the movie *Casino* depicted the Las Vegas casino industry in the 1970's and early 80's. The movie character, Ace, portrayed by Robert DeNiro, was in fact a man named Frank "Lefty" Rosenthal. The character named Nickie in the film was actually a reputed mobster from Chicago, Tony Spilotro. The casino, called the Tangiers in the movie, was in fact the Stardust Casino. Sharon Stone played the part of Frank Rosenthal's wife, named Geri in real life.

Frank Rosenthal was a bookmaker and sports handicapper and was very highly regarded at both endeavors. Basically, Rosenthal survived and prospered because he made money for his partners and, more importantly, he didn't talk. A man doesn't need much more incentive to cooperate with the FBI than to be blown up in his car. That event depicted in the movie actually happened in 1982 at the Tony Roma Rib Shack Restaurant on East Sahara Avenue in Las Vegas. Even after being nearly exploded into the middle of Sahara Avenue, Frank did not cooperate with authorities. Rosenthal is currently living in south Florida and manages a restaurant there, no ribs on the menu (bad joke).

Not so lucky was the fate that befell Tony "The Ant" Spilotro; known on the street as "The Little Man" (no one called him that to his face). Tony ruled over street crime in Las Vegas. The scene in the movie where Tony puts a guy's head in a vice and turns it until his eye popped out was reported to have happened in Chicago. Tony operated a jewelry outlet on West Sahara Avenue called the Gold Factory. He and his brother, real name Michael, also operated the Food Factory, a fast food restaurant on Twain

Avenue in Las Vegas. From all accounts and local gossip, the depiction of
Tony Spilotro was fairly accurate. His crew, known as the "Hole in the Wall
Gang," was responsible for many burglaries and robberies in the Las Vegas
area. The crew was shown burglarizing a store in the movie and made
entrance by breaking a hole in the wall, thus the nickname. The actual
store was Bertha's, an expensive furniture and jewelry store on East Sahara
Avenue. One of the alleged crew members was a former Las Vegas Metro
Police Officer named Joe Blasko.

Bookmaking, extortion, loan sharking and drug dealing were all a part
of this crew's business. Disturbing to many casino employees was the
robbery of many casino executives. The crew members knew that certain
casino executives at that time could not or would not run to the police after
being robbed. According to most accounts, it was the involvement in drugs
that ultimately brought down the crew. This, along with the unwanted
publicity, was also what finally finished off Tony Spilotro. One of the crew
members, Frank Cullotta, turned snitch and went into the Federal Witness
Protection Program. I'm told Cullotta resurfaced to act as a technical
consultant for the movie *Casino*.

Spilotro had been entered into the State of Nevada's List of Excluded
Persons, the Black Book. He was removed from the Black Book when he
was removed from this earth. Frank Rosenthal was entered into the Black
Book in 1988.

In 1986 Tony Spilotro and his brother Michael were found buried in a
corn field in Indiana. They had both been beaten beyond recognition and
buried alive.

Geri, the Sharon Stone character, was reported to have had an affair
with Tony Spilotro. After her divorce, Geri drifted into and out of drugs
and eventually died of an apparent drug overdose.

The naive casino front man, played in the movie by Kevin Pollack, was
a real estate investor named Alan Glick. Glick had secured a loan from the
Teamsters Union Pension Fund in the amount of $67,000,000.00 to

purchase the Stardust, Sahara, Marina and Fremont Hotels. The loan was secured with the help of underworld figures in Chicago. Glick found out very quickly that he was a figurehead and the real power rested in the Chicago mob. (In the end, Glick turned States' witness and testified against the mob.) Glick's business partner was a woman named Tara Banks. Ms. Banks had intended to testify before the Nevada Gaming Commission. Before this could happen, Tony Spilotro allegedly paid her a visit in San Diego and shot her in the head five times.

The part of the Teamsters' boss, played by Alan King, was in fact a Teamsters official named Alan Dorfman. Dorfman was in charge of overseeing the Teamsters' loans in Las Vegas. When the federal indictments came down against the mob in Chicago and Kansas City, Dorfman was thought to be a liability because he knew too much. Alan Dorfman was shot to death in broad daylight in a parking lot outside of a Chicago restaurant.

The casino slot employee (real name Jay Vandermark) who was instrumental in the skim at the Stardust disappeared and has never been seen. Speculation is that he was skimmed (killed) to prevent his testimony. Vandermark's son was killed during that time.

Many of the movie's less dramatic depictions were actual incidents that happened in Las Vegas. The shooting by metro police of the alleged crew member who was holding the submarine sandwich actually happened. There were, of course, two different versions. The real shooting victim was a kid named Stevie Bluestein, a maitre d' at the Hacienda. The police claimed that Bluestein pulled a gun, while most street guys claimed he was holding a submarine sandwich wrapped in tinfoil.

The restaurant shown in the movie represented a place in the 1970's which sat kitty corner from the Aladdin Hotel called the Leaning Tower of Pizza. We used to call it the Leaning Tower of Savings and Loans because of all the loan shark activity which occurred there.

Several Las Vegans portrayed themselves. Entertainers and the Las Vegas Jeweler, Mordechai, did cameo appearances along with local newscaster Gwen Castaldi. The house shared by Ace and Ginger in the movie once belonged to Ash Resnick. Ash was one of the most famous Las Vegas casino executives and sports promoters the town has ever known. The famous mob attorney, Oscar Goodman, portrayed himself. Having moved to Las Vegas in the mid 1970's, it was interesting and fun to see a movie depiction of the way Las Vegas was back then. (Actually, I miss it.)

Question: Why doesn't the mob like the Jehovah Witnesses?
Answer: Because they don't like any witnesses.

Author's Note: In January of 1997, during the second writing of this book, "Fat Herbie" Blitzstein was found dead in his condo. Herb Blitzstein a casual acquaintance, was an alleged member of the "Hole In The Wall Gang." Herb was killed Gangland fashion, a bullet to the back of the head.

Author's Note: During the writing of the second edition of this book attorney Oscar Goodman won a landslide victory in the Las Vegas mayoral election. Congratulations Mayor Goodman. There is no truth however, to the rumor spread by his opponents that "Three Finger Louie" will be the new city treasurer and all city loans will be "6 for 5."

Why don't a lot of the dealers smile?

When I did a survey of casino customers, this question came up often enough to include it in this book.

In the old days in Las Vegas, the casinos were run by private owners. It was much easier to get rid of an unfriendly or annoying employee. There were, of course, many times when innocent employees were fired at the whim of a casino boss or owner, but that was then. Any service oriented business, such as hotel/casinos, have a vested interest in employees being pleasant with the customers. There is such strong competition between hotels for casino customers, convention trade, and tour and travel business that most hotel human resources departments conduct niceness classes with all employees.

Most dealing jobs are boring and monotonous. It is easy for dealers to be on auto pilot and not pay much attention. Many long time dealers have gone through a time when the IRS has cracked down on tip income. In the old days, dealers, bartenders, cocktail servers and valet attendants did not declare the full amount of their tip income to the IRS (not even close). Because of the IRS investigations and subsequent regulations, all heavily tipped income employees are closely monitored. The net result is that many individuals are making the same money they did years ago but are putting less in their pocket. This does not make for a group of happy campers. From the casino's standpoint, however, there is no excuse for any employee to be rude or inattentive to customers. If you should encounter one such employee, the hotel would appreciate knowing about it.

Dealers' joke: I just came back from one of the niceness classes. I was thinking of buying one of those books on the 'Power of Positive Thinking'. Then I thought to myself, "What the hell good could that do?"

Why is the carpet in most casinos so ugly?

There have been a number of studies conducted by marketing research firms to quantify the effects of different types of carpet. Such items as the color scheme, and differing patterns were studied. The point of the research was to discover patterns and color schemes which will be displeasing to the human eye and force, or coax, the customers eyes up from the floor. The ceiling should be uninteresting and coax your eyes down. Well, of course, looking straight ahead brings the customers eyes in sight of the slot machines or table games in the casino. This will hopefully instigate impulse play. In the old days, most casinos were designed like the hub of a wheel. The casino floor was the center of the wheel and all other destinations flowed from the center. In other words, in order to get from any one place to another (dining rooms, swimming pool, hotel elevators, etc.), you had to go through the casino.

Several other studies have been conducted over the years relevant to the psychology of gambling. Such elements as room temperature, lighting and overall color schemes have been studied. Slot machine carousel configurations have also been shown in studies to have a direct correlation to slot machine profit. Carousels that have an interesting design such as ovals or triangles are more profitable than straight rows of slot machines. It is the excitement and intrigue of not knowing what's around the corner. Straight rows of slot machines allow you to see down the entire row and don't create the same excitement. Some casinos have slot machines outfitted with very shallow and noisy coin trays. Coins dropping into the shallow trays make more noise and excitement, and look fuller than the deeper trays.

Note: You'll also notice that there are no clocks in casinos. In addition, most casinos have no outside windows visible to players.

Old gambler's joke: What's the difference between praying in a casino and praying in a church? In a casino you really mean it!

(Special thanks to my friends Frank Shinos of the Leelanau Sands Casino, Gaming Commission, Suttons Bay, Michigan and Fielding West, a wonderful comedy magician and a good friend, for the above joke.)

1 0 1

Who was the greatest heavyweight boxing champion of all time?

At first glance, this may seem an odd question to be included in a book about gambling and Las Vegas. Consider, however, that for the past four decades, Las Vegas has hosted many of the greatest boxing matches in all weight classes that have ever been fought. There is no other special event in Las Vegas that generates as much pure excitement as a heavyweight championship fight. There is a fascinating mixture of celebrities, sport figures, gamblers and the underworld who descend upon Las Vegas to attend a championship bout and the many after-parties. Casinos will rarely have a more profitable event or a greater cash flow.

I have a more selfish reason for including this question in my book. I moved to Las Vegas in the mid 1970's. I had the real honor and pleasure to know

The immortal Joe Louis.

for a short time, the man who fought with the nickname "The Brown Bomber", Joe Louis. I had the even greater pleasure of marrying one of his daughters, Candice.

When asking the question of who was the greatest heavyweight champ of all time, the argument usually splits down two paths. The main thrust of one argument is an emotional appeal based in large part on the age of the people in the discussion, and the fighters they have seen themselves.

Fight fans from the 1960's and 1970's will be partial to Muhammad Ali, while those fans from the 1980's and 1990's will tout Mike Tyson. It is difficult to compare any athlete from one era to another because of such subjective feelings and personal opinions. In any sport where accomplishments can be judged and participants measured against the stopwatch or tape measure, the comparisons become a little more objective. Consider the following facts:

- The average reign of a heavyweight champ is about three years. Joe Louis held the Heavyweight Crown for twelve years (June 22, 1937 through March 1, 1949).
- The average number of times a heavyweight champ successfully defends his title is four. Joe Louis successfully defended his Heavyweight Title a record 25 times.
- Joe Louis defended his Heavyweight Crown more times than the eight previous heavyweight champions combined.
- Joe Louis had more first round knockouts in heavyweight title defenses than any other heavyweight in history (a record total of eight).
- Joe Louis knocked out five former world heavyweight champions (a record).
- Joe Louis knocked out every opponent he ever faced twice in a title bout.
- Joe Louis never fought on an under card. Every one of his fights was a main event.
- Joe Louis defended his title 21 times in four years, then gave four years to the armed forces where his title was on hold. Keep in mind that at the time there were only seven weight divisions and one governing body in boxing—not the 14 weight classes and three governing bodies we have today. It's hard to imagine how many times Joe would have defended his title if it were not for World War II.

Here are a few more interesting *stats* provided by John Grasso, IBRO, Heavyweight Title Fights:

Most Championship Bouts:

Joe Louis 27
Muhammad Ali 25
Larry Holmes 23
Lennox Lewis 18
Mike Tyson 15

Most Championship Bouts Won:

Joe Louis 26
Muhammad Ali 22
Larry Holmes 21
Mike Tyson 12
Tommy Burns 11
Lennox Lewis 11
Joe Frazier 10

Most Consecutive Bouts Won:

Joe Louis 26
Larry Holmes 21
Muhammad Ali 11

Most Knockouts:

Joe Louis 22
Larry Holmes 15
Muhammad Ali 14
Lennox Lewis 12
Tommy Burns 9
Mike Tyson 9
Floyd Patterson 8

Most Consecutive Knockouts:

Joe Louis 14
Tommy Burns 8
Larry Holmes 8
Mike Tyson 6

The emotional argument over who was the greatest heavyweight champ seems to me to be even more clear cut. It is hard to imagine a time when a boxer could ever again mean as much to an entire race of people as Joe Louis did. Long before the black athlete was given a chance to participate in American sports on a real professional level, there was only Joe Louis. Joe was instrumental in the integration of the U.S. Armed Forces. Joe intervened to help clear Jackie Robinson of court martial charges in the army, before Robinson broke the color barrier in baseball. The pride and hope and dignity of all black Americans rested in the fists and accomplishments of one man, Joe Louis. Long before there were civil rights cases, school integration, "I have a dream" speeches and civil rights legislation, there was only Joe Louis. At a time when black people were thought by many white Americans and institutions to be inferior physically and mentally, there was Joe Louis showing the world that a black man was the strongest man in the world.

Joe Louis was also instrumental in integrating the previously segregated world of professional golf. Joe was almost a scratch golfer. He held the annual Joe Louis Golf Tournament during the 1940's. Because of Joe's efforts, great black golfers such as Charlie Sifford and Lee Elders were brought to the forefront of the golf world.

A very sad but telling story illustrates the measure of Joe Louis' importance to blacks at the time. A black inmate in a southern prison was to be the first inmate executed in that state's gas chamber. At the last moment of his life, he could have called out to the governor for mercy, to his mother for comfort, or to God almighty for salvation. Instead he yelled out, "Save me, Joe Louis, save me, Joe Louis."

Will there ever again be a time when hundreds of thousands of people take to the streets after a boxer wins a fight to party and celebrate vicariously through the exploits of one man? Joe was the only black man at the time who could not only stand up to a white man, but could knock him down. Understand, it was not a black athlete outrunning a white athlete, it was a black man touching and knocking out a white fighter. In today's sports world there are hundreds of black athletes to admire and stand as role models for the young. Back then, it was Joe Louis. It seems that Joe Louis was always the champ.

Will there ever again be a time when a heavyweight fight will have such political significance and such distinct moral overtones? In the mid 1930's, Italy had invaded the small and hopelessly unarmed black country of Ethiopia. At the same time, an Italian fighter named Primo Carnera was destroying all combatants in the ring. Carnera, a former circus strongman, was a giant of a man standing over 6 feet 6 inches tall and weighing about 270 pounds. The symbolism was obvious and well-publicized: The huge and very strong Italian taking on the smaller black. Well, Joe Louis destroyed Primo Carnera, knocking him down several times before knocking him out.

An interesting story, during that fight, Carnera was constantly trying to clutch Joe in order to stay away from Joe's tremendous punching power. At one point, Joe literally picked up the giant, turned him around and set him down. Carnera sheepishly said, "I should be doing this to you." In another fight, a boxer once begged the referee, "Please don't let him hit me again." Another boxer once asked the referee to let him leave the ring and go hide on the roof. A journeyman boxer who Joe knocked out with relative ease remarked, "I guess I zigged when I should of zagged." When light heavyweight champ Billy Conn announced his fight plan was to "get on his bicycle and run," Joe answered with a phrase which over fifty years later is still part of American culture, "he can run but he can't hide." Joe was keenly aware of his mortality in the ring, but he was also supremely confidant in his ability. "I always know I can go into the ring and someone could take my title, but not this night and not this guy." There are countless descriptions of Joe's punching power knocking a fighter's teeth into their mouthpiece.

Here are a couple of not so well known examples of Joe's punching power. In the late 1970's, Joe suffered his first stroke and was bedridden most of the time. As kids will often do, Joe's son John-John (about eight or nine years old at the time) jumped into bed with his dad. More accurately, Johnny jumped on top of his sleeping dad. Well, Joe reached out and instinctively caught his young son on the chin and knocked him out cold. John-John tells me all he remembers was seeing white. There are a great number of men that Joe knocked out in the ring, however his son John-John will always have the distinction of being the last man Joe Louis ever knocked out. About 20 years before the John-John knockout, when my wife was about 10 or 12 years old, Joe and the family lived in Los Angeles. Candice and Joe's goddaughter, Cindre, were playing in a tree on the front lawn. Cindre fell from the tree and on the way down caught her nose on a branch. The branch ripped open the flesh between the two nostrils. Joe came running and carried the little girl to a doctor who lived about five houses away. The doctor made a cursory examination and told Joe, "It's not too bad, but we

My wife Candice and her dad.

need to get her to the hospital so I can put her out and put in a couple of stitches." Joe asked, "How long do you want her out for?" The doctor seemed a little confused but replied, "About 15 minutes." Joe took hold of Cindre's neck with his left hand. With two knuckles of his right hand, Joe made a "baby fist." With a backhand like motion, Joe tapped the little girl underneath the chin. She was out for 18 minutes. Had anyone other than my wife told me this story, I would not have believed it. It's the knuckles that really intrigue me. Two knuckles meant 18 minutes. I suppose three knuckles means a half hour, four knuckles puts you to sleep for an hour, and a full fist meant death!

It is hard to imagine how a boxer could ever again symbolize the ideals and courage of an entire free world when pitted against the awful tyranny and destruction of a so called Master Race. Max Schemling, the German former heavyweight world champion, was being touted by Hilter and the Nazi party as proof of Aryan superiority, not over just blacks, but over all non-Aryans. As Nazi forces were systematically walking over the European continent, Joe Louis took Max Schemling apart in two minutes and four seconds of the first round of their title bout. Joe hit Schemling so hard during that one round that Schemling spent two weeks in the hospital in this country and had to be taken by stretcher back to Germany were he spent another six weeks in a hospital there. Years later, Joe's son, Joe Jr. (nicknamed Punchy), spoke with several concentration camp survivors. Many of them told Joe Jr. that they had hope in their hearts that America would save them because Joe Sr. had proven to the world that the Nazi could be beaten.

As the United States was drawn into World War II, it would have been easy for Joe to acquire a deferment, as Jack Dempsey had done in World War I, by claiming sole support and pulling some political strings. Joe Louis, however, enlisted in the army and refused a commission. When asked why he hadn't tried to avoid the service (particularly considering the blatant racial discrimination in the U.S. Armed Forces), Joe replied, "I'm only doing what any red-blooded American would do." Not a black American or white American, but what any American would do.

What other heavyweight champion would risk his world title and give the entire proceeds of the title fight to the Army relief fund? Then again put his title on the line and donate the proceeds to the Navy relief fund? When criticized because he had fought for nothing, Joe replied, "I'm not fighting for nothing, I'm fighting for my country. That's not nothing." When the country needed a slogan to rally support for the war effort, Joe Louis provided it by saying, "We will win because we're on God's side." Today it all sounds pretty corny, right? Well, the world could use that kind of corn again. I know this country could.

Speaking to the heart and integrity of the man, in the 96 fights Joe fought at U.S. Armed Force bases all over the world while in the Army, Joe insisted that the previously segregated audiences be integrated.

During his time in the Army, Joe spent over $200,000.00 of his own money (a value of about $2,000,000.00 by today's standards) buying dinners for and giving money to servicemen who, in Joe's words, "Didn't have it as good as me." It has always been an open wound with Joe's family and friends that much of Joe's tax trouble arose from his unselfish patriotism. The money Joe Louis donated to the war effort was paid to him after his fights by check under his name. Joe simply signed over the checks for their entire amounts to the Army and Navy relief funds. The Internal Revenue Service in one of the monumentally bonehead and cruel moves of all times charged Joe Louis income tax, penalties and interest on the money he gave to the armed forces. Joe knew he was well past his prime, but was forced out of retirement by the IRS who attached his earnings for back taxes. (We have a beautiful old Arabic saying which is quite apropos for such situations—"Yah ahcrute . . . ibbin sitteen alf clab!" Translated means, "You bastards are the sons of sixty thousand dogs! What the hell were you think?" (Sorry, Ma.))

Another corny tribute to the man that most people don't know is that when Joe Louis turned pro, he went to the office of the Detroit Welfare Fund and paid back all the money they had given to his mother. On the other hand, when Joe's boxing career was over, he was offered $50,000.00 to attend a golf tournament in South Africa. Joe was broke, but refused the fifty thousand. "They'll try to use me as an example of how good things are for blacks over there. They will treat me better than their own people."

During a television interview with Muhammad Ali, Joe mentioned that his string of title defenses was known as the "Bum of the Month Club." Ali joked, "You think I'm a bum?" Joe answered, "You'd have been on the tour." Family members tell stories of how when Ali was around, he used to taunt Joe with jibes and paw at him with fake punches. Like lightning, Joe would suddenly throw a left jab slap, which Ali couldn't or wouldn't block, catching the younger fighter on the side of the face, as if to say "See." Years later when Joe had passed away and Ali had retired, a reporter asked Ali about Joe Louis. Ali spoke with warm regard and commented that people everywhere loved Joe. Said Ali, "They all think he was great." When asked by the reporter, "Was Joe Louis the greatest?" Ali added, "Of all times."

Understand that I am not trying to diminish the accomplishments and impact of other fighters. Muhammad Ali made the heavyweight championship *Pay For View* event the spectacular that it is today. Ali made blacks around the world stand up for their black pride, but it was Joe Louis who gave blacks the pride. (The whole family is proud of my nephew, Limmie "Tiger" Young, Joe's grandson. Tiger held the state of Nevada light heavyweight Golden Gloves championship for eight years running and was the PAL National light heavyweight champion. "Keep punching, Tiger.")

Joe Louis was the champion of my father's youth. Joe retired as champion the year I was born.

Joe Louis died April 12, 1981. Quoting from the Detroit Free Press, Monday, April 13, 1981:

"It is unlikely that we will ever again know the magic of those yesterdays when the streets emptied and commerce stopped and America huddled by its radios to listen to the exploits of the man with the jackhammer fists.

To a nation battered by the uncertainties of the Great Depression and World War II, there was comfort in the ring announcer's reassuring affirmation: "The winner and still heavyweight champion of the world...Joe Louis."

He was the champ when Hitler's troops moved into Czechoslovakia and still the champ when Hilter died. He was the champ when scientists split the atom and still the champ when its by-product, the atomic bomb, was dropped on Hiroshima and Nagasaki.

He was champ when Depression victims fled the dust bowls of Oklahoma and when North Korea crossed the 38th Parallel to trigger the Korean War. And to so many he will always remain the champ."

I was in the front row as Rev. Jessie Jackson delivered the eulogy for Joe in April of 1981. Quoting Rev. Jackson, "A champion rides on the shoulders of the people, a hero carries the people on his shoulders." That was Joe Louis. Joe Louis set boxing records, most of which have stood for over fifty years. If however, every one of those records were to fall tomorrow, it could not diminish Joe's place in the history of sports, the history of this country, or in the hearts of those of us who loved the man.

I suppose the question of who was the greatest heavyweight champion of all times will be debated as long as there are sports fans anywhere . . . just not in my house.

Author's note: After the recent heavyweight fight in which Mike Tyson bit the ears of Evander Holyfield, a group of us were arguing the question of great fighters past and present. One wise guy, an obvious Tyson supporter, sarcastically asked how I thought Joe Louis would do against today's heavyweights. Being the even wiser guy I replied, "When Joe fought, he won most of his fights in early round knockouts. If Joe were fighting today, he would win all his fights, but in late round knockouts and by decision." When asked why I felt that way, I answered, "Because Joe would be 80 years old by now...you dumb bastard!"

Epilog

Louis Edward Safi Joseph was born on July 18, 1924. To his family and friends he was known as "Fast Eddie" because of his love of sports betting. Fast Eddie was far from being the biggest sports bettor in Detroit, but he was one of the finest football handicappers around. Louis Edward Joseph is my Dad. More than just a dad, my Dad was always my best friend. Unfortunately, always doesn't mean forever. In gambling terms, my Dad rolled "Ace Deuce" on Super Bowl Sunday, January 31, 1999. In practical terms, my Dad lost his life to cigarettes when he was a teenager. Because he was so strong it just took fifty-five years to kill him. In medical terms my Dad succumbed to congestive heart failure, kidney failure and pneumonia. In sports handicapping terms, Fast Eddie bet the underdog once too often. In selfish terms, on Super Bowl Sunday, 1999 a part of my heart was taken. I'm not writing this epilog because my father died, I'm writing this tribute because he lived. He lived the way he wanted and called all the

My dad "Fast Eddie" and me in 1950.

shots; even knowing the risks, even in spite of the risks. My Dad lived long enough to give us all the gifts we needed to carry on, because, "Ain't none of us are getting out of this thing alive." I wrote in the last chapter of this book about a true sports and American hero, Joe Louis. (Was it fate or coincidence that the son of Louis Joseph married the daughter of Joseph Louis?) Sports heroes are easy to write about. Their accomplishments are documented in books and movies. My Dad was the hero of my life. Everyday he taught me, my brothers Wayne and Larry, and my sister Carmelita, about true unconditional love and protection. He learned much of his unconditional love from my mother, his wife of fifty-three years, Georgia. We all learned a lot about unconditional love from my brother in-law Jim who helped take care of dad (I love you Jim). My Dad was my best friend, my confidant, my critic, my foe, and my hero. He always told me straight...he may have had to defend me first, but he always told me straight. There is no secret that he lived vicariously through my exploits, even the bad ones, even the ones no one else in the family knew about...and never will (sorry Ma), and he always told me straight. You can't ask more from a man, a father, a dad, and a hero. My Dad gave me the strength to hold his hand and watch him die on that Super Bowl Sunday, but he did it his way. He died five minutes after kick off. He bet Atlanta—the "Dog."

Years ago Paul Peterson sang a song titled "My Dad" on the Donna Reed TV Show.

> "He wasn't much in the eyes of the world,
> he never made history.
> He wasn't much in the eyes of the world but
> he was the world to me...my dad.
> When I was small I felt ten feet tall when I
> was by his side...
> And everyone would say that's his son and
> my heart would burst with pride...my dad"

My brother Wayne said all that needs to be said at the eulogy..."Una Behhibuck Biyee."—"I love you Dad."

He Is There

The smell in the tunnel to Canada . . . He's There
The noise in the crowd at Eastern Market . . . He's There
Standing in a garden feeling the earth in my hands . . . He's There
The smell of fresh baking anything . . . He's There
Football Season . . . He's There . . .He's There . . .He's There . . .He's There . . .
Watching the games on TV . . . He's There
His voice fills my head, His spirit my Soul . . . He's There
In the sping, in the fall . . . He's There . . . He's There . . .
And missed more than tears will tell . . . He's There

by Carmelita (Joseph) Carter
His Daughter, My Sister, His Favorite

Author's note: In Arabic we say "Saiken Bee Albee" which translates "He's alive in my heart."

Mao Zedong and China's Revolutions

A Brief History with Documents

Timothy Cheek

University of British Columbia

BEDFORD/ST. MARTIN'S   Boston ♦ New York

To Tessa, who was patient

For Bedford/St. Martin's

Publisher for History: Patricia A. Rossi
Director of Development for History: Jane Knetzger
Developmental Editor: Louise Townsend
Editorial Assistant: Rachel Siegel
Editorial Assistant, Publishing Services: Maria Teresa Burwell
Senior Production Supervisor: Joe Ford
Production Associate: Christie Gross
Marketing Manager: Jenna Bookin Barry
Project Management: Books By Design, Inc.
Text Design: Claire Seng-Niemoeller
Indexing: Books By Design, Inc.
Cover Design: Billy Boardman
Cover Photo: Mao Zedong © Bettmann/CORBIS.
Composition: Stratford Publishing Services, Inc.
Printing and Binding: Haddon Craftsmen, an RR Donnelley & Sons Company

President: Charles H. Christensen
Editorial Director: Joan E. Feinberg
Director of Marketing: Karen R. Melton
Director of Editing, Design, and Production: Marcia Cohen
Manager, Publishing Services: Emily Berleth

Library of Congress Control Number: 2001097845

For information, write: Bedford/St. Martin's, 75 Arlington Street, Boston, MA 02116
(617-399-4000)

ISBN: 0-312-25626-4   (paperback)
       0-312-29429-8   (hardcover)

Acknowledgments

Acknowledgments and copyrights can be found at the back of the book on pages 243–44, which constitutes an extension of the copyright page.

Foreword

The Bedford Series in History and Culture is designed so that readers can study the past as historians do.

The historian's first task is finding the evidence. Documents, letters, memoirs, interviews, pictures, movies, novels, or poems can provide facts and clues. Then the historian questions and compares the sources. There is more to do than in a courtroom, for hearsay evidence is welcome, and the historian is usually looking for answers beyond act and motive. Different views of an event may be as important as a single verdict. How a story is told may yield as much information as what it says.

Along the way the historian seeks help from other historians and perhaps from specialists in other disciplines. Finally, it is time to write, to decide on an interpretation and how to arrange the evidence for readers.

Each book in this series contains an important historical document or group of documents, each document a witness from the past and open to interpretation in different ways. The documents are combined with some element of historical narrative—an introduction or a biographical essay, for example—that provides students with an analysis of the primary source material and important background information about the world in which it was produced.

Each book in the series focuses on a specific topic within a specific historical period. Each provides a basis for lively thought and discussion about several aspects of the topic and the historian's role. Each is short enough (and inexpensive enough) to be a reasonable one-week assignment in a college course. Whether as classroom or personal reading, each book in the series provides firsthand experience of the challenge—and fun—of discovering, recreating, and interpreting the past.

Natalie Zemon Davis
Ernest R. May
Lynn Hunt
David W. Blight

Preface

What can the life of a notable figure tell us about the experience of a people or a country? And how can we get at that life—get access to the thoughts and goals of a leader? This book seeks to provide such an avenue through a brief history and documents by and about Mao Zedong. Mao is probably the greatest figure of twentieth-century China—a hero to some, a demon to others. He led the Chinese Communist party (CCP) to national victory in 1949. He drove the People's Republic of China (PRC) through three decades of tumultuous revolutions, from the Soviet model in the 1950s, to the Cultural Revolution in the 1960s, to rapprochement with the United States in the 1970s. More than twenty-five years after his death in 1976, Mao remains an iconic figure in China today, both as the indispensable legitimator of the troubled CCP and as the object of popular fascination and nationalist hopes.

Mao's writings provide a concrete path into the experience of China's twentieth-century revolutions, as he deals with rural misery in the 1920s, government formation in the 1940s, and social revolution in the late 1950s and 1960s. Earlier histories, in the West as well as in China, have conventionally presented Mao as the embodiment of each stage of *the* Chinese revolution. Now we can ask, When was Mao in synch or out of synch with the social experiences and political aspirations of major groups in China? In the 1920s, Mao was not the most important CCP leader, but his 1927 "Report on the Peasant Movement in Hunan" was an accurate assessment of rural poverty and its potential as a catalyst for social revolution. By 1940, when Mao wrote "On New Democracy," he was a top leader of a revived CCP, and the plan outlined in that essay became the public blueprint for the CCP's takeover of China in 1949. By 1957 Mao was supreme leader and ideological fountainhead, but his assessment of Chinese society, as well as his hypocritical reluctance to follow his own prescriptions, made his "On the Correct Handling of Contradictions among the People" both misrepresent reality and contribute to tragedy. By the era of the Cultural Revolution, beginning in 1966, Mao's writings had been reduced to oracular pronouncements and sound bites from the famous "Little Red Book" *(Quotations from Chairman Mao Zedong)*. These writings did not provide an accurate assessment of Chinese society, but they did contribute to the Mao cult and the emerging chaos of the Cultural Revolution.

The three long essays by Mao referred to above characterize three periods in the life of Mao and China. Briefer selections of the Chairman's writings are also included to provide a sense of Mao's nationalism, poetry, literary policies, and leadership model. In each of these three periods—rural revolution in the 1920s and 1930s, political revolution in the 1940s, and utopian social revolution in the late 1950s and 1960s—we can observe Mao's contributions (for good or for ill) to China's varied revolutions in nationalism, socialism, and economic development.

This collection offers students in an introductory or world studies course a manageable and representative sample of Mao's writings. I have chosen long extracts from the three periods outlined above. As a result, I have omitted some of the topics covered by Mao's extensive corpus, such as his views on the Soviet Union and land reform, his philosophical essays, and his economic plans. These are all available in the new comprehensive collections of Mao's writings edited by Schram and by Kau and Leung (see the bibliography). Some teachers may find the three core texts too long and may choose to focus on certain sections of them. Or they may focus on one of the three main essays (and the related secondary texts in part two) or on certain themes, such as the status of women or changes in rural life. In any case, these three core texts represent complete thoughts by Mao that were published under his scrutiny and were influential both inside and outside China. They remain important primary documents, which intelligent readers can mine for purposes beyond those I suggest.

The Mao texts are followed by several writings about Mao to help describe the contexts in which Mao operated and to indicate something of what Mao meant to Chinese and non-Chinese in the twentieth century. They range from Edgar Snow's famous interview with Mao in 1936, to the memoirs of his doctor, to uses of Mao by Red Guards in the Cultural Revolution and by people in China today. This section also includes a taste of what academics have tried to contribute to our understanding of Mao. The romanization of Chinese names and words has been changed to the pinyin system, except for a few names, such as Chiang Kai-shek and Sun Yat-sen.

The volume begins with a comprehensive introduction, which presents the major issues in modern Chinese history and Mao's growing role in the events of the twentieth century. It includes a small set of photographs and graphic images to give a sense of how Mao was portrayed. In all, this book aims to equip students to make their own readings of Mao's writings and to find for themselves what the "Great Helmsman's" life and work can teach us about China's continuing revolutions.

ACKNOWLEDGMENTS

I wish to thank Jeff Wasserstrom for making this project possible and Louise Townsend for making it happen. I am grateful to the students in my Mao seminar at Colorado College for testing the readings and offering necessary suggestions. I owe a special debt to the five reviewers for Bedford/St. Martin's—Stephen Averill, Jeff Hornibrook, Steven I. Levine, Sandra Loman, and Patricia Stranahan—for their alarmingly detailed and trenchant readings of the first draft of this book. Although I was not able to follow all of their suggestions, to the degree that this book achieves the impossible goal of satisfying both specialist and newcomer, it is due to our collective efforts. Thanks as well to Tim Brook, Nancy Hearst, Nick Knight, David Ownby, Stuart Schram, and Mark Selden for making careful readings of earlier drafts and providing extensive comments and suggestions. Also thanks to the following colleagues for helpful suggestions: Vera Fennell, Anne Hyde, David Kelly, Tony Saich, and Michael Schoenhals. I am grateful to Stuart Schram not only for his prodigious scholarship, on which I have relied, but also for permission to use the forthcoming translation of "On New Democracy" from his *Mao's Road to Power* collection. Sandy Papuga helped bring the manuscript to order, and Jack Hayes researched the photos used in this volume. The professional team at Bedford/St. Martin's made this the best book it can be under the guiding hand of Emily Berleth. Nancy Benjamin at Books By Design served as efficient project manager, Rachel Siegel assisted with permissions, and Billy Boardman created the striking cover art. Special thanks are due to Barbara Jatkola for copyediting above and beyond the call of duty. Finally, thanks to my family for their patience, and especially to my daughter, Tessa.

Timothy Cheek

Contents

Maps and Illustrations

Introduction:
Comrade, Chairman, Helmsman —
The Continuous Revolutions of Mao Zedong

When Mao Zedong was thirteen, he had a huge fight with his strict father during a large party at their home. Mao recalled later, "My father denounced me before the whole group, calling me lazy and useless. This infuriated me. I cursed him and left the house. My mother ran after me and tried to persuade me to return. My father also pursued me, cursing at the same time that he commanded me to come back." But Mao was sick of his father's harsh treatment and refused to obey. In fact, Mao threatened to jump in the nearby pond and kill himself. Faced with this fierce resistance, Mao's father gave in. They agreed: Mao would obey his father if his father would promise to stop beating him. "Thus the war ended," Mao said, "and from it I learned that when I defended my rights by open rebellion my father relented, but when I remained meek and submissive he only cursed and beat me the more."[1] Mao carried this lesson into political life. He always sought revolutionary answers to the social and political problems he encountered. He was the continuous revolutionary—from his early days as a radical student in rural China in the 1910s to his last days as supreme leader in Beijing in the 1970s.

Mao Zedong lived from 1893 to 1976. He is the most famous Chinese of the twentieth century and certainly China's most influential political leader. Mao has been presented by his faithful followers in the Chinese Communist party (CCP) as the embodiment of China's socialist revolution, which brought the Communists to power in the new People's Republic of China (PRC) in 1949. That "story" was extremely compelling—not only to a majority of Chinese over several decades at mid-century, but also to non-Chinese academics trying to explain

[1]As told to Edgar Snow in *Red Star over China* (New York: Grove Press, 1968), 133. See extracts of Snow's interviews with Mao in 1936 in Document 11.

1

Map 1. *China Today*

2

RUSSIA

MONGOLIA

Heilongjiang

Harbin

Changchun

Jilin

Shenyang

Liaoning

Inner Mongolia

Hohhot

Beijing

Beidaihe

Tangshan

Tianjin

Dalian

KOREA

Hebei

Taiyuan

Shijiazhuang

Ningxia

Yan'an

Shanxi

Shandong

Qingdao

nzhou

Jinan

Yellow River

Zhengzhou

ansu

Xi'an

Henan

Jiangsu

Shaanxi

Nanjing

Hefei

Anhui

Shanghai

Sichuan

Hubei

ongqing

Yangtze River

Wuhan

Hangzhou

East China
Sea

Zhejiang

Nanchang

Hunan

Changsha

Jiangxi

Guizhou

Fuzhou

Fujian

Guiyang

Xiamen

Taipei

Guangxi

Guangdong

TAIWAN

Nanning

Guangzhou

Macao

Hong Kong

IETNAM

South China
Sea

HAINAN

Source: Shaun Breslin, *Mao: Profiles in Power* (London: Longman, 1998). Used with permission.

Map 2. *Key Locations in the History of Mao's China*

4

Notes to Map 2

(1) Shaoshan: Mao's birthplace.

(2) Changsha: Where Mao went to school and later worked in the Changsha Normal School. Also the site of Mao's abortive "Autumn Harvest" uprising.

(3) Jingganshan: The original safe haven in Jiangxi province that Mao and others fled to after the failed uprising of 1927.

(4) Ruijin: The capital of the Jiangxi soviet.

(5) Zunyi: The site of the conference in 1935 where Mao began his rise to supreme power in the CCP.

(6) Yan'an: The Communist headquarters after the Long March and throughout the war against Japan.

(7) Xi'an: The site of Chiang Kai-shek's kidnapping by the northern warlords, which led to the creation of the second united front.

(8) Beijing: China's capital before the collapse of the empire in 1911 and once again after the revolution.

(9) Wuhan: Birthplace of the 1911 Revolution and the site of intramilitary conflict at the height of the Cultural Revolution. Also briefly twice China's capital under the Guomindang—first as they moved north before taking Nanjing, and later as the Guomindang fled Nanjing after the Japanese invasion.

(10) Nanchang: Site of a doomed Communist uprising in 1927.

(11) Guangzhou (Canton): The Guomindang's headquarters after Yuan Shikai ignored the national election result in 1912. The scene of many and bitter battles during the 1920s. Also the site of a short-lived commune after the Communist uprising in December 1927.

(12) Nanjing: Capital of China after the 1911 Revolution, and again after the Guomindang established a new national government after the Northern Expedition. Site of the "Rape of Nanjing" after the Japanese invasion and of the puppet regime of Wang Jingwei under Japanese control.

(13) Chongqing: Became the Guomindang's base during the war against Japan.

(14) Taipei: The capital of the Guomindang's Republic of China from 1949 to the present day.

(15) Shanghai: China's major commercial center and one of the centers of radicalism during the Cultural Revolution. The basis of the Gang of Four's power in the early 1960s.

(16) Hangzhou: Another center of radical leftism. Site of a number of important conferences and meetings at the outset of the Cultural Revolution.

China's many social and political changes.[2] It is not so simple now. Mao's faults, the achievements of other CCP leaders, and the contributions of talented Chinese in other arenas are all part of the story of China's several revolutions. The question, then, is how best to use Mao to understand China's revolutions.

[2]Mark Selden, *The Yenan Way in Revolutionary China* (Cambridge: Harvard University Press, 1971). Even those critical of Mao put him at the center of a single Chinese revolution. See Merle Goldman, *Literary Dissent in Communist China* (Cambridge: Harvard University Press, 1967), and Simon Leys, *Chinese Shadows* (New York: Viking, 1977).

This reader seeks to provide students with the means to use writings by and about Mao Zedong to understand China's twentieth-century revolutions. Three of the most important revolutions in which China was engaged were nationalism, socialism, and economic development. Each took root during the twentieth century, and as leader of the CCP, Mao was active in each. One way to begin to use Mao's writings and work as a window on China is to ask, When was Mao in synch or out of synch with the social experiences and political aspirations of major groups in China? This requires us to have some sense of what Mao was thinking and what those around him, as well as people throughout China, were experiencing. The three long texts by Mao and excerpts from some of his other essays in part one, along with the related readings by various Chinese and Western writers in part two, offer sufficient information for the careful reader to approach this goal. They provide some understanding of China's revolutions in nationalism, socialism, and economic development; of Mao's contributions to those revolutions; and of what it meant to be a Chinese revolutionary—one of the millions who followed Mao from dispirited poverty to unimaginable successes and then to unanticipated disasters. This mixed record continues to shape Chinese culture and society today.

CHINA'S REVOLUTIONS

China's leaders today wish to fit in with the international political and economic system, but they wish to do so with "Chinese characteristics." Whereas the leaders of the CCP seek "socialism with Chinese characteristics," the rival Chinese government on Taiwan, run until recently by the Guomindang (GMD), or Nationalist party, has worked to preserve Chinese identity while engaging in global capitalism. Both efforts were part of China's twentieth-century revolutions, which transformed it from a Confucian empire to a modern nation-state.

Mao came to represent the efforts of many Chinese to address the challenges of nationalism, socialism, and economic development, and he brought China a long way toward achieving the success it enjoys today. But in the 1920s, few people thought that China could solve its problems of internal disorder and foreign encroachment, and nearly no one had heard of Mao Zedong.

When Mao was born in 1893, China's Qing dynasty was faltering. In 1895 the empire lost a major war with Japan. Five years later, it fell victim to the Boxer Rebellion of 1900 and the occupation of the capital, Beijing, by European and Japanese forces, which put down the revolt. Finally, the empire collapsed in the 1911 Revolution, which promised a constitutional republic but delivered only militarist rule and competing warlords across China. During these years, Mao grew up as the eldest son of a prosperous farmer in the central Chinese province of Hunan. His father was a harsh patriarch and his mother a devout Buddhist. Mao studied the ancient Confucian classics at a local school but took a greater interest in the new writings of Chinese reformers and anarchists. Meanwhile, his father wanted him to learn the family business. This led to a violent confrontation between father and son, and Mao took his rebellious attitude into the cultural turmoil and political debate of the 1910s.

China in the 1910s and 1920s was in trouble. Politically, economically, and socially, it was on the verge of utter collapse—or at least it appeared to be so. Politically, China had failed in its attempt to turn a dynastic empire into a nation-state run as a constitutional republic. Economically, foreign commercial interests plundered China's raw materials and flooded it with manufactured goods that drove rural handicraft households into bankruptcy. Socially, the links between scholars and the state and between scholar-gentry families and farming communities had been broken, leaving the government to fools and villains and the rural order to thugs.[3] Mao's own account of his youth (see Document 11) gives a vivid sense of these troubled years. Yet these same years were a time of vibrant intellectual and political experimentation, and Mao contributed to that vitality.

From around 1915 on, Chinese scholars and writers increasingly saw the previous century as one long story of decline and failure in China. They worried that China might cease to exist. Since the 1911 Revolution had not made China strong and independent, these scholars came to believe that China needed a "new culture" to restore its glory.

They had a point. In the eighteenth century, China had been a proud and militarily expansionist empire with a vibrant commercial economy and rich urban culture.[4] Yet it was also overpopulated, served by an understaffed bureaucracy, and unwilling to deal with

---

[3]Two excellent textbooks are Jonathan Spence, *The Search for Modern China,* 2nd ed. (New York: W. W. Norton, 2000), and John King Fairbank and Merle Goldman, *China: A New History* (Cambridge: Harvard University Press, 1998).

[4]Susan Naquin and Evelyn Rawski, *Chinese Society in the Eighteenth Century* (New Haven: Yale University Press, 1987).

upstart strangers at its back door—British merchants on the south-east coast. China had maintained commercial links with "Nanyang," the southern seas of Southeast Asia, for well over a thousand years. Threats to its national security, however, had always come from nomads in the north and west,[5] including the Mongols, who success-fully occupied all of China in the thirteenth century, and the Manchus of the Qing dynasty, who ruled from 1644 to 1911. Those invaders had never questioned the cultural-political model of imperial Confucianism. They had added their own practices to Chinese culture, but they largely adopted Chinese institutions and tended to become Chinese in their habits and interests. This was not the case with these new bar-barians from the sea.

From the beginning of direct contact with Europeans in the six-teenth century, China could tolerate Catholic missionaries and trading sea captains from a position of strength. But the decline of Qing administrative efficiency and military might tragically coincided with the unprecedented growth of European means and motives to get wealth out of China and to "save" China's residents from their igno-rance of Christianity and Europe's supposedly superior civilization. Never had China been so profoundly challenged on all three levels of strategic order, economic organization, and social and cultural values.

The Qing dynasty buckled under the weight. The Opium War of 1839–42 was the turning point. After that defeat to British naval power and commercial zeal, the Qing conceded five "treaty ports" where first British and then all foreign merchants and diplomats could set up shop—under their own law. From the foothold of these treaty ports, Western ideas and practices began their slow and unsettling challenge to Chinese government and ways of life. The Qing never really recov-ered. The devastating Taiping Rebellion of 1850–64, fomented by a bizarre pseudo-Christian sect,[6] engulfed more than half of China. Sup-pressing the Taiping rebels required the Qing to give more treaty ports to the Western powers and, fatefully, more military indepen-dence to regional Chinese loyalists.

The Qing finally collapsed in the 1911 Revolution, to be replaced by a short-lived republic under Sun Yat-sen, China's revered father of modern revolution. Sun was a republican revolutionary and is consid-ered the founder of the Nationalist party (the GMD). However, Gen-

[5]Sechin Jagchid and Van Jay Symons, *Peace, War, and Trade along the Great Wall: Nomadic-Chinese Interaction through Two Millennia* (Bloomington: Indiana University Press, 1989).

[6]Jonathan Spence, *God's Chinese Son* (New York: W. W. Norton, 1996).

eral Yuan Shikai, China's first warlord, quickly forced him to resign. China sank into what Mao would later call semifeudal, semicolonial conditions, where no real central government held sway over more than a few of China's twenty-nine provinces and the rest were controlled by a motley crew of militarists and foreign powers.

BATTLE CRY

It was these dire straits that provoked a sense of terminal crisis among China's scholars and writers and led to the New Culture Movement (1915–25). Under the empires, China's scholars were versed in the Confucian canon, vetted by state examinations, and valued as leaders of government and society. That link, however, was broken by 1905, when the Qing discontinued the state examination system, and hopes for its revival or replacement foundered with the fall of the Qing dynasty and the sinking of the republic. On top of all this, China's patriots had to watch Japan—a traditional tributary to China's courts—swagger in as the newest foreign imperialists, taking what they pleased from China. When the Versailles treaty of 1919 gave former German territories in China to the Japanese instead of returning them to China (which, like Japan, had fought with the allies), China's intellectuals hit the streets in protest.

The archetype of militant protests in modern China was the May Fourth Movement.[7] On May 4, 1919, Beijing University students and many others protested the Versailles treaty and forced the Chinese delegation not to sign it (China never did). This political movement gave focus to the broader New Culture Movement. Between 1915 and the mid-1920s, China's new urban educated class tried to reform China's high culture so as to save it from extinction. The essays and magazines Mao read as a youth came from the New Culture Movement, especially Liang Qichao, whose writings were first published at the turn of the century. Chen Duxiu's radical *New Youth* journal was required reading. Hu Shi and other scholars led the vernacularization effort—the shift from the terse and complex classical Chinese of *wenyan* to the easier-to-read *baihua,* which mimicked the spoken language and helped more people learn to read and write.

The battle cry of the New Culture Movement, as Mao recalls, was "Down with the house of Confucius." Yet the West, with its model of

[7]See Jeffery Wasserstrom, *Student Protests in Twentieth-Century China* (Stanford: Stanford University Press, 1991).

parliamentary democracy, was by 1920 neither the only nor the most compelling alternative to stuffy Confucian rituals. Sullied by their association with economic and political imperialism, Western liberal ideals were utterly discredited by the devastation of World War I. Thousands of Chinese students who worked as trench diggers and factory hands in France got a firsthand look at that European disaster. By 1917 China was ripe for the news of the October Revolution in Russia, in which the Communist Bolsheviks led by Lenin toppled the old tsarist regime. By 1919 Marxism, which had been known but not popular in China for a decade, became a viable alternative to what became known in Mao's view as feudalism (Chinese tradition) and imperialism (Western liberal democratic models).

The CCP began to take shape in 1920 in at least four spots around China, ranging from Guangzhou to Sichuan.[8] Mao was an early participant in one of the regional study groups — the New People's Society in Changsha, Hunan province, where he owned a radical bookstore. He served as one of two Hunan delegates to the First Party Congress of the CCP in Shanghai in July–August 1921.[9] From the start, the party was guided by agents of the Comintern — Lenin's Communist International organization. These Soviet agents oversaw the fledgling Chinese leftists in the creation and operation of a Bolshevik party. This brought the prodigious power of Leninist "party cell" organization and the mobilizing ideology of Marxism-Leninism into China.[10] The fit was not good. Soviet theory focused on the industrial working class, or proletariat, but the proletariat in China was tiny. Furthermore, Soviet state policy conflicted with its ideological program. At the same time it helped the CCP, the USSR in fact simultaneously supported the rival Nationalist party, or GMD, as a hedge to guarantee a Chinese government that would be friendly to the Soviets.

The CCP struggled with the GMD, although at first the two worked together. Sun Yat-sen, the erstwhile first president of the republic, had

---

[8] Hans J. van de Ven, *From Friend to Comrade: The Chinese Communist Party, 1920–1927* (Berkeley: University of California Press, 1991), chap. 1.

[9] The best documentary collection and analysis of CCP history is Tony Saich, *The Rise to Power of the Chinese Communist Party: Documents and Analysis* (Armonk, N.Y.: M. E. Sharpe, 1996). On Mao's skill as a bookstore owner, see Jonathan Spence, *Mao Zedong* (New York: Viking Penguin, 1999), 44.

[10] On the considerable organizational powers of Leninism and its contributions to national independence struggles and economic modernization efforts, see Kenneth Jowitt, "The Leninist Response to National Dependency," in Kenneth Jowitt, *New World Disorder: The Leninist Extinction* (Berkeley: University of California Press, 1992), 1–50. On the Comintern and the Chinese revolution, see Tony Saich, *The Origins of the First United Front in China* (Leiden: E. J. Brill, 1991).

retreated after his forced resignation in 1912 to form the GMD, a revolutionary party. By the mid-1920s, it had a foothold in southern China but needed support. Only the new Soviet Union would assist Sun against the northern warlords. The price was a "united front"—political cooperation with the fledgling CCP. When Sun died in 1925, Chiang Kai-shek succeeded him as leader of the GMD.

During the Northern Expedition of 1926–27, forces under Chiang worked with the Communists to reclaim nearly half of China's territory—from Guangdong in the south to central China and even Beijing (see Map 1)—under a central government. Mao refers to the soldiers in this expeditionary force in his 1927 "Report on the Peasant Movement in Hunan" (see Document 1). But the alliance between the CCP and GMD soon crumbled. In April 1927, Chiang, who had visited Soviet Russia and understood the expansionist nature of the Communist party, turned on the CCP in a surprise attack that wiped out the urban party infrastructure.

Into this void stepped Mao Zedong. As outlined in his 1927 report, Mao looked not to the urban revolution of factory workers—the proletariat of Marx and Lenin—but rather to the rural poor, whom Marx had dismissed as "peasants" (see Figure 1). This essay reflects the new conceptual tools that Russian Marxism-Leninism provided Chinese leftists to make sense of their own situation. Mao's breakdown of the rural classes into poor, middle, and rich peasants has become the authoritative statement of Marxist class analysis of the Chinese countryside. Likewise, his description of the peasant associations reflects an attention to the sinews of local power that is a hallmark of Leninism. Mao's genius was to locate the fundamental battleground of this class struggle not at the national or provincial level, but in local society. This view was not, however, popular with either most of his Communist comrades, who believed the proletariat to be the key group, or his Nationalist allies, who did not favor rural insurrection.

Mao's report also reflects the astonishing feminism of some early CCP policy.[11] Mao was certainly a leader in advocating women's liberation from the "masculine authority of husbands," as well as clan, temple, and general religious oppression. That Mao and the CCP did not pursue this feminist agenda for the next several decades had much to do with the life-and-death political confrontation between the

[11] For more on gender and the Chinese revolution, see Christina Gilmartin, *Engendering the Chinese Revolution* (Berkeley: University of California Press, 1995).

Figure 1. *Working in the Rice Paddies*
The backbreaking labor of cultivating rice in flooded paddies provides the
staple crop of much of China, as it has for centuries.
© Michael S. Yamashita/CORBIS.

CCP and the GMD. Likewise, since Marxism-Leninism taught urban
revolution by the proletariat, the CCP did not in the 1920s pursue the
rural revolution that Mao had suggested.

By the early 1930s, what was left of the CCP was running a rural
soviet (an elected government council) in Jiangxi province in south-
east China. Throughout this period, the CCP survived by pursuing
guerrilla warfare—harrying the GMD's (and later Japan's) superior
forces with the "mobile warfare" outlined by Mao in 1936 (see Mao's
interview with Edgar Snow, Document 11).

In 1934 Chiang Kai-shek's modern army and air force drove the
CCP out of Jiangxi and on what became known as the Long March—
a three-thousand-mile retreat into the rugged hills of northwest China.

The survivors who set up shop in 1936 in the dusty county town of Yan'an (see Map 2 and Figure 2), some two thousand miles northwest of Jiangxi in Shaanxi province, were or soon became Mao's men. The Japanese invasion of central China in July 1937 forced Chiang to acquiesce to a second "united front" with the CCP, but this alliance was brief and weakened by mutual mistrust. It mostly gave the CCP protection from further GMD attacks, while both endured the brutal invasion by the Japanese army. Chiang led the national war effort from the GMD stronghold in Chongqing, in the far west of Sichuan province.

CREATING A NEW CHINA

By 1940 the Communist party had successfully passed through a tribulation of biblical proportions. Japan had encroached on Chinese territory since 1895, but in July 1937 the Japanese launched a blitzkrieg that took most of China's rich northern and central provinces. By 1942, after the Japanese attacked Pearl Harbor, the world was embroiled in the Second World War. At the war's end in 1945, China and its two dominant political parties, the Communists and the Nationalists, had endured eight years of bitter fighting. Even so, after a short standoff, the CCP and GMD fell into another civil war.

While resisting Japan, the CCP and GMD had competed for the hearts and minds of China's patriotic urban classes and rural majority. In this atmosphere, Mao wrote "On New Democracy," his blueprint for a "new China" (see Document 2). Published in a CCP journal in Yan'an in January 1940, this essay was not at first CCP policy. Mao's final rise to undisputed authority in the CCP took place in the Yan'an Rectification Movement of 1942–44. The Rectification Movement was an intense study program that focused on CCP history, why the CCP had been crippled by the GMD and forced on the Long March, and why Mao had the right ideas to fulfill the revolutionary promises of the CCP. By the end of this movement, the rank and file of the CCP, as well as its leaders (people called *ganbu,* or cadres), had a clear and compelling set of goals and an understanding of themselves, their role in China's rejuvenation, and even China's role in the liberation of oppressed peoples worldwide. Mao publicly introduced these ideas in "On New Democracy."

Mao cut an impressive figure during these years. Edgar Snow interviewed him in 1936 (see Document 11), shortly after Mao and his colleagues had set up camp in the Yan'an area. Snow saw "a gaunt, rather

Figure 2. *Yan'an and Its Cave Dwellings*
After the Long March and during the anti-Japanese war, CCP leaders worked
in this isolated county seat and lived in the traditional peasant cave dwellings
carved into the rugged hillsides. (Photo, 1981)
© Lowell Georgia/CORBIS.

Lincolnesque figure, above average height for a Chinese, somewhat stooped, with a head of thick black hair grown very long, and with large, searching eyes, a high bridged nose and prominent cheekbones. My fleeting impression was of an intellectual face of great shrewdness" (see Figure 3).

During the next decade, Mao articulated and engineered popular support for what became known inside and outside China as the Yan'an Way. Key aspects of the Yan'an Way are represented in two of Mao's other writings. In "Talks at the Yan'an Conference on Literature and Art" (see Document 3), which he delivered in May 1942, Mao gave his model for intellectuals in the new order and his quintessential example of ideological remolding for everyone. Included in these talks was the mass line, Mao's synthesis of the experience of the CCP administrations in various base areas, or rural soviets. He articulated a coherent policy of populist reform, rent reduction, and honest administration. The mass line also gave Communist leaders and local organizers a common set of goals and a common language—Maoism—with which to analyze China's problems and propose solutions. Mao's brilliant summary of this became the 1943 Central Committee's directive on the mass line (see Document 4), in which "correct leadership comes from the masses and goes to the masses."

Although the discipline the mass line required of cadres may seem extreme to readers today, we must remember the dire straits of both China and the CCP during World War II. Extraordinary danger called for extraordinary efforts, even at the cost of personal liberty. But the mass line was more than a harsh reaction to harsh conditions. Tang Tsou has shown that the mass line was not primarily a means of class struggle but rather a way to connect the goals of the CCP with the interests of ordinary Chinese. Brantly Womack rightly notes that during the years leading up to the Yan'an period, Mao shifted from a position of harsh dictatorship over landlords and other enemies of the CCP to "a politics sensitive to mass opinion within a mobilizational framework."[12]

In Yan'an, Mao found a way to mobilize his followers and increasing numbers of ordinary Chinese to support the nationalist and reformist goals of the CCP. As he said in "On New Democracy," he put off the

---

[12]Tang Tsou, "Reflections on the Formation and Foundations of the Communist Party-State," in Tang Tsou, *The Cultural Revolution and Post-Mao Reforms: A Historical Perspective* (Chicago: University of Chicago Press, 1986), 269–71; Brantly Womack, "The Party and the People: Revolutionary and Post-Revolutionary Politics in China and Vietnam," *World Politics,* 39, no. 4 (July 1987): 479–507.

Figure 3. *Mao Zedong in 1937*
This is how Mao looked when Edgar Snow met him in the late 1930s.
© Bettmann/CORBIS.

radical goals of communism to some future date and instead
addressed the political and psychological concerns of most Chinese:
their need to reside in a China of which they could be proud and to
have enough social peace to live and work. The policies that Mao and
the CCP developed in the Yan'an period addressed these needs con-
vincingly. In the five years from 1944, when the Japanese began to fal-
ter, to 1949, when the CCP took control of Mainland China, the CCP
put the Yan'an Way into practice and defeated the GMD. Mao felt a
connection with these historic changes. In his poem "Snow," most

likely penned in 1944 or 1945, he put himself on a par with China's famous founding emperors (see Document 5).

While in Yan'an, Mao was most in synch with China's revolutions — providing a compelling model for national mobilization, a gradual shift to socialist organization, and a way to reconnect China's educated elite to a government committed both to care for the rural majority and to build the modern industry necessary for economic development. Document 12, a selection from Stuart Schram's biography of Mao, provides a sense of the immense practicality and political success of Mao's model for a new China in Yan'an. This model did not come without a fight and was not without its ugly side. Mao had competitors for leadership, and he was ruthless in suppressing them. The very organization of Mao's writings comes out of the rectification campaign to discredit his enemies and unify the party under his hand. Those who got in his way were, like the party literary critic Wang Shiwei, cut down and vilified.[13]

In fact, during the Chinese civil war (1945–49), the CCP returned to the harsh class warfare in rural China it had carried out in Jiangxi in the early 1930s. The party abandoned the moderate rent reduction campaigns of the Yan'an period and revived full-scale land reform, in conjunction with mass denunciations, and often executions, of landlords. People's courts were held in villages throughout China not only to prosecute common criminals but also to give peasants a chance to "struggle against" local landlords and to distribute the landlords' land to poor peasants. As the CCP took over larger areas of China in the late 1940s, land reform — or land to the tiller — was a basic organizational tool of the party administration.[14] It removed the enemy (landlords allied with the GMD), it built a constituency (farmers freed from

---

[13]Still a valuable study of the politics of Yan'an and the rise of Mao is Raymond F. Wylie, *The Emergence of Maoism: Mao Tse-tung, Ch'en Po-ta, and the Search for Chinese Theory, 1935–1945* (Stanford: Stanford University Press, 1980). David Apter and Tony Saich give a vivid sense of Mao's inspiration to cadres in Yan'an and after in *Revolutionary Discourse in Mao's Republic* (Cambridge: Harvard University Press, 1994); see Document 19 for a review of this book. Finally, the tragic case of Wang Shiwei still haunts the halls of power in China, as seen in Dai Qing's reportage on the case, *Wang Shiwei and "Wild Lilies": Rectification and Purges in the Chinese Communist Party, 1942–1944* (Armonk, N.Y.: M. E. Sharp, 1994).

[14]Saich, *Rise to Power*, 1185–382, provides documents on the CCP's land policy in the context of the 1945–49 civil war. A vivid account of what land reform meant is covered by the American journalist Jack Belden, *China Shakes the World* (New York: Harper & Brothers, 1949), and in the fictional account of a Chinese participant written after she left China, Yuan-tsung Chen, *The Dragon's Village: An Autobiographical Novel of Revolutionary China* (New York: Penguin, 1980).

tenancy and grateful to the party), and it trained administrators in the goals of "serve the people."

Victory in the Chinese civil war brought new challenges for the CCP and for Mao. Chiang Kai-shek and the GMD regime retreated to the island of Taiwan, off the southeast coast of China. National consolidation by the CCP in 1949 solved one of the burning problems of the past century: ending national humiliation and foreign meddling inside China. Indeed, for almost all Chinese, Mao's declaration in September 1949 on the eve of the founding of the People's Republic of China (PRC) still brings a flush of pride: "The Chinese people have stood up!" (see Document 6). On October 1, 1949, Mao officially declared the founding of the PRC (see Figure 4).

But having stood up, the people had to figure where to go and how. The model for a new China outlined in "On New Democracy" was substantially modified on the eve of CCP victory in Mao's "On the People's Democratic Dictatorship."[15] Whereas in 1940 Mao saw the long-range program of the CCP—socialism—as farther off and the short-term program of a democratic united front as more pressing, by the end of the bloody civil war he and the CCP had reversed their emphasis to focus more on the exercise of "dictatorship over reactionary classes."

With increased confidence and revived radicalism, the CCP faced the question of implementing socialism in China and promoting economic recovery and development. Mao and the CCP chose the Soviet model—the Stalinist version of Marxism-Leninism and its centralized planned economy. Scholars have long noted that Mao was not a puppet of Stalin or the Soviet Union, and as we shall see, China would make an acrimonious split with the USSR in 1960. But this should not blind us to the real nature of the political system the CCP instituted in Yan'an and the new PRC. It was based on the Soviet model of the 1930s; it was, and still is, a Stalinist system. Although there were fewer purges and show trials in China than in the Soviet Union in the 1930s, and although China's approach to its farmers was much more solicitous than the Soviet Union's, recent research has confirmed the profound similarities between these two major socialist states.[16]

The central parts of the Soviet model were party hegemony over the government and military (without any constitutional or legal

---

[15]Dated June 30, 1949, in *Selected Works of Mao Tse-tung* (Peking: Foreign Languages Press, 1969), 4:411–24.

[16]Saich, *Rise to Power;* Timothy Cheek and Tony Saich, eds., *New Perspectives on State Socialism in China* (Armonk, N.Y.: M. E. Sharpe, 1997).

Figure 4.   *Mao Speaking on Tiananmen Gate*
Mao declared the founding of the People's Republic of China, atop Tiananmen
Gate in central Beijing, on October 1, 1949.
© Bettmann/CORBIS.

restraints), a centralized state administration that oversaw the operations of an increasingly complex national planned economy, a huge network of mass organizations (such as state-run labor unions, a national women's association, and a youth league), a muscular military, and an omnipresent secret police system. Running through this entire edifice was an independent network of party organizations and cells in every institution, down to the local party office, village, and neighborhood. It was a most amazing and extensive web. It was intended to make good on the promises of national rejuvenation and social equity made by the CCP in the 1940s, and it began with the good intentions of the cadres nurtured on the Yan'an model of rectification study and hands-on experience in the land reform struggle.

This idealistic regime confronted severe challenges. China's economy was wasted by some fifteen years of total war since the Japanese invasion in 1937. The United States enforced an almost immediate embargo on the new PRC. The Korean War broke out within ten months of independence (in June 1950), pulling China into battlefield confrontation with the most powerful nation in the world. These pressures brought out the dark side of the Yan'an Way—the Stalinist purges and inquisitions of those with connections to America, the search for spies, and the demand to conform to party ideology. In Yan'an, Mao had curtailed such purges, and in the early 1950s public campaigns against landlords, corruption, and spies were similarly contained. But the model of using mass campaigns in which millions of people across China followed directions from the national press to attack a particular problem or "enemy" was set.

Mass campaigns were part of a modified Stalinist model in which administrative issues were moralized into political crimes that were then attacked by a national campaign with token negative examples.[17] The early campaigns weakened competing social forces—landlords, capitalists, and bureaucrats left over from the GMD administration— but soon the campaigns became more ideological. Earlier efforts at reeducating intellectuals exploded into harsh media attacks on two leading scholars in 1955. Hu Shi, the great liberal academic and reformer of the New Culture Movement, was denounced as a bourgeois lackey because he had chosen to move to Taiwan with the ousted GMD regime rather than remain on the mainland under CCP

---

[17]The classic study of the origins and application of this rectification model is Frederick C. Teiwes, *Politics and Purges in China: Rectification and the Decline of Party Norms, 1950–1965,* 2nd ed. (Armonk, N.Y.: M. E. Sharpe, 1993).

rule. Hu Feng, the disciple of China's literary revolutionary hero Lu Xun, was attacked for his failure to adhere to the requirements of Mao's "Talks at the Yan'an Conference on Literature and Art" (see Document 3). Both media campaigns were integrated into the mass campaign style of rectification, with study groups in every party cell and office, every workshop and village. Instead of removing or disarming obvious enemies, such campaigns began to "eat the revolution's own." Thus the mass campaign was an effective but dangerous double-edged sword in the armory of militant socialism. It would soon come back to cut Mao and the CCP.

UTOPIAN REVOLUTIONS: THE HUNDRED FLOWERS CAMPAIGN, GREAT LEAP FORWARD, AND CULTURAL REVOLUTION

In 1956 China, the Communist party, and Mao had much to celebrate. The country was more unified, respected, peaceful, productive, and prosperous than it had been in a century and a half. Yet there were shadows lurking, and within a year horrible problems would surface, leading to national purges, the massive famines of the Great Leap Forward, and the political cataclysm of the Cultural Revolution. China had run up against the limitations of the Soviet model. Domestically, there was a shocking rise in bureaucratism: The Yan'an spirit of "serve the people" seemed to decrease in direct proportion to the consolidation of party power over society. Party leaders pushed others around and helped themselves to the fruits of victory. Internationally, socialism was experiencing real problems and challenges. These issues set Mao off in a direction that ultimately proved disastrous for China.[18] One of the first steps was his seminal writing "On the Correct Handling of Contradictions among the People" (see Document 7). It is arguably Mao's most important contribution to the development of state socialism and Marxist-Leninist theory after 1949.[19]

[18]This history and its consequences for China's politics are vividly portrayed in Roderick MacFarquhar, *The Origins of the Cultural Revolution,* vols. 1–3 (New York: Columbia University Press, 1974–97), and Frederick C. Teiwes with Warren Sun, *China's Road to Disaster* (Armonk, N.Y.: M. E. Sharpe, 1999).

[19]The other most obvious candidate is Mao's 1955 speeches, which were combined to become "On the Ten Great Relationships," in *Selected Works of Mao Tse-tung,* vol. 5 (1977). See Stuart Schram, *The Thought of Mao Tse-tung* (Cambridge: Cambridge University Press, 1989), 102.

Figure 5. *Anshan Steel Mill — Mao's Pride*
Anshan Steel Mill was famous for its Maoist workers' constitution in the spirit
of the Great Leap Forward. This picture of Anshan shows the successful
development of some heavy industry by the late 1950s in China.
© Milepost 92½/CORBIS.

Mao presented "On the Correct Handling of Contradictions among
the People" as a keynote lecture on February 27, 1957, to an expanded
group of party leaders. It was then circulated inside party channels
at special study meetings throughout the spring. It was finally published in a drastically edited form in June. The whole affair pointed out
an ominous development in Chinese socialism—the alienation of
the supreme leader from his party, his people, and ultimately from
reality.[20] Mao's concerns about increasing bureaucratism at home

[20]The contentious history of Mao's "Contradictions" speech and his push for a new
rectification movement has been obscured by the party's withholding of Mao's writings
from this period. In the 1980s, Red Guard copies of Mao's unedited speeches and talks
from January to July 1957 confirmed the inner-party struggle that Roderick MacFar-

were heightened by troubles in the international socialist world. First came Soviet premier Nikita Khrushchev's denunciation of Stalin in 1956 and the ensuing de-Stalinization in the Soviet Union and Eastern Europe. Next came the uprisings against Soviet control in Poland and Hungary. Mao accurately saw the likelihood of similar uprisings in China against an increasingly arrogant CCP administration, but his efforts to prevent such uprisings backfired.

Mao's approach to address any major public problem was the mass campaign. In this case, the problem was bureaucratism, the heavy-handed administrative tyranny of the CCP. To combat bureaucratism, Mao declared in early 1956 a reform movement under the slogan "Let a hundred flowers bloom; let a hundred schools contend." The idea was intended to reengage the technical and literary elite that had been chastened by the 1955 campaigns against Hu Shi and Hu Feng. Mao needed this elite to contribute to the next stages of industrialization and socialist transformation of commercial and village life. He sincerely wanted "the masses" of intellectuals and professionals to criticize party errors and excesses. In this aim, he was badly out of step both with his CCP compatriots and with most of China's intellectuals. The rest of the party held to the Leninist notion that the public could hardly comment usefully on the work of socialist transformation because most of the public was of bad, or at best neutral, class background—being mostly peasants and bourgeoisie, rather than working class. The party administration had no interest in soliciting public criticism from these suspect groups, but Mao insisted. In February 1957, using his "Contradictions" speech as a centerpiece, he pushed for a formal rectification movement of the sort that had melded the CCP into a winning team in Yan'an in the 1940s. The party apparatus resisted, but Mao ultimately got his way. A major public criticism campaign was launched in May 1957 as the Hundred Flowers Campaign. What Mao got from the public, however, was not tactical criticism on how to improve the party but strategic attacks on how to get rid of one-party rule. There were calls for parliamentary democracy, multi-party secret-ballot elections, and an end to CCP dictatorship.[21] The party apparatus's fears had come true, and Mao was left with egg on his face in front of his senior colleagues.

---

quhar and others had suspected. The core texts are translated and analyzed in Roderick MacFarquhar, Timothy Cheek, and Eugene Wu, eds., *The Secret Speeches of Chairman Mao: From the Hundred Flowers to the Great Leap Forward* (Cambridge: Harvard Contemporary China Series, 1989).

[21]See Goldman, *Literary Dissent in Communist China,* and Hualing Nieh, *Literature of the Hundred Flowers,* 2 vols. (New York: Columbia University Press, 1981).

The mistake was covered up in public. The open debate and criticism was shut down after barely a month, and the vicious Anti-Rightist Campaign was launched, in which those who had answered Mao's call to criticize the party had their lives ruined. They were fired, sent to virtual prison camps in undeveloped areas, and forever carried the stigma of rightist (that is, someone who opposed the CCP). All this was signaled, once again, by Mao's "Contradictions" piece. On June 6, 1957, it was published in the *People's Daily,* the official newspaper of the CCP, in a heavily edited form that lacked most of his earlier calls for public criticism of the party and included a restrictive litmus test of party loyalty that was to be applied to all such "suggestions." To the Chinese public, not to mention Western scholars bound up in cold war anti-Communist ideology, the Hundred Flowers Campaign appeared to be a particularly cynical attempt to lure opposition out into the open and then cut it off at the knees. Mao's reckless attempt to forestall the intellectual abuses of Soviet Stalinism had achieved the reverse result: It had created the Chinese Stalinist terror.

Understanding the inner history of the Hundred Flowers Campaign is essential in assessing what Roderick MacFarquhar calls the "Yan'an Round Table." King Arthur had fallen out with his knights.[22] From this time forward, Mao distrusted his party, and party leaders felt increasingly terrorized by their charismatic leader. The net result was that Mao became more bizarre and unpredictable, and his bureaucrats became more stodgy and cautious. This combination led to disaster.

Having called upon the intellectuals but found them wanting, Mao next turned to China's farming masses. In 1958 he declared the Great Leap Forward to complete China's two core tasks—finishing the socialist revolution to reach communism (the classless society) and achieving full economic development by overtaking Britain in industrial output. With the technical elite and local party cadres cowed after the Anti-Rightist Campaign, there was no organizational or professional resistance to the unrealistic plans Mao and his emerging circle of sycophants came up with. Mao's August 1958 "Talks at the Beidaihe Conference" (see Document 8) gives a sense of his dizzying imagination: the creation of "people's communes" (pooling the land that farmers had gained in land reform only six years earlier into communal farms), a return to a barter economy, communal dining halls, airstrips in every county, and backyard steel furnaces.

---

[22]See MacFarquhar, *Origins,* 3:471. The detailed history of the Hundred Flowers Campaign is covered in MacFarquhar, *Origins,* vol. 1.

Mao's profound detachment from the realities of life in China is captured by the somewhat tainted memoirs of one of his personal physicians, Dr. Li Zhisui (see Document 14). Mao's sequestered life of autocratic power was proving once again Lord Acton's dictum: "Power tends to corrupt, and absolute power corrupts absolutely." Tragically, the powerful organizational web that the CCP had built in the early 1950s responded loyally to Mao's impossible plans. Local leaders competed in reporting inflated grain harvests, finally claiming that thousands of pounds of rice or wheat were grown per acre. The party center in Beijing praised them and then took more tax revenue on the presumption that there really was more grain. But there was not. There was less, much less, because labor had been diverted to ill-founded industrial projects, such as the backyard steel furnaces. The result was the worst famine of the twentieth century. According to middle estimates, some 20 million Chinese, mostly in rural areas, died between 1959 and 1961.[23] Mao and the CCP were clearly to blame for this disaster.

What is amazing about the debacle of the Great Leap Forward is that the CCP did not fall from power. There was no counterrevolution. This is testimony to the residual legitimacy that the CCP had as the liberators of the Chinese nation from foreign bullies and of the Chinese farmer from tenancy. It is also testimony to the efficacy of centralized propaganda and the harsh political repression of critics in the Anti-Rightist Campaign of 1957–59. Years later, many Chinese reported that they thought the famine occurred only in their county, just an isolated catastrophe. Still, it was more than control of the media that got the recently landed farmers to give up their private land to the new collectives, the people's communes. Most people simply believed in Mao. Land reform was reversed after less than a decade, and the new landlord was the party-state, in the form of local officials who had an interest in making sure all land came back to the "collective."

The legacy of the Great Leap Forward is extensive. Not only did it lead directly to famine and then to the infighting of the Cultural Revolution in 1966, but even today party officials have not extricated themselves from the economy in China. What looks to advocates of trade liberalization with China as increasing privatization of the economy is actually the devolution of party economic control from central

---

[23]See Teiwes and Sun, *China's Road to Disaster,* and Jasper Becker, *Hungry Ghosts* (New York: Henry Holt and Co., 1996).

authorities in Beijing and regional authorities in the provincial capitals to local authorities or, worse, local party strongmen.[24] This profound mixing of business and government in China dates from the Great Leap Forward.

This second major disaster further alienated Mao from the CCP. He had officially "retired" from day-to-day party administration before the Great Leap Forward, but now he really did leave the actual leadership—and the cleanup—to his official successor, Liu Shaoqi. During the early 1960s, the party bureaucracy under Liu tried to pull China from the brink of economic and social collapse through a retreat to moderate social policies (a partial return to private farming and a relaxation in cultural life) and strict Leninist discipline. By 1965 China's economy was on the road to recovery. Yet for Mao, this economic recovery had come at the cost of revolutionary purity. He saw "sprouts of capitalism" in these moderate reforms.

During these years, Mao also picked an acrimonious fight with the leadership of the Soviet Union over ideological orthodoxy. This squabble prompted the departure of all Soviet technical advisers from China in 1960. The two Communist parties suspended relations, although the countries maintained chilly diplomatic channels. Good relations did not return until the late 1980s. Mao brooded over his revolutionary disappointments and concluded that he was surrounded by turncoats, or revisionists. In his view, the party itself was the problem because it was promoting capitalism. It needed to be destroyed and rebuilt.

The final scene in Mao's search to "continue the revolution" through utopian campaigns became the Cultural Revolution in 1966. He tried one more time to redeem the party through revolutionary struggle. Having found China's farmers as incapable as its intellectuals in creating the right sort of society, Mao turned to the youth. With his characteristic tactical brilliance, Mao maneuvered behind the scenes to set up a complex chess game that would bring down his perceived enemies (the party elite, including Liu Shaoqi). When he was ready, he set the game in motion with an attack on academic intellectuals that quickly flared into a full-scale assault on the Beijing party leadership. Mao then called on youth radicals to "Bombard the Head-

---

[24]Dorothy Solinger, "Urban Entrepreneurs and the State: The Merger of State and Society," in *State and Society in China: The Consequences of Reform,* ed. Arthur Lewis Rosenbaum (Boulder, Colo.: Westview Press, 1992).

quarters" (see Document 10). This gave supreme support to student attacks on all elders—teachers, parents, and party officials.[25]

The results in 1966 and 1967 were public terror at the hands of teenage gangs called Red Guards. They were officially sanctioned by Mao, paraded several times before him in Tiananmen Square in central Beijing, and wrought havoc around the country (see Figure 6). Rae Yang's memoir (see Document 15) gives us a glimpse of the madness of the Cultural Revolution. The Red Guards' bible was *Quotations from Chairman Mao Zedong,* commonly known as the "Little Red Book" (see Document 10). Lin Biao, the head of the military, had edited it a few years earlier as a simplified study guide for soldiers. Hundreds of millions of copies of the book were distributed, as the country teetered on the brink of chaos.

The excesses of the Cultural Revolution were not the end of Mao. He lived for another decade. During those years, both he and the CCP reeled in the excesses of the Red Guards by bringing in the People's Liberation Army (PLA) to restore order in China's schools, offices, and villages. Red Guard gangs were broken up in the "rustification movement," in which individual teenagers were "sent down" to villages across China to "learn from the peasants." Since Mao had purged his designated successor, Liu Shaoqi, in 1967, he chose a new successor, Lin Biao. Yet Mao soon came to suspect his new successor as well, and in 1971 Lin Biao died in a plane crash while trying to elude Mao's secret police. During this time, various factions in the CCP competed to get Mao's attention and approval. The two biggest groups were those around his wife, Jiang Qing, who were later known as the Gang of Four, and those around Prime Minister Zhou Enlai. In fact, Mao supported both groups some of the time.

Mao had one more revolution up his sleeve. After two decades of cold war antagonism (see Document 9), Mao surprised everyone by restoring diplomatic relations with the United States. First with secret negotiations with U.S. secretary of state Henry Kissinger in 1971 and then with President Richard Nixon's visit to China in 1972, Mao

[25]The best documentary collection is Michael Schoenhals, ed., *China's Cultural Revolution, 1966–1969: Not a Dinner Party* (Armonk, N.Y.: M. E. Sharpe, 1996). Personal accounts of life during these years are a cottage industry in America. Among the most engaging for students are the memoirs by Gao Yuan, *Born Red* (Stanford: Stanford University Press, 1985), and Rae Yang, *Spider Eaters* (Berkeley: University of California Press, 1997). Also see Anita Chan, *Children of Mao: Personality Development and Political Activism in the Red Guard Generation* (Seattle: University of Washington Press, 1985).

Figure 6.　*Red Guards Parading during the Cultural Revolution*
Red Guard student activists parade in Tiananmen Square, Beijing, in 1967.
They carry a poster of Mao in front, labeled "Long Live Chairman Mao." The
big set of placards reads "Hold High the Great Red Banner of Mao Zedong
Thought," and the smaller banner toward the back reads "Long Live the Great
Proletarian Cultural Revolution." Such mass rallies were common at the begin-
ning of the Cultural Revolution in 1966 and 1967.
© Bettmann/CORBIS.

reversed more than twenty years of animosity between the two countries. With U.S. support, the PRC took the "China seat" on the UN
Security Council, displacing the GMD regime of Chiang Kai-shek
(which occupied Taiwan). The United States and China finally normal-
ized relations and exchanged ambassadors in 1979. Normal diplomatic
relations between China and the United States, despite our various
tensions, are the result of Mao's last, dramatic act of pragmatic leadership of China.

　　When Mao died in September 1976, China was struck with grief. It
was a mixed grief, combining the memory of both Mao's great contri-

butions to the establishment of the nation, the application of socialist goals, and the realization of economic progress, and his cruel persecution of intellectuals, his abandonment of the peasants, his ruinous mass campaigns, and the arbitrary dictatorship of his later years. When Mao was born, China was a failing, backward empire. When he died, it was a respected (or feared) nation on the world scene—a nuclear power with a permanent seat on the UN Security Council and able to feed its people and run a modern economy. The price of this success had been high, and the credit for it belongs to thousands of hardworking Chinese, not just to Mao. But Mao came to represent the noble goals, the grand achievements, and the terrible failures of China in the twentieth century.

EXPERIENCING MAO'S REVOLUTIONS

The readings in part two offer some glimpses of how people inside and outside China experienced Mao. From early on, it was clear that Mao captured people's imaginations as a hero and potential savior. In Document 11, Edgar Snow, his first biographer, records popular stories about Mao as early as 1936. "Mao had the reputation of a charmed life," writes Snow. "He had been repeatedly pronounced dead by his enemies, only to return to the news columns a few days later, as active as ever." Writing before Mao's final rise to power, Snow concludes, "There would never be any one 'savior' of China, yet undeniably one felt a certain force of destiny in Mao."

In the 1930s, Mao was engaged in constant warfare—defending his rural "people's soviet" from local bandits or from the government troops of the GMD, and later resisting the Japanese invasion of China. He was significant mostly to rural people who had to deal with harsh landlords, violent bandits, and corrupt local officials. The Red Army that Mao came to lead, as described in Document 11, shows how effective Mao, Zhu De, and other Communist leaders were in addressing these rural problems.

Stuart Schram's biography (see Document 12) gives us a sense of what it was like to apply Mao's ideas at Yan'an, the Communist capital during World War II. Mao's Thought was a big part of his attraction to many Chinese. He was not just an inspiring figure and a successful general. His way of explaining life made sense to people. Nick Knight offers a good description of how Mao's philosophy applied to broader issues and why it attracted so many Chinese (see Document 13). Mao made Marxism-Leninism—a European ideology developed by Karl Marx, a German, and applied by Lenin, a Russian—into a Chinese system of thought. That is, Mao Sinified Marxism. Coming into the 1950s, a Chinese farmer would be grateful for the land given to him by CCP land reform; a Chinese worker would be happy with better working conditions; a student would be thrilled at the chance to serve China through the CCP, which had brought these good things to pass; and all would be proud that Mao and the CCP had made China stand up as an independent nation at peace for the first time in a century. It is no wonder that Mao's "Sinified Marxism" seemed the right way to ensure China's future growth and development.

Yet the promise was not fulfilled, at least not without a terrible price. By the end of the 1950s, only ten years after their inspiring national victory, Mao and the CCP had developed a police state and caused the biggest famine in China's history. Today researchers can analyze why this happened, but at the time most people could not understand why things were going wrong. The memoir by Li Zhisui, one of Mao's personal doctors (see Document 14), gives one reason: Power corrupts. Mao was a superstar by the 1950s and lost touch not only with the common people but with his colleagues. Yet the more distant Mao became from his people and his peers, the harder it seemed to blame him for what was going wrong. Despite the suffering of the Great Leap Forward, Mao was idolized (see Figure 7). When he unleashed the Cultural Revolution in 1966, hardly a soul thought, or dared, to contradict anything he said.

At the peak of his power, Mao had drifted away from Chinese reality. Whereas his 1927 "Report on the Peasant Movement in Hunan" was a detailed analysis of meticulous field research, the basic Cultural Revolution reading, *Quotations from Chairman Mao Zedong,* provided soothingly simplistic sound bites that were used in often superstitious ways by a confused and troubled public. Red Guards reported a mystical sense of union just by chanting "Long live Chairman Mao," and more recent Chinese scholars note that applying a single Mao sentence to some practical problem continued the superstitions of folk religion (see Documents 15 and 18).

Although Mao's 1957 speech "On the Correct Handling of Contradictions among the People" had failed to create a legitimate arena for public criticism under state socialism (largely due to his own impetuosity), ironically the social disaster of the Cultural Revolution sowed the seeds of democracy in China. A generation of youths learned that it was indeed "right to rebel" (Mao's phrase from his 1927 Hunan

主席是我们心中永远不落的红太阳

Figure 7. *Father Mao Poster from the Cultural Revolution Period*
This is one of literally thousands of colorful propaganda posters idolizing Mao.
He is pictured as the patriarch overseeing the revolutionary masses, who
clutch copies of his red *Quotations from Chairman Mao*. The poster's title, at
the bottom, reads "Chairman Mao Is the Never-Setting Red Sun in Our
Hearts." This particular print is from 1978.
© Ric Ergenbright/CORBIS.

report, which was lionized out of context throughout the Cultural Revolution), but they also learned that the Communist party could be
wrong. Rae Yang, who was one of the youths "sent down" to the
villages during the Cultural Revolution (see Document 15), later reflected on her experience: "Now I agree with Chairman Mao that class
struggle continues to exist in China under socialist conditions—but
not between landlords and poor peasants or capitalists and workers. It

goes on between the Communist Party officials and the ordinary Chinese people!"[26]

In the late 1960s, millions of educated youths were "sent down" to the rural areas ostensibly to "learn from the masses" but actually to disband the Red Guard gangs in the cities. It took nearly ten years for some of these youths to make it back to China's post-Mao universities. Today that cohort of intellectuals and leaders, now in their fifties, has a profound understanding of and link to rural China and a deep-seated distrust of authority.[27] Mao unintentionally provided a solution to two long-standing problems in twentieth-century China—the alienation of the urban elite from China's rural majority and the burden of authoritarian government.

Empowering intellectual independence and reconnecting China's elite with the countryside were not the party's goals in the Cultural Revolution. The CCP was simply trying to survive this final assault by its vengeful founder. When Mao died, he left a wounded institution behind. But it was not mortally wounded, as its survival into the twenty-first century demonstrates. We can see Mao's legacy in the CCP's survival and in the problems it faces. Deng Xiaoping, who was part of Zhou Enlai's faction against Jiang Qing and the Gang of Four, became China's paramount leader after Mao. Deng built his popular support by analyzing and addressing the needs of China's rural majority. He explicitly saw himself as a Maoist in this regard, even though his actual success was based on dismantling Mao's beloved people's communes and restoring the land to those who had originally been awarded it under land reform.

The CCP today uses Mao's united front policies from "On New Democracy" to organize a more relaxed control over public life. In 1988 Li Zehou, a noted philosopher and cultural commentator, invoked "New Democracy" as the right balance of capitalist forces and socialist goals. A decade later, in 1999, senior party historian and CCP establishment spokesman Hu Sheng revisited "On New Democracy" in the flagship journal of the Chinese Academy of Social Sciences, *Chinese Social Sciences*. Hu came to essentially the same conclusion that Li had a decade earlier: New Democracy made the proper use of capitalist energy (farmers and merchants) for socialist goals (a strong and prosperous China) because it focused on the development of productive forces (economic development).[28] As Mao's most senior Western

---

[26]Rae Yang, *Spider Eaters,* 163.

[27]Lisa Rafel, *Other Modernities: Gendered Yearnings in China after Socialism* (Berkeley: University of California Press, 1999).

[28]The interesting thing to note about these two views, aside from their continuity

expert, Stuart Schram, has noted, Mao's core writings from 1935 to 1965 served "as a vehicle of Westernization" that helped China become a modern nation.[29]

Finally, Mao's search for a mechanism for legitimate political opposition under state socialism—the heart of his "On the Correct Handling of Contradictions among the People"—enlivens party leaders today. In 2001 party chairman Jiang Zemin tried to get businessmen to join the CCP.[30] Quite possibly, such an expanded and liberal version of the CCP will become one building block of "democracy with Chinese characteristics."

Mao's legacy is contested. In 1981 the CCP Central Committee passed a resolution on party history and the role of Mao (see Document 16). In this resolution, the Central Committee tried to enforce a formula of 70 percent successes and 30 percent failures in Mao's life and revolutionary leadership. But this resolution has been challenged by writers such as Li Zhisui, who published a denunciation of Mao as an evil emperor in 1994 (see Document 14). This book has been translated into Chinese and circulates widely (albeit illegally) in China today.[31] In Document 17, Jeffrey Wasserstrom provides a sense of how scholars approach Mao today in a review of Li's book and a study by David Apter and Tony Saich of the charismatic authority of Mao in the minds of party cadres. Wasserstrom identifies the major trend in recent studies on Mao and Chinese history: a shift in focus from Mao the man, as representative of a single Chinese socialist revolution, to Mao the image, in the hearts and minds of hundreds of millions of Chinese. We hear some of those unofficial voices from China today in Document 18.

Politically, Mao's legacy is ambiguous. Political scientist Frederick Teiwes notes the reason: "Mao degenerated from pragmatic visionary

---

across the "great divide" of the 1989 Tiananmen protests and repression, is that Li Zehou is considered by Beijing authorities to be a "dissident," while Hu Sheng is an acknowledged establishmentarian. See *Li Zehou wenji* (Works of Li Zehou) (Taipei: Sanmin shuju, 1996), 345, reprinted from *Renmin ribao,* 7 Apr. 1988, and Hu Sheng, "Mao Zedong de Xin minzhuzhuyi lun zai pingjia" (Assessment of Mao's "On New Democracy"), *Zhongguo shehui kexue* (Chinese Social Sciences), 3 (10 May 1999): 4–19.

[29]Schram, *The Thought of Mao Tse-tung,* 192.

[30]Special report on China, *Economist,* 30 June 2001, 9, 21–23; Craig Smith, "Workers of the World, Invest!" *New York Times,* 19 Aug. 2001, WK3.

[31]It is controversial not only with CCP authorities but also with other scholars who feel that the Chinese edition (as well as the English) is distorted. See Geremie R. Barmé, *Shades of Mao: The Posthumous Cult of the Great Leader* (Armonk, N.Y.: M. E. Sharpe, 1996), 53, 72. Li's book has been criticized as bad history by some serious Western scholars, notably Frederick C. Teiwes, "Seeking the Historical Mao," *The China Quarterly,* Mar. 1996.

Figure 8. *Mao Lighter*
One of the popular uses of Mao's memory and image in China today is this striking red cigarette lighter that is still widely available in urban China in the early 2000s. The Chinese characters above Mao's head read "The Red Sun," one of the accolades given to the Chairman during the Cultural Revolution. When opened to light, the red light at the top-center flashes and the tune "The East Is Red" (also of Cultural Revolution vintage) plays. This is a prime example of the commercialization and nostalgia for Mao among a generation that did not actually experience the Cultural Revolution.
Jack Hayes; used with permission.

to paranoid ideologue." On the one hand, Mao's great charisma and authority have stood the test of time, making his leadership style popular even today. On the other hand, the leaders who worked with Mao, and now a new generation that has learned those lessons secondhand, desire "normal politics" without the chaotic mass campaigns and terrifying purges that Mao promoted. Even so, they have inherited political practices that still cause problems today. The CCP still carries a "them and us" attitude as a revolutionary party that feels it cannot trust the ordinary citizen, and it is unwilling to limit its power by establishing a viable legal system. Furthermore, the political methods of Mao continue to haunt the CCP, as is evident in their faith in a now discredited ideology, their reliance on a "core leader," the practice of lower-level leaders clambering to endorse that top leader's "thought," and a mass

Figure 9. *Mao in Temple*

Another use of Mao in contemporary China has been to incorporate him into the vibrant revival of popular religion. Here a Cultural Revolution–period portrait of Mao appears in a local temple in Lahsa, Tibet (1983). Mao clearly remains a potent figure in the popular imagination, but not necessarily for the idealistic policies he advocated or the terrible tragedies he precipitated. What meanings Chinese of the twenty-first century will draw from Mao is an open question, but they are likely to make use of his legacy in some fashion.
© Bettmann/CORBIS.

campaign approach to carrying out policy. "Until these practices are overcome," Teiwes concludes, "it is unlikely that the most important aspect of 'stability and unity'—that between the regime and society—can be achieved."[32]

In all, Mao's revolutions—at first ahead of his contemporaries, then as the best expression of them, and finally as unreasonable dictator—contributed to China's broader revolutions in nationalism,

[32]Frederick C. Teiwes, "Politics at the 'Core': The Political Circumstances of Mao Zedong, Deng Xiaoping and Jiang Zemin," *China Information,* 15, no. 1 (2001): 1–66.

socialism, and economic development. Like other efforts to revolutionize China, Mao's efforts and those of the CCP ran up against the realities of village and urban life that had confronted emperors and mandarins for a thousand years: the importance of family, the thick web of local relationships in villages and urban neighborhoods that defends against efforts by the state to get people to do what it wants, the resilience of "popular religion" that remains out of state control (most recently the Falungong group), and the need to employ and care for a huge and growing population.[33] The clash between these revolutionary impulses and continuing realities has produced not revolutionary change in China today, but evolution—a gradual development of life and thought.

Thus Mao's final legacy is not a simple matter. He will not be forgotten, but he also will no longer likely serve as the charismatic font of all wisdom. Mao has crossed the Taiwan Strait to the home of his Nationalist party rivals, establishing new and developing links between Mainland China and Taiwan. An establishment scholar, Professor Jiang Yihua at Fudan University in Shanghai, edited a volume of Mao's writings that was published in Taiwan in 1994.[34] Radical scholars such as Cui Zhiyuan may call upon Mao's mass campaigns as a model of "extensive democracy" to combat the corruption in China today,[35] and ordinary people may see Mao as a commercial image or as another deity in the pantheon of China's enduring folk religion (see Figures 8 and 9 and Document 18). In the end, some of his contributions will be honored and continued, and others will be discarded. Certainly, his fierce nationalism and faith in China's ordinary people, his focus on the farmers, and his fearless willingness to experiment will likely find a ready audience in the China to come.

[33]On these daily realities and their continuity through centuries of political change, see Lloyd Eastman, *Family, Fields, and Ancestors: Constancy and Change in China's Social and Economic History* (New York: Oxford University Press, 1988); James L. Watson, *Class and Social Stratification in Post-Mao China* (Cambridge: Cambridge University Press, 1984); and David Ownby, "A History for Falungong," *Nova Religio,* Vol. 5, No. 2 (2002, forthcoming).

[34]*Mao Zedong zhuzuo xuan* (Selection of Writings by Mao Zedong), ed. Jiang Yihua (Taipei: Taiwan Shangwu yinshuguan, 1994).

[35]Cui Zhiyuan, quoted in Gloria Davies, ed., *Voicing Concerns: Contemporary Chinese Critical Inquiry* (Lanham, Md.: Rowman & Littlefield, 2001), 52.

PART ONE

Mao Documents

A NOTE ABOUT THE TEXTS

The introduction provides the historical context of Mao Zedong's writings and life. However, it is also the task of historians to assess these texts through source criticism.[1] Historians need to know how the words we read in a document come to us so that we can assess those words. The most obvious point to note here is that the texts in this reader are translations. Mao wrote in modern Chinese; he knew no foreign languages. The translations used here are the best available, by the finest scholars in the field or by the official Beijing translation committee of Mao's *Selected Works*. However, in the case of Mao's writings, evaluation of these documents is complicated by his stature as the "Great Helmsman," the "Savior of the Chinese People," and the author of "Marxism-Leninism Mao Zedong Thought," which is the official ideology of the CCP and thus of China. Thus the problems of the textual transmission and editing of Mao's writings most nearly resemble those of theological texts, such as biblical writings. Fortunately, recent scholarship, especially in China, helps us to know which sort of Mao text we are reading.[2]

Since the advent of "Mao Zedong Thought" in the early 1940s, Mao's writings have been published in China in three kinds of collections. These may be distinguished by the intent of their editors as "collective wisdom" editions, "genius" editions, and "historicist"

[1] John Tosh, *The Pursuit of History,* 3rd ed. (London: Longman, 2000).

[2] For much more detail on the source criticism of Mao's texts, see Timothy Cheek, "Textually Speaking: An Assessment of Newly Available Mao Texts," in *The Secret Speeches of Chairman Mao: From the Hundred Flowers to the Great Leap Forward,* ed. Roderick MacFarquhar, Timothy Cheek, and Eugene Wu (Cambridge: Harvard Contemporary China Series, 1989), 75–103.

editions.[3] First, beginning in 1944, volumes of *Selected Works of Mao Zedong* began to appear by the order of various high-level CCP institutions. They were edited by committee according to a "collective wisdom" criterion: the idea that Mao "represented" the summation of Sinified Marxism-Leninism and thus should reflect the consensus of the party leadership. That this editing relied most heavily on Mao's acquiescence and that the process was highly distorted as early as 1960 did not weaken, in the minds of the editors, the attempt to make official Mao works a "collective" enterprise. Indeed, both Mao himself and advisers from the Soviet Union were active in this process during the early 1950s. Second, during the Cultural Revolution and particularly at the height of the Red Guard movement in 1967, Mao's writings were published by a confusing array of unnamed editors based on the idea that the Chairman was a lone genius and thereby not subject to revision by any collective leadership, least of all by a party riddled with "capitalist roaders." Finally, since Mao's death, party historiographers have published both restricted circulation and publicly available collections of his writings that reflect in varying degrees a "historicist" urge to understand the past as it really was and to place Mao and his writings more firmly in a historical context.

Most of the texts in the first part of this reader are taken from official, or "collective wisdom," editions. I have selected these versions, even though they have been more or less heavily edited from the original, because they are the versions that were studied by hundreds of millions of Chinese as the authoritative word of Mao and the doctrine of the CCP.[4] Some of the shorter extracts come from "historicist" or "genius" editions to give the reader a sense of the difference of these significant but less widely read versions of Mao's writings. The introduction to each document notes its precise source and nature.

The reader of any text that comes from one of Mao's official *Selected Works* needs to keep two points in mind. First, the texts have been freely edited to conform to what the editors considered to be the needs of changing circumstances. That is, in contravention of scholarly standards of accuracy in reprinting historical documents, the texts have been altered. Many well-known studies have documented this

---

[3]These are my categories and not Chinese ones, although they correspond (in order) to the Chinese categories of official (published by the Mao committee), unauthorized, and reference (*yanjiu,* or "research") in the publication of Mao's writings.

[4]As many as 236 million copies of the first four volumes alone were published during Mao's life, according to Michael Y. M. Kau and John Leung, eds., *The Writings of Mao Zedong, 1949–1956* (Armonk, N.Y.: M. E. Sharpe, 1986), 1:xxvi.

phenomenon.[5] For example, Mao's 1957 speech "On the Correct Handling of Contradictions among the People" was massively edited, but I have used the edited version as it appears in volume 5 of his *Selected Works* because that was the version that was widely studied (see Document 7). Among the more common changes in these texts are the deletion of positive comments about the GMD, earthy language, references to policies that did not work, and specific details. Scholars who want to research Mao's role and intentions in specific contexts must seek out the original versions, which are widely available.[6] For those wishing to contemplate the *impact* of the Chairman's writings on the Chinese reading public, the *Selected Works* versions are more appropriate.

Second, the reader should be aware that the official editions of Mao's writings published before his death in 1976 are considered by the CCP leadership to represent "the crystallization of collected wisdom in the CCP."[7] This has been the case since "Mao Zedong Thought" was officially designated as the guiding thought of the CCP in the June 1945 constitution passed at the Seventh Party Congress in Yan'an. This is the trade-off for letting Mao speak for the party: The party can check what he said in print.[8]

[5]See Jerome Chen, *Mao Papers: Anthology and Bibliography* (London: Oxford University Press, 1970), introduction.

[6]Takeuchi Minoru, *Mao Zedongji* (Collected Writings of Mao Zedong), rev. ed., 10 vols. (Tokyo: Hokobosha, 1983), and *Mao Zedong ji bujuan* (Supplements to Collected Writings of Mao Zedong), 10 vols. (Tokyo: Sososha, 1983–86). The tenth volume of *bujuan,* which is unnumbered, contains a chronology of Mao's writings. These sets constitute the most reliable collections of Mao's writings in Chinese, along with *Mao Zedong wenji* (Collected Writings of Mao Zedong), 8 vols. (Beijing: Renmin chubanshe, 1993–99), which goes only through 1957.

The standard references for translations of Mao's collected works are Stuart R. Schram and Nancy J. Hodes, eds., *Mao's Road to Power: Revolutionary Writings, 1912–1949,* planned 10 vols. (Armonk, N.Y.: M. E. Sharpe, 1992–2003), of which five volumes have appeared by 2001, and for September 1949 to December 1957, Michael Y. M. Kau and John K. Leung, eds., *The Writings of Mao Zedong, 1949–1976,* 2 vols. (Armonk, N.Y.: M. E. Sharpe, 1986, 1992). Unfortunately, the Kau and Leung volumes will go no further. The official, or "collected wisdom," edition of *Selected Works of Mao Zedong* in Chinese and English, as edited by the CCP and published in Beijing, is widely available, with a corrected edition released for Mao's centenary in 1993. Finally, full texts of the official English version of *Selected Works* are available on the Web at <http://www.marx2mao.org/Mao/Index.html>.

[7]A classic example of this claim can be found in paragraph 28 of the Central Committee's June 1981 resolution, "On Questions of Party History." For the English version of this resolution, see *Beijing Review,* 6 July 1981, 10–39; paragraph 28 also appears in Helmut Martin, *Cult & Canon: The Origins and Development of State Maoism* (Armonk, N.Y.: M. E. Sharpe, 1982), 213.

[8]See, for example, Martin, *Cult & Canon,* and Joshua A. Fogel, *Ai Ssu-ch'i's Contribution to the Development of Chinese Marxism* (Cambridge: Harvard Council on East Asian Studies, 1987).

The current guide inside China for permissible interpretations of CCP history and Mao's writings is "Resolution on Some Questions on Party History Since the Founding of the Nation," passed by the Central Committee on June 27, 1981 (see Document 16).[9] Perhaps the best preliminary metaphor for the issues surrounding historicist party writings in the 1980s, including those on Mao's works, is that of academic theology in the Christian and Jewish traditions, where "scientific" linguistic and historical analyses seek to contribute to a living faith.

Finally, an assessment of Mao's writings would not be complete without at least a reference to the continuing debate in the West over the interpretations of these texts. Some of the documents in this book reflect these issues (see Documents 13 and 17). The reader should, however, be aware of a few issues in order to mine Mao's texts independently. Stuart Schram's basic text, *The Political Thought of Mao Tse-tung,* and his collection of alternative Cultural Revolution "genius" editions of Mao's works, *Mao Zedong Unrehearsed,* provide ample background on these issues, as does Roderick MacFarquhar and company's *Secret Speeches of Chairman Mao.* In addition, Schram has produced a review of the literature, "Mao Studies: Retrospect and Prospect," which raises problems of interpretation.[10] More provocatively, Nick Knight challenges the reader to confront the problems of relativism and unconscious assumptions in analyzing Mao's texts.[11]

In the selections, footnotes original to the document use footnote symbols (*, †, ‡, etc.); footnotes added by the editor of this volume are numbered.

[9] *Beijing Review,* 6 July 1981, 10–39; Martin, *Cult & Canon,* 180–231.

[10] Stuart Schram, *The Political Thought of Mao Tse-tung,* rev. ed. (New York: Praeger, 1969); Stuart Schram, *Mao Zedong,* rev. ed. (Harmondsworth: Penguin, 1967); Stuart Schram, "Mao Studies: Retrospect and Prospect," *China Quarterly,* 97 (1984): 95–125. See also, Brantly Womack's thoughtful review essay on the first five volumes of Schram and Hodes's *Mao's Road to Power:* "Mao before Maoism," *The Chinese Journal,* no. 46 (July 2001): 95–117.

[11] Nick Knight, "Mao and History: Who Judges and How?" *Australian Journal of Chinese Affairs,* no. 13 (January 1985): 121–36. Knight makes a further contribution in "Mao Zedong: Ten Years After," *Australian Journal of Chinese Affairs,* no. 16 (July 1986): special issue.

1

Report on the Peasant Movement in Hunan
February 1927

This is one of Mao's most famous essays. It sets out to describe the uprising among poor farmers in the counties outside Changsha, in the central province of Hunan, in the winter of 1926–27. The full text of this report was first published in a local CCP journal in March and April 1927. Mao's intended audience was his fellow revolutionaries in the CCP and in the revolutionary wing of the GMD, or Nationalist Party.

The essay is organized into three broad topics: (1) an enthusiastic description and defense of the rural violence that had engulfed the area (and parts of neighboring provinces); (2) a class analysis of the leadership of this violence; and (3) a fourteen-point account of the achievements of the peasant associations that had sprung up to replace the decimated traditional power structure. Throughout the essay, Mao declares that this is the real Chinese revolution, not the urban revolution promised by European Marxism. Mao's genius was to locate the fundamental battleground of this class struggle not at the national or provincial level, but in local society. Mao especially claims that this rural insurrection fulfills the promise of Sun Yat-sen's 1911 Revolution, which had been subverted by militarists.

The essay includes one of Mao's most famous maxims: "Revolution is not a dinner party" (it is phrased slightly differently in this translation). This famous defense of the necessity and appropriateness of revolutionary violence, particularly summary executions of unpopular landlords, marked Mao as a serious and, among the GMD, hated revolutionary. He never looked back.

"Hunan nongmin yundong kaocha baogao," in *Mao Zedong ji,* ed. Takeuchi Minoru (Tokyo: Hokobosha, 1970), 1:207–49, which is taken from the 1944 and 1947 Chinese editions of Mao's *Selected Works.* Translation from Stuart R. Schram and Nancy J. Hodes, eds., *Mao's Road to Power: Revolutionary Writings, 1912–1949: Volume II: National Revolution and Social Revolution, December 1920–June 1927* (Armonk, N.Y.: M. E. Sharpe, 1994), 2:429–64. I have edited the text very lightly to minimize technical terms. I have not included Schram's extensive notations of textual variations between this original and the post-1949 editions of Mao's *Selected Works.*

I. RURAL REVOLUTION

1. The Importance of the Peasant Problem

During my recent visit, I made a first-hand investigation of the five counties of Xiangtan, Xiangxiang, Hengshan, Liling, and Changsha. In the thirty-two days from January 4 to February 5, I called together fact-finding conferences in villages and county towns, which were attended by experienced peasants and by comrades in the peasant movement, and I listened attentively to their reports and collected a great deal of material. Many of the arguments of the peasant movement were the exact opposite of what I had heard from the gentry class in Hankou and Changsha. I saw and heard many strange things of which I had hitherto been unaware. I believe that the same is also true of every province in all of China. Consequently, all criticisms directed against the peasant movement must be speedily set right, and the various erroneous measures adopted by the revolutionary authorities concerning the peasant movement must be speedily changed. Only thus can the future of the revolution be benefited. For the present upsurge of the peasant movement is a colossal event. In a very short time, several hundred million peasants in China's central, southern, and northern provinces will rise like a fierce wind or tempest, a force so swift and violent that no power, however great, will be able to suppress it. They will break through all the trammels that bind them and rush forward along the road to liberation. They will, in the end, send all the imperialists, warlords, corrupt officials, local bullies, and bad gentry to their graves. All revolutionary parties and all revolutionary comrades will stand before them to be tested, to be accepted or rejected as they decide. To march at their head and lead them? To stand behind them, gesticulating and criticizing them? Or to stand opposite them and oppose them? Every Chinese is free to choose among the three, but by the force of circumstances you are fated to make the choice quickly. Here I have written up my investigations and opinions in several sections, for the reference of revolutionary comrades.

2. Get Organized

The peasant movement in Hunan, so far as it concerns the counties in the central and southern parts of the province, where the movement is already developed, can be roughly divided into two periods. The first, from January to September of last year, was one of organization.

Within this period, January to June was a time of secret [activity], and July to September, when the revolutionary army was driving out Zhao,[1] an open time. During this period, the membership of the peasant associations did not exceed 300,000 to 400,000, and the masses directly under their command numbered little more than a million; there was as yet hardly any struggle in the rural areas, and consequently there was very little criticism of the associations in other circles. Because its members served as guides, scouts, and porters, even some of the officers had a good word to say for the peasant associations. The second period, from last October to January of this year, was one of revolution. The membership of the associations jumped to 2 million and the masses directly under their command increased to 10 million. (The peasants generally enter only one name for the whole family on joining a peasant association; therefore a membership of 2 million means a mass following of 10 million.) Almost half the peasants in Hunan are now organized. In counties like Xiangtan, Xiangxiang, Liuyang, Changsha, Liling, Ningxiang, Pingjiang, Xiangyin, Hengshan, Hengyang, Laiyang, Chenxian, and Anhua, nearly all the peasants have gone into the peasant associations or have come under their command. It was on the strength of their extensive organization that the peasants went into action and within four months brought about a great revolution in the countryside, a revolution without parallel in history.

3. Down with the Local Bullies and Bad Gentry! All Power to the Peasant Associations!

Now that the peasants have got themselves organized, they are beginning to take action. The main targets of their attack are the local bullies, the bad gentry, and the lawless landlords, but in passing they also hit out against patriarchal ideas and institutions of all kinds, against the corrupt officials in the cities, and against bad practices and customs in the rural areas. In force and momentum the attack is quite simply tempestuous; those who submit to it survive, and those who resist perish. As a result, the privileges the feudal landlords have enjoyed for thousands of years are being shattered to pieces. Their dignity and prestige are being completely swept away. With the collapse of the power of the gentry, the peasant associations have now become the sole organs of authority, and "All power to the peasant

---

[1]*Zhao:* Zhao Hengti, governor of Hunan until March 1926

associations" has become a reality. Even trifling matters such as quarrels between husband and wife must be brought before the peasant association for settlement. Nothing can be settled in the absence of peasant association representatives. Whatever nonsense the people from the peasant association talk at meetings, that, too, is sacred. The association actually dictates everything in the countryside, all rural affairs, and quite literally, "whatever it says, goes." People outside the associations can only speak well of them and cannot say anything against them. The local bullies, bad gentry, and lawless landlords have completely lost their right to speak, and none of them dares even mutter dissent. Faced by the intimidating force of the peasant associations, the top local bullies and bad gentry have fled to Shanghai, those of the second rank to Hankou, those of the third to Changsha, and those of the fourth to the county towns, while the fifth rank and the still lesser fry surrender to the peasant associations in the villages.

"Here's ten yuan.[2] Please let me join the peasant association," one of the lesser bad gentry will say.

"Ha! Who wants your filthy money?" is the peasants' reply.

Many middle and small landlords, rich peasants, and even some middle peasants, who were formerly opposed to the peasant associations, are now seeking admission. Visiting various places, I often came across such people who pleaded with me, "Mr. Committeeman from the provincial capital, please be my guarantor!"

Under the Qing dynasty, the household census compiled by the local authorities consisted of a regular register and "the other" register, the former for honest people and the latter for burglars, bandits, and similar undesirables. In some places the peasants now use this to scare those who were formerly against the associations. They say, "Put their names down in the other register!"

Afraid of being entered in the other register, such people try various devices to gain admission into the peasant associations. Their minds are entirely set on this, and they do not feel safe until their names are entered in the peasant association register. More often than not the peasant associations turn them down flat, and so they are always on tenterhooks; with the doors of the association barred to them, they are like tramps without a home or, in rural parlance, "mere trash." In short, what was generally sneered at four months ago as the "peasants' gang" has now become something most honorable. Those

---

[2]*yuan:* one Chinese dollar. Its value fluctuated, but it was always a lot of money for poor farmers.

who formerly prostrated themselves before the gentry now all prostrate themselves before the power of the peasants. Everyone, no matter who, admits that the world has changed since last October.

4. It's Terrible and It's Fine

The peasants' revolt in the countryside disturbed the gentry's sweet dreams. When the news from the countryside reached the cities, the urban gentry were immediately in an uproar. When I first arrived in Changsha, I met all sorts of people and picked up a good deal of gossip. From the middle strata of society upwards to the Guomindang right-wingers,[3] there was not a single person who did not sum it all up in the phrase, "It's terrible!" Even very revolutionary people, influenced by the views of the "It's terrible!" school which dominated the climate in the city, became downhearted when they tried to picture the situation in the countryside in their mind's eye and were unable to deny the word "terrible." Even very progressive people could only say, "This kind of thing is inevitable in a revolution, but still it's terrible." In short, no one at all could completely reject this word "terrible." But as I have already said, the fact is that the broad peasant masses have risen to fulfill their historical mission, and that the democratic forces in the countryside have risen to overthrow the forces of feudalism in the countryside. This overthrowing of the feudal forces is the real objective of the national revolution. What Mr. Sun Yatsen wanted, but failed, to accomplish in the forty years he devoted to the national revolution, the peasants have accomplished in a few months. The patriarchal-feudal class of local bullies, bad gentry, and lawless landlords has formed the basis of autocratic government for thousands of years, and is the cornerstone of imperialism, warlordism, and corrupt officialdom. [To overthrow them] is a marvelous feat never before achieved, not just in forty but in thousands of years. It is fine. It is not "terrible" at all. It is anything but "terrible." To give credit where credit is due, if we allot ten points to the accomplishments of the democratic revolution, then the achievements of the city dwellers and the military rate only three points, while the remaining seven points should go to the achievements of the peasants in their rural revolution. "It's terrible!" is obviously a theory for combating the rise

[3] *Guomindang right-wingers:* In 1926 and early 1927, the CCP and GMD cooperated in a united front. Mao was a member of both the GMD and the CCP at the time. Here Mao is criticizing conservative members of the GMD who do not support peasant activism.

of the peasants in the interests of the landlords; it is obviously a theory of the landlord class for preserving the old feudal order and obstructing the establishment of the new democratic order; it is obviously a counterrevolutionary theory. No revolutionary comrade should echo this nonsense. If your revolutionary viewpoint is firmly established, and if you go to the villages and have a look around, you will undoubtedly feel a joy you have never known before. Countless thousands of slaves—the peasants—are there overthrowing their cannibalistic enemies. What the peasants are doing is absolutely right; what they are doing is "fine!" "It's fine!" is the theory of the peasants and of other revolutionaries. Every revolutionary comrade should know that the national revolution requires a great change in the countryside. The Revolution of 1911 did not bring about this change, hence its failure. Now a change is taking place, and this is an important factor for the completion of the revolution. Every revolutionary comrade must support this change or he will be a counterrevolutionary.

5. The Question of "Going Too Far"

Then there is another section of people who say, "Although peasant associations are necessary, their actions at present are undeniably going too far." This is the opinion of the middle-of-the-roaders. But what is the actual situation? True, the peasants are in a sense "unruly" in the countryside. Supreme in authority, the peasant association allows the landlord no say and sweeps away the landlord's prestige. This amounts to striking the landlord down into the dust and trampling on him there. They coined the phrase: "If he has land, he must be a bully, and all gentry are evil." In some of the places even those who own 50 *mu*[4] of fields are called local bullies, and those who wear long gowns are called bad gentry. The peasants threaten, "We will put you in the other register!" They fine the local bullies and bad gentry, they demand contributions from them, and they smash their sedan-chairs.[5] In the case of local bullies and bad gentry who are against the peasant association, a mass of people swarm into their houses, slaughtering their pigs and consuming their grain. They may even loll on the ivory-inlaid beds belonging to the young ladies in the households of the local bullies and bad gentry. At the slightest provocation they make arrests, crown the arrested with tall paper hats, and parade

---

[4]mu: about one-sixth of an acre

[5]*sedan-chairs:* chairs in which rich people traveled in rural China. Two or four porters would lift and carry the chair, which had sides and curtains.

them through the villages, saying, "You dirty landlords, now you know who we are!" Doing whatever they like and turning everything upside down, they have even created a kind of terror in the countryside. This is what ordinary people call "going too far," or "going beyond the proper limits in righting a wrong," or "really too much." Such talk may seem plausible, but in fact it is wrong. First, the local bullies, bad gentry, and lawless landlords have themselves driven the peasants to this. For ages they have used their power to tyrannize over the peasants and trample them underfoot; that is why the peasants have reacted so strongly. The most violent revolts and the most serious disorders have invariably occurred in places where the local bullies, bad gentry, and lawless landlords perpetrated the worst outrages. The peasants are clear-sighted. Who is bad and who is not, who is the worst and who is not quite so vicious, who deserves severe punishment and who deserves to be let off lightly—the peasants keep clear accounts, and very seldom has the punishment exceeded the crime. Therefore, Mr. Tang Mengxiao[6] also said "The peasants are arresting local bullies and bad gentry, nine of ten arrested deserve it." Secondly, a revolution is not like inviting people to dinner, or writing an essay, or painting a picture, or doing embroidery; it cannot be so refined, so leisurely and gentle, so "benign, upright, courteous, temperate and complaisant."* A revolution is an uprising, an act of violence whereby one class overthrows the power of another. A rural revolution is a revolution in which the peasantry overthrows the power of the feudal landlord class. If the peasants do not use extremely great force, they cannot possibly overthrow the deeply rooted power of the landlords, which has lasted for thousands of years. The rural areas must experience a great, fervent revolutionary upsurge, which alone can rouse the peasant masses in their thousands and tens of thousands to form this great force. All the excessive actions mentioned above [result from] the power of the peasants, mobilized by the great, fervent revolutionary upsurge in the countryside. It was highly necessary for such things to be done in the second period of the peasant movement, the period of revolutionary action. Such actions were extremely necessary during the second period of the peasant movement (the period of revolution).

---

[6] *Tang Mengxiao:* Tang Shengzhi, a military commander for Hunan's governor Zhao Hengti. In March 1926, Tang succeeded Zhao as governor and worked with the GMD. In early 1927, Tang supported Mao's work, but he later turned against the Communists.

*These are the qualities that enabled Confucius, according to his disciple Zigong, to obtain information about the government of the countries he visited. See the *Analects,* I, X, 2.

In this period, it was necessary to establish the absolute dominance of the peasants. It was necessary to forbid criticism of the peasant associations. It was necessary to overthrow completely the authority of the gentry, to knock them down and even stamp them underfoot. All excessive actions had revolutionary significance during the second period. To put it bluntly, it is necessary to bring about a brief reign of terror in every rural area; otherwise we could never suppress the activities of the counterrevolutionaries in the countryside or overthrow the authority of the gentry. To right a wrong it is necessary to exceed the proper limits; the wrong cannot be righted without doing so. The argument of this group seems on the surface to differ from that of the group discussed earlier, but essentially they proceed from the same standpoint and likewise voice a landlord theory that upholds the interests of the privileged classes. Since this theory impedes the rise of the peasant movement and so disrupts the revolution, we must firmly oppose it.

II. THE REVOLUTIONARY VANGUARD

1. The Movement of the Riffraff

The right wing of the Guomindang says, "The peasant movement is a movement of the riffraff, a movement of the lazy peasants." This argument has gained much currency in Changsha. When I was in the countryside, I heard the gentry say, "It is all right to set up peasant associations, but the people now running them are no good. They ought to be replaced!" This argument comes to the same thing as what the right-wingers are saying. Both admit that it is all right to have a peasant movement (since the peasant movement has already come into being, no one dare say otherwise), but they regard the people running it as no good. Their hatred is directed particularly against those in charge of the associations at the lower levels, whom they call "riffraff." Those people in the countryside who used to go around in worn-out leather shoes, carry broken umbrellas, wear green gowns, and gamble—in short, all those who were formerly despised and kicked into the gutter by the gentry, who had no social standing, and who were completely deprived of the right to speak, have now dared to lift their heads. Not only have they raised their heads, they have also taken power into their hands. They are now running the township peasant associations (the lowest level of peasant associations), and have turned them into a formidable force. They raise their rough, blackened hands and lay them on the heads of the gentry. They tether the bad gentry with ropes, crown them with tall paper hats, and parade them through the villages. (In Xiangtan and Xiangxiang they call this "parading through the township" and in Liling "parading through the fields.") Every day the coarse, harsh sounds of their denunciations pierce the ears of these gentry. They are giving orders and running everything. They, who used to rank below everyone else, now rank above everybody else—that is what people mean by "turning things upside down."

2. Vanguard of the Revolution or Outstanding Contributors to the Revolution

When there are two different ways of looking at a certain thing, or a certain kind of people, two opposite assessments emerge. "It's terrible!" and "It's fine!" are one example and "riffraff" and "vanguard of the revolution" are another. We said above that the peasants had accomplished a revolutionary task for many years left unaccomplished and had done the principal work in the national revolution. But has this great revolutionary task, this principal work in the revolution, been performed by all the peasants? No. There are three kinds of peasants: the rich, the middle, and the poor peasants. These three categories live in different circumstances and so have different ideas about the revolution. In the first period, what appealed to the rich peasants (those who have surplus money and grain are called rich peasants) was the talk about the Northern Expeditionary Army's sustaining a crushing defeat in Jiangxi, about Chiang Kaishek's being wounded in the leg and flying back to Guangdong, and about Wu Peifu's recapturing Yuezhou.[7] The peasant associations would certainly not last and the Three People's Principles[8] could never prevail, because they had never been heard of before. Thus an official of the township peasant association (generally one of the riffraff type) would walk into the house of a rich peasant, register in hand, and say, "Will you please join the peasant association?" How did the rich peasants reply? "Peasant association? I have lived here for decades, tilling my land. I never saw such a thing before, yet I've managed to live all

[7]These are all rumored setbacks in the Northern Expeditionary Army's military campaigns. Wu Peifu was a northern militarist who at one point reportedly retook the central Chinese city of Yuezhou from the Northern Expeditionary Army.

[8]*Three People's Principles:* socialism, nationalism, and democracy—the goals of Sun Yat-sen and the official ideology of the Northern Expeditionary Army

right," says a rich peasant with a tolerably decent attitude. "I advise you to give it up!" A really vicious rich peasant says, "Peasant association! Nonsense! Association for getting your head chopped off! Don't get people into trouble!" Yet, surprisingly enough, the peasant associations have now been established for several months and have even dared to stand up to the gentry. The gentry of the neighborhood who refused to hand over their opium pipes were arrested by the associations and paraded through the villages. In the county towns, moreover, some big landlords were put to death (such as Yan Rongqiu of Xiangtan and Yang Zhize of Ningxiang). On the anniversary of the October Revolution, at the time of the anti-British rally and of the great celebrations of the victory of the Northern Expedition, tens of thousands of peasants, holding high their banners, big and small, along with their carrying poles and hoes, demonstrated in massive, streaming columns. The rich peasants began to get perplexed and alarmed in their hearts. During the great victory celebrations of the Northern Expedition, they learned that [the city of] Jiujiang had also been taken, that Chiang Kaishek had not been wounded in the leg, and that Wu Peifu had been defeated after all. What is more, they saw "Long live the Three People's Principles!" "Long live the peasant associations!" "Long live the peasants!" and so on and so forth clearly written on the red and green proclamations (slogans).

"What?" wondered the rich peasants, greatly perplexed and alarmed, "'Long live the peasants!' Are these people now to be regarded as emperors?"* So the peasant associations are putting on grand airs. People from the associations say to the rich peasants:

"We'll enter you in the other register!"

"In another month, the admission fee will be ten yuan a head!"

Only under the impact and intimidation of all this are the rich peasants tardily joining the associations, some paying fifty cents or one yuan for admission (the regular fee being a mere ten coppers), some securing admission only after asking other people to put in a good word for them. But there are quite a number of diehards who have not joined to this day. When the rich peasants join the associations, they generally enter the name of some sixty- or seventy-year-old member of the family, for they are in constant dread of conscription. After joining, the rich peasants are not keen on doing any work for the association. They remain inactive throughout. How about the middle peasants?

---

*The most common expression in Chinese for "Long live!" is *wansui,* literally "ten thousand years," which was used of the emperor.

(Those who do not have any surplus money and rice, are not in debt, and are able to assure themselves of clothing, food, and shelter every year are called the middle peasants.) The attitude of the middle peasants is a vacillating one. They think that the revolution will not bring much good to them. They have rice cooking in their pots and no creditors knocking on their doors at midnight. They, too, judging a thing by whether it ever existed before, knit their brows and think to themselves, "Can the peasant association really last?" "Can the Three People's Principles prevail?" Their conclusion is, "Afraid not!" They imagine it all depends on the will of Heaven and think, "A peasant association? Who knows if Heaven wills it or not?" In the first period, people from the association would call on a middle peasant, register in hand, and say, "Will you please join the peasant association?" The middle peasant replied, "There's no hurry!" It was not until the second period, when the peasant associations were already exercising great power, that the middle peasants came in. Even though they are somewhat better in the peasant associations than the rich peasants, they are never very enthusiastic, and retain their vacillating attitude. The only kind of people in the countryside who have always put up the bitterest fight are the poor peasants. From the period of underground work straight through to the period of open activity, it is they who have fought. As for organization, it is they who are organizing things there, and as for revolution, it is they who are making revolution there. They alone are the deadly enemies of the local tyrants and evil gentry, and they strike them without the slightest hesitation. They alone are capable of carrying out the work of destruction. They say to the rich and middle peasants:

"We joined the peasant association long ago, why are you still hesitating?"

The rich and the middle peasants answer mockingly:

"What is there to keep you from joining? You people have neither a tile over your heads nor a speck of land under your feet!"

It is true that the poor peasants are not afraid of losing anything. They are the disinherited or semidisinherited in rural life. Some of them really have "neither a tile over their heads nor a speck of land under their feet." What, indeed, is there to keep them from joining the associations? According to the survey of Changsha county, the poor peasants comprise 70 percent, the middle peasants 20 percent, and the rich peasants 10 percent. The 70 percent, the poor peasants, may be subdivided into two categories, the utterly destitute and the less destitute. The "utterly destitute" are the completely dispossessed, that is, people who have neither land nor capital, are without any means of livelihood, and are forced to leave home and become mercenaries or hired laborers and wandering beggars, or commit crimes and become robbers and thieves. They make up 20 out of the 70 [percent]. The less destitute are the partially dispossessed, that is, people with just a little land or a little capital who eat up more than they earn and live in toil and distress the year round, such as the handicraftsmen, the tenant-peasants (not including the rich tenant-peasants), and the semitenant-peasants. These make up 50 out of the 70 [percent]. (The number of poor peasants in other counties may be smaller than in Changsha, but there should not be a big discrepancy.) This great mass of poor peasants constitute the backbone of the peasant associations, the vanguard in overthrowing the feudal forces, and the foremost heroes who have performed the great revolutionary task which for long years was left undone. Without the poor peasant class (the riffraff, as the gentry call them), it would never have been possible to bring about the present revolutionary situation in the countryside, or to overthrow the local bullies and bad gentry and to complete the democratic revolution. The poor peasants (especially the portion who are utterly destitute), being the most revolutionary group, have gained the leadership of the peasant associations. In both the first and second periods almost all the chairmen and committee members in the peasant associations at the lowest level (i.e., the township associations) were poor peasants (of the officials in the township associations in Hengshan county the class of the utterly destitute comprise 50 percent, the class of the less destitute 40 percent, and poverty-stricken intellectuals 10 percent). This leadership by the poor peasants is extremely necessary. Without the poor peasants there would be no revolution. To deny their role is to deny the revolution. To attack them is to attack the revolution. From beginning to end, the general direction they have given to the revolution has never been wrong. They have discredited the local bullies and bad gentry. They have knocked down the local bullies and bad gentry, big and small, and trampled them underfoot. Many of their "excessive" deeds in the period of revolutionary action were in fact the very things the revolution required. Some county governments, county headquarters of the Guomindang, and county peasant associations in Hunan have already made a number of mistakes; some have even sent soldiers to arrest officials of the lower-level associations at the landlords' request. A good many chairmen and committee members of township associations in Hengshan and Xiangxiang counties have been thrown in jail. This mistake is very serious and unintentionally feeds the arrogance of the reactionaries. To judge whether or not it is a mistake, you have only to see how joyful the lawless landlords become and how reactionary sentiments grow whenever the chairmen or committee members of local peasant associations are arrested. We must combat the counterrevolutionary slogan of a "movement of riffraff" and a "movement of lazy peasants," but at the same time we should be especially careful not to help the local bullies and bad gentry (however unintentionally) in their attacks on the leadership of the poor peasant class. In fact, though a few of the poor peasant leaders undoubtedly did "gamble, play cards, and not earn their living by hard work," most of them have changed by now. They themselves are energetically prohibiting gambling and suppressing banditry. Where the peasant association is powerful, gambling has stopped altogether and the peril of banditry has vanished. In some places it is literally true that people do not take articles left by the wayside and that doors are not bolted at night. According to the Hengshan survey, 85 percent of the poor peasant leaders have made great progress and have proved themselves capable and hard-working. Only 15 percent retain some bad habits. The most one can call them is "an unhealthy minority," and we must not echo the local bullies and bad gentry in undiscriminatingly condemning them as "riffraff." As to dealing with the "unhealthy minority," we can proceed only under the peasant associations' own slogan of "strengthen discipline," by conducting propaganda among their masses, by training the "unhealthy minority," and by improving the discipline of the associations; in no circumstances should soldiers be arbitrarily sent to make such arrests as would weaken the faith [in] the poor peasants and feed the arrogance of the local bullies and bad gentry. This point requires careful attention.

III. PEASANTS AND THE PEASANT ASSOCIATIONS

Most critics of the peasant associations allege that they have done a great many bad things. I have already pointed out in the preceding two sections that the peasants' attack on the local bullies and bad gentry is entirely revolutionary behavior and in no way blameworthy. But the peasants have done a great many things, and we must closely examine all their activities to see whether or not what they have done is really all bad, as is being said from without. I have summed up their activities of the last few months; in all, the peasants under the command of the peasant associations have the following fourteen great achievements to their credit.

1. Organizing the Peasants under Peasant Associations

This is the first great thing the peasants have achieved. In counties such as Xiangtan, Xiangxiang, and Hengshan, nearly all the peasants are organized and there is hardly a remote corner where they are not on the move; these are the best places. In some counties like Yiyang and Huarong, the bulk of the peasants have arisen, with only a small section not yet arisen; these places are in the second grade. In other counties, like Chengbu and Lingling, while a small section has arisen, the bulk of the peasants have still not arisen; these places are in the third grade. Western Hunan, which is under the control of Yuan Zuming, has not yet been reached by the associations' propaganda, and the peasants of many of its counties have completely failed to rise; these form a fourth grade. Roughly speaking, the counties in central Hunan, with Changsha as the center, are the most advanced, those in southern Hunan come second, and western Hunan is only just beginning to organize. According to the figures compiled by the provincial peasants' association last November, organizations with a total membership of 1,367,727 have been set up in thirty-seven of the province's seventy-five counties. Of these members, about one million were organized during the time of October and November when the power of the associations rose high, while up to September the membership had only been 300,000 to 400,000. Then came the two months of December and January, and the peasant movement continued its brisk growth. By the end of the month the membership must have reached at least two million. As a family generally enters only one name when joining and has an average of five members, the mass following must have reached ten million. This astonishing and accelerating rate of expansion explains why the local bullies, bad gentry, and corrupt officials have been isolated; why society has been amazed at how different the world was before and after; and why a great revolution has been wrought in the countryside. This is the first great thing that the peasants have achieved under the command of the peasant associations.

The table [on pp. 56–58] gives the membership of the peasant associations in all the counties in Hunan province as of last November [1926].

2. Dealing Political Blows to the Landlords

After the peasants are organized, the first thing they do is to smash the political prestige of the landlord class, and especially of the local bullies and bad gentry, that is, to pull down the power and influence of the landlords and build up the power and influence of the peasants in rural society. This is a most serious and urgent struggle; it is the central struggle in the second period, the period of revolution. If this struggle is not victorious, there can be no possibility of victory in any of the economic struggles, such as the struggle for rent and interest reduction, or for capital and land, and so on. In many places in Hunan like Xiangxiang, Hengshan, and Xiangtan counties, this is of course no problem since the power of the landlords has been overturned and the peasants constitute the sole power. But in counties like Liling, there are still some places (such as the two western and southern counties of Liling) where the power of the landlords seems weaker than that of the peasants but, because the political struggle has not been sharp, landlord power is in fact surreptitiously opposing peasant power. In such places it is still too early to say that the peasants have gained political victory; they must wage the political struggle more vigorously until the power of the landlords is completely cast down. . . .

[In the remaining part of this item, Mao catalogs the methods used by peasants to attack landlord power in Hunan: auditing accounts, imposing fines, levying contributions, holding minor and major demonstrations, parading landlords in dunce caps, jailing, banishment, and execution. In the next item, Item 3, Mao covers the economic powers of the peasant associations, including keeping grain in the county, limiting rents, protecting tenants' rights, and lowering interest on loans.]

4. Overthrowing the Feudal Politics of the Local Bullies and Bad Gentry in the Rural Areas — Smashing the Districts and the Townships

The old organs of rural administration in the districts and townships, and especially at the district level (namely just below the county level), used to be almost exclusively in the hands of the local bullies and bad gentry. They had jurisdiction over a population of from ten to fifty or sixty thousand people. They had their own independent armed forces, such as the township defense corps; their own independent fiscal

Comparative Table of Peasant Association Membership by County

NAME OF COUNTY	NO. OF QU ASSNS[a]	NO. OF XIAN ASSNS[b]	SOCIAL STATUS OF MEMBERS									NO. OF MEMBERS
			AGR. LABORERS	SHARE CROPPERS	SEMI-OWNER PEASANTS	OWNER PEASANTS	HANDI-CRAFT WORKERS	PRIMARY SCHOOL TEACHERS	SMALL MERCHANT	WOMEN	OTHER	
Xiangxiang	44	499	16,400	91,500	41,000	13,100	28,000	450				190,544
Xiangyin		67	15,857	87,590	52,635	14,793	12,514	151	634	57	400	176,000
Liuyang	21	568										139,190
Xiangtan	17	450	27,000	54,100	12,400	8,460	7,400	1,100				120,460
Hengyang	23	244	17,358	37,725	7,532	5,628	6,135	2,256			1,579	88,223
Changsha	12	640	17,527	25,948	9,131	5,381	4,915	1,425	1,463	643		66,415
Anhua	15	120										62,300
Liling	15	323	6,746	35,460	6,920	3,998	3,643	230	601	195	683	58,476
Ningxiang	18	400	5,000	20,000	10,000	4,000	8,400	600				58,000
Chenxian	14	696	19,725	26,898	2,124	2,550	5,711	118	100	16		57,262
Hengshan	13	203	3,623	16,933	2,965	2,174	3,328				1,133	30,016
Suburbs		169	9,509	10,646	3,563	2,893	1,794	332	582	156		29,475
Linwu	6	32	2,183	10,143	4,146	2,291	933	254				20,000
Youxian		29										18,400
Yiyang	7	67	1,568	5,017	6,586	1,586	784	32	126			15,680
Huarong	6	49	2,000	6,595	2,453	1,887	401	1,216				14,652
Yizhang	10	185	1,438	8,936	1,637	1,283	802	87				14,183
Laiyang	9	149	1,145	6,865	2,684	1,844	342	66				12,946
Linli	6	49	2,000	3,000	2,400	4,000	200	60				11,660
Chaling	4	124	500	7,000	2,500	1,000	200	60				11,260
Yongxing	16	107	1,200	2,800	4,020	2,200	200	30				10,450

Pingjiang	17	162	1,023	4,298	1,781	1,612	1,093	214	85	4	42	10,152
Xinning	9	25	1,722	6,533	858	375	184	74				9,746
Changde	3	59	890	2,800	2,080	3,500	310	65				9,545
Baoqing	7	136	1,438	2,367	1,481	1,744	771					9,377
Wugang	8	40	1,800	4,500	900	900	900	900				9,000
Rucheng	6	46	406	4,195	2,957	1,228	41	38				8,865
Hanshou	69	1,125	3,276	1,047	1,378	228	33	61	78		7,226	
Nanxian	6	49	1,384	4,064	907	406	69	89	45		36	7,000
Zhuping Lu		21	997	3,152	732	539	687	50	297	10		6,464
Xinhua	6		1,526	3,246	497	424	472	202				6,377
Guiyang	4	52	445	274	1,673	1,525	402	24				6,245
Qiyang	15	70										6,000
Lingxian	12	48	1,312	1,917	601	492	546	218	382			5,468
Zixing	5	79	2,148	1,123	891	341	699	122				5,324
Guidong	7	95	816	1,156	1,022	1,507	94	62	204	297	25	5,193
Xintian	8	47	456	2,927	955	488	299	25				5,150
Changning		78	486	2,378	823	536	96	12		34	178	4,549
Cili	11	48	263	1,550	601	1,806	236	40				4,496
Linxiang	7	95	624	995	847	1,195	47	31	105	152	81	4,077
Taoyuan	7	36										4,000
Yuanjiang	3	19	241	1,174	520	1,615	243	46				3,839
Lanshan	4	51	765	1,499	604	385	41	21			35	3,350
Lixian	4	16	597	1,033	389	249	215	66				2,549
Jiahe	3	27	295	598	588	850	89	32				2,452

[a] A *qu* is a subdistrict of a county.
[b] A *xiang* is a subdistrict of a *qu*.

57

Comparative Table of Peasant Association Membership by County (continued)

NAME OF COUNTY	NO. OF QU ASSNS[a]	NO. OF XIAN ASSNS[b]	AGR. LABORERS	SHARE CROPPERS	SEMI-OWNER PEASANTS	OWNER PEASANTS	SOCIAL STATUS OF MEMBERS HANDI-CRAFT WORKERS	PRIMARY SCHOOL TEACHERS	SMALL MERCHANT	WOMEN	OTHER	NO. OF MEMBERS
Anxiang	6	13	280	760	680	440	120	18				2,298
Yongming	5	31	58	522	1,150	420	21	11				2,182
Yueyang	7	47	136	830	410	558	65	11				2,010
Xupu	2	11	540	775	331	204	108	7				1,965
Daoxian	13	39	136	540	282	403	56	18				1,435
Luxi	3	17	102	350	520	240	82	12				1,306
Suining	4	15	121	314	332	297	13	34				1,111
Ningyuan	8	13	86	480	105	159	42	20				892
Chengbu	1	8	130	195	372	101	74	13	14			889
Lingling	4	15	23	133	167	251	8	28	29		58	697
Mayang		9	130	348	36	19	4	3	21	21	48	630
Zhijiang		4		118	76	73		7				274
Total	461	6,867										1,367,727

[a] A *qu* is a subdistrict of a county.
[b] A *xiang* is a subdistrict of a *qu*.

58

powers, such as the power to levy taxes; and their own judiciary, which could freely arrest, imprison, try, and punish the peasants and so on. The bad gentry who ran these organs of rural administration were virtual monarchs of the countryside. Comparatively speaking, the peasants were not so much concerned with the president of the republic, the provincial military governor, or the county magistrate; their real "bosses" were these rural monarchs. A mere snort, and the peasants all knew they had to watch their step. As a consequence of the present revolt in the countryside, the authority of the landlord class has been struck down everywhere, and the organs of rural administration dominated by the local bullies and bad gentry have naturally collapsed in its wake. The heads of the districts and the townships all steer clear of the people, dare not show their faces and hand all local matters over to the peasant associations. They put people off with the remark, "It is none of my business!"

Whenever their conversation turns to the heads of the districts and the townships, the peasants say angrily, "That bunch! They are finished!"

Yes, the term "finished" truly describes the state of the old organs of rural administration wherever the storm of revolution has raged.

5. Overthrowing the Armed Forces of the Landlords and Establishing Those of the Peasants

The armed forces of the landlord class were smaller in central Hunan than in the western and southern parts of the province. An average of 600 rifles for each county would make a total of 45,000 rifles for all the seventy-five counties; there may, in fact, be more than this number. In the southern and central parts where the peasant movement is being developed, the landlord class cannot hold its own because of the overwhelming momentum with which the peasants have risen, and its armed forces have largely capitulated to the peasant associations and taken the side of the peasants; examples of this are to be found in such counties as Ningxiang, Pengjiang, Liuyang, Changsha, Liling, Xiangtan, Xiangxiang, Anhua, Hengshan, and Hengyang. In some counties such as Baoqing and so on, a small number of the landlords' armed forces are taking a neutral stand, though still with a tendency to capitulate. Another small section are opposing the peasant associations, but the peasants are attacking them and may wipe them out before long, as, for example, in such counties as Yichang, Linwu, and Jiahe. At the present time, stronger measures are being taken against these forces, which may all be eradicated soon. The armed forces thus taken over from the reactionary landlords are all being reorganized into a "standing household militia" and are under the new organs of rural self-government, which are organs of the political power of the peasantry. This "taking over these old armed forces" is one part of building up an armed force of the peasantry. Even though some of them are still struggling, the various counties in southern and central Hunan have no problems anymore. There are some problems only in western Hunan. In addition, there is a new way for establishing an armed force of the peasants, which is through the setting up of spear corps under the peasant associations. The spears have pointed, double-edged blades mounted on long shafts, and there are now 100,000 of these weapons in Xiangxiang county alone. Other counties such as Xiangtan, Hengshan, Liling, and Changsha have 70,000 to 80,000, or 50,000 to 60,000, or 30,000 to 40,000 each. In every county where there is a peasant movement, the spears are spreading rapidly. These peasants thus armed form an "irregular household militia." This multitude equipped with spears, which is larger than the old armed forces mentioned above, is a newborn "thing," the mere sight of which makes the local tyrants and evil gentry shiver. The revolutionary authorities in Hunan should see to it that this kind of thing is built up on a really extensive scale among the more than 20 million peasants in the seventy-five counties of the province, that every peasant, whether young or in his prime, possesses a spear, and that no restrictions are imposed as though a spear were something dreadful. Anyone who is scared at the sight of the spear corps is indeed a weakling! Only the local bullies and bad gentry are frightened of them, but no revolutionaries should take fright.

6. Overthrowing the Political Power of the County Magistrate and His Bailiffs

That only if the peasants rise can the county government be cleaned up has already been proved in Haifeng, Guangdong province. On this occasion in Hunan, we have obtained further ample proof. In a county that is under the sway of the local bullies and bad gentry, the magistrate, whoever he may be, is always a corrupt official. In a county where the peasants have risen there is clean government, whoever the magistrate may be. In the counties I visited, the magistrates had to consult the peasant associations on everything in advance. In counties where the power of the peasant movement was very strong, the word of the peasant association worked miracles. If the peasant association demanded the arrest of a local bully in the morning, the magistrate dared not delay till noon; if they demanded it by noon, he dared not delay till the afternoon. When the power of the peasants was just beginning to make itself felt in the countryside, the magistrate worked in league with the local bullies and bad gentry. When the peasants' power grew till it matched that of the landlords, the magistrate took the position of trying to accommodate both sides, accepting some of the peasant association's suggestions while rejecting others. The remark that "the word of the peasants works miracles" applies only when the power of the landlords has been completely beaten down by that of the peasants. At present the political situation in counties such as Xiangxiang, Xiangtan, Liling, and Hengshan is as follows:

a. All decisions are made by a joint council consisting of the magistrate and the representatives of the revolutionary mass organizations. The council is convened by the magistrate and meets in his office. In some counties it is called the "joint council of public bodies and the local government," and in others the "council of county affairs." Besides the magistrate himself, those attending but not voting are the representatives of the county peasant association, trade union council, merchant association, women's association, school staff association, student association, and Guomindang party office. At such council meetings the magistrate is influenced by the views of the public organizations and "invariably does their bidding." The adoption of a democratic committee system of county government does not, therefore, present the slightest problem in Hunan. The present county governments are already quite "democratic" both in form and substance. This situation has been brought about only in the last two or three months, that is, since the peasants have risen all over the countryside and overthrown the power of the local bullies and bad gentry. It has now come about that the magistrates, seeing their old props collapse and needing new props to retain their posts, have begun to curry favor with the public organizations, and the situation has changed as described above.

b. The judicial assistant has scarcely any cases to handle. The judicial system in Hunan remains one in which the county magistrate is concurrently in charge of judicial affairs, with an assistant to help him in handling cases. To get rich, the magistrate and his underlings used to rely entirely on "collecting taxes and levies, procuring men and provisions for the armed forces," and "extorting money in civil and criminal lawsuits by confounding right and wrong," the last being the most regular and reliable source of income. In the last few months, with the downfall of the local bullies and bad gentry, all the legal petti-foggers have disappeared. What is more, the peasants' problems, big and small, are now all settled in the peasant associations at the various levels. Thus the county judicial assistant simply has nothing to do. The one in Xiangxiang told me, "When there were no peasant associations, an average of sixty civil or criminal suits were brought to the county government each day; now it receives an average of only four or five suits a day." So it is that the purses of the magistrates and their under-lings perforce remain empty.

c. The armed guards, the police, and the bailiffs all keep out of the way and dare not go near the villages to practice their extortions. In the past the people in the villages were afraid of the people in the towns, but now the people in the towns are afraid of the people in the villages. In particular the vicious curs kept by the county govern-ment—the police, the armed guards, and the bailiffs—are afraid of going to the villages, or if they do so, they no longer dare to practice their extortions. They tremble at the sight of the peasants' spears.

7. Overthrowing the Clan Authority of the Ancestral Temples and Clan Elders, the Religious Authority of Town and Village Gods, and the Masculine Authority of Husbands

A man in China is usually subjected to the domination of three sys-tems of authorities: (1) the state system (political authority), ranging from the national, provincial, and county government down to that of the township; (2) the clan system (clan authority), ranging from the central ancestral temple and its branch temples down to the head of the household; and (3) the supernatural system (religious authority), ranging from the King of Hell down to the town and village gods belonging to the nether world, and from the Emperor of Heaven down to all the various gods and spirits belonging to the celestial world. As for women, in addition to being dominated by these three, they are also dominated by men (the authority of the husband). These four authorities—political, clan, religious, and masculine—are the embod-iment of the whole feudal-patriarchal ideological system, and are the four thick ropes binding the Chinese people, particularly the peasants. How the peasants have overthrown the political authority of the land-lords in the countryside has been described above. The political authority of the landlords is the backbone of all the other systems of authority. With the politics of the landlords overturned, the clan authority, the religious authority, and the authority of the husband all begin to totter. Where the peasant association is powerful, the clan elders and administrators of temple funds no longer dare oppress those lower in the clan hierarchy or embezzle clan funds. The worst clan elders and administrators, being local bullies, have been thrown out. No one any longer dares to practice the corporal and capital punishments that used to be inflicted in the ancestral temples, such as flogging, drowning, and burying alive. The old rule barring women and poor people from the banquets in the ancestral temples has also been broken. The women of Baiguo in Hengshan county gathered in force and swarmed into their ancestral temple, firmly planted their backsides on the seats, and joined in the eating and drinking, while the venerable clan bigwigs had willy-nilly to let them do as they pleased. At another place, where poor peasants had been excluded from temple banquets, a group of them flocked in and ate and drank their fill, while the local bullies and bad gentry and other long-gowned gentlemen all took to their heels in fright. Everywhere religious authority totters as the peasant movement develops. In many places the peasant associations have taken over the temples of the gods as their offices. Everywhere they advocate the appropriation of temple property for peasant schools and to defray the expenses of the associations, calling it "public revenue from superstition." In Liling county, prohibiting superstitious practices and smashing idols have become quite the vogue. In its northern districts the peasants have prohibited the incense-burning processions to propitiate the god of pestilence. There were many idols in the Daoist temple on Fubo Hill in Lukou, but when extra premises were needed for the district party offices [of the Guomindang], they were all piled up in a corner, big and small together, and no peasant raised any objection. Since then, sacrifices to the gods, the performance of religious rites, and the offering of sacred lamps have rarely been practiced when a death occurs in a family. Because the initiative in this matter was taken by the chairman of the peasant association, Sun Xiaoshan, he is hated by the local Daoist priests. In the Longfeng Nunnery in the North Third District, the peasants and primary school teachers chopped up the wooden idols and actually used the wood to cook meat. More than thirty idols in the Dongfu Monastery in the Southern District were burned by the students and peasants together, and only two small images of Bao Gong were snatched up by an old peasant who said, "Don't commit a sin!" Everywhere it has always been the case that only the older peasants and the women believe in the gods; all the younger peasants do not. Since the latter control the associations, the overthrow of religious authority and the eradication of superstition are going on everywhere. As to the authority of the husband, this has always been weaker among the poor peasants because, out of economic necessity, their womenfolk have to do more manual labor than the women of the richer classes and therefore have more say and greater power of decision in family matters. In sexual matters, they also have relatively more freedom. Among the poor peasants in the countryside, triangular and multilateral relationships are almost universal. With the increasing bankruptcy of the rural economy in recent years, the basis for men's domination over women has already been weakened. With the rise of the peasant movement, the women in many places have now begun to organize rural women's associations; the opportunity has come for them to lift up their heads, and the authority of the husband is getting shakier every day. In a word, the whole feudal-patriarchal ideological system is tottering with the growth of the peasants' power. But in the past and at the present time, the peasants are concentrating entirely on destroying the landlords' political authority. Wherever it has been wholly destroyed, they are beginning to press their attack in the three other spheres of the clan, the gods, and male domination. But such attacks have only just "begun," and there can be no thorough overthrow of all three until the peasants have won complete victory in the economic fight. Therefore, our present task is to lead the peasants to put their greatest efforts into the political struggle, so that the landlords' authority is entirely overthrown. The economic struggle should follow immediately, so that the economic problems of the poor peasants may be fundamentally solved. As for smashing the clan system, superstitious ideas, and one-sided concepts of chastity, this will follow as a natural consequence of victory in the political and economic struggles. If too much of an effort is made arbitrarily and prematurely to abolish these things, then the local bullies and bad gentry will seize the pretext to put forward such slogans as "the peasant association has no piety towards ancestors," "the peasant association is blasphemous and is destroying religion," and "the peasant association stands for the communization of wives," all for the purpose of undermining the peasant movement. A case in point is the recent events at Xiangxiang, Hunan, and Yangxin, Hubei, where the landlords exploited the opposition of some peasants to smashing idols. It is the peasants who made the idols, and when the time comes they will cast the idols aside with their own hands; there is no need for anyone else to do it for them prematurely. Our propaganda policy in such matters is, "Draw the bow but do not release the arrow, having seemed to leap."* The idols should be removed by the peasants themselves, the ancestral tablets should be smashed by the peasants themselves, the temples to martyred virgins and arches for chaste and filial widows and daughters-in-law should be demolished by the peasants themselves.

While I was in the countryside, I did some propaganda against superstition among the peasants. I said: "If you believe in the Eight Characters,[9] you hope for good luck; if you believe in geomancy,[10] you hope to benefit from the location of your ancestral graves. This year within the space of a few months the local bullies, bad gentry, and corrupt officials have all fallen from power. Is it possible that until a few months ago they all had good luck and enjoyed the benefit of well-sited ancestral graves, while suddenly in the last few months their luck has turned and their ancestral graves have ceased to exert a beneficial influence?

"The local bullies and bad gentry jeer at your peasant association and say, 'How odd! Today, the world is a world of committeemen. Look, you can't even go to pass water without bumping into a committeeman!' Quite true, the towns and the villages, the peasant associations and the labor unions, the Guomindang and the Communist Party, all without exception have their executive committee members—it is indeed a world of committeemen. But is this caused by the Eight Characters and the location of the ancestral graves? How strange! The Eight Characters of all the poor wretches in the countryside have suddenly turned auspicious! And their ancestral graves have suddenly started exerting beneficial influences!

"The gods? Worship them by all means. But if you had only Lord Guan and the Goddess of Mercy and no peasant association, could you have overthrown the local tyrants and evil gentry? The 'gods' and 'goddesses' are indeed miserable objects. You have worshipped them for several thousand years, and they have not overthrown a single one of the local bullies or bad gentry for you! Now you want to have your

---

*Mao here takes his text from the *Mencius,* VII, I, XLI, 3. The moral that Mao wished to draw from the passage is clear, in any case: the master illustrates the action to be taken, driving home the message with dramatic gestures, but leaves it to the disciples to carry out the action.

[9]*Eight Characters:* a written record of the astrological moment of a person's birth and thus his or her fate

[10]*geomancy:* a practice in which the placement of household furniture, buildings, and even family graves is chosen to produce auspicious effects; also known as feng shui

rent reduced. Let me ask you, what method will you use? Will you place your faith in the gods, or in the peasant associations?"

When I spoke these words, the peasants laughed, and in the midst of their laughter, I imagined that the gods and idols all fled from sight.

8. Spreading Political Propaganda

Even if ten thousand schools of law and political science had been opened, could they have brought as much political education to the people, men and women, young and old, all the way into the poorest and remotest corners of the countryside, as the peasant associations have done in so short a time? I think they certainly could not have. Down with imperialism! Down with the warlords! Down with the corrupt officials! Down with the local bullies and bad gentry!—these political slogans have grown wings, they have found their way to the young, the middle-aged, and the old, to the women and children in countless villages, they have penetrated into their minds and flowed back from their minds into their mouths. Suppose, for example, you watch a group of children at play. If one gets angry with another, if he glares, stamps his foot, and shakes his fist, you will then immediately hear from the other the shrill cry: "Down with imperialism!"

In the Xiangtan area, when the children who pasture the cattle get into a fight, one will take the part of Tang Shengzhi and the other that of Ye Kaixin.[11] When, after a while, one is defeated and runs away with the other chasing him, it is the pursuer who is Tang Shengzhi and the pursued Ye Kaixin. As to the song "Down with the Imperialist Powers. . . ," of course almost every child in the towns can sing it, and now many village children can sing it too. Some of the peasants can also recite a little of Mr. Sun Yatsen's Testament. They pick out from it the terms "freedom," "equality," "the Three People's Principles," and "unequal treaties" and apply them, if rather crudely, in their life. When somebody who looks like one of the gentry encounters a peasant on the road and stands on his dignity, refusing to make way along a pathway, the peasant will say angrily, "Hey, you local bully, don't you know the Three People's Principles?"

Formerly, when the peasants from the vegetable farms on the outskirts of Changsha entered the city to sell their produce, they used to be pushed around by the police. Now they can find a weapon, which is no other than the Three People's Principles. When a policeman strikes or swears at a peasant from a vegetable farm, the peasant from the

---

[11] *Ye Kaixin:* a competitor of Tang Shengzhi in Hunan

vegetable farm immediately answers back by invoking the Three People's Principles and the policeman has not a word to say. Once in Xiangtan, when a district peasant association and a township peasant association could not see eye to eye about a certain matter, the chairman of the township association declared: "Down with the district peasant association's unequal treaties!"

The spread of political propaganda throughout the rural area is entirely an achievement of the peasant associations. Simple slogans, cartoons, and speeches have produced such a widespread and speedy effect among the peasants that it is as though every one of them had been to a political school. According to the reports of comrades engaged in rural work, the influence of extensive political propaganda was to be found in the three great mass movements: the anti-British demonstration, the celebration of the October Revolution, and the victory celebration for the Northern Expedition. In these movements, political propaganda was conducted extensively wherever there were peasant associations, arousing the whole countryside. Consequently, the impact was very great. From now on, care should be taken to make use of every opportunity gradually to enrich the content and clarify the meaning of the simple slogans mentioned above!

9. Peasant Bans and Prohibitions

When the peasant associations establish their authority in the countryside, the peasants begin to forbid strictly or to restrict the things they dislike. Gaming, gambling, and opium smoking are the three things that are most strictly forbidden.

> Gaming: Where the peasant association is powerful, mahjong,[12] dominoes, and card games are wholly banned.
> The peasant association in the Fourteenth District of Xiangxiang burned two basketfuls of mahjong [pieces].
> If you go to the countryside, you will find none of these games played; anyone who violates the ban is promptly and strictly punished.
> Gambling: Former hardened gamblers are now themselves forcefully suppressing gambling; this abuse, too, has been swept away in places where the peasant association is powerful.
> Opium smoking: The prohibition is extremely strict. When the peasant association orders the surrender of opium pipes, no

[12] *mahjong:* a board game using small tiles on which bets can be made

one dares to raise the least objection. In Liling county, one of the bad gentry who did not surrender his pipes was arrested and paraded through the villages.

The peasants' campaign to "disarm the opium smokers" is no less impressive than the disarming of the troops of Wu Peifu and Sun Chuanfang by the Northern Expeditionary Army. Quite a number of venerable fathers of officers in the revolutionary army, old men who were opium addicts and inseparable from their pipes, have been disarmed by the "emperors" (as the peasants are called derisively by the bad gentry). The "emperors" have banned not only the growing and smoking of opium, but also trafficking in it. A great deal of the opium transported from Guizhou to Jiangxi via the various counties of Baoqing, Xiangxiang, Yuoxian, and Liling has been intercepted on the way and burned. This has affected government revenues. As a result, out of consideration for the army's need for funds in the Northern Expedition, the provincial peasant association ordered the associations at the lower levels "temporarily to postpone the ban on opium traffic." This, however, has upset and displeased the peasants.

There are many other things besides these three that the peasants have prohibited or restricted, the following being some examples:

The flower drum. An obscene and vulgar local opera. Its performances are forbidden in many places.

Sedan-chairs. In many counties, especially Xiangxiang, there have been cases of smashing sedan-chairs. A prohibition on taking sedan-chairs has become a vogue. The only people who can take sedan-chairs are the peasant movement officials; otherwise, they will be smashed. The peasants, detesting the people who use this conveyance, are always ready to smash the chairs, but the peasant associations forbid them to do so. Peasant movement officials tell the peasants, "If you smash the chairs, you only save the rich money and lose the carriers their jobs. And the carriers will be out of a job if they have no work to do. Will that not hurt yourselves?" Seeing the point, the peasants answer, "That's right." They then adopt a new [policy on] sedan chairs—"to increase considerably the fares charged by the chair-carriers" so as to penalize the rich.

Distilling and sugar-making. The use of grain for distilling spirits and making sugar is everywhere prohibited, and therefore the distillers and sugar refiners are constantly complaining. Distilling is not banned in Futianpu, Hengshan county, but prices are fixed very low, and the wine and spirits dealers, seeing no prospect of profit, have had to stop it.

Pigs. The number of pigs a family can keep is limited, for they consume grain.

Chickens and ducks. In Xiangxiang county the raising of chickens and ducks is prohibited, but the women object. In Hengshan county, each family in Yangtang is allowed to keep only three chickens, and in Futianpu five chickens. In many places the raising of ducks is completely banned, for ducks not only consume grain but also ruin the rice plants and so are worse than chickens.

Feasts. Sumptuous feasts are generally forbidden. In Shaoshan, Xiangtan county, it has been decided that guests are to be served only three kinds of animal food, namely, chicken, fish, and pork. It is also forbidden to serve bamboo shoots, kelp, and lentil noodles. In Hengshan county it has been resolved that eight dishes and no more may be served at a banquet, and not even one more is allowed. Only five dishes are allowed in the East Third District in Liling county, and only three meat and three vegetable dishes in North Second District, while in the West Third District New Year feasts are forbidden entirely. In Xiangxiang county, there is a ban on all "egg-cake feasts," which are by no means sumptuous. When Tie Jiawan in the Second District gave an "egg-cake feast" at a son's wedding, the peasants, seeing the ban violated, swarmed into the house and destroyed the "egg-cake feast." In the town of Jiamuo, Xiangxiang county, the people have refrained from eating expensive foods and use only fruit when offering ancestral sacrifices.

Oxen. Oxen are treasured possessions of the peasants in the South. "Slaughter an ox in this life and you will be an ox in the next" has become almost a religious tenet; oxen must never be killed. Before the peasants had power, they could only appeal to religious taboos in opposing the slaughter of cattle and had no real power to ban it. People in the towns always want to eat beef, and therefore people in the towns always want to kill cattle. Since the rise of the peasant associations, their real jurisdiction has extended even to the cattle, and they have prohibited the slaughter of cattle in the towns. Of the six butcheries that formerly existed in the county town of Xiangtan, five are now closed and the remaining merchant slaughters only enfeebled or disabled animals. The slaughter of cattle is totally prohibited throughout Hengshan county. No one in the county town dares slaughter either. A peasant whose ox fell from a high place, broke a leg, and is now disabled dared not kill it. He consulted the peasant association and got their permission before he dared kill it. When the chamber of commerce of Zhuzhou rashly slaughtered a cow, the peasants one day swarmed into town and demanded an explanation. As a result, the chamber, besides paying a fine, had to let off firecrackers by way of apology.

Vagrant ways. A resolution passed in Liling county prohibited the drumming of New Year greetings or the chanting of praises to the local deities or the singing of lotus rhymes.[13] Various other counties have passed resolutions prohibiting this; in other places, these practices have disappeared of themselves, and no one engages in them anymore. The "beggar-bullies" or "vagabonds," who used to be extremely evil, now have no alternative but to submit to the peasant associations. In Shaoshan, Xiangtan county, the vagabonds used to make the temple of the Rain God their regular haunt and could not be persuaded by anyone, but since the rise of the associations they have all stolen away. The peasant association in Huti township in the same county caught three such vagabonds and made them carry clay for the brick kilns. Resolutions have been passed prohibiting the wasteful customs associated with New Year calls and gifts.

Besides these, a great many other minor prohibitions have been introduced in various places, such as the Liling prohibitions on incense-burning processions to propitiate the god of pestilence, on buying preserves and fruit for ritual presents, on burning ritual paper garments during the Festival of the Dead, and on pasting up good-luck posters at the New Year. At Gushui in Xiangxian county, there is even a prohibition on smoking water pipes. In the Second District, letting off firecrackers and ceremonial guns is forbidden, with a fine of 1.20 yuan for the former and 2.40 yuan for the latter. Religious rites for the dead are prohibited in the Seventh and Twentieth Districts. In the Eighteenth District, it is forbidden to make funeral gifts of money. Things like these, which defy enumeration, may be generally called "peasant bans and prohibitions." They are of great significance in two

---

[13]*lotus rhymes:* popular Buddhist chants

respects. First, they represent a revolt against bad customs, such as gaming, gambling, and opium smoking. These customs arose out of the rotten political environment of the landlord class and are swept away once its authority is overthrown. Second, the prohibitions are a form of self-defense against exploitation by city merchants; such are the prohibitions on feasts and on buying preserves and fruit for ritual presents. Because manufactured goods are extremely dear and agricultural products are extremely cheap, the peasants are very ruthlessly exploited by the merchants, and they must therefore engage in passive resistance. The reason for all this is that the unscrupulous merchants exploited them; it is not a matter of their rejecting manufactured goods in order to uphold the Doctrine of Oriental Culture.[14] The peasants' economic protection of themselves necessitates that the peasants organize consumers' cooperatives for collective sale and production. Furthermore, it is also necessary for the government to provide help to the peasant associations in establishing credit cooperatives. If these things were done, the peasants would naturally find it unnecessary to ban the outflow of grain as a method of keeping down the price; nor would they have to prohibit the inflow of manufactured goods as the sole method of economic self-defense.

10. Eliminating Banditry

In my opinion, no ruler in any dynasty from Yao, Shun, Yu, and Tang [in ancient times] down to the Qing emperors and the presidents of the Republic has ever shown as much prowess in eliminating banditry as have the peasant associations today. Wherever the peasant associations are powerful, there is not even the shadow of a bandit. It is truly amazing! In many places there are no longer even those pilferers who stole vegetables at night. Though there are still pilferers in some places, in the counties I visited, even including those that were formerly bandit-ridden, there was no trace of bandits. The reasons are: First, the members of the peasant associations are spread out everywhere over the hills and dales, spear or cudgel in hand, ready to go into action in their hundreds, so that the bandits have nowhere to hide. Second, since the peasants have prohibited the outflow of rice, the price of rice is extremely modest. It was six yuan a

---

[14]*Doctrine of Oriental Culture:* a belief that foreign (that is, Western) things are inferior to Chinese or Oriental things. Mao is making fun of the doctrine and claiming that peasants reject modern things not because of the doctrine but because merchants are overcharging for them.

picul[15] of rice last spring but only two yuan last winter. The poor peasants can buy more grain with less money. And the problem of food has become less serious than in the past for the people. Third, members of the secret societies have all joined the peasant associations, in which they can openly play the hero and vent their grievances, so that there is no further need for the secret "mountain," "lodge," "shrine," and "river" forms of organization. In killing the pigs and sheep of the local tyrants and evil gentry and imposing heavy levies and fines, they have adequate outlets for their feelings against those who oppressed them. Fourth, the armies are recruiting large numbers of soldiers and many of the "unruly" have joined up. Thus the evil of banditry has been eliminated with the rise of the peasant movement. On this point, even the well-to-do approve of the peasant associations. Their comment is:

> The peasant associations? Well, to be fair, there is also something to be said for them.

In prohibiting gaming, gambling, and opium smoking, and in eliminating banditry, the peasant associations have won general approval.

11. Abolishing Exorbitant Levies

As the whole country has not yet been unified and the authority of the imperialists and the warlords has not been overthrown, there is as yet no way of removing the heavy burden of government taxes and levies on the peasants or, more explicitly, of removing the burden of expenditure for the revolutionary army. However, the exorbitant levies imposed on the peasants when the local bullies and bad gentry dominated rural administration, for example, the surcharge on each *mu* of land, have been abolished or at least reduced with the rise of the peasant movement and the downfall of the local bullies and bad gentry. This too should be counted among the achievements of the peasant associations.

12. The Movement for Education

In China education has always been the exclusive preserve of the landlords, and the peasants have had no access to it. But the landlords' culture is completely created by the peasants, for its sole source

---

[15]*picul:* about 133 pounds

is the peasants' sweat and blood that they plundered. In China, more than 90 percent of the citizens have had no access to culture, and of these the overwhelming majority are peasants. The moment the power of the exploiting class was overthrown in the rural areas, the peasants' movement for education began. See how the peasants who hitherto detested the schools are today zealously setting up evening classes! They always disliked the "foreign-style school." When I was going to school and saw that the peasants were against the "foreign-style school," I, too, used to identify myself with the general run of "foreign-style students and teachers" and stand up for it, feeling always that the peasants were "stupid and detestable people." Only in the 14th year of the Republic [1925], when I lived in the country-side for half a year, did I realize that I had been wrong and the peasants' reasoning was extremely correct. The texts used in the rural primary schools were entirely about urban things and unsuited to rural needs. Besides, the attitude of the primary school teachers toward the peasants was very bad and, far from being helpful to the peasants, they came to be disliked by the peasants. Hence the peasants preferred the old-style schools (the so-called "Chinese classes") to the modern schools and the old-style teachers to the ones in the primary schools. Now the peasants are enthusiastically establishing evening classes, which they call "peasant schools." Some have already been opened, others are being organized, and on the average there is one school for every township peasant association. The peasants are very enthusiastic about setting up these evening schools and regard them, and only them, as truly their own. The sources of funds for the evening schools come from the local "public revenue from superstition," from ancestral temple funds, and from other idle public funds or property. The county education boards wanted to use this money to establish national primary schools (that is, "foreign-style schools" not suited to the needs of the peasants), while the peasants wanted to set up peasant schools. Inevitably, there were clashes between the two sides, and the result was generally that both got some of the money, though there were places where the peasants got it all. The development of the peasant movement has naturally resulted in raising their cultural level. Before long, several schools will have sprung up in the villages throughout the province; this is quite different from the empty talk about "universal education," which the intelligentsia and the so-called "educationalists" have been bandying back and forth and which after all this time remains an empty phrase.

13. The Cooperative Movement

The peasants really need cooperatives, especially consumers', marketing, and credit cooperatives. When they buy goods, the merchants exploit them; when they sell their farm produce, the merchants cheat them; when they borrow money or rice, they are fleeced by the usurers; and they are eager to find a solution to these three problems. During the fighting in the Yangtse valley last winter, when trade routes were cut and the price of salt went up in Hunan, a great many peasants organized cooperatives for salt. When the landlords deliberately stopped lending, there were many attempts by the peasants to organize credit agencies because they needed to borrow money. A major problem is the absence of detailed, standard rules of organization. In all localities, many of these spontaneously organized peasant cooperatives fail to conform to cooperative principles; as a result, the comrades engaged in the peasant movement are always eagerly enquiring about "rules and regulations." Given proper guidance, the cooperative movement can spread everywhere along with the growth of the peasant associations. Because the term *hezuo* is not at all familiar to the peasants, [the idea] could also be rendered as *hehuopu*.*

14. Building Roads and Embankments

This, too, is one of the achievements of the peasant associations. Before there were peasant associations the roads in the countryside were terrible. Because roads cannot be repaired without money, and the wealthy were unwilling to dip into their purses, the roads were left in bad shape. If there was any road work done at all, it was done as an act of charity; a little money was collected from families "wishing to gain merit in the next world," and a few narrow, skimpily paved roads were built. With the rise of the peasant associations, orders have been given specifying the required width—three, five, seven, or ten feet, according to the requirements of the different routes—and each landlord along a road has been ordered to build a section. Once the order is given, who dares to disobey? In a short time many good roads have appeared. This is no work of charity but the result of compulsion, and

*Hezuo (cooperate, literally "work together"), and *hezuoshe* (cooperative) have been the standard Chinese terms since the 1920s. The alternative that Mao suggests, *hehuopu,* means literally joint goods shop." It is in fact this coinage which he used for "cooperative" in the title of this section of his report in the original version.

a little compulsion of this kind is not at all a bad thing. The same is true of the embankments. The ruthless landlords were always out to take what they could from the tenant-peasants and would never spend even a few copper cash on embankment repairs; they would leave them to dry up and the tenant-peasants to starve, caring about nothing but the rent. Now that there are peasant associations, they can be bluntly ordered to repair the embankments. When a landlord refuses, the association will tell him very affably:

"Very well! If you won't do the repairs, you will contribute grain, a *dou*[16] for each workday." As this is a bad bargain for the landlord, he hastens to do the repairs. Consequently many defective embankments have been turned into good ones.

The fourteen deeds enumerated above have all been accomplished by the peasants under the command of the peasant associations; would the reader please consider and say whether any of them is bad? Only the local bullies and bad gentry, I think, will call them bad. Curiously enough, it is reported from Nanchang that Chiang Kaishek, Zhang Jingjiang, and other such gentlemen do not altogether approve of the activities of the Hunan peasants. This opinion is shared by Liu Yuezhi and other right-wing leaders in Hunan, all of whom say, "They have simply gone Red." But where would the national revolution be without this bit of Red? To talk about arousing the masses of the people day in and day out and then to be scared to death when the masses do rise—what difference is there between this and Lord She's love of dragons?*

[16]dou: thirty pounds

*The reference is to an anecdote in the *Xin xu* (New Prefaces) of Liu Xiang (76–5 B.C.E.), a descendant of Liu Bang. Lord She professed such a love of dragons that he decorated his whole palace with drawings and carvings of them. Pleased by this report, a real dragon paid him a visit and frightened Lord She out of his wits.

2

On New Democracy

January 15, 1940

In this essay, Mao begins his effort to organize and categorize the experience of China over the past generation by casting it in a broader narrative of imperialist aggression and "feudal" collaboration with invaders going back a century to the Opium War of 1839–42. "On New Democracy" seeks nothing less than to create a meaningful "history" out of "experience," to tell the national story of the new China for a broader public in 1940. The telling, naturally, puts the CCP at the center of the story as the savior that can bring the nation back together and lead it to a prosperous and just future. Mao convinced both inner-party audiences of cadres and the broader public of students, urban professionals, independent political activists, and enough of China's rural population to gain popular support for the CCP in the 1940s as it fought against the GMD (Nationalist party) for the right to rule China.

The essay was first published in January 1940 in a small party journal in Yan'an. Through the Rectification Movement of 1942–44, Mao's ideas became the dominant philosophy of the CCP, and "On New Democracy" contains the core of those ideas. The main audience for Mao's "story" were educated Chinese, who would be needed to staff the new state run by the CCP. This massive expansion of personnel required a coherent set of goals. Just as Mao had tried to claim the mantle of Sun Yat-sen's 1911 Revolution in his 1927 "Report on the Peasant Movement in Hunan," (see Document 1), so did he seek to capture the spirit of the most important intellectual event of his generation—the May Fourth Movement or New Culture Movement—in this essay. Indeed, his description of the events around the famous 1919 student demonstration and associated cultural trends is so detailed and coherent that Western scholars long accepted it as completely accurate.

"*Lun xin minzhuzhuyi,*" in *Mao Zedong ji,* ed. Takeuchi Minoru (Tokyo: Hokobosha, 1970), 7:143–202, which is taken from the 1944 Chinese edition of Mao's *Selected Works.* This translation by Stuart Schram in Stuart R. Schram and Nancy J. Hodes, eds., *Mao's Road to Power: Revolutionary Writings, 1912–1949: Vol. VII, 1940–1941* (Armonk, N.Y.: M. E. Sharpe, forthcoming). I have edited the text very lightly to minimize technical terms. I have not included Schram's extensive notations of textual variations between this original and the post-1949 editions of Mao's *Selected Works.*

The essay is organized as a lecture, explaining what New Democracy is and why it is the right path for China in a series of questions and answers. Throughout the essay, Mao assumes that democracy *means a government that reflects the interests of China's ordinary people; he does not mean elected representative government in the American sense. Along the way, Mao gives a detailed review of modern Chinese history and its stages of development. The turning point from "old democratic revolution" to "new democratic revolution" was the May Fourth Movement. In Mao's version of the story, the shift makes sense in Marxist terms—from bourgeois leadership of the old revolution, which achieved national independence in 1911, to proletarian (that is, CCP) leadership of the new revolution, which was to achieve socialism in the future. He adapts Sun Yat-sen's "Three People's Principles" (nationalism, democracy, and people's livelihood) by adding the "Three Great Policies"— alliance with Soviet Russia, cooperation with the CCP, and attention to the needs of workers and peasants. Mao appeals to his non-CCP audience by putting the party's "maximum program" (communism) into the more distant future and guaranteeing a long period of the "minimum program" (a democratic alliance of all nationalist parties).*

Two of Mao's most famous lines appear in this essay. The first, "The history of modern China is a history of imperialist aggression," summarizes the broad appeal of Mao's leadership across China. He successfully casts himself and the CCP as nationalists and anti-imperialists. In this the CCP was true to its word, ejecting foreigners and nationalizing foreign industries after 1949. Mao's second famous quotation reflects his militant nature: "There is no construction without destruction." Yet this comment is made in reference not to social or political order but to culture and ideology (it would later be used to justify social violence in the Cultural Revolution). Also, it is important to note that these words evoke the ancient Chinese philosophy of yin and yang (flowing and damming; motion and rest), indicating the fit between the Marxist philosophy of dialectics and the traditional Chinese worldview. Mao's story gave the Chinese a way of understanding their place in the world and told them what to do about it.

I. WHITHER CHINA?

A lively atmosphere has prevailed throughout the country ever since the War of Resistance[1] began. There is a general feeling that a way out of the impasse has been found, and people no longer knit their brows in despair. Of late, however, the dust and din of compromise and anti-Communism have once again filled the air, and once again the people are thrown into bewilderment. Most susceptible, and the first to be affected, are the intellectuals and the young students. So the questions "What is to be done?" and "Where is China headed?" have once again arisen. On the occasion of the publication of *Chinese Culture,*[2] it may therefore be profitable to clarify the political and cultural trends in China. I am a layman in matters of culture; I would like to study them, but have only just begun to do so. Fortunately, there are many comrades in Yan'an who have written at length in this field, so that my rough and ready words may serve the same purpose as the beating of the gongs before a theatrical performance. Our observations may contain a grain of truth for the nation's advanced cultural workers and may serve as a modest spur to induce them to come forward with valuable contributions of their own. We hope that they will join in the discussion to reach correct conclusions which will meet our national needs. To "seek truth from facts"[3] is the scientific approach, and presumptuously to claim infallibility and lecture people will *assuredly* never settle anything. The disaster that has befallen our nation is extremely grave, and only a scientific approach and a spirit of responsibility can lead it on to the road of liberation. There is but one truth, and the question of whether or not one has it depends not on subjective boasting but on objective practice. The only yardstick of truth is the revolutionary practice of millions of people. This, I think, can be regarded as the attitude of *Chinese Culture.*

[1] *War of Resistance:* China's war against Japan, which began with Japan's invasion in July 1937 and ended with the end of World War II in August 1945

[2] Chinese Culture: the journal in Yan'an in which Mao first published this essay

[3] *seek truth from facts:* one of the most famous phrases in Chinese communism. This credo of one school of Neo-Confucianism was carved over the door of Mao's high school. The phrase is especially famous for its use in the early post-Mao period of the late 1970s to reverse the excesses of the Cultural Revolution.

II. WE WANT TO BUILD A NEW CHINA

For many years we Communists have struggled not only for a political and economic revolution, but for a cultural revolution as well. The goal of all these revolutions is to build a new society and a new state for the Chinese nation. That new society and new state will have not only a new politics and a new economy but a new culture. In other words, not only do we want to change a China that is politically oppressed and economically exploited into a China that is politically free and economically prosperous, we also want to change the China which is being kept ignorant and backward under the sway of the old culture into an enlightened and progressive China under the sway of a new culture. In short, we want to build a new China. Our aim in the cultural sphere is to build a new Chinese national culture.

III. CHINA'S HISTORICAL CHARACTERISTICS

We want to build a new national culture, but what kind of culture should it be?

Any given culture (as an ideological form) is a reflection of the politics and economics of a given society, and the former in turn has a tremendous influence upon the latter; politics is the concentrated expression of economics. This is our fundamental view of the relation of culture to politics and economics and of the relation of politics to economics. It follows that the form of culture is first determined by the political and economic form, and only then does it influence the given political and economic form. Marx says, "It is not the consciousness of men that determines their being, but, on the contrary, their social being that determines their consciousness."[4] He also says, "The philosophers have only interpreted the world in various ways; the point, however, is to change it."[5] For the first time in human history, these scientific formulations correctly solved the problem of the relationship between consciousness and existence, and they are the basic points of departure underlying the dynamic revolutionary theory of knowledge as the reflection of reality which was later elaborated so

[4]Karl Marx, "Preface to *A Contribution to the Critique of Political Economy,*" in *Selected Works of Marx and Engels,* English ed. (Moscow: Foreign Languages Publishing House, 1958), 1:363.
[5]Karl Marx, "Theses on Feuerbach," in *Selected Works of Marx and Engels,* 2:405.

profoundly by Lenin. These basic points of departure must be kept in mind in our discussion of China's cultural problems.

Thus it is quite clear that the old national culture we want to eliminate is inseparable from the old national politics and economics, while the new national culture which we want to build up is inseparable from the new national politics and economics. The old politics and economics of the Chinese nation form the basis of its old culture, just as its new politics and economics will form the basis of its new culture.

What are China's old politics and economics? And what is her old culture?

From the Zhou and Qin dynasties[6] onward, Chinese society was feudal, as were its politics and its economy. And the culture, reflecting the politics and economy, was feudal culture.

Since the invasion of foreign capitalism and the gradual growth of capitalist elements in Chinese society, that is, during the hundred years from the Opium War to the Sino-Japanese War, the country has changed by degrees into a colonial, semi-colonial, and semi-feudal society. China today is colonial in the enemy-occupied areas and basically semi-colonial in the non-occupied areas, and it is predominantly feudal in both. Such, then, is the character of present-day Chinese society and the state of affairs in our country. The politics and the economy of this society are predominantly colonial, semi-colonial, and semi-feudal, and the culture, reflecting the politics and economy, is also colonial, semi-colonial, and semi-feudal.

It is precisely against these predominant political, economic, and cultural forms that our revolution is directed. What we want to get rid of is the old colonial, semi-colonial, and semi-feudal politics and economy and the old culture. And what we want to build up is their direct opposite, i.e., the new politics, the new economy, and the new culture of the Chinese nation.

What, then, are the new politics and the new economy of the Chinese nation, and what is its new culture?

In the course of its history the Chinese revolution must go through two stages, first, the democratic revolution, and second, the socialist revolution, and by their very nature they are two different revolutionary processes. But what I call democracy no longer belongs to the old category, it is not the old democracy; it belongs to the new category, it is New Democracy.

___

[6]The Zhou and Qin dynasties ruled from the eleventh to the third centuries B.C.E., setting the model for later Chinese empires.

It can thus be affirmed that China's new politics are the politics of New Democracy, that China's new economy is the economy of New Democracy, and that China's new culture is the culture of New Democracy.

Such are the historical characteristics of the Chinese revolution at the present time. Any political party, group, or person taking part in the Chinese revolution that fails to understand this will not be able to direct the revolution and lead it to victory, but will be cast aside by the people and left to grieve out in the cold.

IV. THE CHINESE REVOLUTION IS PART OF THE WORLD REVOLUTION

The historical characteristic of the Chinese revolution lies in its division into the two stages, democracy and socialism, the first being no longer democracy in general, but democracy of the Chinese type, a new and special type, namely, New Democracy. How, then, has this historical characteristic come into being? Has it been in existence for the past hundred years, or is it of recent origin?

A brief study of the historical development of China and of the world shows that this characteristic did not emerge immediately after the Opium War, but took shape later, after the First Imperialist World War and the October Revolution[7] in Russia. Let us now examine the process of its formation.

Clearly, it follows from the colonial, semi-colonial, and semi-feudal character of present-day Chinese society that the Chinese revolution must be divided into two stages. The first step is to change the colonial, semi-colonial, and semi-feudal form of society into an independent, democratic society. The second is to carry the revolution forward and build a socialist society. At present the Chinese revolution is taking the first step.

The first step began with the Opium War in 1840, that is to say, when China's feudal society started changing into a semi-colonial and semi-feudal one. Then came the Movement of the Taiping Heavenly Kingdom, the Coup of 1898,* the Sino-French War, the Sino-Japanese

---

[7]The October Revolution in 1917 brought Lenin and the Bolsheviks to power in Russia and led to the formation of the USSR.

*Here, as in his speech of May 4, 1939, Mao refers to the events of 1898 as a "coup." Obviously he was thinking of the suppression of the Reform Movement, rather than of that movement itself. In the *Selected Works* version, this event has been moved to its

War, the Revolution of 1911, the May Fourth Movement, the May Thirtieth Movement, the Northern Expedition, the Agrarian Revolution, the December Ninth Movement, and the present War of Resistance against Japan.[8] Together these have taken up a whole century and in a sense they represent that first step, being struggles waged by the Chinese people, on different occasions and in varying degrees, against imperialism and the feudal forces in order to build up an independent, democratic society and complete the first revolution. The Revolution of 1911 was in a fuller sense the beginning of that revolution. In its social character, this revolution is a bourgeois-democratic and not a proletarian-socialist revolution. It is still unfinished and still demands great efforts, because to this day its enemies are still very strong. When Mr. Sun Yat-sen said, "The revolution is not yet completed, all my comrades must struggle on," he was referring to the bourgeois-democratic revolution.

A change, however, occurred in China's bourgeois-democratic revolution after the outbreak of the First Imperialist World War in 1914 and the founding of a socialist state on one-sixth of the globe as a result of the Russian October Revolution of 1917.

Before these events, the Chinese bourgeois-democratic revolution came within the old category of the bourgeois-democratic world revolution, of which it was a part.

Since these events, the Chinese bourgeois-democratic revolution has changed, it has come within the new category of bourgeois-democratic revolutions and, as far as the alignment of revolutionary forces is concerned, forms part of the proletarian-socialist world revolution.

Why? Because the First Imperialist World War and the first victorious socialist revolution, the October Revolution, have changed the whole course of world history and ushered in a new era.

In an era in which the world capitalist front has collapsed in one corner of the globe (a corner which occupies one-sixth of the world's surface), and has fully revealed its decadence everywhere else, in an era in which the remaining capitalist portions cannot survive without relying more than ever on the colonies and semi-colonies, in an era in which a socialist state has been established and has proclaimed its readiness to fight in support of the liberation movement of all colonies and semi-colonies, and in which the proletariat of the capitalist coun-

---

proper chronological place, after the Sino-French and Sino-Japanese wars, but it remains a coup.

⁸This list of events, from the Opium War to the War of Resistance, reflects the major events in Chinese foreign relations from 1839 to 1940.

tries is steadily freeing itself from the social-imperialist influence of the social-democratic parties and has proclaimed its support for the liberation movement in the colonies and semi-colonies—in such an era, a revolution in any colony or semi-colony that is directed against imperialism, that is to say, against the international bourgeoisie and international capitalism, no longer comes within the old category of the bourgeois-democratic world revolution, but within the new category. It is no longer part of the old bourgeois and capitalist world revolution, but is part of the new world revolution, the proletarian-socialist world revolution. Such revolutionary colonies and semi-colonies can no longer be regarded as allies of the counter-revolutionary front of world capitalism; they have become allies of the revolutionary front of world socialism.

Although during its first stage or step, such a revolution in a colonial and semi-colonial country is still fundamentally bourgeois-democratic in its social character, and although its objective demand is still basically to clear the path for the development of capitalism, it is no longer a revolution of the old type, led entirely by the bourgeoisie, with the aim of establishing a capitalist society and a state under bourgeois dictatorship. It is rather a revolution of the new type, in which the proletariat participates in or exercises the leadership, and having as its aim, in the first stage, the establishment of a new-democratic society and a state under the joint dictatorship of all the revolutionary classes. In the course of its progress, there may be a number of further sub-stages, because of changes on the enemy's side and within the ranks of our allies, but the fundamental character of the revolution remains unchanged and it will remain the same until the time of the socialist revolution.

Such a revolution attacks imperialism at its very roots, and is therefore not acceptable to imperialism, which on the contrary opposes it. But it is acceptable to socialism, and is supported by the land of socialism[9] and by the international socialist proletariat.

Therefore, such a revolution cannot but become part of the proletarian-socialist world revolution.

The correct thesis that "the Chinese revolution is part of the world revolution" was put forward as early as 1924–27 during the period of China's Great Revolution.[10] It was put forward by the Chinese Communists and endorsed by all those taking part in the anti-imperialist

[9]*land of socialism:* the Soviet Union

[10]*China's Great Revolution:* another name for the Northern Expedition of 1926–27, which brought GMD rule to central China and the establishment of the capital of the Republic of China in Nanjing

and anti-feudal struggle of the time. At that time, however, the significance of this thesis was not fully expounded, and consequently it was
only vaguely understood. I remember that during his eastern expedition against Cheng Jiongming in 1925, Mr. Chiang Kai-shek made a
speech on reaching Chao Shan,* in which he also said, "China's revolution is part of the world revolution."

The "world revolution" no longer refers to the old world revolution,
for the old bourgeois world revolution has long been a thing of the
past; it refers to the new world revolution, the socialist world revolution. Similarly, to form "part of" means to form part not of the old
bourgeois revolution, but of the new socialist revolution. This is a
tremendous change unparalleled in the history of China and of the
world.

The Chinese Communists put forward this correct thesis on the
basis of Stalin's theory.

As early as 1918, in an article commemorating the first anniversary
of the October Revolution, Stalin wrote:

> The great world-wide significance of the October Revolution chiefly
> consists of the following three points. First, it has widened the scope
> of the national question and converted it from the particular ques-
> tion of national oppression to the general question of emancipating
> the oppressed peoples, colonies, and semi-colonies from imperial-
> ism. Second, it has opened up wide possibilities for their emancipa-
> tion and the right paths towards it, has thereby greatly facilitated
> the cause of the emancipation of the oppressed peoples of the West
> and the East, and has drawn them into the common path of the vic-
> torious struggle against imperialism. Third, it has thereby erected a
> bridge between the socialist West and the enslaved East, thus creat-
> ing a new front of revolutions against world imperialism, extending
> from the proletarians of the West, through the Russian Revolution,
> to the oppressed peoples of the East. (Zhang Zhongshi, *Stalin on the
> National Question,* Liberation Press, Yan'an, p. 130.)[11]

Since writing this article, Stalin has again and again expounded
the theory that revolutions in the colonies and semi-colonies have broken away from the old category and become part of the proletarian-
socialist revolution. The clearest and most precise explanation is given
in an article published on June 30, 1925, in which Stalin carried on a

---

*The reference is to Chaoxian and Shantou, two small cities in the northeastern cor-
ner of Guangdong, or to the short railroad connecting them.

[11]Translated in J. V. Stalin, "The October Revolution and the National Question," in
Works, English ed. (Moscow: Foreign Languages Publishing House, 1953), 4:169–70.

controversy with the Yugoslav nationalists of the time. Entitled "The National Question Once Again," it is included in a book translated by Chang Zhongshi and published under the title *Stalin on the National Question.* It contains the following passage:

> Comrade Semich refers to a passage in Stalin's book *Marxism and the National Question,* written at the end of 1912. There it says that "the national struggle is a struggle of the bourgeois classes among themselves." Evidently, by this Semich is trying to suggest that his formula defining the social significance of the national movement under the present historical conditions is correct. But Stalin's pamphlet was written before the imperialist war, when the national question was not yet regarded by Marxists as a question of world significance, when the Marxists' fundamental demand for the right to self-determination was regarded not as part of the proletarian socialist revolution, but as part of the bourgeois-democratic revolution. It would be ridiculous not to see that since then the international situation has radically changed, that the war in Europe, on the one hand, and the October Revolution in Russia, on the other, transformed the national question from a part of the bourgeois-democratic revolution into a part of the proletarian-socialist revolution. As far back as October 1916, in his article, "The Discussion on Self-Determination Summed Up," Lenin said that the main point of the national question, the right to self-determination, had ceased to be a part of the general democratic movement, that it had already become a component part of the general proletarian, socialist revolution. I do not even mention many other profound works on the national question by Lenin and by other representatives of Russian communism. What significance can Semich's reference to the passage in Stalin's book, written in the period of the bourgeois-democratic revolution in Russia, have at the present time, when as a consequence of the new historical situation, we have entered a new epoch, the present epoch of world proletarian revolution? It can only signify that Comrade Semich completely quotes outside of space and time, without reference to the living historical situation, and thereby violates the elementary requirements of dialectics, and ignores the saying that what is right for one historical situation may prove to be wrong in another historical situation.[12]

From this it can be seen that there are two kinds of world revolutions. The first belongs to the bourgeois or capitalist category. The era of this kind of world revolution is long past; it came to an end as far

[12]Translated in J. V. Stalin, "The National Question Once Again," in *Works,* English ed. (Moscow: Foreign Languages Publishing House, 1954), 7:225–27.

back as 1914, when the First Imperialist World War broke out, and above all in 1917, when the Russian October Revolution took place. The second kind, namely the proletarian-socialist world revolution, thereupon began. This type of revolution has the proletariat of the capitalist countries as its main force, and the oppressed peoples of the colonies and semi-colonies as its allies. No matter what classes, parties, or individuals in an oppressed nation join the revolution, and no matter whether they are conscious of this point or understand it subjectively, so long as they oppose imperialism, their revolution becomes part of the proletarian-socialist world revolution and they become its allies.

Today, the Chinese revolution has taken on still greater significance. This is a time when the economic and political crises of capitalism are dragging the world more and more deeply into the Second Imperialist War,[13] when the Soviet Union has reached the period of transition from socialism to communism and is capable of leading and helping the proletariat, oppressed nations, and all revolutionary people of the whole world in their fight against imperialist war and capitalist reaction, when the proletariat of the capitalist countries is preparing to overthrow capitalism and establish socialism, and when the proletariat, the peasantry, the intellectuals, and the petty bourgeoisie in China have become a mighty independent political force under the leadership of the Chinese Communist Party. Situated as we are in this day and age, should we not make the appraisal that the Chinese revolution has taken on still greater world significance? I think we should. The Chinese revolution is a great part of the world revolution.

Although the Chinese revolution in this first stage (with its many sub-stages) is a new type of bourgeois-democratic revolution and is not yet itself the newest type of proletarian-socialist revolution in its social character, it has long become a part of the proletarian-socialist world revolution and now even a very important part and a great ally of this world revolution. The first step or stage in our revolution is definitely not, and cannot be, the establishment of a capitalist society under the dictatorship of the Chinese bourgeoisie, but will result in the establishment of a new-democratic society under the joint dictatorship of all the revolutionary classes of China. The revolution will then be carried forward to the second stage, in which a socialist society will be established in China.

---

[13] *Second Imperialist War:* World War II

This is the fundamental characteristic of the Chinese revolution of today, of the new revolutionary process of the past twenty years (counting from the May Fourth Movement), and its concrete living essence.

V. THE POLITICS OF NEW DEMOCRACY

The new historical characteristic of the Chinese revolution is its division into two stages, the first being the new-democratic revolution. How does this manifest itself concretely in internal political and economic relations? Let us consider the question.

Before the May Fourth Movement of 1919 (which occurred after the First Great Imperialist War of 1914 and the Russian October Revolution of 1917), the petty bourgeoisie and the bourgeoisie (through their intellectuals) were the political leaders of the bourgeois-democratic revolution. The Chinese proletariat had not yet appeared on the political scene as an awakened and independent class force, but participated in the revolution only as a follower of the petty bourgeoisie and the bourgeoisie. Such was the case with the proletariat at the time of the Revolution of 1911.

After the May Fourth Movement, the chief political leader of China's bourgeois-democratic revolution was no longer the single class of the bourgeoisie, and the proletariat also participated in the political leadership. The Chinese proletariat rapidly became an awakened and independent political force as a result of its maturing and of the influence of the Russian Revolution. It was the Chinese Communist Party that put forward the slogan "Down with imperialism" and the thoroughgoing program for the whole of the bourgeois-democratic revolution, and it was the Chinese Communist Party alone that carried out the Agrarian Revolution.

Because the Chinese bourgeoisie is the bourgeoisie of a colonial and semi-colonial country, and because it is oppressed by imperialism, it retains at certain periods and to a certain degree — even in the era of imperialism — a certain revolutionary nature which leads it to fight against foreign imperialism and the domestic governments of bureaucrats and warlords (instances of opposition to the latter can be found in the periods of the Revolution of 1911 and the Northern Expedition, that is to say at periods when the bourgeoisie itself did not exercise power). It can ally itself with the proletariat and the petty bourgeoisie against such enemies as it is ready to oppose. In this respect the Chinese bourgeoisie differs from the bourgeoisie of the old Russian empire. Since the old Russian empire was itself already a military-feudal imperialism which carried on aggression against other countries, the Russian bourgeoisie was entirely lacking in revolutionary quality. There, the task of the proletariat was to oppose the bourgeoisie, not to unite with it. But because China is a colonial and semi-colonial country which is a victim of aggression, the Chinese bourgeoisie has a revolutionary quality at certain periods and to a certain degree. Here, the task of the proletariat is not to neglect this revolutionary quality of the bourgeoisie, or the possibility of establishing a united front with it against imperialism and the bureaucrat and warlord governments.

At the same time, however, precisely because the Chinese bourgeoisie is the bourgeoisie of a colonial and semi-colonial country, it is extremely flabby economically and politically, and it also has another quality, namely a proneness to compromise with the enemies of the revolution. The Chinese bourgeoisie, and especially the big bourgeoisie, even when it takes part in the revolution, is unwilling to break with imperialism completely, and is, moreover, closely associated with exploitation through the land in the rural areas. Thus it is neither willing nor able to overthrow imperialism thoroughly, still less to overthrow the feudal forces thoroughly. So neither of the two basic problems or tasks of China's bourgeois-democratic revolution can be solved or accomplished by the bourgeoisie. During the long period between 1927 and 1936, it nestled in the arms of the imperialists, formed an alliance with the feudal forces, betrayed its own revolutionary programs, and opposed the revolutionary people of the time.[14] During the War of Resistance, the section of the big bourgeoisie represented by Wang Jingwei[15] has once again capitulated to the enemy. This constitutes a fresh betrayal on the part of the big bourgeoisie. This is also a point with respect to which the bourgeoisie in China differs from the earlier bourgeoisie of the advanced countries in Europe and America, especially France. When the European and American countries were still in their revolutionary era, the bourgeoisie of those countries, and especially of France, was comparatively thorough in

[14]Mao is describing and criticizing the actions of the Nationalist government under Chiang Kai-shek.

[15]*Wang Jingwei:* a leader of the Guomindang who was sidelined by Chiang Kai-shek and then became head of the collaborationist regime in Nanjing during the Sino-Japanese War

carrying out the revolution. In China, the bourgeoisie does not possess even this degree of thoroughness.

On the one hand revolutionary nature, and on the other hand proneness to conciliation—such is the dual character of the Chinese bourgeoisie, which faces both ways. Even the bourgeoisie in European and American history shared this dual character. When confronted by a formidable enemy, they united with the workers and peasants against him, but when the workers and peasants awakened, they turned round to unite with the enemy against the workers and peasants. This is a general rule applicable to the bourgeoisie everywhere in the world, but the trait is more pronounced in the Chinese bourgeoisie.

In China, the situation is extremely clear. Whoever can lead the people in overthrowing imperialism and the feudal forces will be able to win the people's confidence, for the mortal enemies of the people are imperialism and the feudal forces, especially imperialism. Today, whoever can lead the people in driving out Japanese imperialism and introducing democratic government will be the savior of the people. If the Chinese bourgeoisie can fulfill this responsibility, no one will be able to refuse his admiration; but if it cannot do so, the responsibility will inevitably fall upon the shoulders of the proletariat.

Therefore, the proletariat, the peasantry, the intellectuals, and the other sections of the petty bourgeoisie undoubtedly constitute the basic forces determining China's fate. These classes, some already awakened and others in the process of awakening, will necessarily become the basic components of the state and governmental structure in the democratic republic of China. The Chinese democratic republic which we now desire to establish can only be a democratic republic under the joint dictatorship of all the anti-imperialist and anti-feudal people. That is to say that it will be a new-democratic republic, a republic of the genuinely revolutionary new Three People's Principles with their Three Great Policies.

This new-democratic republic will be different from the old European-American form of capitalist republic under bourgeois dictatorship, which is the old democratic form and already out-of-date. On the other hand, it will also be different from the socialist republic of the newest Soviet type under the dictatorship of the proletariat which is already flourishing in the USSR, and which, moreover, will be established in all the capitalist countries and will undoubtedly become the dominant form of state and governmental structure in all the advanced countries. For a certain historical period, however, this form is not suitable for the colonial and semi-colonial countries. During this period, therefore, a third form of state must be adopted in all colonial and semi-colonial countries, namely, the new-democratic republic. This is a form suited to a certain historical period, and is therefore a transitional form; nevertheless, it is a form which is necessary and cannot be dispensed with.

Thus the multifarious types of state system in the world, classified according to their social character, can be reduced to three basic kinds: (1) republics under bourgeois dictatorship; (2) republics under the dictatorship of the proletariat; and (3) republics under the joint dictatorship of several revolutionary classes.

The first kind comprises the old democratic states. Today, after outbreak of the second imperialist war, there is already not the slightest trace of democracy in any of the capitalist countries. They have all been transformed, or are about to be transformed, into bloody military dictatorships of the bourgeoisie. Certain countries under the joint dictatorship of the landlords and the bourgeoisie can be grouped with this kind.

Apart from the Soviet Union, the second kind is ripening in capitalist countries, and in the future, it will be the dominant form throughout the world for a certain period.

The third kind is the transitional form of state in the revolutionary colonies and semi-colonies. To be sure, the various colonies and semi-colonies will necessarily have different characteristics, but these are only minor differences within the general framework of uniformity. So long as they are revolutionary colonial or semi-colonial countries, their state and governmental structure will of necessity be basically the same, namely, a new-democratic state under the joint dictatorship of several anti-imperialist classes. In China today, the new-democratic state takes the form of the Anti-Japanese United Front. It is anti-Japanese and anti-imperialist; it is also a united front, an alliance of several revolutionary classes. But unfortunately, despite the fact that the War of Resistance has been going on for so long, the work of democratizing the state has hardly started, and the Japanese imperialists have exploited this fundamental weakness to stride into our country. If nothing is done about it, our national future will be gravely imperiled. We hope that the Movement for Constitutional Government that has just started will prevent this danger.

The question under discussion here is that of the "state system." After several decades of wrangling since the last years of the Qing dynasty, it has still not been cleared up. Actually it is simply a question of the status of the various social classes within the state. The bourgeoisie, as a rule, conceals the problem of class status and carries out its one-class dictatorship under the "national" label. Such concealment is of no advantage to the revolutionary people and the matter should be clearly explained to them. The term "national" can be used, but the people of the nation do not include counterrevolutionaries and Chinese traitors, and are comprised of all revolutionary people. The kind of state we need today is a dictatorship of all the revolutionary classes over the counterrevolutionaries and Chinese traitors.

The so-called democratic system in modern states is usually monopolized by the bourgeoisie and has become simply an instrument for oppressing the common people. On the other hand, the Guomindang's Principle of Democracy means a democratic system shared by all the common people and not privately owned by the few. Such was the solemn declaration made in the Manifesto of the First National Congress of the Guomindang, held in 1924. For sixteen years the Guomindang has violated this declaration and as a result it has created the present grave national crisis. This is a gross blunder, which we hope the Guomindang will correct in the cleansing flames of resistance to Japan.

As for the question of "political power," this is a matter of how political power is organized, the form in which one social class or another chooses to arrange its apparatus of political power to oppose its enemies and protect itself. There is no state which does not have an appropriate apparatus of political power to represent it. China may now adopt a system of congresses, from the national congress down to the provincial, county, district, and township congresses, with all levels electing their respective governmental bodies. But if there is to be proper representation for each revolutionary class according to its status in the state, a proper expression of the people's will, a proper direction for revolutionary struggles, and a proper manifestation of the spirit of New Democracy, then a system of really universal and equal suffrage, irrespective of sex, creed, property, or education, must be introduced. Such is the system of democratic centralism. Only a government based on democratic centralism can fully express the will of all the revolutionary people and fight the enemies of the revolution most effectively. There must be a spirit of refusal to be "privately owned by the few" in the government and the army; without a genuinely democratic system this cannot be attained and the system of government and the state system will be out of harmony.

The state system, a joint dictatorship of all the revolutionary classes, and the system of government, democratic centralism—these constitute the politics of New Democracy, the republic of New Democracy, the republic of the Anti-Japanese United Front, the republic of the new Three People's Principles with their Three Great Policies, the Republic of China in reality as well as in name. Today we have a Republic of China in name but not in reality, and our present task is to create the reality that will fit the name.

Such are the internal political relations which a revolutionary China, a China fighting Japanese aggression, should and must establish without fail; such is the orientation, the only correct orientation, for our present work of national reconstruction.

VI. THE ECONOMY OF NEW DEMOCRACY

If such a republic is to be established in China, it must be new-democratic not only in its politics but also in its economy.

The big banks and the big industrial and commercial enterprises will become state-owned.

> Enterprises such as banks, railways, and airlines, whether Chinese-owned or foreign-owned, which are either monopolistic in character or too big for private management, shall be operated and administered by the state, so that private capital cannot dominate the livelihood of the people: this is the main principle of the regulation of capital.

This is another solemn declaration in the Manifesto of the Guomindang's First National Congress, and it is the correct policy for the economic structure of the new-democratic republic. But at the same time the republic will neither confiscate capitalist private property in general nor forbid the development of such capitalist production as does not "dominate the livelihood of the people," for China's economy is still very backward.

The republic will take certain necessary steps to confiscate the land of the big landlords and distribute it to those peasants having little or no land, carry out Mr. Sun Yat-sen's slogan of "land to the tiller," abolish feudal relations in the rural areas, and turn the land over to the private ownership of the peasants without establishing a socialist agriculture. A rich peasant economy will be allowed in the rural areas. Such is the policy of "equalization of land ownership." "Land to the tiller" is the correct slogan for this policy.

China's economy must develop along the path of the "regulation of capital" and the "equalization of landownership," and must never be "privately owned by the few"; we must never permit the few capitalists and landlords to "dominate the livelihood of the people"; we must never establish a capitalist society of the European-American type or allow the old semi-feudal society to survive. Whoever dares to go counter to this line of advance will certainly not succeed but will run into a brick wall.

Such are the internal economic relations which a revolutionary China, a China fighting Japanese aggression, must and necessarily will establish.

Such is the economy of New Democracy.

And the politics of New Democracy are the concentrated expression of the economy of New Democracy.

VII. REFUTATION OF BOURGEOIS DICTATORSHIP

More than 90 percent of the people are in favor of a republic of this kind with its new-democratic politics and new-democratic economy; "without such a republic, nothing can be achieved, for it accords with the natural principles and people's sentiments, goes with the trend of the world, meets the demands of the people, and has been pursued resolutely by people of foresight" (Sun Yat-sen's words). There is no alternative road.

What about the road to a capitalist society under bourgeois dictatorship? To be sure, that was the old road taken by the European and American bourgeoisie, but whether one likes it or not, neither the international nor the domestic situation allows China to do the same.

Judging by the international situation, that road is blocked. In its fundamentals, the present international situation is one of a struggle between capitalism and socialism, in which capitalism is on the downgrade and socialism on the upgrade. In the first place international capitalism, or imperialism, will not permit it. Indeed the history of modern China is a history of imperialist aggression, of imperialist opposition to China's independence and to her development of capitalism. Earlier revolutions failed in China because imperialism strangled them, and innumerable revolutionary martyrs died, bitterly lamenting the non-fulfillment of their mission. Today a powerful Japanese imperialism is forcing its way into China and wants to reduce her to a colony; it is not China that is developing Chinese capitalism but Japan that is developing Japanese capitalism in our country; and it is not the Chinese bourgeoisie but the Japanese bourgeoisie that is exercising dictatorship in our country. True enough, this is the period of the final struggle of dying imperialism—imperialism is "moribund capitalism." But just because it is dying, it is all the more dependent on colonies and semi-colonies for survival and will certainly not allow any colony or semi-colony to establish anything like a capitalist society under the dictatorship of its own bourgeoisie. Just because Japanese imperialism is bogged down in serious economic and political crises, just because it is dying, it must invade China and reduce her to a colony, thereby blocking the road to bourgeois dictatorship and national capitalism in China. . . .

[For the rest of Section VII, and through Sections VIII and IX, Mao spends six pages refuting alternate ideas for what China should do—from liberals, to extreme leftists, to die-hard conservatives.]

X. THE THREE PEOPLE'S PRINCIPLES, OLD AND NEW

The bourgeois die-hards have no understanding whatsoever of historical change; their knowledge is so poor that it is practically nonexistent. They do not know the difference either between communism and the Three People's Principles or between the new Three People's Principles and the old.

We Communists recognize "the Three People's Principles as the political basis for the Anti-Japanese United Front," we acknowledge that "the Three People's Principles being what China needs today, our Party is ready to fight for their complete realization," and we admit the basic agreement between the Communist minimum program and the political tenets of the Three People's Principles. But which kind of Three People's Principles? The Three People's Principles as reinterpreted by Mr. Sun Yat-Sen in the Manifesto of the First National Congress of the Guomindang, and no other. I wish the die-hard gentlemen would spare a moment from the work of "restricting communism," "corroding communism," and "combating communism," in which they are so gleefully engaged, to glance through this manifesto. In the manifesto Mr. Sun Yat-sen said: "Here is the true interpretation of the Guomindang's Three People's Principles." Hence these are the only genuine Three People's Principles and all others are spurious. The only "true interpretation" of the Three People's Principles is the one contained in the Manifesto of the First National Congress of the Guomindang, and all other interpretations are false. Presumably this is no Communist fabrication, for many Guomindang members and I myself personally witnessed the adoption of the manifesto.

The manifesto marks off the two epochs in the history of the Three People's Principles. Before it, they belonged to the old category; they were the Three People's Principles of the old bourgeois-democratic revolution in a semi-colony, the Three People's Principles of old democracy, the old Three People's Principles.

After it, they came within the new category; they became the Three People's Principles of the new bourgeois-democratic revolution in a semi-colony, the Three People's Principles of New Democracy, the new Three People's Principles. These and these alone are the revolutionary Three People's Principles of the new period.

The revolutionary Three People's Principles of the new period, the new or genuine Three People's Principles, embody the Three Great Policies of alliance with Russia, cooperation with the Communist Party, and assistance to the peasants and workers. Without each and every one of these Three Great Policies, the Three People's Principles become either false or incomplete in the new period.

In the first place, the revolutionary, new, or genuine Three People's Principles must include alliance with Russia. The present situation is perfectly clear. If there is no policy of uniting with Russia, if we do not unite with the land of socialism, there will inevitably be a policy of uniting with imperialism, we will inevitably unite with imperialism. Is it not evident that this is exactly what happened after 1927? During the first two years of the War of Resistance against Japan, because the Great Imperialist War had not yet broken out, the contradictions between Britain, the United States, and other countries and Japan could still be exploited. Since the outbreak of the Imperialist World War, these contradictions, although they have not entirely disappeared, have greatly diminished. If we were to make improper use of them, then England and the United States could demand that China participate in their struggle against the Soviet Union. If China then complied with their demand, she would immediately place herself on the side of the reactionary front of imperialism, thus putting an end to all national independence. Once the conflict between the socialist Soviet Union and imperialist Britain and the United States grows sharper, China will have to take her stand on one side or the other. This is an inevitable trend. Is it not possible to avoid leaning to either side? No, that is an illusion. The entire globe will be swept into one or the other of these two fronts, and henceforth "neutrality" will be merely a deceptive term. Especially is this true of China, which is fighting an imperialist power that has penetrated deep into her territory; her final victory is inconceivable without the assistance of the Soviet Union. If alliance with Russia is sacrificed for the sake of alliance with imperialism, the word "revolutionary" will have to be expunged from the Three People's Principles, which will then become reactionary. In the last analysis, there can be no "neutral" Three People's Principles; they can only be either revolutionary or counter-revolutionary. Would it not be more heroic to "fight against attacks from both sides" as Wang Jingwei once remarked, and to have the kind of Three People's Principles that serves this "fight"? Unfortunately, even its inventor Wang Jingwei himself has abandoned (or "folded up") this kind of Three People's Principles, for he has adopted the Three People's Principles of alliance with imperialism. If it is argued that there is a difference between Eastern and Western imperialism, and that, unlike Wang Jingwei who has allied himself with Eastern imperialism, you should ally yourself with some motherfucking Western imperialists to march eastward and attack, then would not such conduct be quite revolutionary? But whether you like it or not, the Western imperialists are determined to oppose the Soviet Union and communism, and if you ally yourself with them, they will ask you to march northward and attack, and your revolution will come to nothing. All these circumstances make it essential for the revolutionary, new, and genuine Three People's Principles to include alliance with Russia, and under no circumstances alliance with imperialism against Russia.

In the second place, the revolutionary, new, and genuine Three People's Principles must include cooperation with the Communist Party. Either you cooperate with the Communist Party or you oppose it. Opposition to communism is the policy of the Japanese imperialists and Wang Jingwei, and if that is what you want, very well, they will invite you to join their Anti-Communist Company. But wouldn't that look suspiciously like turning traitor? You may say, "I am not following Japan, but some other country." That is just ridiculous. No matter whom you follow, the moment you oppose the Communist Party you become a traitor, because you can no longer resist Japan. If you say, "I am going to oppose the Communist Party independently," that is arrant nonsense. How can the "heroes" in a colony or semi-colony tackle a counterrevolutionary job of this magnitude without depending on the strength of imperialism? For ten long years, virtually all the imperialist forces in the world were enlisted against the Communist Party, but in vain. How can you suddenly oppose it "independently"?

Some people outside the Border Region, we are told, are now saying: "Opposing the Communist Party is good, but you can never succeed in it." This remark, if it is not simply hearsay, is only half wrong, for what "good" is there in opposing the Communist Party? But the other half is true, you certainly can "never succeed in it." Basically, the reason lies not with the Communists but with the common people, who like the Communist Party and do not like "opposing" it. If you oppose the Communist Party at a juncture when our national enemy is penetrating deep into our territory, the people will be after your hide; they will certainly show you no mercy. This much is certain, whoever wants to oppose the Communist Party must be prepared to be ground to dust. If you are not keen on being ground to dust, you had certainly better drop this opposition. This is our sincere advice to all the anti-Communist "heroes." Thus it is as clear as can be that the Three People's Principles of today must include cooperation with the Communist Party, or otherwise those Principles will perish. It is a question of life and death for the Three People's Principles. Cooperating with the Communist Party, they will survive; opposing the Communist Party, they will perish. Can anyone prove the contrary?

In the third place, the revolutionary, new, and genuine Three People's Principles must include the policy of assisting the peasants and workers. Rejection of this policy, failure whole-heartedly to assist the peasants and workers or failure to carry out the behest in Mr. Sun Yat-sen's Testament to "arouse the masses of the people," amounts to preparing the way for the defeat of the revolution, and one's own defeat into the bargain. Stalin has said that "in essence, the question of colonies and semi-colonies is a peasant question."[16] This means that the Chinese revolution is essentially a peasant revolution and that the resistance to Japan now going on is essentially peasant resistance. Essentially, the politics of New Democracy means giving the peasants their rights. The new and genuine Three People's Principles are essentially the principles of a peasant revolution. Essentially, mass culture means raising the cultural level of the peasants. The anti-Japanese war is essentially a peasant war. We are now living in a time when the "doctrine of going up to the

---

[16]Translated in J. V. Stalin, "Concerning the National Question in Yugoslavia," in *Works,* 7:71–72.

mountains"[17] applies; everyone is on the top of the hills; meetings, work, classes, newspaper publication, the writing of books, theatrical performances—everything is done up in the hills, and all essentially for the sake of the peasants. And essentially it is the peasants who provide everything that sustains the resistance to Japan and keeps us going. By "essentially" we mean basically, not ignoring the other sections of the people, as Stalin himself has explained. As every schoolboy knows, 80 percent of China's population are peasants, more than 80 percent after the fall of the big cities. So the peasant problem becomes the basic problem of the Chinese revolution and the strength of the peasants is the main strength of the Chinese revolution. In the Chinese population the workers rank second to the peasants in number. There are several million industrial workers in China and several tens of millions of handicraft workers and agricultural laborers. China cannot live without them, because they are the producers in the industrial sector of the economy. And the revolution cannot succeed without them, because they are the leaders of the Chinese revolution and the most revolutionary class. In these circumstances, the revolutionary, new, and genuine Three People's Principles must include the policy of assisting the peasants and workers. Any other kind of Three People's Principles which lack this policy, do not give the peasants and workers wholehearted assistance, or do not carry out the behest to "arouse the masses of the people" will certainly perish.

Thus it is clear that there is no future for any Three People's Principles which depart from the Three Great Policies of alliance with Russia, cooperation with the Communist Party, and assistance to the peasants and workers. Every conscientious follower of the Three People's Principles must seriously consider this point.

The Three People's Principles comprising the Three Great Policies—in other words, the revolutionary, new, and genuine Three People's Principles—are the Three People's Principles of New Democracy, a development of the old Three People's Principles, a great contribution of Mr. Sun Yat-sen, and a product of the era in which the Chinese revolution has become part of the world socialist revolution. It is only the Three People's Principles which the Chinese Communist Party regards as "being what China needs today" and for whose "complete realization" it declares itself pledged "to fight." These are the only Three People's Principles which are in basic agree-

---

[17]*going up to the mountains:* forming base areas in remote places, such as Shaan-Gan-Ning

ment with the Communist Party's political program for the stage of democratic revolution, namely with its minimum program.

As for the old Three People's Principles, they were a product of the old period of the Chinese revolution. Russia was then an imperialist power, and naturally there could be no policy of alliance with her; there was then no Communist Party in existence in our country and naturally there could be no policy of cooperation with it; the movement of the workers and peasants had not yet revealed its full political significance and aroused people's attention, and naturally there could be no policy of alliance with them. Hence the Three People's Principles of the period before the reorganization of the Guomindang in the thirteenth year of the Republic [1924] belonged to the old category, and they became obsolete. The Guomindang could not have gone forward unless it had developed them into the new Three People's Principles. Mr. Sun Yat-sen in his wisdom saw this point, secured the help of Lenin and the Chinese Communist Party, and reinterpreted the Three People's Principles so as to endow them with new characteristics suited to the times. As a result, a united front was formed between the Three People's Principles and communism, Guomindang-Communist cooperation was established for the first time, the sympathy of the people of the whole country was won, and the First Great Revolution was launched.

The old Three People's Principles were revolutionary in the old period and reflected its historical features. But if the old stuff is repeated in the new period after the new Three People's Principles have been established, or alliance with Russia is opposed after the socialist state has been established, or cooperation with the Communist Party is opposed after the Communist Party has come into existence, or the policy of assisting the peasants and workers is opposed after they have awakened and demonstrated their political strength, then that is reactionary and shows ignorance of the times. The period of reaction after 1927 was the result of such ignorance. The old proverb says, "Whosoever understands the signs of the times is a great man." I hope the followers of the Three People's Principles today will bear this in mind.

Were the Three People's Principles to fall within the old category, then they would have nothing basically in common with the Communist minimum program, because they would belong to the past and be obsolete. Any sort of Three People's Principles that oppose Russia, the Communist Party, or the peasants and workers are definitely reactionary; they not only have absolutely nothing in common with the

Communist minimum program but are the enemy of communism, and there is no common ground at all. This, too, the followers of the Three People's Principles should carefully consider.

In any case, people with a conscience will never forsake the new Three People's Principles until the task of opposing imperialism and feudalism is basically accomplished. The only ones who do are people like Wang Jingwei. No matter how energetically they push their spurious Three People's Principles which oppose Russia, the Communist Party, and the peasants and workers, there will surely be no lack of people with a conscience and sense of justice who will continue to support Sun Yat-sen's genuine Three People's Principles. Many followers of the genuine Three People's Principles continued the struggle for the Chinese revolution even after the reaction of 1927, and the numbers will undoubtedly swell to tens upon tens of thousands now that the national enemy has penetrated deep into our territory. We Communists will always persevere in long-term cooperation with all the true followers of the Three People's Principles and, while rejecting the traitors and the sworn enemies of communism, will never forsake any of our friends.

XI. THE CULTURE OF NEW DEMOCRACY

In the foregoing we have explained the historical characteristics of Chinese politics in the new period and the question of the new democratic republic. We can now proceed to the question of culture.

A given culture is the ideological reflection of the politics and economics of a given society. There is in China an imperialist culture which is a reflection of imperialist rule, or partial rule, in the political and economic fields. This culture is fostered not only by the cultural organizations run directly by the imperialists in China but by a number of Chinese who have lost all sense of shame. Into this category falls all culture embodying a slave ideology. China also has a semi-feudal culture which reflects her semi-feudal politics and economy and whose exponents include all those who advocate the worship of Confucius, the study of the Confucian canon, the old ethical code, and the old ideas in opposition to the new culture and new ideas. Imperialist culture and semi-feudal culture are devoted brothers and have formed a reactionary cultural alliance against China's new culture. This kind of reactionary culture serves the imperialists and the feudal class and must be swept away. Unless it is swept away, no new culture of any kind can be built up. There is no construction without destruction, no flowing without damming, and no motion without rest; the two are locked in a life-and-death struggle.

As for the new culture, it is the ideological reflection of the new politics and the new economy which it sets out to serve.

As we have already stated in Section III, Chinese society has gradually changed in character since the emergence of a capitalist economy in China; it is no longer an entirely feudal but a semi-feudal society, although the feudal economy still predominates. Compared with the feudal economy, this capitalist economy is a new one. The political forces of the bourgeoisie, the petty bourgeoisie, and the proletariat are the new political forces which have emerged and grown simultaneously with this new capitalist economy. Various revolutionary parties, the Guomindang and the Communist Party being the most important among them, are the representatives of the awakened bourgeoisie, the petty bourgeoisie, and the proletariat. And the new culture reflects these new economic and political forces in the field of ideology and serves them. Without the capitalist economy, without the bourgeoisie, the petty bourgeoisie, and the proletariat, and without the political parties of these classes, the new ideology or new culture could not have emerged.

These new political, economic, and cultural forces are all revolutionary forces which are opposed to the old politics, the old economy, and the old culture. The old is composed of two parts, one being China's own semi-feudal politics, economy, and culture, and the other the politics, economy, and culture of imperialism, with the latter heading the alliance. Both are bad and should be completely destroyed. The struggle between the new and the old in Chinese society is a struggle between the new forces of the people (the various revolutionary classes) and the old forces of imperialism and the feudal class. It is a struggle between revolution and counterrevolution. This struggle has lasted a full hundred years starting from the Opium War, and nearly thirty years starting from the Revolution of 1911.

But as already indicated, revolutions too can be classified into old and new, and what is new in one historical period becomes old in another. The century of China's bourgeois-democratic revolution can be divided into two main stages, a first stage of eighty years and a second of twenty years. Each has its basic historical characteristics. China's bourgeois-democratic revolution in the first eighty years belongs to the old category, while in the last twenty years, owing to the change in the international and domestic political situation, it belongs to the new category. Old democracy is the characteristic of the first eighty years. New Democracy is the characteristic of the last twenty. This distinction holds good in culture as well as in politics. How does it manifest itself in the field of culture? We shall explain this next.

XII. THE HISTORICAL CHARACTERISTICS OF CHINA'S CULTURAL REVOLUTION

On the cultural or ideological front, the two periods preceding and following the May Fourth Movement form two distinct historical periods.

Before the May Fourth Movement, the struggle on China's cultural front was one between the new culture of the bourgeoisie and the old culture of the feudal class. The struggles between the modern school system and the imperial examination system, between the new learning and the old learning, and between Western learning and Chinese learning, were all of this nature. The so-called modern schools or new learning or Western learning of that time concentrated mainly (we say mainly, because in part pernicious vestiges of Chinese feudalism still remained) on the bourgeois natural sciences and social sciences. In addition to the natural sciences at the time, the new schools before the May Fourth Movement were dominated by the ideology represented by Darwin's theory of evolution, Adam Smith's classical economics, Mill's formal logic, and French Enlightenment scholar Montesquieu's socialism introduced to China by Yan Fu.[18] At the time, this ideology played a revolutionary role in fighting the Chinese feudal ideology, and it served the bourgeois-democratic revolution of the old period. But because the Chinese bourgeoisie lacked strength and the world had already entered the era of imperialism, this bourgeois ideology was only able to last out a few rounds and was beaten back by the reactionary alliance of the enslaving ideology of foreign imperialism and the "back to the ancients" ideology of Chinese feudalism; as soon as this reactionary ideological alliance started a minor counteroffensive, the so-called new learning lowered its banners, muffled its drums, and beat a retreat, retaining its outer form but losing its soul. The old bourgeois-democratic culture became enervated and decayed in the era of imperialism, and its failure was inevitable.

---

[18] *Yan Fu:* the translator and interpreter of some of the most influential European thinkers at the turn of the twentieth century. Mao and others read Yan's translations of Charles Darwin, Herbert Spencer, John Stuart Mill, and others.

But since the May Fourth Movement things have been different. A brand-new cultural force came into being in China, that is, the Communist culture and ideology guided by the Chinese Communists, or the Communist world outlook and theory of social revolution. The May Fourth Movement occurred in 1919, and in 1921 came the founding of the Chinese Communist Party and the real beginning of China's labor movement—all in the wake of the First World War and the October Revolution, i.e., at a time when the national problem and the colonial movements of the world underwent a change, and the connection between the Chinese revolution and the world revolution became quite obvious. The new political force of the proletariat and the Communist Party mounted the Chinese political stage, and as a result, the new cultural force, in new uniform and with new weapons, mustering all possible allies and deploying its ranks in battle array, launched heroic attacks on imperialist culture and feudal culture. Although this vital force has not yet had the time to occupy the field of natural sciences and carry out a fight in it, in general allowing the bourgeois world outlook to dominate it temporarily, it has aroused a great revolution in the social science field, which provides the most important ideological weapons in the era of revolutions in the colonies and semi-colonies. This new force has made great strides in the domain of the social sciences, whether of philosophy, economics, political science, military science, history, literature, or art (including the theater, the cinema, music, sculpture, and painting). For the last twenty years, wherever this new cultural force has directed its attack, a great revolution has taken place both in ideological content and in form (for example, in the written language[19]). Its influence has been so great and its impact so powerful that it is invincible wherever it goes. The numbers it has rallied behind it have no parallel in Chinese history. Lu Xun[20] was the greatest and the most courageous standard-bearer of this new cultural force. The chief commander of China's cultural revolution, he was not only a great man of letters but a great thinker and revolutionary. Lu Xun was a man of unyielding integrity, free from all sycophancy or obsequiousness; this quality is invaluable among colonial and semi-colonial peoples. Representing the great

[19]Mao is referring to changes in written Chinese from the complex classical language to the vernacular, or *baihua*. This was a major cultural change, as it contributed to a rapid rise in popular literacy.

[20]*Lu Xun:* China's most famous man of letters in the 1920s and 1930s; considered China's foremost writer of the twentieth century. He was a biting social critic and came to support the Communist cause, although he never joined the CCP.

majority of the nation, Lu Xun breached and stormed the enemy citadel; on the cultural front he was the bravest and most correct, the firmest, the most loyal and the most ardent national hero, a hero without parallel in our history. The road he took was the very road of China's new national culture.

Prior to the May Fourth Movement, China's new culture was a culture of the old-democratic kind and part of the capitalist cultural revolution of the world bourgeoisie. Since the May Fourth Movement, it has become new-democratic and part of the socialist cultural revolution of the world proletariat.

Prior to the May Fourth Movement, China's new cultural movement, her cultural revolution, was led by the bourgeoisie, which still had a leading role to play. After the May Fourth Movement, the culture and ideology of this class became even more backward than its politics, and it was incapable of playing any leading role; at most, it could serve to a certain extent as an ally during revolutionary periods, while inevitably the responsibility for leading the alliance rested on proletarian culture and ideology. This is an undeniable fact.

The new-democratic culture is the anti-imperialist and anti-feudal culture of the broad masses; today it is the culture of the Anti-Japanese United Front. This culture can be led only by the culture and ideology of the proletariat, by the ideology of communism, and not by the culture and ideology of any other class. In a word, new-democratic culture is the proletarian-led, anti-imperialist, and anti-feudal culture of the broad masses.

XIII. THE FOUR PERIODS

A cultural revolution is the ideological reflection of the political and economic revolutions, and serves them. In China there is a united front in the cultural as in the political revolution.

The history of the united front in the cultural revolution during the last twenty years can be divided into four periods. The first covers the two years from 1919 to 1921, the second the six years from 1921 to 1927, the third the nine years from 1927 to 1936, and the fourth the three years from 1937 to the present.

The first period extended from the May Fourth Movement of 1919 to the founding of the Chinese Communist Party in 1921. The May Fourth Movement was its chief landmark.

The May Fourth Movement was an anti-imperialist as well as an anti-feudal movement. Its outstanding historical significance is to be seen in a feature which was absent from the Revolution of 1911, namely its thorough and uncompromising opposition to imperialism as well as to feudalism. The May Fourth Movement possessed this quality because capitalism had developed a step further in China and because new hopes had arisen for the liberation of the Chinese nation as China's revolutionary intellectual class saw the collapse of three great imperialist powers—Russia, Germany, and Austria-Hungary—and the weakening of two others, Britain and France, while the Russian proletariat had established a socialist state and the German, Hungarian, and Italian proletariat had risen in revolution. The May Fourth Movement came into being at the call of the world revolution of the time, of the Russian Revolution, and of Lenin. It was part of the world proletarian revolution of the time. Although at the time of the May Fourth Movement the Chinese Communist Party had not yet come into existence, there were already large numbers of intellectuals who approved of the Russian Revolution and had the rudiments of Communist ideology. In the beginning the May Fourth Movement was a revolutionary movement of the united front of three sections of people— Communist intellectuals, revolutionary petty-bourgeois intellectuals, and bourgeois intellectuals (the last forming the right wing at that time). Its weak point was that it was confined to the intellectuals, and the workers and peasants did not participate in it. But as soon as it developed into the June Third Movement,[21] not only the intellectuals but the mass of the proletariat, the petty bourgeoisie, and the bourgeoisie joined in, and it became a nationwide revolutionary movement. The cultural revolution ushered in by the May Fourth Movement was uncompromising in its opposition to feudal culture; there had never been such a great and thoroughgoing cultural revolution since the dawn of Chinese history. Raising aloft the two great banners of the day, "Down with the old ethics and up with the new!" and "Down with the old literature and up with the new!" the cultural revolution had great achievements to its credit. At that time it was not yet possible for this cultural movement to become widely diffused among the workers and peasants. The slogan of "Literature for the common people" was

[21]*June Third Movement:* an important extension of the demonstrations of May 4, 1919, in which students linked with workers to hold labor strikes in defiance of police repression

advanced, but in fact the "common people" then could only refer to the petty-bourgeois and bourgeois intellectuals in the cities, that is, the so-called urban intelligentsia. Both in ideology and in the matter of cadres, the May Fourth Movement paved the way for the founding of the Chinese Communist Party in 1921, for the May Thirtieth Movement of 1925,[22] and for the Northern Expedition. The bourgeois intellectuals, who constituted the right wing of the May Fourth Movement, mostly compromised with the enemy in the second period and went over to the side of reaction.

In the second period, whose landmarks were the founding of the Chinese Communist Party, the May Thirtieth Movement, and the Northern Expedition, the united front of the three classes formed during the May Fourth Movement was continued and expanded. This united front also took form politically, this being the first instance of Guomindang-Communist cooperation. Mr. Sun Yat-sen was a great man not only because he led the great Revolution of 1911 (although it was only a democratic revolution of the old period), but also because, "adapting himself to the trends of the world and meeting the needs of the masses," he had the capacity to bring forward the revolutionary Three Great Policies of alliance with Russia, cooperation with the Communist Party, and assistance to the peasants and workers, give new meaning to the Three People's Principles, and thus institute the new Three People's Principles with their Three Great Policies. Previously, the Three People's Principles had exerted little influence on the educational and academic world or with youth, because they had not raised the issues of opposition to imperialism or to the feudal social system and feudal culture. They were the old Three People's Principles which people regarded as the time-serving banner of a group of men bent on seizing power, in other words, on securing official positions, a banner used purely for political maneuvering. Then came the new Three People's Principles with their Three Great Policies. The cooperation between the Guomindang and the Communist Party and the joint efforts of the revolutionary members of the two parties spread the new Three People's Principles all over China, extending to a section of the educational and academic world and the mass of student youth. This was entirely because the original Three People's Principles had developed into the anti-imperialist, anti-feudal,

---

[22] *May Thirtieth Movement of 1925:* started with a violent confrontation between protesters and British soldiers in Shanghai and touched off nationwide demonstrations and boycotts against foreign goods in China

and new-democratic Three People's Principles with their Three Great Policies. Without this development it would have been impossible to disseminate the ideas of the Three People's Principles.

During this period, the revolutionary Three People's Principles became the political basis of the united front of the Guomindang and the Communist Party and of all the revolutionary classes, and since "communism is the good friend of the Three People's Principles," a united front was formed between the two of them. In terms of social classes, it was a united front of three classes of the proletariat, the petty bourgeoisie, and the bourgeoisie. Using the Guomindang's *Republican Daily News* of Shanghai and other newspapers in various localities as their bases of operations, the two parties jointly advocated anti-imperialism, jointly combated feudal education based upon the worship of Confucius and upon the study of the Confucian canon, and jointly opposed feudal literature and the classical language and promoted the new literature and the vernacular style of writing with an anti-imperialist and anti-feudal content. During the wars in Guangdong and during the Northern Expedition, they reformed China's armed forces by the inculcation of anti-imperialist and anti-feudal ideas. The slogans, "Down with the corrupt officials" and "Down with the local bullies and bad gentry," were first raised among the peasant millions, and great peasant revolutionary struggles were aroused. Thanks to all this and to the assistance of the Soviet Union, the Northern Expedition was victorious. But no sooner did the bourgeoisie climb to power with the help of workers and peasants than it put an end to this great revolution, thus creating an entirely new political situation.

The third period was the new revolutionary period of 1927–36. As a result of the changes which had taken place within the revolutionary camp at the end of the previous period, with the bourgeoisie going over to the counterrevolutionary camp of the imperialist and feudal forces, only two of the three classes formerly within the revolutionary camp remained, namely, the proletariat and the petty bourgeoisie (including the peasantry, the revolutionary intellectuals, and other sections of the petty bourgeoisie). Thus the Chinese revolution inevitably entered a new period in which the Chinese Communist Party alone exercised the leadership. This period was one of reactionary campaigns of "encirclement and suppression," on the one hand, and of the deepening of the revolution, on the other. There were two kinds of reactionary campaigns of "encirclement and suppression," the military and the cultural. The deepening of the revolution was of two kinds; both the agrarian and the cultural revolutions were deepened. At the instigation of the imperialists, the reactionary forces of the whole country and of the whole world were mobilized for both kinds of campaigns of "encirclement and suppression," which lasted no less than ten years and were unparalleled in their ruthlessness; hundreds of thousands of Communists and young students were slaughtered and millions of workers and peasants suffered cruel persecution. The people responsible for all this apparently had no doubt that communism and the Communist Party could be "exterminated once and for all." However, the outcome was different; both kinds of "encirclement and suppression" campaigns failed miserably. The military campaign resulted in the northern march of the Red Army to resist the Japanese,[23] and the cultural campaign resulted in the outbreak of the December Ninth movement of the revolutionary youth in 1935. And the common result of both was the awakening of the people of the whole country. These were three positive results. But the negative result was the attack by a powerful enemy; this is the key reason why the people of the whole country to this day bitterly detest the anti-communism of those ten years. The most amazing thing of all was that the Guomindang's cultural "encirclement and suppression" campaign failed completely in the Guomindang areas as well, although the Communist Party was in an utterly defenseless position in all the cultural and educational institutions there. Why did this happen? Does it not give food for prolonged and deep thought? It was in the very midst of such campaigns of "encirclement and suppression" that Lu Xun, who believed in communism, became the giant of China's cultural revolution.

In the struggles of this period, the revolutionary side firmly upheld the people's anti-imperialist and anti-feudal New Democracy and their new Three People's Principles, while the counterrevolutionary side, under the direction of imperialism, imposed the despotic regime of the coalition of the landlord class. That despotic regime butchered Mr. Sun Yat-sen's Three Great Policies and his new Three People's Principles both politically and culturally, with catastrophic consequences to the Chinese nation.

The fourth period is that of the present anti-Japanese war. Pursuing its zigzag course, the Chinese revolution has again arrived at a united front of the three classes. But this time the scope is much broader.

---

[23]Mao is referring to the Long March of 1934–35, which ultimately brought the main CCP forces to Yan'an.

Among the upper classes it includes all the rulers. Among the middle classes, it includes the petty bourgeoisie in its totality. Among the lower classes, it includes the entire proletariat. All classes and strata of the country have become allies, and are resolutely resisting Japanese imperialism. The first stage of this period lasted until the fall of Wuhan. During that stage, there was a lively atmosphere in the country in every field; politically there was a trend toward democracy and culturally there was widespread activity. With the fall of Wuhan [in October 1938] the second stage began, during which the political situation has undergone many changes, with one section of the big bourgeoisie capitulating to the enemy and another desiring an end to the War of Resistance. In the cultural movement, this situation has been reflected in the reactionary activities of Ye Qing,[24] Zhang Junmai, and others, and in the suppression of freedom of speech and of the press.

To overcome this crisis, a firm struggle is necessary against all ideas opposed to resistance, unity, and progress, and unless these reactionary ideas are crushed, there will be no hope of victory. How will this struggle turn out? This is the big question in the minds of the people of the whole country. Judging by the domestic and international situation, the Chinese people are bound to win, however numerous the obstacles on the path of resistance. If we consider Chinese history as a whole, the progress achieved during the twenty years since the May Fourth Movement not only surpasses that of the preceding eighty years, it truly surpasses that achieved of several millennia. Can we not visualize what further progress China will make in another twenty years? The unbridled violence of all the forces of darkness, whether domestic or foreign, has brought disaster to our nation; but this very violence indicates that while the forces of darkness still have some strength left, they are already in their death throes, and that the people are gradually approaching victory. This is true in the East and in the entire world. . . .

[In Section XIV Mao reviews in about two pages what he sees as wrong ideas about culture and how Communists and their supporters should struggle against these errors by spreading Marxism-Leninism.]

---

[24] *Ye Qing:* a former leftist who used Marxist theory to attack CCP policies

XV. A NATIONAL, SCIENTIFIC, AND MASS CULTURE

New-democratic culture is national. It opposes imperialist oppression and upholds the dignity and independence of the Chinese nation. It belongs to this nation of ours, and bears our own national characteristics. It links up with the socialist and new-democratic cultures of other nations, and establishes with them the relations whereby they can absorb something from each other and help each other to develop, mutually forming a part of a new world culture. But it can absolutely not link up with any reactionary imperialist culture of whatever nation, for our culture is a revolutionary national culture. China must assimilate on a large scale the progressive culture of foreign countries, as an ingredient for enriching her own culture. Not enough of this was done in the past. We should assimilate whatever is useful to us today not only from the present-day socialist and new-democratic cultures, but also from the older cultures of foreign countries, for example, from the culture of the various capitalist countries in the Age of Enlightenment. However, we absolutely cannot gulp down any of this foreign material uncritically, but must treat it as we do our food—first chewing it in the mouth, then subjecting it to the working of the stomach and intestines with their juices and secretions, and separating it into essence to be absorbed and waste matter to be discarded—before it can nourish us. So-called "wholesale Westernization" is wrong. China has suffered a great deal in the past from the formalist absorption of foreign things. Similarly, in applying Marxism to China, Chinese Communists must fully and properly integrate the universal truth of Marxism with the concrete practice of the Chinese revolution, or in other words, the universal truth of Marxism must have a national form if it is to be useful, and in no circumstances can it be applied subjectively as a mere formula. Marxists who make a fetish of formulas are simply playing with Marxism and the Chinese revolution, and there is no room for them in the ranks of the Chinese revolution. Chinese culture should have its own form, its own national form. National in form and new-democratic in content—such is our new culture today.

New-democratic culture is scientific. Opposed as it is to all feudal and superstitious ideas, it stands for "seek truth from facts," for objective truth, and for the unity of theory and practice. On this point, the possibility exists of a united front against imperialism, feudalism, and superstition between the scientific thought of the Chinese proletariat and those Chinese bourgeois materialists and natural scientists who are progressive, but in no case is there a possibility of a united front with any reactionary idealism. In the field of political action Communists may form an anti-imperialist united front with some idealists and even religious people, but we can never approve of their idealism or religious doctrines. A splendid ancient culture was created during the long period of China's feudal society. Therefore, to clarify the process of development of this ancient culture, to discard its feudal dross and assimilate its democratic essence, is a necessary condition for developing our new national culture and increasing our national self-confidence, but we absolutely cannot swallow anything and everything uncritically. We must separate the fine, old popular culture which had a more or less democratic and revolutionary character from all the rotten things of the old feudal ruling class. China's present new politics and new economy have developed out of her old politics and old economy, and her present new culture, too, has developed out of her old culture. Consequently, we must respect our own history and can absolutely not mutilate history. Respect for history means, however, giving it its proper place as a science, respecting its dialectical development, and not eulogizing the past at the expense of the present or praising every drop of feudal poison. As far as the masses and the young students are concerned, the essential thing is to guide them to look forward and not backward.

New-democratic culture belongs to the broad masses and is therefore democratic. It should serve the toiling masses of workers and peasants who make up more than 90 percent of the nation's population and should gradually become their very own. There is a difference of degree, as well as a close link, between the knowledge imparted to the revolutionary cadres and the knowledge imparted to the revolutionary masses, between the raising of cultural standards and popularization. Revolutionary culture is a powerful revolutionary weapon for the broad masses of the people. It prepares the ground ideologically before the revolution comes and is an important, indeed essential, fighting front in the general revolutionary front during the revolution. People engaged in revolutionary cultural work are the commanders at various levels on this cultural front. "Without revolutionary theory there can be no revolutionary movement"; one can thus see how important the cultural movement is for the practical revolutionary movement. Both the cultural and practical movements must be of the masses. Therefore all progressive cultural workers in the anti-Japanese war must have their own cultural battalions, that is, the broad masses. A cultural worker or a cultural ideology detached from the popular masses is a "shadow" commander without an army, whose firepower cannot bring the enemy down. To attain this objective, written Chinese must be reformed, given the requisite conditions, and our spoken language brought closer to that of the people, for the people, it must be stressed, are the inexhaustible source of our revolutionary culture.

A national, scientific, and mass culture—such is the anti-imperialist and anti-feudal culture of the people, the culture of New Democracy and the new Three People's Principles, the new culture of the Chinese nation.

Combine the politics, the economy, and the culture of New Democracy, and you have the new-democratic republic, the Republic of China both in name and in reality, the new China we want to create.

Behold, New China is within sight. Let us all hail her!
Her masts have already risen above the horizon. Let us all cheer in
welcome!
Raise both your hands. New China is ours!

3

Talks at the Yan'an Conference on Literature and Art

1942

As Mao consolidated his power over the CCP in Yan'an in the early 1940s, he was unexpectedly confronted by biting criticism of the party's failure to live up to its own egalitarian goals. These criticisms came from the CCP's left-wing intellectuals, hundreds of whom had come to Yan'an after the outbreak of war with Japan in 1937. In May 1942, Mao paused the Rectification Movement—his broader campaign to eliminate his senior party rivals and mobilize the party rank and file to the ideals of his "On New Democracy" (see Document 2)—to discipline his way-

"Zai Yan'an wenyi zuotanhui shangde jianghua," Jiefang ribao, 19 Oct. 1943. Translation from Bonnie S. McDougall, Mao Zedong's "Talks at the Yan'an Conference on Literature and Art": A Translation of the 1943 Text with Commentary (Ann Arbor: Michigan Studies in Chinese Studies, 1980), 57–58, 60–61, 69–70, 75. McDougall carefully notes the changes made for the official 1951 Selected Works edition in her endnotes, which are not retained here.

ward left-wing critics. The result was the Yan'an Conference on Literature and Art.

The brief extracts here from Mao's talks at the conference focus on two fundamental points: First, the importance of the social role of art (in service of the revolution) and the need for art to subordinate itself to politics. Mao's view of art is not romantic. He sees "cultural workers" as just another brigade in the revolutionary army. Yet he acknowledges that they are a necessary "screw" in the revolutionary machine. Second, Mao outlines what artists need to do to "serve the people." They need to "become one with the masses" by the physical act of living, working, and fighting against the Japanese with the poor farmers of China. Mao underlines this with a most astonishing autobiographical story of his "conversion" from bourgeois pride to solidarity with the working poor. It is a noble image of reaching out beyond one's social class, but it is chilling when we remember that Mao fully expected everyone to have the identical experience.

The translation here comes from the original published version of 1943 in Yan'an's party newspaper, Liberation Daily. *Bonnie McDougall's careful translation retains the feel of Mao's 1940s writings and his earthy style much better than the overly polished and sanitized 1951* Selected Works *version.*

INTRODUCTION

(2 May 1942)

Comrades! I have invited you to this conference today for the purpose of exchanging opinions with you on the correct relationship between work in literature and art and revolutionary work in general, to obtain the correct development of revolutionary literature and art and better assistance from them in our other revolutionary work, so that we may overthrow our national enemy and accomplish our task of national liberation.

There are a number of different fronts in our struggle for the national liberation of China, civil and military, or, we might say, there is a cultural as well as an armed front. Victory over the enemy depends primarily on armies with guns in their hands, but this kind of army alone is not enough. We still need a cultural army, since this kind of army is indispensable in achieving unity among ourselves and winning victory over the enemy. Since May Fourth, when this cultural army took shape in China, it has aided the Chinese revolution by gradually limiting the sphere of China's feudal culture and the slavish culture that serves imperialist aggression, and weakening their strength, so that now reactionaries are reduced to resisting new culture by "meeting quality with quantity": reactionaries aren't short of money, and with some effort they can turn out a lot even if they can't come up with anything worthwhile. Literature and art have formed an important and successful part of the cultural front since May Fourth. . . . Our meeting today is to ensure that literature and art become a component part of the whole revolutionary machinery, so they can act as a powerful weapon in uniting and educating the people while attacking and annihilating the enemy, and help the people achieve solidarity in their struggle against the enemy. What are the problems which must be solved in order to achieve this purpose? They are questions relating to our position, attitude, audience, work, and study. . . .

Since the audience for literature and art consists of workers, peasants, soldiers, and their cadres, the question then arises of how to get to understand and know these people properly. To do this, we must carry out a great deal of work in Party and government organs, in villages and factories, in the Eighth Route Army and the New Fourth Army,[1] getting to understand all sorts of situations and all sorts of people and making ourselves thoroughly familiar with them. Our workers in literature and art must carry out their own work in literature and art, but the task of understanding people and getting to know them properly has the highest priority. How have our workers in literature and art performed in this respect until now? I would say that until now they have been heroes without a battlefield, remote and uncomprehending. What do I mean by remote? Remote from people. Workers in literature and art are unfamiliar with the people they write about and with the people who read their work, or else have actually become estranged from them. Our workers in literature and art are not familiar with workers, peasants, soldiers, or even their cadres. What do I mean by uncomprehending? Not comprehending their language. Yours is the language of intellectuals, theirs is the language of the popular masses. I have mentioned before that many comrades like

---

[1]The Eighth Route Army and the New Fourth Army were the two major military forces of the CCP after the start of the Second United Front in 1937. The New Fourth Army was all but destroyed by GMD forces in 1941, but the Eighth Route Army survived and grew to become the People's Liberation Army, which conquered all of China by 1949.

to talk about "popularization," but what does popularization mean? It means that the thoughts and emotions of our workers in literature and art should become one with the thoughts and emotions of the great masses of workers, peasants, and soldiers. And to get this unity, we should start by studying the language of the masses. If we don't even understand the masses' language, how can we talk about creating literature and art? "Heroes without a battlefield" refers to the fact that all your fine principles are not appreciated by the masses. The more you parade your qualifications before the masses, the more you act like "heroes," and the harder you try to sell your principles to them, the more the masses will resist buying. If you want the masses to understand you, if you want to become one with the masses, you must make a firm decision to undergo a long and possibly painful process of trial and hardship. At this point let me relate my own experience in how feelings are transformed. I started off as a student at school, and at school I acquired student habits, so that I felt ashamed to do any manual labor such as carry my own bags in front of all those students who were incapable of carrying anything for themselves. I felt that intellectuals were the only clean people in the world, and that workers, peasants, and soldiers were in general rather dirty. I could wear clothes borrowed from an intellectual, because I considered them clean, but I would not wear workers', peasants', or soldiers' clothes, because I thought they were dirty. When I joined the revolution and lived among workers, peasants, and soldiers, I gradually became familiar with them and they got to know me in return. Then and only then the bourgeois and petty bourgeois feelings taught to me in bourgeois schools began to undergo a fundamental change. Comparing intellectuals who have not yet reformed with workers, peasants, and soldiers, I came to feel that intellectuals are not only spiritually unclean in many respects but even physically unclean, while the cleanest people are workers and peasants; their hands may be dirty and their feet soiled with cow dung, but they are still cleaner than the big and petty bourgeoisie. This is what I call a transformation in feelings, changing over from one class to another. If our workers in literature and art who come from the intelligentsia want their work to be welcomed by the masses, they must see to it that their thoughts and feelings undergo transformation and reform. Otherwise, nothing they do will turn out well or be effective. . . .

CONCLUSION

(23 May 1942)

. . . Revolutionary Chinese writers and artists, the kind from whom we expect great things, must go among the masses; they must go among the masses of workers, peasants, and soldiers and into the heat of battle for a long time to come, without reservation, devoting body and soul to the task ahead; they must go to the sole, the broadest, and the richest source, to observe, experience, study, and analyze all the different kinds of people, all the classes and all the masses, all the vivid patterns of life and struggle, and all literature and art in their natural form, before they are ready for the stage of processing or creating, where you integrate raw materials with production, the stage of study with the stage of creation. Otherwise, there won't be anything for you to work on, since without raw materials or semiprocessed goods you have nothing to process and will inevitably end up as the kind of useless writer or artist that Lu Xun in his will earnestly instructed his son never to become.

. . . In the world today, all culture or literature and art belongs to a definite class and party, and has a definite political line. Art for art's sake, art that stands above class and party, and fellow-travelling or politically independent art do not exist in reality. In a society composed of classes and parties, art obeys both class and party and it must naturally obey the political demands of its class and party, and the revolutionary task of a given revolutionary age; any deviation is a deviation from the masses' basic need. Proletarian literature and art are a part of the whole proletarian revolutionary cause; as Lenin said, they are "a screw in the whole machine,"[2] and therefore, the party's work in literature and art occupies a definite, assigned position within the party's revolutionary work as a whole. Opposition to this assignment must lead to dualism or pluralism, and in essence resembles Trotsky's "Politics—Marxist; art—bourgeois."[3] We do not support excessive emphasis on the importance of literature and art, nor do we

[2]Lenin, in his 1902 goals for press and propaganda, used this mechanical metaphor, with soldiers, politicians, and publicists serving as coordinated parts of the revolutionary machine. Mao goes farther than Lenin by extending this machine to include creative literature.
[3]Leon Trotsky, the hero of the Russian Revolution who lost out to Stalin in factional fighting in the late 1920s, was known for his liberal views on fine arts and literature. Mao characterizes them as "politics—Marxist; art—bourgeois" to emphasize the lack of control over art and literature favored by Trotsky. By the 1940s, anything associated with Trotsky was bad news inside the Communist movement.

support their underestimation. Literature and art are subordinate to politics, and yet in turn exert enormous influence on it. Revolutionary literature and art are a part of the whole work of revolution; they are a screw, which of course doesn't compare with other parts in importance, urgency, or priority, but which is nevertheless indispensable in the whole machinery, an indispensable part of revolutionary work as a whole. If literature and art did not exist in even the broadest and most general sense, the revolution could not advance or win victory; it would be incorrect not to acknowledge this. Furthermore, when we speak of literature and art obeying politics, politics refers to class and mass politics and not to the small number of people known as politicians. Politics, both revolutionary and counterrevolutionary alike, concerns the struggle between classes and not the behavior of a small number of people. Ideological warfare and literary and artistic warfare, especially if these wars are revolutionary, are necessarily subservient to political warfare, because class and mass needs can only be expressed in a concentrated form through politics.

4

Resolution of the Central Committee of the Chinese Communist Party on Methods of Leadership

June 1, 1943

This resolution of the CCP's politburo of the Central Committee was passed in Yan'an on June 1, 1943. It is attributed to Mao Zedong and is included in volume 3 of his Selected Works *as "Some Questions Concerning Methods of Leadership." We have every reason to believe that he did write it or that it captures what he was telling his comrades. The resolution sums up the organizational lessons of the 1942–44 Rectification Movement in Yan'an and outlines in some detail how the party should organize mass mobilization. It is a blueprint of how to run the revolution at the local level, thus answering the challenge Mao set forth in his 1927*

"Zhonggong zhongyang guanyu lingdao fangfade jueding," in *Zhengfeng wenxian* (Rectification Documents) (Yan'an, 1944). Translation from Boyd Compton, ed., *Mao's China: Party Reform Documents, 1942–44* (Seattle: University of Washington Press, 1952), 176–83.

"Report on the Peasant Movement in Hunan" (see Document 1). It was extremely effective in the 1940s as the CCP extended its sway into new regions of China.

The lessons of coordinated but flexible organizing outlined in the resolution have been applied to social movements elsewhere, from the Vietcong in Vietnam to Che Guevara in Latin America to Marxist insurgents in Nepal. The key points are (1) a version of "think globally, act locally," but with a strong Leninist chain of command; (2) a hardheaded assessment of the "masses" one wants to mobilize (usually, 10 percent activists, 80 percent average, 10 percent backward); (3) a focus on nurturing that activist 10 percent to get the movement going; and (4) the importance of coordinated propaganda to guide leadership and motivate the rank and file. The philosophical method of this approach to changing society requires "theory-practice-theory," in which an ideology (Marxism) is tested by actual efforts to do something and then modified on the basis of the practical results of one's efforts. (Nick Knight provides a helpful chart of this process in Document 13.)

The most famous phrase from this resolution is the populist credo of Maoism: "Correct leadership must come from the masses and go to the masses." When the CCP followed this heartfelt populist method by taking the time to research local conditions and talk in advance to local people, it was extremely successful. When the increasingly powerful CCP apparatus bypassed the laborious "people's democratic methods" outlined in the resolution, it made mistakes, culminating in Mao's colossal errors in the Great Leap Forward (see Documents 8 and 14).

(Passed by the Political Bureau of the Central Committee, June 1, 1943)

1. Two methods must be adopted in accomplishing any task: the first is to combine the general and the particular, and the second is to unite leadership with the masses.

2. If any work or mission lacks a general, universal slogan, the broad masses cannot be moved to action, but if there is nothing more than a general slogan and the leaders do not make a concrete, direct, and thorough application of it with those from a particular unit who have been rallied around the slogan, [if the leaders] fail to break through at some point and gain experience, or fail to use acquired experience in later guiding other units, there is then no way for the leaders to test the correctness of the general slogan and there is no

way for them to carry out its contents; there is then the danger that the general slogan will have no effect.

For example, in the general reform of 1942, all those who met with success had adopted the method of combining a general slogan with particular guidance. All those who were unsuccessful had failed to adopt this method. In the reform movement of 1943, all Central Committee bureaus and subbureaus, cultural committees, and district and local Party committees must not only present general slogans (the reform plan for the entire year), but also acquire experience by selecting two or three units from their own organization, nearby organizations, schools, and military groups (the number need not be large), studying them thoroughly, gaining a detailed understanding of the process whereby reform and study have developed within these units, gaining a detailed understanding of the characteristics of the history, experience, thought, etc., the diligence in study and the quality of work of certain specific typical cadres from among these units (the number need not be large), and in addition personally guiding the leaders of these units to come to concrete solutions of the actual problems facing the units. The same should be done with a number of units within these organs, schools, or military groups, and the leaders of these organs, schools, or military groups should also utilize the method described above. This is also the method to be used by leaders to combine guidance and study. Any leader who, in his studies, fails to observe specific units and specific individuals at the lower levels or fails to refer to concrete cases, will never be able to give the units general guidance. This method must be universally promoted so that it can be mastered and applied by leaders and cadres at all levels.

3. The experience of the reform movement of 1942 has also proved that in the process of reform, the reform of each concrete unit must produce a leading nucleus of minority activists who are the core of the administrative leadership of that unit and it must also bring this leading nucleus into close union with the broad masses engaged in study; in this way only can reform fulfill its mission. If there is only a positive spirit on the part of the leading nuclei, it [the reform] becomes an empty flurry of activity on the part of a minority; yet if there is only a positive spirit on the part of the broad masses, with no powerful leading nucleus to organize the positive spirit of the masses properly, the masses' spirit then cannot endure, nor can it move in a correct direction or be elevated to a high standard.

Wherever there are masses, there are in all probability three groups: those who are comparatively active, those who are average, and those who are backward. In comparing the three groups, the two extremes are in all probability small, while the middle group is large. As a result, leaders must be skillful at consolidating the minority activists to act as a leading nucleus, and must rely on this nucleus to elevate the middle group and capture the backward elements. A truly consolidated, uniform, and united nucleus for the leadership of the masses must materialize gradually from the mass struggle (for example, in reform and study); it cannot materialize apart from the mass struggle.

In the process of any great struggle, the leading nucleus in the initial, intermediate, and final stages should not be, and cannot be, entirely the same; activists (heroes) in the struggle must be constantly recruited to replace those elements which were originally part of the nucleus, but which have been found wanting on closer inspection, or have degenerated. A fundamental reason that the work in many areas and many organs has not progressed has been the lack of just such a constantly healthy leading nucleus, which is unified and connected with the masses.

If a school of one hundred persons does not have among its teachers, experts, and students a leading nucleus of a few or a few dozen individuals, which is formed naturally (and not assembled by compulsion) by those who are comparatively the most active, orthodox, and intelligent, the school will then be difficult to manage. In all organs, schools, or units of any size, we should start with an application of Stalin's comments on the establishment of leadership, to be found in the ninth section of his discussion of the "Bolshevization of the Party." The standards for this leading nucleus should be the four points raised by Dimitrov[1] in his discussion of cadre policy (unlimited loyalty, relation to the masses, ability to do independent work, observation of discipline). Whether the mission is concerned with war, production, or education (including reform), or whether the work is reform and study, supervision of work, the investigation of cadres, or any other task, we must adopt not only the method of combining a general slogan with particular guidance, but also the method of combining the leading nuclei with the broad masses.

4. In all our Party's actual work, correct leadership must come from the masses and go to the masses. This means taking the views of the

---

[1]*Dimitrov:* Georgi Dimitrov, the leader of the Comintern, the Communist International that ran Russia's program for international Communist revolution from 1919 to 1943. Dimitrov was the key leader in the 1930s, and his writings were used by Mao and the CCP in Yan'an.

masses (unintegrated, unrelated views) and subjecting them to concentration (they are transformed through research into concentrated systematized views), then going to the masses with propaganda and explanation in order to transform the views of the masses, and seeing that these [views] are maintained by the masses and carried over into their activities. It also means an examination of mass activities to ascertain the correctness of these views. Then again, there is concentration from the masses and maintenance among the masses. Thus the process is repeated indefinitely, each time more correctly, vitally, and fruitfully. This is the epistemology and methodology of Marxism-Leninism.

5. The idea that correct relations should be created between the leading nucleus and the broad masses in organization, in the struggle, and in action; the idea that correct guiding views can result only from the process of concentrating from the masses and maintaining among the masses; and the idea of combining a general slogan with particular guidance when the views of the leadership are being carried out . . . these ideas must be universally propagated in the current reform movement, so that mistaken views existing among the cadres on these questions can be corrected. Many comrades neglect or are unskillful in the task of consolidating activists and organizing a leading nucleus and neglect or are unskillful in the task of closely uniting the leading nucleus and the broad masses. As a consequence, their leadership becomes a bureaucratic leadership separated from the masses. Many comrades neglect or are unskillful at summarizing the experience of the mass struggle and delight in showing off by expressing many subjectivistic views; as a consequence, their own views become impractical nonsense. Many comrades are satisfied with the general slogan for their task, and either neglect or are unskillful at providing close, direct, specific, and concrete leadership after the slogan has been adopted. As a consequence, the slogan goes no further than talk, a piece of paper, or a meeting, and becomes bureaucratic leadership. The current reform movement must correct these defects. In reform of study, the supervision of work, and the investigation of cadres, [we must] learn the methods of uniting leadership and the masses and combining the general and the particular; we must then adopt these methods in all our work.

6. Correct guiding views are those which are concentrated from the masses then maintained among the masses; this is a fundamental method. In concentrating and maintaining, the method of combining a general slogan and particular guidance must be adopted. This is an

integral part of the foregoing method. From many specific [experiences] of leadership, a general view is formulated (a general slogan): this general view is then tested in particular units (you must not only do this yourself, but must also ask others to do the same); then new experiences can be concentrated (summarized experiences) and established as a new guide for the general leadership of the masses. Comrades should do this in the current reform movement and should do the same in any work they undertake. Comparatively good leadership results from comparative skill in this method.

7. In any type of work (military work, production, education, reform and study, supervision, the investigation of cadres or propaganda, organizational work, counterespionage, etc.), higher-level guiding organs should work through persons in responsible positions in lower-level organs connected with that work, see that they assume responsibilities, bring about a division of labor, and at the same time achieve a unified objective (centralization). It is not enough for the individual departments merely to contact individual lower-level departments (for example, the higher-level Organizational Bureau contacts only the lower-level Organizational Bureau, the higher-level Propaganda Bureau contacts only the lower-level Propaganda Bureau; the higher-level Counterespionage Bureau contacts only the lower-level Counterespionge Bureau) so that those primarily responsible in lower-level organs (for example, secretaries, chairmen, department heads, and school principals, etc.) do not understand or accept responsibility; they should see that both those with primary and secondary responsibilities understand and accept responsibility. . . .

8. According to the concrete historical and environmental conditions of each district, leaders should plan and control the general program and make correct decisions on central tasks and the order of work during a given period, sticking rigidly to this order until definite results are achieved. This is one of the arts of leadership. It is also a problem which must be closely considered in determining methods of leadership, while applying the principles of uniting leadership with the masses and combining the general and the particular.

9. Systematic attention has not been given here to questions of detail concerning methods of leadership. On the basis of the principles and directives presented in this resolution, comrades in all areas should reflect carefully and develop their own creative abilities. The more bitter the struggle becomes, the more necessary is the

demand for close union between men of the Communist Party and the broad masses, the more necessary to Communist Party members is the close union between general slogans and particular guidance, and [the more necessary is] the thorough disruption of subjectivistic and bureaucratic methods of leadership. All leading comrades of our Party must forthwith adopt scientific methods of leadership and oppose them to subjective and bureaucratic methods of leadership, overcoming the latter with the former. Subjectivists and bureaucratists who do not understand the principles of uniting leadership with the masses and combining the general and the particular, greatly hamper the development of Party work. We must therefore oppose subjectivistic and bureaucratic methods of leadership, and universally and profoundly promote methods of leadership which are scientific.

5

Snow

1945

This is Mao's most famous poem, written in the Yan'an area of northwest China near the Yellow River, a dry and rugged region. Here Mao has adopted the voice of classical Chinese poetry, which is short and lyrical. The first stanza should be read like a Chinese painting—dabs of ink outlining the mental picture of Mao viewing this grandiose landscape. The second stanza reveals Mao's feelings. He stands where great emperors of the past have stood, both literally by the Yellow River and figuratively on the verge of taking power. His conclusion is resolutely revolutionary: "For men of vision/We must seek among the present generation." Written after his consolidation of power inside the CCP, as the Japanese war effort was flagging and the CCP "base areas" were growing, this poem conveys his confidence and elation.

Xue, in *Mao Zedong shici xuan* (Beijing: Renmin wenxue chubanshe, 1986), 61–62. Translated by Michael Bullock and Jerome Ch'en in Jerome Ch'en, *Mao and the Chinese Revolution* (London: Oxford University Press, 1965), 340–41. Chinese editions date this poem to 1936, but I follow Bullock and Ch'en's dating of 1945.

The northern scene:
A thousand leagues locked in ice,
A myriad leagues of fluttering snow.
On either side of the Great Wall
Only one vastness to be seen.
Up and down this broad river
Torrents flatten and stiffen.
The mountains* are dancing silver serpents
And hills, like waxen elephants, plod on the plain,
Challenging heaven with their heights.
A sunny day is needed
For seeing them, with added elegance,
In red and white.

Such is the beauty of these mountains and rivers
That has been admired by unnumbered heroes—
The great emperors of Qin and Han
Lacking literary brilliance,
Those of Tang and Song
Having but few romantic inclinations,
And the prodigious Gengis Khan[1]
Knowing only how to bend his bow
    and shoot at vultures.
All are past and gone!
For men of vision
We must seek among the present generation.

---

*The highlands are those of Shaanxi and Shanxi.
[1]*Gengis Khan:* Genghis Khan (ca. 1162–1227), Mongol conqueror who became emperor of China

6

The Chinese People Have Stood Up

September 1949

By September 1949, the CCP had clearly defeated the GMD and set about establishing its new government, the People's Republic of China (PRC). Part of that system, drawing on the promise of a united front of Communists and non-Communists made in Mao's 1940 "On New Democracy" (see Document 2), was the formation of the Chinese Political Consultative Congress, which brought together a range of left-wing and independent parties willing to work with the new CCP government. This selection comes from Mao's speech at the preparatory session of the Consultative Congress. The tone of the speech is celebratory. After decades of turmoil and the near eradication of the CCP, victory was at hand. Mao's themes are nationalist rather than socialist; he dwells on China's new prestige and its national success in throwing off the Japanese, the Europeans (referred to as imperialists), and the corrupt government of the GMD. This was the high point of Mao's popular prestige, because he was widely seen as the savior who had delivered China's hard-earned independence and stature. Yet Mao hints at the continuing need to maintain "vigilance" against unnamed "reactionaries," leaving the door open for the terrible political purges and mass campaigns of the future.

This talk is the source of one of Mao's most remembered—and misremembered—statements: "We [the Chinese people] have stood up." Popular memory has it that Mao said this from the top of Tiananmen Gate on October 1, 1949, but he actually said it at this meeting in September. The title here comes from the editors of the most complete Chinese edition of Mao's writing, published in the 1990s and thus reflecting the continued power of the words.

"Zhongguo ren congci zhanqi laile," in Mao Zedong wenji (Beijing: Renmin chubanshe, 1996), 5:342–46, based on the People's Daily version of September 22, 1949. Translation from Stuart Schram, The Political Thought of Mao Tse-tung, 2nd ed. (New York: Praeger, 1969), 167–68.

. . . Our conference is one of great nationwide popular unity.

Such great nationwide popular unity has been achieved because we have vanquished the Guomindang reactionary government, which is aided by American imperialism. In the course of little more than three years, the heroic Chinese People's Liberation Army, an army such as the world has seldom seen, crushed the offensive of the several million troops of the American-supported Guomindang reactionary government, thereby enabling us to swing over to the counter-offensive and the offensive. . . .

We have a common feeling that our work will be recorded in the history of mankind, and that it will clearly demonstrate that the Chinese, who comprise one quarter of humanity, have begun to stand up. The Chinese have always been a great, courageous, and industrious people. It was only in modern times that they have fallen behind, and this was due solely to the oppression and exploitation of foreign imperialism and the domestic reactionary government.

For more than a century, our predecessors never paused in their indomitable struggles against the foreign and domestic oppressors. These struggles include the Revolution of 1911, led by Sun Yat-sen, the great pioneer of China's revolution. Our predecessors instructed us to carry their work to completion. We are doing this now. We have united ourselves and defeated both our foreign and domestic oppressors by means of the people's liberation war and the people's great revolution, and we proclaim the establishment of the People's Republic of China.

Henceforth, our nation will enter the large family of peace-loving and freedom-loving nations of the world. It will work bravely and industriously to create its own civilization and happiness, and will, at the same time, promote world peace and freedom. Our nation will never again be an insulted nation. We have stood up. Our revolution has gained the sympathy and acclamation of the broad masses throughout the world. We have friends the world over.

Our revolutionary work is not yet concluded. . . . The imperialists and the domestic reactionaries will certainly not take their defeat lying down. . . . Daily, hourly, they will try to restore their rule in China. . . . We must not relax our vigilance. . . .

The people's democratic dictatorship and unity with international friends will enable us to obtain rapid success in our construction work. . . . Our population of 475 million and our national territory of 9,597 million square kilometres are factors in our favour. It is true that there are difficulties ahead of us, a great many of them. But we firmly believe that all the difficulties will be surmounted by the heroic struggle of all the people of our country. The Chinese people has had ample experience in overcoming difficulties. If we and our predecessors could come through the long period of extreme difficulties and defeat the powerful domestic and foreign reactionaries, why can we not build up a prosperous and flourishing country after our victory? . . .

An upsurge in cultural construction will inevitably follow in the wake of the upsurge of economic construction. The era in which the Chinese were regarded as uncivilized is now over. We will emerge in the world as a nation with a high culture.

Our national defence will be consolidated and no imperialist will be allowed to invade our territory again. . . .

Let the domestic and foreign reactionaries tremble before us. Let them say that we are no good at this and no good at that. Through the Chinese people's indomitable endeavours, we will steadily reach our goal.

7

On the Correct Handling of Contradictions among the People

June 1957

This is arguably Mao Zedong's most important single contribution to the development of state socialism and Marxist-Leninist theory after 1949. Here Mao confronts directly the ultimately fatal flaw of the Leninist state: the lack of political feedback (such as that provided by secret-ballot elections in liberal democracies). Since the CCP claims access to truth as the scientific voice of the working class, to oppose the CCP is to oppose all that is good and right. Yet everyone, including the CCP leadership, knew that the CCP was not infallible despite its formal claims. In our terms, if a government does not find a way to get accurate feedback on how its policies work in practice, it will soon crash — like a pilot

"Guanyu zhengque chuli renmin neibu maodun de wenti," Renmin ribao, 19 June 1957. Translation from Selected Works of Mao Tse-tung (Peking: Foreign Languages Press, 1977), 5:384–421.

flying blind. Mao set out in February 1957 to solve this problem for China.

This is the most philosophical of Mao's writings included in this reader. His line of argument, especially in the first several pages, is a model of his application of Marxist dialectics to a pressing political problem. Thus he concludes his first review of the economy by saying, "The ceaseless emergence and ceaseless resolution of contradictions constitute the dialectical law of the development of things." Throughout the text, Mao analyzes the whole range of social issues in China—from agriculture to industry to intellectuals to foreign policy—in these philosophical terms. He begins his practical consideration of "contradictions among the people" by dispensing with counterrevolutionaries (subjects, of course, of antagonistic contradictions). He then turns to major social groups in China: various agrarian classes (poor, middle, and rich peasants), businessmen and industrialists, and intellectuals. Mao and the CCP needed the talents of all these social classes, but especially the technical skills of China's intellectual elite, to move China's economic modernization program forward.

Mao offered this comprehensive philosophical and political blueprint at a time of challenge for the new Communist government of China. The first seven years of CCP had gone quite well, and Mao was the revered leader of the nation. But now there were problems. De-Stalinization in the USSR and anti-Soviet rebellions in Communist Poland and Hungary in 1956 added urgency to Mao's conviction that the CCP had succumbed to bureaucratism—rule by a heartless and all-powerful state administration.

Mao's solution was to give the party a dose of self and mutual criticism, one of the techniques of rectification study from the Yan'an period, but with a twist—he would ask a new part of the "masses," China's literate public and intellectuals, to improve the party through public criticism in the press. This required an explanation, in terms of Marxist theory, of why it might be permissible to criticize "the voice of the people." Mao provides that theoretical development in this speech. He posits two kinds of contradictions—antagonistic ones between "us" and the enemy (such as relations between China and the United States) and non-antagonistic ones within the ranks of the people.

It was a brilliant idea, and one that promised to make the Communist government more open to public opinion and more aware of the trade-offs necessary in administering a modernizing nation. Indeed, in the February 1957 version of the speech, Mao essentially guaranteed

*immunity from political prosecution if professionals and intellectuals (in
several nominal and powerless "democratic parties") would speak up.*[1]
   *The chronology of the spring of 1957 is covered in the introduction.
When the public "blooming" Mao called for finally occurred in May, it
was much more harshly critical of the CCP than he had anticipated. The
party promptly shut down these criticisms, and the Anti-Rightist Campaign started in late June to prosecute those who had spoken up. The
betrayal of Mao's promise to intellectuals was embodied in the published
version of "On the Correct Handling of Contradictions" on June 19 in the*
People's Daily, *the CCP's national newspaper. There it appeared in a
highly edited form minus the guarantees of immunity and with a new set
of six criteria "for distinguishing fragrant flowers from poisonous weeds"
that made the May critics guilty after the fact. Thus the politics around
the text negated its promising content. Mao's practice was out of step
with his pronouncements.*
   This translation is the official Selected Works *version based on the*
People's Daily *article in June 1957. This is the version approved by the
party as a "collective wisdom" edition (see "A Note about the Texts"),
and it is the version studied by millions of Chinese, even though it is not
the version Mao first presented in February 1957. The revised version is
important for more than the deletion of Mao's promise to respect all public criticism. The "speaking notes" version from February is rambling
and, at points, incoherent. Party editors and Mao clearly put a great
deal of effort into systematizing Mao's thoughts on the nature of contradictions in this public version.*

Our general subject is the correct handling of contradictions among
the people. For convenience, let us discuss it under twelve sub-
headings. Although reference will be made to contradictions between
ourselves and the enemy, this discussion will center on contradictions
among the people.

---

[1]The "speaking notes" of Mao's February 27, 1957, "Contradictions" talk is translated in Roderick MacFarquhar, Timothy Cheek, and Eugene Wu, eds., *The Secret
Speeches of Chairman Mao: From the Hundred Flowers to the Great Leap Forward* (Cambridge: Harvard Contemporary China Series, 1989), 131–90.

I. TWO TYPES OF CONTRADICTIONS DIFFERING IN NATURE

Never before has our country been as united as it is today. The victories of the bourgeois-democratic revolution and of the socialist revolution and our achievements in socialist construction have rapidly changed the face of the old China. A still brighter future lies ahead for our motherland. The days of national disunity and chaos which the people detested are gone, never to return. Led by the working class and the Communist Party, our 600 million people, united as one, are engaged in the great task of building socialism. The unification of our country, the unity of our people and the unity of our various nationalities—these are the basic guarantees for the sure triumph of our cause. However, this does not mean that contradictions no longer exist in our society. To imagine that none exist is a naive idea which is at variance with objective reality. We are confronted with two types of social contradictions—those between ourselves and the enemy and those among the people. The two are totally different in nature.

To understand these two different types of contradictions correctly, we must first be clear on what is meant by "the people" and what is meant by "the enemy.". . . At the present stage, the period of building socialism, the classes, strata and social groups which favour, support and work for the cause of socialist construction all come within the category of the people, while the social forces and groups which resist the socialist revolution and are hostile to or sabotage socialist construction are all enemies of the people.

The contradictions between ourselves and the enemy are antagonistic contradictions. Within the ranks of the people, the contradictions among the working people are non-antagonistic, while those between the exploited and the exploiting classes have a non-antagonistic as well as an antagonistic aspect. There have always been contradictions among the people, but they are different in content in each period of the revolution and in the period of building socialism. In the conditions prevailing in China today, the contradictions among the people comprise the contradictions within the working class, the contradictions within the peasantry, the contradictions within the intelligentsia, the contradictions between the working class and the peasantry, the contradictions between the workers and peasants on the one hand and the intellectuals on the other, the contradictions between the working class and other sections of the working people on the one hand and the national bourgeoisie on the other, the contradictions within the national bourgeoisie, and so on. Our People's Government is one that genuinely represents the people's interests, it is a government that serves the people. Nevertheless, there are still certain contradictions between this government and the people. These include the contradictions between the interests of the state and the interests of the collective on the one hand and the interests of the individual on the other, between democracy and centralism, between the leadership and the led, and the contradictions arising from the bureaucratic style of work of some of the state personnel in their relations with the masses. All these are also contradictions among the people. Generally speaking, the fundamental identity of the people's interests underlies the contradictions among the people.

In our country, the contradiction between the working class and the national bourgeoisie comes under the category of contradictions among the people. By and large, the class struggle between the two is a class struggle within the ranks of the people, because the Chinese national bourgeoisie has a dual character. In the period of the bourgeois-democratic revolution, it had both a revolutionary and a conciliationist side to its character. In the period of the socialist revolution, exploitation of the working class for profit constitutes one side of the character of the national bourgeoisie, while its support of the Constitution and its willingness to accept socialist transformation constitute the other. The national bourgeoisie differs from the imperialists, the landlords and the bureaucrat-capitalists. The contradiction between the national bourgeoisie and the working class is one between exploiter and exploited, and is by nature antagonistic. But in the concrete conditions of China, this antagonistic contradiction between the two classes, if properly handled, can be transformed into a non-antagonistic one and be resolved by peaceful methods. However, the contradiction between the working class and the national bourgeoisie will change into a contradiction between ourselves and the enemy if we do not handle it properly and do not follow the policy of uniting with, criticizing and educating the national bourgeoisie, or if the national bourgeoisie does not accept this policy of ours.

Since they are different in nature, the contradictions between ourselves and the enemy and the contradictions among the people must be resolved by different methods. To put it briefly, the former entail drawing a clear distinction between ourselves and the enemy, and the latter entail drawing a clear distinction between right and wrong. It is of course true that the distinction between ourselves and the enemy is also one of right and wrong. For example, the question of who is in the right, we or the domestic and foreign reactionaries, the imperialists, the feudalists and bureaucrat-capitalists, is also one of right and wrong, but it is in a different category from questions of right and wrong among the people.

Our state is a people's democratic dictatorship led by the working class and based on the worker-peasant alliance. What is this dictatorship for? Its first function is internal, namely, to suppress the reactionary classes and elements and those exploiters who resist the socialist revolution, to suppress those who try to wreck our socialist construction, or in other words, to resolve the contradictions between ourselves and the internal enemy. For instance, to arrest, try and sentence certain counter-revolutionaries, and to deprive landlords and bureaucrat-capitalists of their right to vote and their freedom of speech for a certain period of time—all this comes within the scope of our dictatorship. To maintain public order and safeguard the interests of the people, it is necessary to exercise dictatorship as well over thieves, swindlers, murderers, arsonists, criminal gangs and other scoundrels who seriously disrupt public order. The second function of this dictatorship is to protect our country from subversion and possible aggression by external enemies. In such contingencies, it is the task of this dictatorship to resolve the contradiction between ourselves and the external enemy. The aim of this dictatorship is to protect all our people so that they can devote themselves to peaceful labour and make China a socialist country with modern industry, modern agriculture, and modern science and culture. Who is to exercise this dictatorship? Naturally, the working class and the entire people under its leadership. Dictatorship does not apply within the ranks of the people. The people cannot exercise dictatorship over themselves, nor must one section of the people oppress another. Law-breakers among the people will be punished according to law, but this is different in principle from the exercise of dictatorship to suppress enemies of the people. What applies among the people is democratic centralism. Our Constitution lays it down that citizens of the People's Republic of China enjoy freedom of speech, the press, assembly, association, procession, demonstration, religious belief, and so on. Our Constitution also provides that the organs of state must practise democratic centralism, that they must rely on the masses and that their personnel must serve the people. Our socialist democracy is the broadest kind of democracy, such as is not to be found in any bourgeois state. Our dictatorship is the people's democratic dictatorship led by the working class and based on the worker-peasant alliance. That is to say, democracy operates within the ranks of the people, while the working class, uniting with all others enjoying civil rights, and in the first place with the peasantry, enforces dictatorship over the reactionary classes and elements and all those who resist socialist transformation and oppose socialist construction. By civil rights, we mean, politically, the rights of freedom and democracy.

But this freedom is freedom with leadership and this democracy is democracy under centralized guidance, not anarchy. Anarchy does not accord with the interests or wishes of the people.

Certain people in our country were delighted by the Hungarian incident.[2] They hoped that something similar would happen in China, that thousands upon thousands of people would take to the streets to demonstrate against the People's Government. Their hopes ran counter to the interests of the masses and therefore could not possibly win their support. Deceived by domestic and foreign counter-revolutionaries, a section of the people in Hungary made the mistake of resorting to violence against the people's government, with the result that both the state and the people suffered. The damage done to the country's economy in a few weeks of rioting will take a long time to repair. In our country there were some others who wavered on the question of the Hungarian incident because they were ignorant of the real state of affairs in the world. They think that there is too little freedom under our people's democracy and that there is more freedom under Western parliamentary democracy. They ask for a two-party system as in the West, with one party in office and the other in opposition. But this so-called two-party system is nothing but a device for maintaining the dictatorship of the bourgeoisie; it can never guarantee freedoms to the working people. As a matter of fact, freedom and democracy exist not in the abstract, but only in the concrete. In a society where class struggle exists, if there is freedom for the exploiting classes to exploit the working people, there is no freedom for the working people not to be exploited. If there is democracy for the bourgeoisie, there is no democracy for the proletariat and other working people. The legal existence of the Communist Party is tolerated in some capitalist countries, but only to the extent that it does not endanger the fundamental interests of the bourgeoisie; it is not tolerated beyond that. Those who demand freedom and democracy in the

---

[2]*Hungarian incident:* In October 1956, reformist leaders in socialist Hungary, mobilized by student protests, expelled Stalinist leaders and declared military independence from the Soviet Union. The Soviets quickly crushed the reform government and reasserted control over Hungary by military force.

abstract regard democracy as an end and not as a means. Democracy as such sometimes seems to be an end, but it is in fact only a means. Marxism teaches us that democracy is part of the superstructure and belongs to the realm of politics. That is to say, in the last analysis, it serves the economic base. The same is true of freedom. Both democracy and freedom are relative, not absolute, and they come into being and develop in specific historical conditions. Within the ranks of the people, democracy is correlative with centralism and freedom with discipline. They are the two opposites of a single entity, contradictory as well as united, and we should not one-sidedly emphasize one to the exclusion of the other. Within the ranks of the people, we cannot do without freedom, nor can we do without discipline; we cannot do without democracy, nor can we do without centralism. This unity of democracy and centralism, of freedom and discipline, constitutes our democratic centralism. Under this system, the people enjoy broad democracy and freedom, but at the same time they have to keep within the bounds of socialist discipline. All this is well understood by the masses.

In advocating freedom with leadership and democracy under centralized guidance, we in no way mean that coercive measures should be taken to settle ideological questions or questions involving the distinction between right and wrong among the people. All attempts to use administrative orders or coercive measures to settle ideological questions or questions of right and wrong are not only ineffective but harmful. We cannot abolish religion by administrative order or force people not to believe in it. We cannot compel people to give up idealism, any more than we can force them to embrace Marxism. The only way to settle questions of an ideological nature or controversial issues among the people is by the democratic method, the method of discussion, criticism, persuasion and education, and not by the method of coercion or repression. To be able to carry on their production and studies effectively and to lead their lives in peace and order, the people want their government and those in charge of production and of cultural and educational organizations to issue appropriate administrative regulations of an obligatory nature. It is common sense that without them the maintenance of public order would be impossible. Administrative regulations and the method of persuasion and education complement each other in resolving contradictions among the people. In fact, administrative regulations for the maintenance of public order must be accompanied by persuasion and education, for in many cases regulations alone will not work.

This democratic method of resolving contradictions among the people was epitomized in 1942 in the formula "unity—criticism—unity." To elaborate, that means starting from the desire for unity, resolving contradictions through criticism or struggle, and arriving at a new unity on a new basis. In our experience this is the correct method of resolving contradictions among the people. In 1942 we used it to resolve contradictions inside the Communist Party, namely, the contradictions between the dogmatists and the great majority of the membership, and between dogmatism and Marxism. The "Left" dogmatists had resorted to the method of "ruthless struggle and merciless blows" in inner-Party struggle. It was the wrong method. In criticizing "Left" dogmatism, we did not use this old method but adopted a new one, that is, one of starting from the desire for unity, distinguishing between right and wrong through criticism or struggle, and arriving at a new unity on a new basis. This was the method used in the rectification movement of 1942. Within a few years, by the time the Chinese Communist Party held its Seventh National Congress in 1945, unity was achieved throughout the Party as anticipated, and consequently the people's revolution triumphed. Here, the essential thing is to start from the desire for unity. For without this desire for unity, the struggle, once begun, is certain to throw things into confusion and get out of hand. Wouldn't this be the same as "ruthless struggle and merciless blows"? And what Party unity would there be left? It was precisely this experience that led us to the formula "unity—criticism—unity." Or, in other words, "learn from past mistakes to avoid future ones and cure the sickness to save the patient." We extended this method beyond our Party. We applied it with great success in the anti-Japanese base areas in dealing with the relations between the leadership and the masses, between the army and the people, between officers and men, between the different units of the army, and between the different groups of cadres. The use of this method can be traced back to still earlier times in our Party's history. Ever since 1927 when we built our revolutionary armed forces and base areas in the south, this method had been used to deal with the relations between the Party and the masses, between the army and the people, between officers and men, and with other relations among the people. The only difference was that during the anti-Japanese war we employed this method much more consciously. And since the liberation of the whole country, we have employed this same method of "unity—criticism—unity" in our relations with the democratic parties[3] and with industrial and commercial circles. Our task now is to continue to extend and make still better use of this method throughout the ranks of the people; we want all our factories, co-operatives, shops, schools, offices and people's organizations, in a word, all our 600 million people, to use it in resolving contradictions among themselves.

In ordinary circumstances, contradictions among the people are not antagonistic. But if they are not handled properly, or if we relax our vigilance and lower our guard, antagonism may arise. In a socialist country, a development of this kind is usually only a localized and temporary phenomenon. The reason is that the system of exploitation of man by man has been abolished and the interests of the people are fundamentally identical. The antagonistic actions which took place on a fairly wide scale during the Hungarian incident were the result of the operations of both domestic and foreign counter-revolutionary elements. This was a particular as well as a temporary phenomenon. It was a case of the reactionaries inside a socialist country, in league with the imperialists, attempting to achieve their conspiratorial aims by taking advantage of contradictions among the people to foment dissension and stir up disorder. The lesson of the Hungarian incident merits attention.

Many people seem to think that the use of the democratic method to resolve contradictions among the people is something new. Actually it is not. Marxists have always held that the cause of the proletariat must depend on the masses of the people and that Communists must use the democratic method of persuasion and education when working among the labouring people and must on no account resort to commandism or coercion. The Chinese Communist Party faithfully adheres to this Marxist-Leninist principle. It has been our consistent view that under the people's democratic dictatorship two different methods, one dictatorial and the other democratic, should be used to resolve the two types of contradictions which differ in nature—those between ourselves and the enemy and those among the people. This idea has been explained again and again in many Party documents and in speeches by many leading comrades of our Party. In my article "On the People's Democratic Dictatorship," written in 1949, I said, "The combination of these two aspects, democracy for the people and

---

[3]*democratic parties:* in the 1950s, remnants of truly independent political parties active before 1949. Under the Communist government, they served more as interest groups for professionals. They were retained by the CCP as reminders of the promise of New Democracy, and here Mao is trying to use that legitimacy to reform the CCP.

dictatorship over the reactionaries, is the people's democratic dictatorship." I also pointed out that in order to settle problems within the ranks of the people "the method we employ is democratic, the method of persuasion, not of compulsion." Again, in addressing the Second Session of the First National Committee of the Political Consultative Conference in June 1950, I said:

> The people's democratic dictatorship uses two methods. Towards the enemy, it uses the method of dictatorship, that is, for as long a period of time as is necessary it does not permit them to take part in political activity and compels them to obey the law of the People's Government, to engage in labour and, through such labour, be transformed into new men. Towards the people, on the contrary, it uses the method of democracy and not of compulsion, that is, it must necessarily let them take part in political activity and does not compel them to do this or that but uses the method of democracy to educate and persuade. Such education is self-education for the people, and its basic method is criticism and self-criticism.

Thus, on many occasions we have discussed the use of the democratic method for resolving contradictions among the people; furthermore, we have in the main applied it in our work, and many cadres and many other people are familiar with it in practice. Why then do some people now feel that it is a new issue? Because, in the past, the struggle between ourselves and the enemy, both internal and external, was most acute, and contradictions among the people therefore did not attract as much attention as they do today.

Quite a few people fail to make a clear distinction between these two different types of contradictions—those between ourselves and the enemy and those among the people—and are prone to confuse the two. It must be admitted that it is sometimes quite easy to do so. We have had instances of such confusion in our work in the past. In the course of cleaning out counter-revolutionaries good people were sometimes mistaken for bad, and such things still happen today. We are able to keep mistakes within bounds because it has been our policy to draw a sharp line between ourselves and the enemy and to rectify mistakes whenever discovered.

Marxist philosophy holds that the law of the unity of opposites is the fundamental law of the universe. This law operates universally, whether in the natural world, in human society, or in man's thinking. Between the opposites in a contradiction there is at once unity and struggle, and it is this that impels things to move and change.

Contradictions exist everywhere, but their nature differs in accordance with the different nature of different things. In any given thing, the unity of opposites is conditional, temporary and transitory, and hence relative, whereas the struggle of opposites is absolute. Lenin gave a very clear exposition of this law. It has come to be understood by a growing number of people in our country. But for many people it is one thing to accept this law and quite another to apply it in examining and dealing with problems. Many dare not openly admit that contradictions still exist among the people of our country, while it is precisely these contradictions that are pushing our society forward. Many do not admit that contradictions still exist in socialist society, with the result that they become irresolute and passive when confronted with social contradictions; they do not understand that socialist society grows more united and consolidated through the ceaseless process of correctly handling and resolving contradictions. For this reason, we need to explain things to our people, and to our cadres in the first place, in order to help them understand the contradictions in socialist society and learn to use correct methods for handling them.

Contradictions in socialist society are fundamentally different from those in the old societies, such as capitalist society. In capitalist society contradictions find expression in acute antagonisms and conflicts, in sharp class struggle; they cannot be resolved by the capitalist system itself and can only be resolved by socialist revolution. The case is quite different with contradictions in socialist society; on the contrary, they are not antagonistic and can be ceaselessly resolved by the socialist system itself.

In socialist society the basic contradictions are still those between the relations of production and the productive forces and between the superstructure and the economic base.[4] However, they are fundamentally different in character and have different features from the contradictions between the relations of production and the productive forces and between the superstructure and the economic base in the old societies. The present social system of our country is far superior to that of the old days. If it were not so, the old system would not have been overthrown and the new system could not have been established. In saying that the socialist relations of production correspond

---

[4]Mao uses the terms *relations of production* and *productive forces* to express the Marxist view of who owns the factories, farms, and businesses and how that form of ownership relates to how things are made—that is, the level of modernization of industry and agriculture. Similarly, he uses *superstructure* and *economic base* to talk about the relationship between the economy and politics.

better to the character of the productive forces than did the old relations of production, we mean that they allow the productive forces to develop at a speed unattainable in the old society, so that production can expand steadily and increasingly meet the constantly growing needs of the people. Under the rule of imperialism, feudalism and bureaucrat-capitalism, the productive forces of the old China grew very slowly. For more than fifty years before liberation, China produced only a few tens of thousands of tons of steel a year, not counting the output of the northeastern provinces. If these provinces are included, the peak annual steel output only amounted to a little over 900,000 tons. In 1949, the national steel output was a little over 100,000 tons. Yet now, a mere seven years after the liberation of our country, steel output already exceeds 4,000,000 tons. In the old China, there was hardly any machine-building industry, to say nothing of the automobile and aircraft industries; now we have all three. When the people overthrew the rule of imperialism, feudalism and bureaucrat-capitalism, many were not clear as to which way China should head — towards capitalism or towards socialism. Facts have now provided the answer: Only socialism can save China. The socialist system has promoted the rapid development of the productive forces of our country, a fact even our enemies abroad have had to acknowledge.

But our socialist system has only just been set up; it is not yet fully established or fully consolidated. In joint state-private industrial and commercial enterprises, capitalists still get a fixed rate of interest on their capital, that is to say, exploitation still exists. So far as ownership is concerned, these enterprises are not yet completely socialist in nature. A number of our agricultural and handicraft producers' cooperatives are still semi-socialist, while even in the fully socialist co-operatives certain specific problems of ownership remain to be solved. Relations between production and exchange in accordance with socialist principles are being gradually established within and between all branches of our economy, and more and more appropriate forms are being sought. . . . To sum up, socialist relations of production have been established and are in correspondence with the growth of the productive forces, but these relations are still far from perfect, and this imperfection stands in contradiction to the growth of the productive forces. Apart from correspondence as well as contradiction between the relations of production and the growth of the productive forces, there is correspondence as well as contradiction between the superstructure and the economic base. The superstructure, comprising the state system and laws of the people's democratic dictatorship and the socialist ideology guided by Marxism-Leninism, plays a positive role in facilitating the victory of socialist transformation and the socialist way of organizing labour; it is in correspondence with the socialist economic base, that is, with socialist relations of production. But the existence of bourgeois ideology, a certain bureaucratic style of work in our state organs and defects in some of the links in our state institutions are in contradiction with the socialist economic base. We must continue to resolve all such contradictions in the light of our specific conditions. Of course, new problems will emerge as these contradictions are resolved. And further efforts will be required to resolve the new contradictions. For instance, a constant process of readjustment through state planning is needed to deal with the contradiction between production and the needs of society, which will long remain an objective reality. Every year our country draws up an economic plan in order to establish a proper ratio between accumulation and consumption and achieve an equilibrium between production and needs. Equilibrium is nothing but a temporary, relative, unity of opposites. By the end of each year, this equilibrium, taken as a whole, is upset by the struggle of opposites; the unity undergoes a change, equilibrium becomes disequilibrium, unity becomes disunity, and once again it is necessary to work out an equilibrium and unity for the next year. Herein lies the superiority of our planned economy. As a matter of fact, this equilibrium, this unity, is partially upset every month or every quarter, and partial readjustments are called for. Sometimes, contradictions arise and the equilibrium is upset because our subjective arrangements do not conform to objective reality; this is what we call making a mistake. The ceaseless emergence and ceaseless resolution of contradictions constitute the dialectical law of the development of things.

Today, matters stand as follows. The large-scale, turbulent class struggles of the masses characteristic of times of revolution have in the main come to an end, but class struggle is by no means entirely over. While welcoming the new system, the masses are not yet quite accustomed to it. Government personnel are not sufficiently experienced and have to undertake further study and investigation of specific policies. In other words, time is needed for our socialist system to become established and consolidated, for the masses to become accustomed to the new system, and for government personnel to learn and acquire experience. It is therefore imperative for us at this juncture to raise the question of distinguishing contradictions among the people from those between ourselves and the enemy, as well as the question of the correct handling of contradictions among the people, in order to unite the people of all nationalities in our country for the new battle, the battle against nature, develop our economy and culture, help the whole nation to traverse this period of transition relatively smoothly, consolidate our new system and build up our new state.

II. THE QUESTION OF ELIMINATING COUNTER-REVOLUTIONARIES

The elimination of counter-revolutionaries is a struggle of opposites as between ourselves and the enemy. Among the people, there are some who see this question in a somewhat different light. Two kinds of people hold views differing from ours. Those with a Right deviation in their thinking make no distinction between ourselves and the enemy and take the enemy for our own people. They regard as friends the very persons whom the masses regard as enemies. Those with a "Left" deviation in their thinking magnify contradictions between ourselves and the enemy to such an extent that they take certain contradictions among the people for contradictions with the enemy and regard as counter-revolutionaries persons who are actually not. Both these views are wrong. Neither makes possible the correct handling of the problem of eliminating counter-revolutionaries or a correct assessment of this work.

To form a correct evaluation of our work in eliminating counter-revolutionaries, let us see what repercussions the Hungarian incident has had in China. After its occurrence there was some unrest among a section of our intellectuals, but there were no squalls. Why? One reason, it must be said, was our success in eliminating counter-revolutionaries fairly thoroughly.

Of course, the consolidation of our state is not due primarily to the elimination of counter-revolutionaries. It is due primarily to the fact that we have a Communist Party and a Liberation Army both tempered in decades of revolutionary struggle, and a working people likewise so tempered. Our Party and our armed forces are rooted in the masses, have been tempered in the flames of a protracted revolution and have the capacity to fight. Our People's Republic was not built overnight, but developed step by step out of the revolutionary base areas. A number of democratic personages have also been tempered in the struggle in varying degrees, and they have gone through troubled times together with us. Some intellectuals were tempered in the struggles against imperialism and reaction; since liberation many have gone through a process of ideological remoulding[5] aimed at enabling them to distinguish clearly between ourselves and the enemy. In addition, the consolidation of our state is due to the fact that our economic measures are basically sound, that the people's life is secure and steadily improving, that our policies towards the national bourgeoisie and other classes are correct, and so on. Nevertheless, our success in eliminating counter-revolutionaries is undoubtedly an important reason for the consolidation of our state. For all these reasons, with few exceptions our college students are patriotic and support socialism and did not give way to unrest during the Hungarian incident, even though many of them come from families of nonworking people. The same was true of the national bourgeoisie, to say nothing of the basic masses—the workers and peasants.

After liberation, we rooted out a number of counter-revolutionaries. Some were sentenced to death for major crimes. This was absolutely necessary, it was the demand of the masses, and it was done to free them from long years of oppression by the counter-revolutionaries and all kinds of local tyrants, in other words, to liberate the productive forces. If we had not done so, the masses would not have been able to lift their heads. . . .

In our work of eliminating counter-revolutionaries successes were the main thing, but there were also mistakes. In some cases there were excesses and in others counter-revolutionaries slipped through our net. Our policy is: "Counter-revolutionaries must be eliminated wherever found, mistakes must be corrected whenever discovered." Our line in the work of eliminating counter-revolutionaries is the mass line. Of course, even with the mass line mistakes may still occur, but they will be fewer and easier to correct. The masses gain experience through struggle. From the things done correctly they gain the experience of how things are done correctly. From the mistakes made they gain the experience of how mistakes are made. . . .

The present situation with regard to counter-revolutionaries can be described in these words: There still are counter-revolutionaries, but not many. In the first place, there still are counter-revolutionaries.

---

[5]*ideological remoulding:* one of the core aspects of Maoism, this is the process of changing the way a person thinks, known in the West as brainwashing. Drawing on the ideological study sessions of Yan'an, this effort by the CCP was an orchestrated way to effect the change in class attitude Mao talked about in "Talks at the Yan'an Conference on Literature and Art" (see Document 3).

Some people say that there aren't any more left and all is well and that we can therefore lay our heads on our pillows and just drop off to sleep. But this is not the way things are. The fact is, there still are counter-revolutionaries (of course, that is not to say you'll find them everywhere and in every organization), and we must continue to fight them. It must be understood that the hidden counter-revolutionaries still at large will not take things lying down, but will certainly seize every opportunity to make trouble. The U.S. imperialists and the Chiang Kai-shek clique are constantly sending in secret agents to carry on disruptive activities. Even after all the existing counter-revolutionaries have been combed out, new ones are likely to emerge. If we drop our guard, we shall be badly fooled and shall suffer severely. Counter-revolutionaries must be rooted out with a firm hand wherever they are found making trouble. . . .

III. THE QUESTION OF THE CO-OPERATIVE TRANSFORMATION OF AGRICULTURE

We have a rural population of over 500 million, so how our peasants fare has a most important bearing on the development of our economy and the consolidation of our state power. In my view, the situation is basically sound. The co-operative transformation of agriculture has been successfully accomplished,[6] and this has resolved the great contradiction in our country between socialist industrialization and the individual peasant economy. As the co-operative transformation of agriculture was completed so rapidly, some people were worried and wondered whether something untoward might occur. There are indeed some faults, but fortunately they are not serious and on the whole the movement is healthy. The peasants are working with a will, and last year there was an increase in the country's grain output despite the worst floods, droughts and gales in years. Now there are people who are stirring up a miniature typhoon, they are saying that co-operation is no good, that there is nothing superior about it. Is co-operation superior or not? Among the documents distributed at today's meeting there is one about the Wang Guofan Co-operative in Zunhua County,

---

[6]*Agricultural cooperativization* was the CCP-sponsored movement to bring the newly independent farmers of China into closer economic cooperation. This process began in the mid-1950s but took off, with Mao's encouragement, in 1956. By 1957 Mao was thinking of the next step, which would become the people's communes of the Great Leap Forward in 1958.

Hebei Province, which I suggest you read. This co-operative is situated in a hilly region which was very poor in the past and which for a number of years depended on relief grain from the People's Government. When the co-operative was first set up in 1953, people called it the "paupers' co-op." But it has become better off year by year, and now, after four years of hard struggle, most of its households have reserves of grain. What was possible for this co-operative should also be possible for others to achieve under normal conditions in the same length of time or a little longer. Clearly there are no grounds for saying that something has gone wrong with agricultural co-operation.

It is also clear that it takes hard struggle to build co-operatives. New things always have to experience difficulties and setbacks as they grow. It is sheer fantasy to imagine that the cause of socialism is all plain sailing and easy success, with no difficulties and setbacks, or without the exertion of tremendous efforts.

Who are the active supporters of the co-operatives? The overwhelming majority of the poor and lower-middle peasants who constitute more than 70 per cent of the rural population. Most of the other peasants are also placing their hopes on the co-operatives. Only a very small minority are really dissatisfied. . . .

The co-operatives are now in the process of gradual consolidation. There are certain contradictions that remain to be resolved, such as those between the state and the co-operatives and those in and between the co-operatives themselves.

To resolve these contradictions we must pay constant attention to the problems of production and distribution. On the question of production, the co-operative economy must be subject to the unified economic planning of the state, while retaining a certain flexibility and independence that do not run counter to the state's unified plan or its policies, laws and regulations. At the same time, every household in a co-operative must comply with the over-all plan of the co-operative or production team to which it belongs, though it may make its own appropriate plans in regard to land allotted for personal needs and to other individually operated economic undertakings. On the question of distribution, we must take the interests of the state, the collective and the individual into account. We must properly handle the three-way relationship between the state agricultural tax, the co-operative's accumulation fund and the peasants' personal income, and take constant care to make readjustments so as to resolve contradictions between them. Accumulation is essential for both the state and the co-operative, but in neither case should it be excessive. We should do everything possible to enable the peasants in normal years to raise their personal incomes annually through increased production. . . .

IV. THE QUESTION OF THE INDUSTRIALISTS AND BUSINESSMEN

With regard to the transformation of our social system, the year 1956 saw the conversion of privately owned industrial and commercial enterprises into joint state-private enterprises as well as the co-operative transformation of agriculture and handicrafts. The speed and smoothness of this conversion were closely bound up with our treating the contradiction between the working class and the national bourgeoisie as a contradiction among the people. Has this class contradiction been completely resolved? No, not yet. That will take a considerable period of time. However, some people say the capitalists have been so remoulded that they are now not very different from the workers and that further remoulding is unnecessary. Others go so far as to say that the capitalists are even better than the workers. Still others ask, if remoulding is necessary, why isn't it necessary for the working class? Are these opinions correct? Of course not.

In the building of a socialist society, everybody needs remoulding — the exploiters and also the working people. Who says it isn't necessary for the working class? Of course, the remoulding of the exploiters is essentially different from that of the working people, and the two must not be confused. The working class remoulds the whole of society in class struggle and in the struggle against nature, and in the process it remoulds itself. It must ceaselessly learn in the course of work, gradually overcome its shortcomings and never stop doing so. Take for example those of us present here. Many of us make some progress each year, that is to say, we are remoulding ourselves each year. For myself, I used to have all sorts of non-Marxist ideas, and it was only later that I embraced Marxism. I learned a little Marxism from books and took the first steps in remoulding my ideology, but it was mainly through taking part in class struggle over the years that I came to be remoulded. And if I am to make further progress, I must continue to learn, otherwise I shall lag behind. Can the capitalists be so good that they need no more remoulding?

Some people contend that the Chinese bourgeoisie no longer has two sides to its character, but only one side. Is this true? No. While members of the bourgeoisie have become administrative personnel in joint state-private enterprises and are being transformed from exploiters into working people living by their own labour, they still get a fixed rate of interest on their capital in the joint enterprises, that is, they have not yet cut themselves loose from the roots of exploitation. Between them and the working class there is still a considerable gap in ideology, sentiments and habits of life. How can it be said that they no longer have two sides to their character? Even when they stop receiving their fixed interest payments and the "bourgeois" label is removed, they will still need ideological remoulding for quite some time. If, as is alleged, the bourgeoisie no longer has a dual character, then the capitalists will no longer have the task of studying and of remoulding themselves.

It must be said that this view does not tally either with the actual situation of our industrialists and businessmen or with what most of them want. During the past few years, most of them have been willing to study and have made marked progress. As their thorough remoulding can be achieved only in the course of work, they should engage in labour together with the staff and workers in the enterprises and regard these enterprises as the chief places in which to remould themselves. But it is also important for them to change some of their old views through study. Such study should be on a voluntary basis. When they return to the enterprises after being in study groups for some weeks, many industrialists and businessmen find that they have more of a common language with the workers and the representatives of state ownership, and so there are better possibilities for working together. They know from personal experience that it is good for them to keep on studying and remoulding[7] themselves. The idea mentioned above that study and remoulding are not necessary reflects the views not of the majority of industrialists and businessmen but of only a small number.

V. THE QUESTION OF THE INTELLECTUALS

The contradictions within the ranks of the people in our country also find expression among the intellectuals. The several million intellectuals who worked for the old society have come to serve the new society, and the question that now arises is how they can fit in with the needs of the new society and how we can help them to do so. This, too, is a contradiction among the people.

Most of our intellectuals have made marked progress during the last seven years. They have shown they are in favour of the socialist

[7]*studying and remoulding:* ideological remolding in CCP-organized study groups

system. Many are diligently studying Marxism, and some have become communists. The latter, though at present small in number, are steadily increasing. Of course, there are still some intellectuals who are sceptical about socialism or do not approve of it, but they are a minority.

China needs the services of as many intellectuals as possible for the colossal task of building socialism. We should trust those who are really willing to serve the cause of socialism and should radically improve our relations with them and help them solve the problems requiring solution, so that they can give full play to their talents. Many of our comrades are not good at uniting with intellectuals. They are stiff in their attitude towards them, lack respect for their work and interfere in certain scientific and cultural matters where interference is unwarranted. We must do away with all such shortcomings.

Although large numbers of intellectuals have made progress, they should not be complacent. They must continue to remould themselves, gradually shed their bourgeois world outlook and acquire the proletarian, communist world outlook so that they can fully fit in with the needs of the new society and unite with the workers and peasants. The change in world outlook is fundamental, and up to now most of our intellectuals cannot be said to have accomplished it. We hope that they will continue to make progress and that in the course of work and study they will gradually acquire the communist world outlook, grasp Marxism-Leninism and become integrated with the workers and peasants. . . . But a thorough change in world outlook takes a very long time, and we should spare no pains in helping them and must not be impatient. Actually, there are bound to be some who ideologically will always be reluctant to accept Marxism-Leninism and communism. We should not be too exacting in what we demand of them; as long as they comply with the requirements laid down by the state and engage in legitimate pursuits, we should let them have opportunities for suitable work.

Among students and intellectuals there has recently been a falling off in ideological and political work, and some unhealthy tendencies have appeared. Some people seem to think that there is no longer any need to concern themselves with politics or with the future of the motherland and the ideals of mankind. It seems as if Marxism, once all the rage, is currently not so much in fashion. To counter these tendencies, we must strengthen our ideological and political work. Both students and intellectuals should study hard. In addition to the study of their specialized subjects, they must make progress ideologically and politically, which means they should study Marxism, current events and politics. Not to have a correct political orientation is like not having a soul. The ideological remoulding in the past was necessary and has yielded positive results. But it was carried on in a somewhat rough-and-ready fashion and the feelings of some people were hurt—this was not good. We must avoid such shortcomings in future. All departments and organizations should shoulder their responsibilities for ideological and political work. This applies to the Communist Party, the Youth League,[8] government departments in charge of this work, and especially to heads of educational institutions and teachers. Our educational policy must enable everyone who receives an education to develop morally, intellectually and physically and become a worker with both socialist consciousness and culture. We must spread the idea of building our country through diligence and thrift. We must help all our young people to understand that ours is still a very poor country, that we cannot change this situation radically in a short time, and that only through decades of united effort by our younger generation and all our people, working with their own hands, can China be made prosperous and strong. The establishment of our socialist system has opened the road leading to the ideal society of the future, but to translate this ideal into reality needs hard work. Some of our young people think that everything ought to be perfect once a socialist society is established and that they should be able to enjoy a happy life ready-made, without working for it. This is unrealistic.

VI. THE QUESTION OF THE MINORITY NATIONALITIES

The minority nationalities in our country number more than thirty million. Although they constitute only 6 per cent of the total population, they inhabit extensive regions which comprise 50 to 60 per cent of China's total area. It is thus imperative to foster good relations between the Han[9] people and the minority nationalities. The key to this question lies in overcoming Han chauvinism. At the same time, efforts should also be made to overcome local-nationality chauvinism,

---

[8] *Youth League:* the organization to train future CCP members. It was very important under Mao as the only legal nationwide organization besides the CCP and the People's Liberation Army (PLA).

[9] *Han:* Chinese name for the dominant ethnic group in China. The Han make up about 96 percent of China's population. The remaining citizens of the People's Republic of China (PRC) come from other ethnic groups, or nationalities, such as the Mongols, Manchus, or Uighurs, or from one of dozens of tribes.

wherever it exists among the minority nationalities. Both Han chauvinism and local-nationality chauvinism are harmful to the unity of the nationalities; they represent one kind of contradiction among the people which should be resolved. We have already done some work to this end. In most of the areas inhabited by minority nationalities, there has been considerable improvement in the relations between the nationalities, but a number of problems remain to be solved. In some areas, both Han chauvinism and local-nationality chauvinism still exist to a serious degree, and this demands full attention. As a result of the efforts of the people of all nationalities over the last few years, democratic reforms and socialist transformation have in the main been completed in most of the minority nationality areas. Democratic reforms have not yet been carried out in Tibet because conditions are not ripe. According to the seventeen-article agreement reached between the Central People's Government and the local government of Tibet, the reform of the social system must be carried out, but the timing can only be decided when the great majority of the people of Tibet and the local leading public figures consider it opportune, and one should not be impatient. It has now been decided not to proceed with democratic reforms in Tibet during the period of the Second Five-Year Plan.[10] Whether to proceed with them in the period of the Third Five-Year Plan can only be decided in the light of the situation at the time. . . .

[Section VII provides a one-page general reflection on "Overall consideration and proper arrangements."]

VIII. ON "LET A HUNDRED FLOWERS BLOSSOM, LET A HUNDRED SCHOOLS OF THOUGHT CONTEND" AND "LONG-TERM COEXISTENCE AND MUTUAL SUPERVISION"

"Let a hundred flowers blossom, let a hundred schools of thought contend" and "long-term coexistence and mutual supervision"—how did these slogans come to be put forward? They were put forward in the light of China's specific conditions, in recognition of the continued

---

[10]The First Five-Year Plan (1953–57) was modeled on the central economic planning of the Soviet Union. Such a planned economy replaced the market economy as the mechanism for determining investment, production, and spending. The Second Five-Year Plan ran from 1958 to 1962. China has followed such plans ever since, but their relevance has decreased with market reform in the post-Mao period.

existence of various kinds of contradictions in socialist society and in response to the country's urgent need to speed up its economic and cultural development. Letting a hundred flowers blossom and a hundred schools of thought contend is the policy for promoting progress in the arts and sciences and a flourishing socialist culture in our land. Different forms and styles in art should develop freely and different schools in science should contend freely. We think that it is harmful to the growth of art and science if administrative measures are used to impose one particular style of art or school of thought and to ban another. Questions of right and wrong in the arts and sciences should be settled through free discussion in artistic and scientific circles and through practical work in these fields. They should not be settled in an over-simple manner. A period of trial is often needed to determine whether something is right or wrong. Throughout history, at the outset new and correct things often failed to win recognition from the majority of people and had to develop by twists and turns through struggle. Often, correct and good things were first regarded not as fragrant flowers but as poisonous weeds. Copernicus' theory of the solar system and Darwin's theory of evolution were once dismissed as erroneous and had to win out over bitter opposition. Chinese history offers many similar examples. In a socialist society, the conditions for the growth of the new are radically different from and far superior to those in the old society. Nevertheless, it often happens that new, rising forces are held back and sound ideas stifled. Besides, even in the absence of their deliberate suppression, the growth of new things may be hindered simply through lack of discernment. It is therefore necessary to be careful about questions of right and wrong in the arts and sciences, to encourage free discussion and avoid hasty conclusions. We believe that such an attitude will help ensure a relatively smooth development of the arts and sciences.

Marxism, too, has developed through struggle. At the beginning, Marxism was subjected to all kinds of attack and regarded as a poisonous weed. This is still the case in many parts of the world. In the socialist countries, it enjoys a different position. But non-Marxist and, what is more, anti-Marxist ideologies exist even in these countries. In China, although socialist transformation has in the main been completed as regards the system of ownership, and although the large-scale, turbulent class struggles of the masses characteristic of times of revolution have in the main come to an end, there are still remnants of the overthrown landlord and comprador[11] classes, there is still a bourgeoisie, and the remoulding of the petty bourgeoisie has only just started. Class struggle is by no means over. The class struggle between the proletariat and the bourgeoisie, the class struggle between the various political forces, and the class struggle between the proletariat and the bourgeoisie in the ideological field will still be protracted and tortuous and at times even very sharp. The proletariat seeks to transform the world according to its own world outlook, and so does the bourgeoisie. In this respect, the question of which will win out, socialism or capitalism, is not really settled yet. Marxists remain a minority among the entire population as well as among the intellectuals. Therefore, Marxism must continue to develop through struggle. Marxism can develop only through struggle, and this is not only true of the past and the present, it is necessarily true of the future as well. What is correct invariably develops in the course of struggle with what is wrong. The true, the good and the beautiful always exist by contrast with the false, the evil and the ugly, and grow in struggle with them. As soon as something erroneous is rejected and a particular truth accepted by mankind, new truths begin to struggle with new errors. Such struggles will never end. This is the law of development of truth and, naturally, of Marxism.

It will take a fairly long period of time to decide the issue in the ideological struggle between socialism and capitalism in our country. The reason is that the influence of the bourgeoisie and of the intellectuals who come from the old society, the very influence which constitutes their class ideology, will persist in our country for a long time. If this is not understood at all or is insufficiently understood, the gravest of mistakes will be made and the necessity of waging struggle in the ideological field will be ignored. Ideological struggle differs from other forms of struggle, since the only method used is painstaking reasoning, and not crude coercion. Today, socialism is in an advantageous position in the ideological struggle. The basic power of the state is in the hands of the working people led by the proletariat. The Communist Party is strong and its prestige high. Although there are defects and mistakes in our work, every fair-minded person can see that we are loyal to the people, that we are both determined and able to build up our motherland together with them, and that we have already

---

[11]*comprador:* a nineteenth-century Chinese who worked with European merchants as a middleman in one of the various ports of China. Compradors were widely held to be unpatriotic, if not outright traitors. Many became wealthy and were among the new class of industrial leaders.

achieved great successes and will achieve still greater ones. The vast majority of the bourgeoisie and the intellectuals who come from the old society are patriotic and are willing to serve their flourishing socialist motherland; they know they will have nothing to fall back on and their future cannot possibly be bright if they turn away from the socialist cause and from the working people led by the Communist Party.

People may ask, since Marxism is accepted as the guiding ideology by the majority of the people in our country, can it be criticized? Certainly it can. Marxism is scientific truth and fears no criticism. If it did, and if it could be overthrown by criticism, it would be worthless. In fact, aren't the idealists criticizing Marxism every day and in every way? And those who harbour bourgeois and petty-bourgeois ideas and do not wish to change—aren't they also criticizing Marxism in every way? Marxists should not be afraid of criticism from any quarter. Quite the contrary, they need to temper and develop themselves and win new positions in the teeth of criticism and in the storm and stress of struggle. Fighting against wrong ideas is like being vaccinated—a man develops greater immunity from disease as a result of vaccination. Plants raised in hothouses are unlikely to be hardy. Carrying out the policy of letting a hundred flowers blossom and a hundred schools of thought contend will not weaken, but strengthen, the leading position of Marxism in the ideological field.

What should our policy be towards non-Marxist ideas? As far as unmistakable counter-revolutionaries and saboteurs of the socialist cause are concerned, the matter is easy, we simply deprive them of their freedom of speech. But incorrect ideas among the people are quite a different matter. Will it do to ban such ideas and deny them any opportunity for expression? Certainly not. It is not only futile but very harmful to use crude methods in dealing with ideological questions among the people, with questions about man's mental world. You may ban the expression of wrong ideas, but the ideas will still be there. On the other hand, if correct ideas are pampered in hothouses and never exposed to the elements and immunized against disease, they will not win out against erroneous ones. Therefore, it is only by employing the method of discussion, criticism and reasoning that we can really foster correct ideas and overcome wrong ones, and that we can really settle issues.

It is inevitable that the bourgeoisie and petty bourgeoisie will give expression to their own ideologies. It is inevitable that they will stubbornly assert themselves on political and ideological questions by every possible means. You cannot expect them to do otherwise. We should not use the method of suppression and prevent them from expressing themselves, but should allow them to do so and at the same time argue with them and direct appropriate criticism at them. Undoubtedly, we must criticize wrong ideas of every description. It certainly would not be right to refrain from criticism, look on while wrong ideas spread unchecked and allow them to dominate the field. Mistakes must be criticized and poisonous weeds fought wherever they crop up. However, such criticism should not be dogmatic, and the metaphysical method should not be used, but instead the effort should be made to apply the dialectical method. What is needed is scientific analysis and convincing argument. Dogmatic criticism settles nothing. We are against poisonous weeds of whatever kind, but we must carefully distinguish between what is really a poisonous weed and what is really a fragrant flower. Together with the masses of the people, we must learn to differentiate carefully between the two and use correct methods to fight the poisonous weeds.

At the same time as we criticize dogmatism, we must direct our attention to criticizing revisionism. Revisionism, or Right opportunism, is a bourgeois trend of thought that is even more dangerous than dogmatism. The revisionists, the Right opportunists, pay lip-service to Marxism; they too attack "dogmatism." But what they are really attacking is the quintessence of Marxism. They oppose or distort materialism and dialectics, oppose or try to weaken the people's democratic dictatorship and the leading role of the Communist Party, and oppose or try to weaken socialist transformation and socialist construction. Even after the basic victory of our socialist revolution, there will still be a number of people in our society who vainly hope to restore the capitalist system and are sure to fight the working class on every front, including the ideological one. And their right-hand men in this struggle are the revisionists.

Literally the two slogans—let a hundred flowers blossom and let a hundred schools of thought contend—have no class character; the proletariat can turn them to account, and so can the bourgeoisie or others. Different classes, strata and social groups each have their own views on what are fragrant flowers and what are poisonous weeds. Then, from the point of view of the masses, what should be the criteria today for distinguishing fragrant flowers from poisonous weeds? In their political activities, how should our people judge whether a person's words and deeds are right or wrong? On the basis of the principles of our Constitution, the will of the overwhelming majority of our people and the common political positions which have been proclaimed on various occasions by our political parties, we consider that, broadly speaking, the criteria should be as follows:

1. Words and deeds should help to unite, and not divide, the people of all our nationalities.
2. They should be beneficial, and not harmful, to socialist transformation and socialist construction.
3. They should help to consolidate, and not undermine or weaken, the people's democratic dictatorship.
4. They should help to consolidate, and not undermine or weaken, democratic centralism.
5. They should help to strengthen, and not shake off or weaken, the leadership of the Communist Party.
6. They should be beneficial, and not harmful, to international socialist unity and the unity of the peace-loving people of the world.

Of these six criteria, the most important are the two about the socialist path and the leadership of the Party. These criteria are put forward not to hinder but to foster the free discussion of questions among the people. Those who disapprove these criteria can still state their own views and argue their case. However, so long as the majority of the people have clear-cut criteria to go by, criticism and self-criticism can be conducted along proper lines, and these criteria can be applied to people's words and deeds to determine whether they are right or wrong, whether they are fragrant flowers or poisonous weeds. These are political criteria. Naturally, to judge the validity of scientific theories or assess the aesthetic value of works of art, other relevant criteria are needed. But these six political criteria are applicable to all activities in the arts and sciences. In a socialist country like ours, can there possibly be any useful scientific or artistic activity which runs counter to these political criteria?

The views set out above are based on China's specific historical conditions. Conditions vary in different socialist countries and with different Communist Parties. Therefore, we do not maintain that they should or must adopt the Chinese way.

The slogan "long-term coexistence and mutual supervision" is also a product of China's specific historical conditions. It was not put forward all of a sudden, but had been in the making for several years. The idea of long-term coexistence had been there for a long time. When the socialist system was in the main established last year, the slogan was formulated in explicit terms. Why should the bourgeois and petty-bourgeois democratic parties be allowed to exist side by side with the party of the working class over a long period of time? Because we have no reason for not adopting the policy of long-term coexistence with all those political parties which are truly devoted to the task of uniting the people for the cause of socialism and which enjoy the trust of the people. . . . It is the desire as well as the policy of the Communist Party to exist side by side with the democratic parties for a long time to come. But whether the democratic parties can long remain in existence depends not merely on the desire of the Communist Party but on how well they acquit themselves and on whether they enjoy the trust of the people. Mutual supervision among the various parties is also a long-established fact, in the sense that they have long been advising and criticizing each other. Mutual supervision is obviously not a one-sided matter; it means that the Communist Party can exercise supervision over the democratic parties, and vice versa. Why should the democratic parties be allowed to exercise supervision over the Communist Party? Because a party as much as an individual has great need to hear opinions different from its own. We all know that supervision over the Communist Party is mainly exercised by the working people and the Party membership. But it augments the benefit to us to have supervision by the democratic parties too. Of course, the advice and criticism exchanged by the Communist Party and the democratic parties will play a positive supervisory role only when they conform to the six political criteria given above. Thus, we hope that in order to fit in with the needs of the new society, all the democratic parties will pay attention to ideological remoulding and strive for long-term coexistence with the Communist Party and mutual supervision.

IX. ON THE QUESTION OF DISTURBANCES CREATED BY SMALL NUMBERS OF PEOPLE

In 1956, small numbers of workers or students in certain places went on strike. The immediate cause of these disturbances was the failure to satisfy some of their demands for material benefits, of which some should and could have been met, while others were out of place or excessive and therefore could not be met for the time being. But a more important cause was bureaucracy[12] on the part of the leadership. In some cases, the responsibility for such bureaucratic mistakes fell

---

[12]*bureaucracy:* the excessive and oppressive use of bureaucratic power by government officials. The term Mao used here, *guanliaozhuyi,* is more often translated as "bureaucratism."

on the higher authorities, and those at the lower levels were not to blame. Another cause of these disturbances was lack of ideological and political education among the workers and students. The same year, in some agricultural co-operatives there were also disturbances created by a few of their members, and here too the main causes were bureaucracy on the part of the leadership and lack of educational work among the masses.

It should be admitted that among the masses some are prone to pay attention to immediate, partial and personal interests and do not understand, or do not sufficiently understand, long-range, national and collective interests. Because of lack of political and social experience, quite a number of young people cannot readily see the contrast between the old China and the new, and it is not easy for them thoroughly to comprehend the hardships our people went through in the struggle to free themselves from the oppression of the imperialists and Guomindang reactionaries, or the long years of hard work needed before a fine socialist society can be established. That is why we must constantly carry on lively and effective political education among the masses and should always tell them the truth about the difficulties that crop up and discuss with them how to surmount these difficulties.

We do not approve of disturbances, because contradictions among the people can be resolved through the method of "unity—criticism—unity," while disturbances are bound to cause some losses and are not conducive to the advance of socialism. We believe that the masses of the people support socialism, conscientiously observe discipline and are reasonable, and will certainly not take part in disturbances without cause. But this does not mean that the possibility of disturbances by the masses no longer exists in our country. On this question, we should pay attention to the following. (1) In order to root out the causes of disturbances, we must resolutely overcome bureaucracy, greatly improve ideological and political education, and deal with all contradictions properly. If this is done, generally speaking there will be no disturbances. (2) When disturbances do occur as a result of poor work on our part, then we should guide those involved onto the correct path, use the disturbances as a special means for improving our work and educating the cadres and the masses, and find solutions to those problems which were previously left unsolved. In handling any disturbance, we should take pains and not use over-simple methods, or hastily declare the matter closed. The ringleaders in disturbances should not be summarily expelled, except for those who have committed criminal offences or are active counter-revolutionaries and have to be punished by law. In a large country like ours, there is nothing to get alarmed about if small numbers of people create disturbances; on the contrary, such disturbances will help us get rid of bureaucracy.

There are also a small number of individuals in our society who, flouting the public interest, wilfully break the law and commit crimes. They are apt to take advantage of our policies and distort them, and deliberately put forward unreasonable demands in order to incite the masses, or deliberately spread rumours to create trouble and disrupt public order. We do not propose to let these individuals have their way. On the contrary, proper legal action must be taken against them. Punishing them is the demand of the masses, and it would run counter to the popular will if they were not punished.

X. CAN BAD THINGS BE TURNED INTO GOOD THINGS?

In our society, as I have said, disturbances by the masses are bad, and we do not approve of them. But when disturbances do occur, they enable us to learn lessons, to overcome bureaucracy and to educate the cadres and the masses. In this sense, bad things can be turned into good things. Disturbances thus have a dual character. Every disturbance can be regarded in this way.

Everybody knows that the Hungarian incident was not a good thing. But it too had a dual character. Because our Hungarian comrades took proper action in the course of the incident, what was a bad thing has eventually turned into a good one. Hungary is now more consolidated than ever, and all other countries in the socialist camp have also learned a lesson. . . .

People all over the world are now discussing whether or not a third world war will break out. On this question, too, we must be mentally prepared and do some analysis. We stand firmly for peace and against war. But if the imperialists insist on unleashing another war, we should not be afraid of it. Our attitude on this question is the same as our attitude towards any disturbance: first, we are against it; second, we are not afraid of it. The First World War was followed by the birth of the Soviet Union with a population of 200 million. The Second World War was followed by the emergence of the socialist camp with a combined population of 900 million. If the imperialists insist on launching a third world war, it is certain that several hundred million more will turn to socialism, and then there will not be much room left on earth for the imperialists; it is also likely that the whole structure of imperialism will completely collapse.

In given conditions, each of the two opposing aspects of a contradiction invariably transforms itself into its opposite as a result of the struggle between them. Here, it is the conditions which are essential. Without the given conditions, neither of the two contradictory aspects can transform itself into its opposite. Of all the classes in the world the proletariat is the one which is most eager to change its position, and next comes the semi-proletariat, for the former possesses nothing at all while the latter is hardly any better off. The United States now controls a majority in the United Nations and dominates many parts of the world—this state of affairs is temporary and will be changed one of these days. China's position as a poor country denied its rights in international affairs will also be changed—the poor country will change into a rich one, the country denied its rights into one enjoying them—a transformation of things into their opposites. Here, the decisive conditions are the socialist system and the concerted efforts of a united people. . . .

[In Section XI, Mao uses a page and a half to urge the party to economize and "share weal and woe with the masses."]

XII. CHINA'S PATH TO INDUSTRIALIZATION

In discussing our path to industrialization, we are here concerned principally with the relationship between the growth of heavy industry, light industry and agriculture. It must be affirmed that heavy industry is the core of China's economic construction. At the same time, full attention must be paid to the development of agriculture and light industry. . . .

I do not propose to dwell on economic questions today. With barely seven years of economic construction behind us, we still lack experience and need to accumulate it. Neither had we any experience in revolution when we first started, and it was only after we had taken a number of tumbles and acquired experience that we won nation-wide victory. What we must now demand of ourselves is to gain experience in economic construction in a shorter period of time than it took us to gain experience in revolution, and not to pay as high a price for it. Some price we will have to pay, but we hope it will not be as high as that paid during the period of revolution. We must realize that there is a contradiction here—the contradiction between the objective laws of economic development of a socialist society and our subjective cognition of them—which needs to be resolved in the course of practice. This contradiction also manifests itself as a contradiction between different people, that is, a contradiction between those in whom the reflection of these objective laws is relatively accurate and those in whom the reflection is relatively inaccurate; this, too, is a contradiction among the people. Every contradiction is an objective reality, and it is our task to reflect it and resolve it in as nearly correct a fashion as we can.

In order to turn China into an industrial country, we must learn conscientiously from the advanced experience of the Soviet Union. The Soviet Union has been building socialism for forty years, and its experience is very valuable to us. Let us ask: Who designed and equipped so many important factories for us? Was it the United States? Or Britain? No, neither the one nor the other. Only the Soviet Union was willing to do so, because it is a socialist country and our ally. In addition to the Soviet Union, the fraternal countries in East Europe have also given us some assistance. It is perfectly true that we should learn from the good experience of all countries, socialist or capitalist, about this there is no argument. But the main thing is still to learn from the Soviet Union. Now there are two different attitudes towards learning from others. One is the dogmatic attitude of transplanting everything, whether or not it is suited to our conditions. This is no good. The other attitude is to use our heads and learn those things which suit our conditions, that is, to absorb whatever experience is useful to us. That is the attitude we should adopt.

To strengthen our solidarity with the Soviet Union, to strengthen our solidarity with all the socialist countries—this is our fundamental policy, this is where our basic interests lie. Then there are the Asian and African countries and all the peace-loving countries and peoples— we must strengthen and develop our solidarity with them. United with these two forces, we shall not stand alone. As for the imperialist countries, we should unite with their people and strive to coexist peacefully with those countries, do business with them and prevent a possible war, but under no circumstances should we harbour any unrealistic notions about them.

8

Talks at the Beidaihe Conference
August 1958

Mao's talks at the Beidaihe conference of the CCP politburo have never been officially published in China. But scholars have long known that this meeting in August 1958 produced the big push for Mao's utopian scheme, the "people's communes," and ushered in the high tide of the Great Leap Forward. This text contains extracts from a "draft transcript" of Mao's five long, rambling talks given between August 17 and 30 at the beachside party retreat. The transcript appears in a Cultural Revolution–period "genius" Mao edition that came to light in the 1980s (see "A Note about the Texts"). The extracts here are taken in chronological order from the forty-five-page text, with an emphasis on Mao's comments on the people's communes.

Mao's utopian visions were at their height at the Beidaihe Conference. His wild romanticizing of the Yan'an experience and his equating public dining halls and a nonmonetary economy with communism are startling aspects of the speeches. This shows how little concern Mao had for proper Marxist terms. His colleagues were perplexed by the blending of his noble ideas (such as the dignity of manual labor and a better deal for women and youth) with his unrealistic musings on "deep ploughing" and "airports" for every commune. This selection also includes his tragic call to increase China's population. Two long-term results of Mao's utopian visions have been noted: The improvement of women's place in China has been needlessly linked to the excesses of the Cultural Revolution (and neatly ignored in post-Mao China), and China now wrestles with a severe overpopulation problem.

---

17 AUGUST

This is an enlarged Politburo conference; responsible comrades from all provinces and autonomous regions are participating. The topics are

---

Xuexi wenxuan (Study Selections) (n.p., n.d.), 295–321. Translation from Roderick Mac-Farquhar, Timothy Cheek, and Eugene Wu, eds., *The Secret Speeches of Chairman Mao: From the Hundred Flowers to the Great Leap Forward* (Cambridge: Harvard Council on East Asian Studies, 1989), 397–400, 403, 408, 418–19, 429–30, 434–36, 441.

listed in the documents distributed here, and comrades may refer to them.

The key point is the first problem: the problem of the Five Year Economic Plan next year—mainly it has to do with industry, but it's also somewhat relevant to agriculture. It's unfair just to issue reference figures; we should be fairer and more correct with our figures. Let's take three days to work on it; Comrade Li Fuchun* will be responsible. . . .

The eighth problem: the problem of cadres participating in manual labor. Officials, no matter who, whether big or small, including us here, all should participate in manual labor as long as they're physically able, excepting only those too old or too weak. We have millions of officials; adding those in the army there are more than ten million. We don't even have a clear idea as to exactly how many officials. Cadre children number in the tens of millions, and they are in a favored position from which to become officials. When one has been an official for a long time, it's easy to get separated from reality and the masses. The construction of the Ming Tombs Reservoir has been completed; many people went to the reservoir to perform manual labor for a few days.† Can we do manual labor for one month a year, making assignments according to the four seasons of the year? Workers, peasants, and commercial personnel are all able to combine manual labor and their ordinary work; everybody should be like that. If other people can do manual labor, is it acceptable that our officials should not? And then there are all those many cadre children. In the Soviet Union, graduates of agricultural colleges don't want to go to the countryside. Isn't it absurd to run agricultural colleges in the cities! Agricultural colleges should all move to the countryside. All schools should run factories. Even the Tianjin Conservatory is running a few factories; that's very good. Participating in manual labor is easy for cadres at the county and township levels, but it's hard to manage for those at the level of the Center, provinces, and prefectures; they probably can't operate a machine! How is it that people who can eat with chopsticks and write with brushes can't operate a machine? Is it easier to operate a machine or to climb a mountain? . . .

The fifteenth problem: the problem of deep ploughing. Currently the main orientation in agriculture is the problem of deep ploughing.

---

*_Li Fuchun:_ Chairman, State Planning Commission
†Mao himself had led his senior colleagues to work there in May to symbolize the importance he placed on manual labor.

Ploughing deeply is like creating a big reservoir for water and a big cistern for manure, otherwise no amount of water and manure will work. In the north we should deep plough to a depth of over a foot, in the south to 7 or 8 inches, then apply manure in different layers so as to enhance the granular structure of the soil. Every granule is both a small reservoir, and small manure cistern. Deep ploughing brings water above ground into contact with underground water. Close planting is based on deep ploughing: otherwise it is useless. Deep ploughing helps weeding. Digging up roots in turn helps eliminate insects so that one *mou*[1] of land can produce as much as three *mou*. Now each person nationwide has three *mou* of land. Once we go down to the grass roots, we can increase production. What's the use of planting that much land? In the future we can use one-third of the land for afforestation, and after a few years again decrease the acreage for grain by another *mou* per capita. In the past we weren't able to afforest the plains, but by that time we will be able to. Without deep ploughing there's no such possibility.

Our views on population should change. In the past I said that we could manage with 800 million. Now I think that one billion plus would be no cause for alarm. This shouldn't be recommended for people with many children. When people's level of education increases, they will really practice birth control. . . .

Now on the problem of the people's communes: What should they be called? They may be called people's communes, or they may not. My inclination is to call them people's communes. This name is still socialist in nature, not at all overemphasizing communism. They're called people's communes, first, because they're big and, second because they're public. Lots of people, a vast area of land, large scale of production, and all their undertakings are done in a big way. They integrate government administration with commune management to establish public mess halls, and private plots are eliminated. But chickens, ducks, and the young trees in front and behind a house are still private. These, of course, won't exist in the future. If we have more grain, we can practice the supply system; for the present it's still reward according to one's work. Wages will be given to individuals according to their ability and won't be given to the head of the family, which makes the youth and women happy. This will be very beneficial for the liberation of the individual. In establishing the people's communes, as I see it, once again it's been the countryside that's taken

[1]mou: *mu*

the lead; the cities haven't started yet, because the workers' wage scales are a complicated matter. Whether in urban or rural areas, the aim should be the socialist system plus communist ideology. The Soviet Union practices the use of high rewards and heavy punishments, emphasizing only material incentives. We now practice socialism, and have the sprouts of communism. Schools, factories, and neighborhoods can all establish people's communes. In a few years big communes will be organized to include everyone. . . .

The people's communes contain the sprouts of communism. When products are bountiful, we will implement communist distribution of grain, cotton, and edible oils. By that time morality will have greatly improved. Labor will no longer require supervision; even if you want someone to rest, he won't. The Jianhua Machinery Plant practices the *"ba wu."** In the people's communes, people practice cooperation in a big way, bringing their own tools and food. The workers beat drums and gongs and don't ask for piece-rate wages. All of these are the sprouts of communism, and they destroy the system of bourgeois right. I hope everyone will publicize this way of looking at the problem, read the two relevant documents, and publicize the actual situations in which there is increasing growth of the elements of communist morality.

In the past during the revolution numerous people died without asking anything in return. Why can't it be like that now? If we can eat without paying for it, this will be a tremendous change. Probably in about ten years our production will be very bountiful and the people's morality will be very noble; then we can practice communism in eating, clothing, and housing. Eating without paying in public mess halls is communism. In the future everything will be called a commune. We won't say factories; for instance, Anshan Steel Mill will be called Anshan Commune. Cities and villages will be called communes, and universities and neighborhoods will establish communes. Townships will be integrated with communes, local government will be integrated with commune management; temporarily we put up two signs. Set up a "department of the interior" (administrative section) in the people's communes to administer registry of birth and death, marriage, census, and civil administration. . . . The characteristics of the people's

---

*Ba wu: literally, eight have-nots. This term is obscure, but one Chinese respondent who was a high school student during the Great Leap Forward partially recalls learning a chant, "The Eight Proletarian Points" *(bage wuchanjieji zhuzhang)*. . . . *Ba wu* would not be an unusual contraction, just as *si hua* is the contraction for *sige xiandai hua* (the four modernizations slogan).

communes are one, big, and two, public; most important is that many cooperatives combine into one big commune. The several comments in *Socialist Upsurge in the Countryside** said big cooperatives were good; mountain areas could establish big cooperatives, too, in order to develop a diversified economy and to ensure all-round development. However, establishing slightly small cooperatives to begin with also had its advantages. The youth and women are happy about the new wage system. The rationale of increasing private plots and so on were all proposed by the party's Rural Work Department.† As early as 1955 I recommended establishing big cooperatives. Establish 15,000 to 25,000 communes nationwide averaging 5,000 to 6,000 households or 20,000 to 30,000 people per commune—rather large and convenient for running industry, agriculture, commerce, education, and military affairs side by side, as well as farming, forestry, animal husbandry, sideline production and fisheries. With this way of doing things, I think in the future a few large cities will be dispersed; residential areas of 20,000 to 30,000 people will have everything; villages will become small cities where the majority of philosophers and scientists will be assigned. Every large commune will have highways constructed, wider roads of cement or asphalt, with no trees planted alongside so that airplanes can land—they will be airports. In the future, every province should have a couple of hundred airplanes, averaging two planes per township. Large provinces will set up their own factories for aircraft construction‡ . . .

30 AUGUST, MORNING

The first precondition for communism is plenty; the second is to have a communist spirit. Once an order is issued, everyone automatically goes to their work, idlers are few or none. Communism does not differentiate between superiors and subordinates. We have a twenty-two year history of war communism, with no salaries, which is different from the Soviet Union. In the Soviet Union it's called the system of

---

*The full title of this collection of essays on collectivization edited by Mao and published in January 1956 was *Socialist Upsurge in China's Countryside (Zhongguo nongcun de shehui-zhuyi gaochao)*. Mao seems to be concerned here to demonstrate the consistency between his views of late 1955, when he completed his editorial notes to this book, and August 1958.

†This is a dig at the then head of the department, Deng Zihui, who was criticized in 1955 for being too cautious on collectivization.

‡This utopian vision seems redolent of Sun Yat-sen's earlier visions of the industrialization of China; see C. Martin Wilbur, *Sun Yat-sen, Frustrated Patriot* (New York: Columbia University Press, 1976), 23–26.

surplus grain collection. We didn't practice that. Ours was called the supply system, in which army and civilians, officers and men are equal, and there are also the three great democracies.* Originally we divided up the leftovers from the mess and had small subsidies. After we came into the cities, it was said that the supply system was backward, guerrillaism, a rural work style, and that it couldn't boost initiative, nor stimulate progress. They wanted to establish a salary system. They endured for three years, and in 1952 the salary system was established. They said bourgeois ranks and rights and such were very fine and called our old supply system a backward method, a guerrilla practice that affected activism. In effect they turned the supply system into a system of bourgeois right, thereby promoting bourgeois ideology. Did initiating the 25,000 *li* Long March, the Land Revolution and the War of Liberation rely on salaries? Two to three million people during the anti-Japanese war, from four to five million during the War of Liberation lived a life of war communism, no Sundays off—didn't they all risk their lives? The party, the administration, the army, the civilians—numbering several million—all were together with the masses, supporting the administration and loving the people. The party, the administration, and the army under a unified leadership had nothing "to spend," but with unity between officers and men, and between the army and civilians, and the support for the administration and love for the people, we drove off the Japanese devils and defeated Chiang Kai-shek. Nor did we have anything "to spend" when we fought the United States. Can it be said we did all this because we handed out salaries? Now we have something "to spend," issuing salaries according to rank, dividing them into generals, field rank officers, and junior officers; but some of them have not even been in battle. Whether or not they're any good has yet to be tested. The result is divorce from the masses; the men don't love their officers, and the masses don't love their cadres. Because of this we're not much different from the Nationalist party: our garments are in three colors, our food is divided into five grades, even the desks and chairs of our offices are ranked; and so the workers and peasants don't like us, saying, "You're officials—party officials, government officials, military officials, commercial officials"—so many officials, how can there be no "isms"?† Too many bureaucratic airs, too little politics, so

---

*Democracy in military affairs, politics, and economics.
†Mao is presumably referring to the three sins combatted in the previous year's Rectification Campaign: bureaucratism, sectarianism, and subjectivism.

bureaucratism emerges. Since the Rectification Campaign we have been rectifying bureaucratic airs and putting politics in command. Since then the cases of competing for rank and scrambling for special treatment have not been many. I think we should get rid of this thing. The salary system does not have to be abolished immediately, because there are professors. But we should prepare for it in one or two years. Once the people's communes are established, this will force us gradually to abolish the salary system. Since we came into the cities, we have been under the influence of the bourgeoisie. When we launched a campaign, it was a really Marxist practice and a democratic work style, but they branded us as using "rural work style" and "guerrilla practices." "Guerrilla practices" are capitalists' words. It was probably during the period from 1953 to mid 1957* when they did things together with the bourgeoisie, local tyrants, and evil gentry that they began to straighten their clothes, sit properly, and study the bourgeois style—having haircuts and shaves, shaving three times a day—all learned from the same source. . . .

On eliminating the four pests:† We can focus on this during the National Day holidays, the New Year, and the Lunar New Year. The less we have of these four pests, the better for us; because these four pests harm the people and directly affect the health of the people. We must wipe out various kinds of diseases on a large scale. At one place in Hangzhou, only one person took sick last year. The rate of attendance at work exceeded 90 percent. When the physicians have nothing to do, they can go till the fields and do research. The day China eliminates the four pests we should hold a celebration. It should be recorded in history books. The capitalist states have not done it; those so-called civilized states still have many flies and mosquitoes.

---

*In mid 1957 the bourgeoisie was counterattacked in the Anti-Rightist Campaign.
†*four pests:* rats, sparrows, flies, mosquitoes. In 1960, bed bugs were substituted for sparrows when it was realized that the extermination of these birds had permitted insect pests to flourish.

9

American Imperialism Is Closely Surrounded by the Peoples of the World

1964

China and the United States were enemies in the cold war. Since the Communist victory in China in 1949, the United States enforced an embargo on the People's Republic of China. The 1960s were a time of increasing tension, as the United States became involved in a land war in Southeast Asia, as well as various adventures in Africa. In this short message of support to the people of the Congo, Mao reflects his and the Chinese government's view of America as the world's biggest imperialist aggressor. Yet Mao draws on Chinese revolutionary experience to claim that protracted resistance by people in any area of the world will ultimately prevail over American imperialism. In hindsight we can see that Mao was more accurate in his hopes for the Vietnamese than the African fighters, but his call still rings around the world for groups that take up arms against what they see as a U.S.-dominated international economic order (such as the Shining Path in Peru and Marxist rebels in Nepal). In this message, Mao also makes one version of his famous claim that U.S. strength is a "paper tiger." The virulent anti-Americanism of this piece is representative of the rhetoric of the 1960s (paralleled by American denunciations of "Red China"). Thus it was stunning when a few years later, in the early 1970s, Mao and U.S. president Richard Nixon opened trade relations and joined forces against the Soviet Union.

The U.S. imperialist armed aggression against the Congo (Leopold-ville) is a very grave matter.

The United States has all along attempted to control the Congo. It used the United Nations forces to carry out every sort of evil deed there. It murdered the Congolese national hero Lumumba, it subverted the lawful Congolese government. It imposed the puppet Tshombe on the Congolese people, and dispatched mercenary troops

Originally translated in *Peking Review*. Adaptation from Stuart Schram, *The Political Thought of Mao Tse-tung*, rev. ed. (New York: Praeger, 1969), 383–84.

to suppress the Congolese national liberation movement. And now, it is carrying out direct armed intervention in the Congo in collusion with Belgium and Britain. In so doing, the purpose of U.S. imperialism is not only to control the Congo, but also to enmesh the whole of Africa, particularly the newly independent African countries, in the toils of U.S. neo-colonialism once again. U.S. aggression has encountered heroic resistance from the Congolese people and aroused the indignation of the people of Africa and of the whole world.

U.S. imperialism is the common enemy of the people of the whole world. It is engaged in aggression against South Vietnam, it is intervening in Laos, menacing Cambodia and blustering about extending the war in Indochina. It is trying everything to strangle the Cuban revolution. It wants to turn West Germany and Japan into two important nuclear bases of the United States. It ganged up with England in creating so-called Malaysia to menace Indonesia and other south-east Asian countries. It is occupying South Korea and China's Taiwan province. It is dominating all Latin America. It rides roughshod everywhere. U.S. imperialism has over-extended its reach. It adds a new noose around its neck every time it commits aggression anywhere. It is closely surrounded by the people of the whole world.

In their just struggle, the Congolese people are not alone. All the Chinese people support you. All the people throughout the world who oppose imperialism support you. U.S. imperialism and the reactionaries of all countries are paper tigers. The struggle of the Chinese people proved this. The struggle of the Vietnamese people is now proving it. The struggle of the Congolese people will certainly prove it too. Strengthening national unity and persevering in protracted struggle, the Congolese people will certainly be victorious, and U.S. imperialism will certainly be defeated.

People of the world, unite and defeat the U.S. aggressors and all their running dogs! People of the world, be courageous, dare to fight, defy difficulties and advance wave upon wave. Then the whole world will belong to the people. Monsters of all kinds shall be destroyed.

10

Cultural Revolution Readings
1960s

The Cultural Revolution saw the apotheosis of Chairman Mao. Although party leaders were aware of the tensions between the Chairman and his closest colleagues over the best ways to achieve socialism, and especially over how to recover from the Great Leap Forward, the public saw only their revered, godlike leader—the "Great Helmsman," the "Savior of the Chinese People." For reasons that still defy simple explanations, many Chinese acted irrationally in the Cultural Revolution (1966–69).[1] *Senior leaders found it impossible to bring themselves to stop Mao in the beginning and were helpless to save themselves soon thereafter. "Bombard the Headquarters" is the title of Mao's August 5, 1966, "big-character poster" denouncing "some leading comrades" for arrogance and opposing the proletariat. Big-character posters are essays written on big sheets of paper and hung on the walls of factories, schools, or other places where people lived and worked. Anyone could write and post these essays. Mao's big-character poster galvanized the emerging Red Guard movement of college and high school students. Leaders, from politburo members to local schoolteachers, were paraded through the streets in the dunce caps that Hunan rebels had used on evil landlords in Mao's 1927 "Report on the Peasant Movement in Hunan" (see Document 1). The Cultural Revolution was under way.*

The bible for the Red Guards was Quotations from Chairman Mao Zedong, *more commonly known as the "Little Red Book." Hundreds of millions of copies were printed and distributed during the Cultural Revolution.* Quotations *was a collection of brief quotations from Mao's published works on thirty-three topics, ranging from "The Communist Party"*

---

[1]Today most people refer to the "Cultural Revolution decade" of 1966–76, as Mao's radical policies and the political infighting he instigated in 1966 dominated the decade. However, Mao declared the Cultural Revolution over—that is, "a success"—at the Ninth Congress in April 1969.

"Bombard the Headquarters," New China News Agency, 4 Aug. 1967; *Quotations from Chairman Mao Tse-tung* (Peking: Foreign Languages Press, 1968), i–iv, 1–3, 8–10, 294–98, 312; "Just a Few Words," in *"Zai Zhongyang gongzuo huiyi shang de jianghu"* (Talk at the Central Work Conference), 25 Oct. 1966, translation from Stuart R. Schram, ed., *Mao Tse-tung Unrehearsed: Talks and Letters 1956–1971* (Harmondsworth: Penguin, 1974), 270–74.

to *"People's War"* to *"Unity"* to *"Women"* to *"Study."* Lin Biao, the defense minister, had created it as a basic primer for People's Liberation Army soldiers in the early 1960s. In December 1966, Lin penned a new preface to a second edition of Quotations lauding Chairman Mao. He would become Mao's heir apparent in 1969, replacing Liu Shaoqi, who became the most prominent victim of the Cultural Revolution. Lin's effusive preface to Quotations is a perfect example of the doublespeak that came to dominate the Cultural Revolution. Faith had outstripped reason, and Lin's epigraph to Quotations sums up the mind-set well: *"Study Chairman Mao's writings, follow his teachings and act according to his instructions."*

Even though the quotations themselves carry citations to the original texts from which they are drawn, one cannot escape the fact that Mao's long essays have been reduced to *"sound bites"* taken out of context. Nonetheless, the section on women does reflect some of Mao's calls for the fairer treatment of women. Unfortunately, the repudiation of Mao's utopian policies in the post-Mao period has resulted in the neglect of many of his more sensible ideas on women's liberation.

Mao realized early on that the Cultural Revolution was getting out of hand. *"Just a Few Words,"* his comments at a Central Party Work Conference on October 25, 1966, seems reasonable and self-critical, but as with his 1957 *"Contradictions"* speech (see Document 7), his apparent reasonableness was belied by his ruthless political maneuvering. By 1966 all CCP officials knew this, and his final words in this talk are apt: *"Does anyone else want to speak? I guess that's all for today. The meeting is adjourned."*

BOMBARD THE HEADQUARTERS, AUGUST 5, 1966

China's first Marxist-Leninist big-character poster and commentator's article on it in the *People's Daily*[2] are indeed superbly written! Comrades, please read them again. But in the last fifty days or so some leading comrades from the central down to the local levels have acted in a diametrically opposite way. Having the reactionary stand of the bourgeoisie, they have enforced a bourgeois dictatorship and struck

---

[2]Mao is referring to the big-character poster written by Nie Yuanzi at Beijing University in June 1966, which began the attacks on party leaders characteristic of the Cultural Revolution. Liu Shaoqi, president of China, and other leaders had limited this movement in June and July, but this August 5 big-character poster by Mao himself gave the new Red Guards permission to renew the attack.

down the surging movement of the Great Cultural Revolution of the Proletariat. They have stood facts on their head and juggled black and white, encircled and suppressed revolutionaries, stifled opinions differing from their own, imposed a white terror, and felt very pleased with themselves. They have puffed up the arrogance of the bourgeoisie and deflated the morale of the proletariat. How vicious they are! Viewed in connection with the right deviation in 1962 and the wrong tendency of 1964 which was "left" in form but right in essence, shouldn't this prompt one to deep thought?

QUOTATIONS FROM CHAIRMAN MAO ZEDONG, 1968

Study Chairman Mao's writings, follow his teachings and act according to his instructions.   —Lin Biao

Foreword to the Second Edition

Comrade Mao Zedong is the greatest Marxist-Leninist of our era. He has inherited, defended and developed Marxism-Leninism with genius, creatively and comprehensively and has brought it to a higher and completely new stage.

Mao Zedong's thought is Marxism-Leninism of the era in which imperialism is heading for total collapse and socialism is advancing to world-wide victory. It is a powerful ideological weapon for opposing imperialism and for opposing revisionism and dogmatism. Mao Zedong's thought is the guiding principle for all the work of the Party, the army and the country.

Therefore, the most fundamental task in our Party's political and ideological work is at all times to hold high the great red banner of Mao Zedong's thought, to arm the minds of the people throughout the country with it and to persist in using it to command every field of activity. The broad masses of the workers, peasants and soldiers and the broad ranks of the revolutionary cadres and the intellectuals should really master Mao Zedong's thought; they should all study Chairman Mao's writings, follow his teachings, act according to his instructions and be his good fighters.

In studying the works of Chairman Mao, one should have specific problems in mind, study and apply his works in a creative way, combine study with application, first study what must be urgently applied so as to get quick results, and strive hard to apply what one is studying. In order really to master Mao Zedong's thought, it is essential to study many of Chairman Mao's basic concepts over and over again, and it is best to memorize important statements and study and apply them repeatedly. The newspapers should regularly carry quotations from Chairman Mao relevant to current issues for readers to study and apply. The experience of the broad masses in their creative study and application of Chairman Mao's works in the last few years has proved that to study selected quotations from Chairman Mao with specific problems in mind is a good way to learn Mao Zedong's thought, a method conducive to quick results.

We have compiled *Quotations from Chairman Mao Zedong*[3] in order to help the broad masses learn Mao Zedong's thought more effectively. In organizing their study, units should select passages that are relevant to the situation, their tasks, the current thinking of their personnel, and the state of their work.

In our great motherland, a new era is emerging in which the workers, peasants and soldiers are grasping Marxism-Leninism, Mao Zedong's thought. Once Mao Zedong's thought is grasped by the broad masses, it becomes an inexhaustible source of strength and a spiritual atom bomb of infinite power. The large-scale publication of *Quotations from Chairman Mao Zedong* is a vital measure for enabling the broad masses to grasp Mao Zedong's thought and for promoting the revolutionization of our people's thinking. It is our hope that all comrades will learn earnestly and diligently, bring about a new nationwide high tide in the creative study and application of Chairman Mao's works and, under the great red banner of Mao Zedong's thought, strive to build our country into a great socialist state with modern agriculture, modern industry, modern science and culture and modern national defence!

LIN BIAO

1. The Communist Party

The force at the core leading our cause forward is the Chinese Communist Party.

The theoretical basis guiding our thinking is Marxism-Leninism.
— *Opening address at the First Session of the First National People's Congress of the People's Republic of China (September 15, 1954).*

---

[3]In 1968, this official translation used the older romanization of Mao Zedong's name, Mao Tse-tung, but we have used the *pinyin* system here and throughout this text.

If there is to be revolution, there must be a revolutionary party. Without a revolutionary party, without a party built on the Marxist-Leninist revolutionary theory and in the Marxist-Leninist revolutionary style, it is impossible to lead the working class and the broad masses of the people in defeating imperialism and its running dogs.[4]

—*"Revolutionary Forces of the World Unite, Fight Against Imperialist Aggression!" (November 1948)*, Selected Works, *Vol. IV, p. 284.*

Without the efforts of the Chinese Communist Party, without the Chinese Communists as the mainstay of the Chinese people, China can never achieve independence and liberation, or industrialization and the modernization of her agriculture.

—*"On Coalition Government" (April 24, 1945)*, Selected Works, *Vol. III, p. 318.*

The Chinese Communist Party is the core of leadership of the whole Chinese people. Without this core, the cause of socialism cannot be victorious.

—*Talk at the general reception for the delegates to the Third National Congress of the New-Democratic Youth League of China (May 25, 1957).*

A well-disciplined Party armed with the theory of Marxism-Leninism, using the method of self-criticism and linked with the masses of the people; an army under the leadership of such a Party; a united front of all revolutionary classes and all revolutionary groups under the leadership of such a Party—these are the three main weapons with which we have defeated the enemy.

—*"On the People's Democratic Dictatorship" (June 30, 1949)*, Selected Works, *Vol. IV, p. 422.*

We must have faith in the masses and we must have faith in the Party. These are two cardinal principles. If we doubt these principles, we shall accomplish nothing.

—On the Question of Agricultural Co-operation *(July 31, 1955), 3rd ed., p. 7.*

---

[4] *running dogs:* Chinese or others who serve the enemy in the way dogs follow a hunter and do his bidding. The Chinese term, *zougou,* is sometimes translated as "lackeys."

2. Classes and Class Struggle

Classes struggle, some classes triumph, others are eliminated. Such is history, such is the history of civilization for thousands of years. To interpret history from this viewpoint is historical materialism; standing in opposition to this viewpoint is historical idealism.

—*"Cast Away Illusions, Prepare for Struggle" (August 14, 1949),* Selected Works, *Vol. IV, p. 428.*

In class society everyone lives as a member of a particular class, and every kind of thinking, without exception, is stamped with the brand of a class.

—*"On Practice" (July 1937),* Selected Works, *Vol. I, p. 296.*

Changes in society are due chiefly to the development of the internal contradictions in society, that is, the contradiction between the productive forces and the relations of production, the contradiction between classes and the contradiction between the old and the new; it is the development of these contradictions that pushes society forward and gives the impetus for the supersession of the old society by the new.

—*"On Contradiction" (August 1937),* Selected Works, *Vol. I, p. 314.*

The ruthless economic exploitation and political oppression of the peasants by the landlord class forced them into numerous uprisings against its rule. . . . It was the class struggles of the peasants, the peasant uprisings and peasant wars that constituted the real motive force of historical development in Chinese feudal society.

—*"The Chinese Revolution and the Chinese Communist Party" (December 1939),* Selected Works, *Vol. II, p. 308.*

In the final analysis, national struggle is a matter of class struggle. Among the whites in the United States it is only the reactionary ruling circles who oppress the black people. They can in no way represent the workers, farmers, revolutionary intellectuals and other enlightened persons who comprise the overwhelming majority of the white people.

—*"Statement Supporting the American Negroes in Their Just Struggle Against Racial Discrimination by U.S. Imperialism" (August 8, 1963),* People of the World, Unite and Defeat the U.S. Aggressors and All Their Lackeys, *2nd ed., pp. 3–4.*

31. Women

A man in China is usually subjected to the domination of three systems of authority [political authority, clan authority and religious authority]. . . . As for women, in addition to being dominated by these three systems of authority, they are also dominated by the men (the authority of the husband). These four authorities—political, clan, religious and masculine—are the embodiment of the whole feudal-patriarchal ideology and system, and are the four thick ropes binding the Chinese people, particularly the peasants. How the peasants have overthrown the political authority of the landlords in the countryside has been described above. The political authority of the landlords is the backbone of all the other systems of authority. With that overturned, the clan authority, the religious authority and the authority of the husband all begin to totter. . . . As to the authority of the husband, this has always been weaker among the poor peasants because, out of economic necessity, their womenfolk have to do more manual labour than the women of the richer classes and therefore have more say and greater power of decision in family matters. With the increasing bankruptcy of the rural economy in recent years, the basis for men's domination over women has already been undermined. With the rise of the peasant movement, the women in many places have now begun to organize rural women's associations; the opportunity has come for them to lift up their heads, and the authority of the husband is getting shakier every day. In a word, the whole feudal-patriarchal ideology and system is tottering with the growth of the peasants' power.

—*"Report on an Investigation of the Peasant Movement in Hunan"* (*March 1927*), Selected Works, *Vol. I, pp. 44–46.*

Unite and take part in production and political activity to improve the economic and political status of women.

—*Inscription for the magazine* Women of New China, *printed in its first issue, July 20, 1949.*

Protect the interests of the youth, women and children—provide assistance to young students who cannot afford to continue their studies, help the youth and women to organize in order to participate on an equal footing in all work useful to the war effort and to social progress, ensure freedom of marriage and equality as between

men and women, and give young people and children a useful education. . . .
— "*On Coalition Government*" *(April 24, 1945),* Selected Works, *Vol. III, p. 288.*

[In agricultural production] our fundamental task is to adjust the use of labour power in an organized way and to encourage women to do farm work.
— "*Our Economic Policy*" *(January 23, 1934),* Selected Works, *Vol. I, p. 142.*

In order to build a great socialist society, it is of the utmost importance to arouse the broad masses of women to join in productive activity. Men and women must receive equal pay for equal work in production. Genuine equality between the sexes can only be realized in the process of the socialist transformation of society as a whole.
— *Introductory note to "Women Have Gone to the Labour Front" (1955),* The Socialist Upsurge in China's Countryside, *Chinese ed., Vol. I.*

With the completion of agricultural co-operation, many co-operatives are finding themselves short of labour. It has become necessary to arouse the great mass of women who did not work in the fields before to take their place on the labour front. . . . China's women are a vast reserve of labour power. This reserve should be tapped in the struggle to build a great socialist country.
— *Introductory note to "Solving the Labour Shortage by Arousing the Women to Join in Production" (1955),* The Socialist Upsurge in China's Countryside, *Chinese ed., Vol. II.*

Enable every women who can work to take her place on the labour front, under the principle of equal pay for equal work. This should be done as quickly as possible.
— *Introductory note to "On Widening the Scope of Women's Work in the Agricultural Co-operative Movement" (1955),* The Socialist Upsurge in China's Countryside, *Chinese ed., Vol. I.*

33. Study

In order to have a real grasp of Marxism, one must learn it not only from books, but mainly through class struggle, through practical work and close contact with the masses of workers and peasants. When in addition to reading some Marxist books our intellectuals have gained some understanding through close contact with the masses of workers and peasants and through their own practical work, we will all be speaking the same language, not only the common language of patriotism and the common language of the socialist system, but probably even the common language of the communist world outlook. If that happens, all of us will certainly work much better.

—Speech at the Chinese Communist Party's National Conference on Propaganda Work *(March 12, 1957), 1st pocket ed., p. 12.*

JUST A FEW WORDS, OCTOBER 25, 1966

I have just a few words to say about two matters.

For the past seventeen years there is one thing which in my opinion we haven't done well. Out of concern for state security and in view of the lessons of Stalin in the Soviet Union, we set up a first and second line.[5] I have been in the second line, other comrades in the first line. Now we can see that wasn't so good; as a result our forces were dispersed. When we entered the cities we could not centralize our efforts, and there were quite a few independent kingdoms. Hence the Eleventh Plenum carried out changes. This is one matter. I am in the second line, I do not take charge of day-to-day work. Many things are left to other people so that other people's prestige is built up, and when I go to see God there won't be such a big upheaval in the State. Everybody was in agreement with this idea of mine. It seems that there are some things which the comrades in the first line have not managed too well. There are some things I should have kept a grip on which I did not. So I am responsible, we cannot just blame them. Why do I say that I bear some responsibility?

First, it was I who proposed that the Standing Committee be divided into two lines and that a secretariat be set up. Everyone agreed with this. Moreover I put too much trust in others. It was at the time of the Twenty-three Articles that my vigilance was aroused.* I could do nothing in Beijing; I could do nothing at the Center. Last

---

[5]*First line* means active leadership of the country, and *second line* means serving as top leader for general policy issues but not day-to-day administration. This was set up in China by Mao and Liu Shaoqi to provide an orderly transition of power and to avoid the tribulations of Stalin's last years in the Soviet Union.

*When Mao put forward his new twenty-three-point directive for the Socialist Education Campaign in January 1965 and Liu Shaoqi refused to accept it.

September and October I asked, If revisionism appeared at the Center, what could the localities do? I felt that my ideas couldn't be carried out in Beijing. Why was the criticism of Wu Han[6] initiated not in Beijing but in Shanghai? Because there was nobody to do it in Beijing. Now the problem of Beijing has been solved.

Second, the Great Cultural Revolution wreaked havoc after I approved Nie Yuanzi's big-character poster in Beijing University and wrote a letter to Qinghua University Middle School, as well as writing a big-character poster of my own.* It all happened within a very short period, less than five months in June, July, August, September, and October. No wonder the comrades did not understand too much. The time was so short and the events so violent. I myself had not foreseen that as soon as the Beijing University poster was broadcast, the whole country would be thrown into turmoil. Even before the letter to the Red Guards had gone out, Red Guards had mobilized throughout the country, and in one rush they swept you off your feet. Since it was I who caused the havoc, it is understandable if you have some bitter words for me. Last time we met I lacked confidence and I said that our decisions would not necessarily be carried out. Indeed all that time quite a few comrades still did not understand things fully, though now after a couple of months we have had some experience, and things are a bit better. This meeting has had two stages. In the first stage the speeches were not quite normal, but during the second stage, after speeches and the exchange of experience by comrades at the Center, things went more smoothly and the ideas were understood a bit better. It has only been five months. Perhaps the movement may last another five months, or even longer. . . .

There have been quite a few brief reports presented at this meeting. I have read nearly all of them. You find it difficult to cross this pass and I don't find it easy either. You are anxious and so am I. I can-

---

[6]The criticism of Wu Han, a Beijing historian and official, in late 1965 started the series of events that opened the Cultural Revolution. Wu Han was criticized by radicals for opposing Mao, and the mayor of Beijing, Peng Zhen, was then denounced as Wu Han's protector.

*A translation of the big-character poster "What Are Song Shuo, Lu Ping, and Peng Peiyun Up To in the Great Cultural Revolution?" is in *Survey of China Mainland Press,* no. 3719, 16 June 1966, 6–8. A translation of Mao's "Letter to the Red Guards of Qinghua University Middle School" is in Stuart R. Schram, ed., *Mao Tse-tung Unrehearsed: Talks and Letters 1956–1971* (Harmondsworth: Penguin, 1974), 260–61. A translation of Mao's big-character poster "Bombard the Headquarters" appears earlier in this document.

not blame you, comrades, time has been so short. Some comrades say that they did not intentionally make mistakes, but did it because they were confused. This is pardonable. Nor can we put all the blame on Comrade Shaoqi and Comrade Xiaoping.[7] They have some responsibility, but so has the Center. The Center has not run things properly. The time was so short. We were not mentally prepared for new problems. Political and ideological work was not carried out properly. I think that after this seventeen-day conference things will be a bit better.

Does anyone else want to speak? I guess that's all for today. The meeting is adjourned.

[7]*Comrade Xiaoping:* Deng Xiaoping, who became China's paramount leader after Mao (1977–1997)

PART TWO

Documenting Mao

11

EDGAR SNOW

Interview with Mao

1937

Edgar Snow's interviews with Mao in 1936 have the status of a classic in both China and the West. These were the first public comments by Mao about himself and his life. Snow, a progressive American journalist, had lived and worked in China since 1929. In June 1936, he set out to visit the "Reds" who had recently made their famous Long March from southeast China to the northwest. Snow published his observations in a book, Red Star over China, *that became an instant bestseller in the West and was quickly translated into Chinese. Although the book includes his impressions of the Communist administration in general, it is his interviews with Mao that have always attracted the most attention.*

Mao proves himself a brilliant storyteller, and Snow a faithful transmitter. The selections from Red Star over China *printed here include Snow's memorable impressions of Mao as a man and portions of Mao's own story about his youth and the activities of the Red Army in the late 1920s and early 1930s. In all, Mao manages to weave his story with that of the CCP, thus beginning his ultimately successful effort to make himself the embodiment of the party.*

. . . Here at last I found the Red leader whom Nanjing had been fighting for ten years—Mao Zedong, chairman of the "Chinese People's Soviet Republic," to employ the official title which had recently been adopted. The old cognomen, "Chinese Workers' and Peasants' Soviet Republic," was dropped when the Reds[1] began their new policy of struggle for a united front. . . .

Mao had the reputation of a charmed life. He had been repeatedly pronounced dead by his enemies, only to return to the news columns a few days later, as active as ever. The Guomindang had also officially

[1] *Reds:* the common name for the Communists at that time

Edgar Snow, *Red Star over China* (New York: Grove Press, 1968), 89–96, 130–33, 172–74.

"killed" and buried Zhu De[2] many times, assisted by occasional corroborations from clairvoyant missionaries. Numerous deaths of the two famous men, nevertheless, did not prevent them from being involved in many spectacular exploits, including the Long March. Mao was indeed in one of his periods of newspaper demise when I visited Red China,[3] but I found him quite substantially alive. There were good reasons why people said that he had a charmed life, however; although he had been in scores of battles, was once captured by enemy troops and escaped, and had the world's highest reward on his head, during all these years he had never once been wounded.

I happened to be in Mao's house one evening when he was given a complete physical examination by a Red surgeon—a man who had studied in Europe and who knew his business—and pronounced in excellent health. He had never had tuberculosis or any "incurable disease," as had been rumored by some romantic travelers. His lungs were completely sound, although, unlike most Red commanders, he was an inordinate cigarette smoker. During the Long March, Mao and Li De[4] had carried on original botanical research by testing out various kinds of leaves as tobacco substitutes. . . .

Mao Zedong was forty-three years old when I met him in 1936. He was elected chairman of the provisional Central Soviet Government at the Second All-China Soviet Congress, attended by delegates representing approximately 9,000,000 people then living under Red laws. . . .

The influence of Mao Zedong throughout the Communist world of China was probably greater than that of anyone else. He was a member of nearly everything—the revolutionary military committee, the political bureau of the Central Committee, the finance commission, the organization committee, the public health commission, and others. His real influence was asserted through his domination of the political bureau, which had decisive power in the policies of the Party, the government, and the army. Yet, while everyone knew and respected him, there was—as yet, at least—no ritual of hero worship built up around him. I never met a Chinese Red who drooled "our-great-leader" phrases; I did not hear Mao's name used as a synonym for the

---

[2]*Zhu De:* founder of the Red Army who fought alongside Mao in southern China and became one of the most respected leaders of the new CCP government

[3]*Red China:* the base area in northwest China that was controlled by the CCP and would soon be known as Yan'an

[4]*Li De:* Otto Braun, an adviser from the Comintern, or Communist International, to the CCP from 1933 to 1937; the only foreign participant to complete the Long March

Chinese people, but still I never met one who did not like "the Chairman"—as everyone called him—and admire him. The role of his personality in the movement was clearly immense.

Mao seemed to me a very interesting and complex man. He had the simplicity and naturalness of the Chinese peasant, with a lively sense of humor and a love of rustic laughter. His laughter was even active on the subject of himself and the shortcomings of the soviets— a boyish sort of laughter which never in the least shook his inner faith in his purpose. He was plain-speaking and plain-living, and some people might have considered him rather coarse and vulgar. Yet he combined curious qualities of naïveté with incisive wit and worldly sophistication.

I think my first impression—dominantly one of native shrewdness—was probably correct. And yet Mao was an accomplished scholar of Classical Chinese, an omnivorous reader, a deep student of philosophy and history, a good speaker, a man with an unusual memory and extraordinary powers of concentration, an able writer, careless in his personal habits and appearance but astonishingly meticulous about details of duty, a man of tireless energy, and a military and political strategist of considerable genius. It was interesting that many Japanese regarded him as the ablest Chinese strategist alive.

The Reds were putting up some new buildings in Bao'an,[5] but accommodations were very primitive while I was there. Mao lived with his wife in a two-room *yaofang*[6] with bare, poor, map-covered walls. He had known much worse, and as the son of a "rich" peasant in Hunan he had also known better. The Maos' chief luxury was a mosquito net. Otherwise Mao lived very much like the rank and file of the Red Army. After ten years of leadership of the Reds, after hundreds of confiscations of property of landlords, officials, and tax collectors, he owned only his blankets and a few personal belongings, including two cotton uniforms. Although he was a Red Army commander as well as chairman, he wore on his coat collar only the two red bars that are the insignia of the ordinary Red soldier.

I went with Mao several times to mass meetings of the villagers and the Red cadets, and to the Red theater. He sat inconspicuously in the midst of the crowd and enjoyed himself hugely. I remember once, between acts at the Anti-Japanese Theater, there was a general

[5]*Bao'an:* the town in Shaanxi province where Snow interviewed Mao. In a few months, Mao and the CCP leadership would move to the larger town of Yan'an.
[6]yaofang: a style of cave house common in northern Shaanxi province

demand for a duet by Mao Zedong and Lin Biao, the twenty-eight-year-old president of the Red Army University and formerly a famed young cadet on Chiang Kai-shek's staff. Lin blushed like a schoolboy and got them out of the "command performance" by a graceful speech, calling upon the women Communists for a song instead.

Mao's food was the same as everybody's, but being a Hunanese he had the southerner's *ai-la,* or "love of pepper." He even had pepper cooked into his bread. Except for this passion, he scarcely seemed to notice what he ate. One night at dinner I heard him expand on a theory of pepper-loving peoples being revolutionaries. He first submitted his own province, Hunan, famous for the revolutionaries it has produced. Then he listed Spain, Mexico, Russia, and France to support his contention, but laughingly had to admit defeat when somebody mentioned the well-known Italian love of red pepper and garlic, in refutation of his theory. One of the most amusing songs of the "bandits," incidentally, was a ditty called "The Hot Red Pepper." It told of the disgust of the pepper with his pointless vegetable existence, waiting to be eaten, and how he ridiculed the contentment of the cabbages, spinach, and beans with their invertebrate careers. He ends up by leading a vegetable insurrection. "The Hot Red Pepper" was a great favorite with Chairman Mao.

He appeared to be quite free from symptoms of megalomania, but he had a deep sense of personal dignity, and something about him suggested a power of ruthless decision when he deemed it necessary. I never saw him angry, but I heard from others that on occasions he had been roused to an intense and withering fury. At such times his command of irony and invective was said to be classic and lethal.

I found him surprisingly well informed on current world politics. Even on the Long March, it seems, the Reds received news broadcasts by radio, and in the Northwest they published their own newspapers. Mao was exceptionally well read in world history and had a realistic conception of European social and political conditions. He was very interested in the Labour Party of England, and questioned me intensely about its present policies, soon exhausting all my information. It seemed to me that he found it difficult fully to understand why, in a country where workers were enfranchised, there was still no workers' government. I was afraid my answers did not satisfy him. He expressed profound contempt for Ramsay MacDonald,[7] whom he designated as a *han-chien* — an archtraitor of the British people.

---

[7] *Ramsay MacDonald:* former British prime minister. MacDonald had founded the Labour party and promoted the sort of parliamentary and moderate socialism that Mao felt betrayed the revolutionary interests of the working class.

His opinion of President Roosevelt was rather interesting. He believed him to be anti-Fascist, and thought China could cooperate with such a man. He asked innumerable questions about the New Deal,[8] and Roosevelt's foreign policy. The questioning showed a remarkably clear conception of the objectives of both. He regarded Mussolini and Hitler as mountebanks, but considered Mussolini intellectually a much abler man, a real Machiavellian, with a knowledge of history, while Hitler was a mere willless puppet of the reactionary capitalists.[9]

Mao had read a number of books about India and had some definite opinions on that country. Chief among these was that Indian independence would never be realized without an agrarian revolution. He questioned me about Gandhi, Jawaharlal Nehru, Suhasini Chattopadhyaya,[10] and other Indian leaders I had known. He knew something about the Negro question in America, and unfavorably compared the treatment of Negroes and American Indians with policies in the Soviet Union toward national minorities. He was interested when I pointed out certain great differences in the historical background of the Negro in America and that of minorities in Russia.

Mao was an ardent student of philosophy. Once when I was having nightly interviews with him on Communist history, a visitor brought him several new books on philosophy, and Mao asked me to postpone our engagements. He consumed those books in three or four nights of intensive reading, during which he seemed oblivious to everything else. He had not confined his reading to Marxist philosophers, but also knew something of the ancient Greeks, of Spinoza, Kant, Goethe, Hegel, Rousseau, and others.

I often wondered about Mao's own sense of responsibility over the question of force, violence, and the "necessity of killing." He had in his youth had strongly liberal and humanistic tendencies, and the transition from idealism to realism evidently had first been made philosophically. Although he was peasant-born, he did not as a youth personally suffer much from oppression of the landlords, as did many Reds, and, although Marxism was the core of his thought, I deduced that class hatred was for him probably an intellectually acquired mechanism in the bulwark of his philosophy, rather than an instinctive impulse to action.

[8] *New Deal:* the set of economic and social policies pursued by Roosevelt in the 1930s to combat the Depression

[9] Hitler and Mussolini were by 1936 the fascist leaders of Germany and Italy. Mao was not alone in thinking that Mussolini was the more significant of the two.

[10] Jawaharlal Nehru and Suhasini Chattopadhyaya were prominent leaders of the nationalist movement in India, which was seeking independence from British rule. Nehru became independent India's first prime minister in 1947.

There seemed to be nothing in him that might be called religious feeling. He was a humanist in a fundamental sense; he believed in man's ability to solve man's problems. I thought he had probably on the whole been a moderating influence in the Communist movement where life and death were concerned. . . .

Yet I doubted very much if he would ever command great respect from the intellectual elite of China, perhaps not entirely because he had an extraordinary mind, but because he had the personal habits of a peasant. The Chinese disciples of Pareto[11] might have thought him uncouth. Talking with Mao one day, I saw him absent-mindedly turn down the belt of his trousers and search for some guests[12]—but then it is just possible that Pareto might have done a little searching himself if he had lived in similar circumstances. But I am sure that Pareto would never have taken off his trousers in the presence of the president of the Red Army University—as Mao did once when I was interviewing Lin Biao. It was extremely hot inside the little cave. Mao lay down on the bed, pulled off his pants, and for twenty minutes carefully studied a military map on the wall—interrupted occasionally by Lin Biao, who asked for confirmation of dates and names, which Mao invariably knew. His nonchalant habits fitted with his complete indifference to personal appearance, although the means were at hand to fix himself up like a chocolate-box general or a politician's picture in *Who's Who in China.*

Except for a few weeks when he was ill, he walked most of the 6,000 miles of the Long March, like the rank and file. He could have achieved high office and riches by "betraying" to the Guomindang, and this applied to most Red commanders. The tenacity with which these Communists for ten years clung to their principles could not be fully evaluated unless one knew the history of "silver bullets"[13] in China, by means of which other rebels were bought off.

I was able to check up on many of Mao's assertions, and usually found them to be correct. He subjected me to mild doses of political propaganda, but it was interesting compared to what I had received in nonbandit quarters. He never imposed any censorship on me, in either my writing or my photography, courtesies for which I was grateful. He did his best to see that I got facts to explain various aspects of soviet life.

[11]*Pareto:* Vilfredo Pareto, the noted leftist theorist who critiqued parliamentary democracy and promoted Marx's vision of class struggle but was a thoroughly bourgeois professor in Switzerland

[12]*search for some guests:* hunt for lice

[13]*silver bullets:* bribes

[Mao gave his story to Edgar Snow, who recorded it as follows.]

"I was born in the village of Shaoshan, in Xiangtan county, Hunan province, in 1893. My father's name was Mao Rensheng, and my mother's maiden name was Wen Qimei.

"My father was a poor peasant and while still young was obliged to join the army because of heavy debts. He was a soldier for many years. Later on he returned to the village where I was born, and by saving carefully and gathering together a little money through small trading and other enterprise he managed to buy back his land. . . .

"I began studying in a local primary school when I was eight and remained there until I was thirteen years old. In the early morning and at night I worked on the farm. During the day I read the Confucian Analects and the Four Classics.[14] My Chinese teacher belonged to the stern-treatment school. He was harsh and severe, frequently beating his students. Because of that I ran away from the school when I was ten. I was afraid to return home for fear of receiving a beating there, and set out in the general direction of the city, which I believed to be in a valley somewhere. I wandered for three days before I was finally found by my family. Then I learned that I had circled round and round in my travels, and in all my walking had got only about eight *li* from my home.

"After my return to the family, however, to my surprise conditions somewhat improved. My father was slightly more considerate and the teacher was more inclined to moderation. The result of my act of protest impressed me very much. It was a successful 'strike.'

"My father wanted me to begin keeping the family books as soon as I had learned a few characters. He wanted me to learn to use the abacus. As my father insisted upon this I began to work at those accounts at night. He was a severe taskmaster. He hated to see me idle, and if there were no books to be kept he put me to work at farm tasks. He was a hot-tempered man and frequently beat both me and my brothers. He gave us no money whatever, and the most meager food. On the fifteenth of every month he made a concession to his laborers and gave them eggs with their rice, but never meat. To me he gave neither eggs nor meat.

"My mother was a kind woman, generous and sympathetic, and ever ready to share what she had. She pitied the poor and often gave them rice when they came to ask for it during famines. But she could

[14]The *Analects* is the record of the teachings of Confucius. Since the twelfth century, it has been considered one of the Four Books that all scholars should study, the other three being *The Mencius, The Great Learning,* and *The Doctrine of the Mean.*

not do so when my father was present. He disapproved of charity. We had many quarrels in my home over this question.

"There were two 'parties' in the family. One was my father, the Ruling Power. The Opposition was made up of myself, my mother, my brother, and sometimes even the laborer. In the 'united front' of the Opposition, however, there was a difference of opinion. My mother advocated a policy of indirect attack. She criticized any overt display of emotion and attempts at open rebellion against the Ruling Power. She said it was not the Chinese way.

"But when I was thirteen I discovered a powerful argument of my own for debating with my father on his own ground, by quoting the Classics. My father's favorite accusations against me were of unfilial conduct and laziness. I quoted, in exchange, passages from the Classics saying that the elder must be kind and affectionate. Against his charge that I was lazy I used the rebuttal that older people should do more work than younger, that my father was over three times as old as myself, and therefore should do more work. And I declared that when I was his age I would be much more energetic.

"The old man continued to 'amass wealth,' or what was considered to be a great fortune in that little village. He did not buy more land himself, but he bought many mortgages on other people's land. His capital grew to two or three thousand Chinese dollars.*

"My dissatisfaction increased. The dialectical struggle in our family was constantly developing.† One incident I especially remember. When I was about thirteen my father invited many guests to his home, and while they were present a dispute arose between the two of us. My father denounced me before the whole group, calling me lazy and useless. This infuriated me. I cursed him and left the house. My mother ran after me and tried to persuade me to return. My father also pursued me, cursing at the same time that he commanded me to come back. I reached the edge of a pond and threatened to jump in if he came any nearer. In this situation demands and counterdemands were presented for cessation of the civil war. My father insisted that I apologize and *koutou*‡ as a sign of submission. I agreed to give a one-knee *koutou* if he would promise not to beat me. Thus the war ended,

---

*Mao used the Chinese term *yuan,* which was often translated as "Chinese dollars"; 3,000 yuan in cash in 1900 was an impressive sum in rural China.

†Mao used all these political terms humorously in his explanations, laughing as he recalled such incidents.

‡Literally, to "knock head." To strike one's head to the floor or earth was expected of son to father and subject to emperor, in token of filial obedience.

and from it I learned that when I defended my rights by open rebellion my father relented, but when I remained meek and submissive he only cursed and beat me the more.

"Reflecting on this, I think that in the end the strictness of my father defeated him. I learned to hate him, and we created a real united front against him. At the same time it probably benefited me. It made me most diligent in my work; it made me keep my books carefully, so that he should have no basis for criticizing me. . . ."

[Snow resumes Mao's story.]

"Gradually the Red Army's work with the masses improved, discipline strengthened, and a new technique in organization developed. The peasantry everywhere began to volunteer to help the revolution. As early as Jingganshan[15] the Red Army had imposed three simple rules of discipline upon its fighters, and these were: prompt obedience to orders; no confiscations whatever from the poor peasantry; and prompt delivery directly to the government, for its disposal, of all goods confiscated from the landlords. After the 1928 Conference [second Maoping Conference] emphatic efforts to enlist the support of the peasantry were made, and eight rules were added to the three listed above. These were as follows:

"1. Replace all doors when you leave a house;*
"2. Return and roll up the straw matting on which you sleep;
"3. Be courteous and polite to the people and help them when you can;
"4. Return all borrowed articles;
"5. Replace all damaged articles;
"6. Be honest in all transactions with the peasants;
"7. Pay for all articles purchased;
"8. Be sanitary, and, especially, establish latrines a safe distance from people's houses.

"The last two rules were added by Lin Biao. These eight points were enforced with better and better success, and today are still

[15]*Jingganshan:* the CCP's first substantial base area, formed in the rugged mountains of rural Jiangxi province in southern China. Mao and Zhu De retreated there in late 1927 after the failure of urban insurrections and together developed the Red Army and basic approaches to running a rural soviet.

*This order is not so enigmatic as it sounds. The wooden doors of a Chinese house are easily detachable, and are often taken down at night, put across wooden blocks, and used for an improvised bed.

the code of the Red soldier, memorized and frequently repeated by him. Three other duties were taught to the Red Army, as its primary purpose: first, to struggle to the death against the enemy; second, to arm the masses; third, to raise money to support the struggle. . . .

"It was at this time that the First Army Corps was organized, with Zhu De as commander and myself as political commissar. It was composed of the Third Army, the Fourth Army commanded by Lin Biao, and the Twelfth Army, under Luo Pinghui. Party leadership was vested in a Front Committee, of which I was chairman. There were already more than 10,000 men in the First Army Corps then, organized into ten divisions. Besides this main force, there were many local and independent regiments, Red Guards and partisans.

"Red tactics, apart from the political basis of the movement, explained much of the successful military development. At Jingganshan four slogans had been adopted, and these give the clue to the methods of partisan warfare used, out of which the Red Army grew. The slogans were:

"1. When the enemy advances, we retreat!
"2. When the enemy halts and encamps, we trouble them!
"3. When the enemy seeks to avoid a battle, we attack!
"4. When the enemy retreats, we pursue!

"These slogans [of four characters each in Chinese] were at first opposed by many experienced military men, who did not agree with the type of tactics advocated. But much experience proved that the tactics were correct. Whenever the Red Army departed from them, in general, it did not succeed. Our forces were small, exceeded from ten to twenty times by the enemy; our resources and fighting materials were limited, and only by skillfully combining the tactics of maneuvering and guerrilla warfare could we hope to succeed in our struggle against the Guomindang, fighting from vastly richer and superior bases.

"The most important single tactic of the Red Army was, and remains, its ability to concentrate its main forces in the attack, and swiftly divide and separate them afterwards. This implied that positional warfare was to be avoided, and every effort made to meet the living forces of the enemy while in movement, and destroy them. On the basis of these tactics the mobility and the swift, powerful 'short attack' of the Red Army was developed.

12

STUART SCHRAM

The Struggle on Two Fronts
1967

Stuart Schram is the dean of Mao studies in the West. Beginning in the mid-1960s, he produced an excellent biography of Mao, from which this brief selection is taken, as well as several editions of selected translations of Mao's writings and other studies on Mao and modern China. Although many biographies of Mao have been written in the past thirty-five years, Schram's has retained its reputation among scholars as one of the most reliable and well researched.

This selection describes the context out of which the famous Yan'an Rectification Movement emerged. Mao and the CCP faced a struggle on two fronts—against the Japanese invaders and against their erstwhile allies, the Nationalists, under Chiang Kai-shek. Both wanted to see the end of the CCP. Mao's response was ideological and educational, as well as military and organizational. This was the context of Mao's successful effort to Sinify (adapt to Chinese conditions) Russian Marxism-Leninism. (See Nick Knight's analysis of Mao's "Sinification of Marxism" in Document 13.) No matter how one regrets the excesses of Mao's later career, Schram's biography gives a vivid sense of what Mao and the CCP had to overcome to reunify the nation.

The years in the North-West saw Mao's emergence as a public figure, both in China and abroad. Though often mentioned in the press during the previous decade, he had remained little more than a name: a bandit chieftain for some, a revolutionary hero for others, but in either case an abstraction. Now, following Edgar Snow's pioneering journey in the summer of 1936, a succession of visitors contrived to reach the "Border Region," and to bring back first-hand reports on its inhabitants.

The portraits they painted of Mao were varied, except in one respect: he left no one indifferent. Edgar Snow, the first foreign

---

Stuart R. Schram, *Mao Tse-tung* (Harmondsworth: Penguin, 1967), 209–20. I have edited Schram's footnotes lightly to limit scholarly detail.

journalist to interview him, described Mao justly as characterized by a combination of intellectual depth and peasant shrewdness. Though the cult of the leader was not to develop seriously for another five years, Snow noted Mao's "deep sense of personal dignity," as well as his "power of ruthless decision." One of the most perceptive accounts of Mao's personality has been left by an intense and highly sensitive woman, Agnes Smedley. She found him, at their first meeting, effeminate and vaguely repellent. "Whatever else he might be," she wrote, "he was an aesthete." Later she discovered the strength behind the mobile features and graceful gestures, and the human warmth and simplicity behind the dignified reserve. But though he could communicate intensely with a few intimate friends, he remained on the whole reserved and aloof. "The sinister quality I had at first felt so strongly in him," continued Agnes Smedley, "proved to be a spiritual isolation. As Zhu De was loved, Mao Zedong was respected. The few who came to know him best had affection for him, but his spirit dwelt within itself, isolating him.". . .

The Yan'an period, especially the two years from the beginning of 1938 to the beginning of 1940, is an altogether exceptional one in Mao's literary career. Not only was his total output very high, but it consisted more of relatively long and systematic writings and less of reports, speeches, and directives than at any other time in his life. It is not difficult to understand the reasons for this. On the one hand, the stable situation in the base area resulting from the accord with the Guomindang, and the fact that he was not personally involved in combat against the Japanese, gave him more leisure than he had enjoyed since his student days, except perhaps for a year or two during the heyday of the Jiangxi Soviet Republic. And on the other hand, he was at last achieving the grasp of Marxist theory, the self-confidence, and the breadth of vision necessary to deal globally with the problems of the Chinese revolution. . . .

In his analysis of the anti-Japanese war as a whole Mao envisaged three phases. During the first, which was nearly completed, the Japanese would be on the offensive and the Chinese on the defensive. During the second, which would be the longest, there would be a certain equilibrium, and the Chinese would carry on guerrilla warfare behind the Japanese lines. During the third and last phase the guerrilla units which had been organized and forged in the course of the preceding phases would swing over to the offensive and abandon their guerrilla tactics for conventional mobile warfare on a large scale. But final victory would be possible only if their efforts were supported both by the conventional forces of the Nationalist army, and by other democratic powers opposed to Japanese imperialism.

In the uncertain and rapidly changing international situation on the eve of the Second World War it was difficult for Mao, or for anyone else, to know exactly on whose support China could count. As late as the beginning of 1939 he professed to believe that, despite Chamberlain's policy of appeasement[1] and his "cowardly attitude towards Japan," the "broad popular masses, including all progressive people from the various social strata who sympathize with China," would in the end succeed in convincing the governments of England, France, and America that it was in their own interests to oppose Japanese aggression. In September 1939, following the Nazi-Soviet pact,[2] he condemned all the "imperialist powers" with equal violence as "mad dogs" who could not do otherwise than "hurl themselves pell mell against their enemies and against the walls of the world." He even suggested that Chamberlain, the leader of "the most reactionary country in the world," was worse than Hitler. . . .

To be sure, the development of the guerrilla base areas was the most effective manner in which Mao and his comrades could fight the Japanese. But Chiang Kai-shek could not be blind to the enormous increase in the Communists' power which resulted from these activities, and which would fortify their bargaining position with the Nationalists once the invaders were expelled. As Chalmers Johnson has put it: "Although the Communist Army was actually continuing to fight the Japanese, its methods left no room for more than one Chinese victor over Japan."*

. . . This judgement in fact sums up the whole subsequent course of the anti-Japanese war, during which Mao and his comrades ceased to make even a pretence of obeying Guomindang directives, yet continuously increased their prestige as the staunchest defenders of China's national interests.

At the same time that their relations with the Guomindang thus deteriorated the Communists found themselves under increasingly fierce attack by the Japanese. The latter, who had already been building blockhouses to separate and isolate the guerrilla areas, intensified

---

[1]Schram is referring to British prime minister Neville Chamberlain, who turned a blind eye to Japanese aggression in China.

[2]*Nazi-Soviet pact:* the nonaggression pact between Germany and the Soviet Union, signed August 23, 1939.

*Chalmers Johnson, *Peasant Nationalism and Communist Power* (Stanford: Stanford University Press, 1962).

this policy in order to prevent any recurrence of the Hundred Regiments' Offensive.[3] In July 1941 the notorious "three-all policy" (burn all, kill all, loot all) was adopted in North China. The result was to reduce the size of the Eighth Route Army from 400,000 to 300,000 men, and to diminish the population of the Communist areas in North China from 44 millions to 25 millions.

The mass burning and killing associated with the "three-all" policy on the whole intensified the peasants' will to resist, and thus aided the Communist cause. But at the same time the Japanese construction of blockhouses, walls, and barbed-wire enclosures, with the virtually total economic blockade of the Communist areas henceforth imposed by the Guomindang, produced increasingly difficult economic and political problems for Mao and his comrades. The economic challenge was met by a successful drive to increase production in the base areas themselves, involving the encouragement of mutual-aid teams among the peasantry, and the participation of the army in industrial and agricultural work. The political challenge was met by the *"Zhengfeng"* or rectification campaign, which was formally launched in February 1942.

The rectification campaign had a dual purpose, neither aspect of which should be ignored. On the one hand, it was designed to strengthen the unity and discipline of the Chinese Communist Party in difficult circumstances, imparting a minimum knowledge of Marxism-Leninism and the political methods developed in the Soviet Union to the large number of new recruits who had been taken into the party in the course of its wartime expansion. But it was also designed to give to the ideological consciousness of party members a special and characteristic quality directly inspired by Mao Zedong himself. In short, Mao's aim was "sinification" of Marxism. . . .

Launching the rectification campaign in February 1942, Mao once more energetically denounced party formalism in general, and "foreign formalism" in particular. In the second of his two long speeches he complained that his appeal of 1938 for the adaptation of Marxism to Chinese conditions had not been heard, and demanded that it be put into practice immediately.

The previous May Mao had criticized only the students returned from Europe, America, or Japan; but now it was clear that the "foreign formalism" he desired to eliminate consisted in the imitation of Soviet models. The rectification campaign was thus directed in part against

---

[3] *Hundred Regiments Offensive:* the surprise Communist attack on Japanese forces in northern China in the summer of 1940. At first it was a great success, turning back Japanese forces at the margin, but it brought a cruel series of counteroffensives in the fall of 1940 and all of 1941 that nearly crushed the CCP.

the predominance of Soviet influence in the party. The most recent official history of the Chinese Communist Party makes this quite clear when it explains that the campaign was aimed at "doctrinaires as represented by Comrade Wang Ming" who were "ignorant of the Party's historical experience," and could "only quote words or phrases from Marxist writings."

To be sure, the fact that the rectification campaign was designed to make the Chinese Communists more aware of their own history and traditions, and teach them to deal with the problems of the Chinese revolution in an independent and original manner, does not mean that it was, properly speaking, *anti*-Soviet. Approximately one fourth of the materials eventually put together in a volume for study by party members consisted of translations from Lenin, Stalin, and Dimitrov.* But if the Chinese Communists were to be instructed in the ideas and methods of their Soviet comrades, they were instructed as well to regard all such with detachment, to choose and assimilate only what was useful to them. A fully autonomous Communist movement in China, with its own ideology specifically adapted to Chinese conditions, was Mao's goal.

*See Boyd Compton ed., *Mao's China: Party Reform Documents, 1942–1944* (Seattle: University of Washington Press, 1952).

13

NICK KNIGHT

Mao Zedong's "Sinification of Marxism"
1985

Nick Knight's essay is a philosophical study of Mao's "theory of practice" that helps us see why Mao's version of Marxism made sense to many Chinese as a social theory and a guide to action—not only during World War II but even today. Sinification *means making something from outside China adapt or integrate into Chinese society and thought. Mao did this with Communist ideology—Marxism-Leninism—in the Yan'an*

Nick Knight, "Mao Zedong and the 'Sinification of Marxism'" in *Marxism in Asia,* ed. Colin Mackerras and Nick Knight (New York: St. Martin's Press, 1985), 83–90.

period (1936–47). Knight is a senior Mao scholar among Western China specialists, and his empathetic analysis of Mao's use of "particular laws" and "universal laws" (of nature, history, and how to wage war) reveals the reasonableness of Mao's ideas on how to make a revolution. Knight's chart on page 203 maps out the cycle of theory-practice-theory presented in Mao's "Methods of Leadership" (1943, see Document 4). When the CCP carefully applied this method, it was often quite success-ful—both in gaining power and in improving the lives of most people in a given locality. The tragedy is that Mao and the CCP soon abandoned this time-consuming method in favor of the simple and disastrous method of dictatorship. Even so, Mao's call to combine theory and practice in the search for social justice remains a compelling ideal that still attracts some Chinese and many revolutionaries elsewhere in the world today.

In . . . October 1938, Mao called for the Sinification of Marxism in the following terms:

> A communist is a Marxist internationalist, but Marxism must take on a national form before it can be applied. There is no such thing as abstract Marxism, but only concrete Marxism. What we call Marxism is Marxism that has taken on a national form, that is, Marxism applied to the concrete struggle in the concrete conditions prevailing in China, and not Marxism abstractly used. If a Chinese communist, who is a part of the great Chinese people, bound to his people by his very flesh and blood, talks of Marxism apart from Chinese peculiarities, this Marxism is merely an empty abstraction. Consequently, the Sinification of Marxism—that is to say, making certain that in all of its manifestations it is imbued with Chinese peculiarities, using it according to these peculiarities—becomes a problem that must be understood and solved by the whole party without delay.*

How is this Sinification of Marxism to be interpreted? Western cri-tiques have tended to cluster around two lines of explication. The first suggests that the Sinification of Marxism entailed the elevation of Chi-nese tradition and realities at the expense of Marxism's universal truths. Stuart Schram, for example, has argued that Mao denied alto-gether the existence of "a universally valid form of Marxism," and that

---

*Stuart Schram, *The Political Thought of Mao Tse-tung*, rev. ed. (Harmondsworth: Penguin, 1969), 172.

his "preoccupation with the glory of China" led to a Sinification of Marxism which was "hermetic."* The second argues that the Sinification of Marxism was a ploy used by Mao to enhance his own position in the power struggle with the Moscow-oriented Returned Students' Faction[1] which had favoured a more orthodox European and Soviet reading of Marxism. According to Robert North, Mao was "adapting Russian communist political theory to meet peculiar Chinese requirements and the convenience of his own climb to power."[†] However, a third explanation is possible: that Mao was attempting to establish a formula by which a universal theory such as Marxism could be utilised in a particular national context and culture *without abandoning the universality of that theory.*[‡]

How can such an interpretation be justified? It is important to point out that Mao believed it possible to discover particular "laws" (of nature, society, history, war) which unlike the universal laws of Marxism, have no universal applicability. This belief in the existence of particular "laws" describing the regularities present in particular or localised contexts comes across clearly in the following interesting passage from "Problems of Strategy in China's Revolutionary War," written by Mao in 1936:

> . . . the different laws for directing wars are determined by the different circumstances of those wars—differences in their time, place and nature *(xingzhi)*. As regards the time factor, both war and its laws develop; each historical stage has its special characteristics, and hence the laws in each historical stage have their special characteristics and cannot be mechanically applied in another stage. As for the nature of war, since revolutionary war and counter-revolutionary war both have their special characteristics, the laws governing them also have their own characteristics, and those applying to one cannot be mechanically transferred to the other. As for the factor of place, since each country or nation, especially a large country or nation, has its own characteristics, the laws of war for each country or nation also have their own characteristics, and

---

*Ibid., 112–16.

[1]*Returned Students' Faction:* refers to Chinese Communists who studied in Moscow in the 1920s and early 1930s. They became competitors to Mao for leadership of the CCP.

[†]Robert C. North, *Moscow and Chinese Communists* (Stanford: Stanford University Press, 1953 & 1963), 193.

[‡]The following analysis is a truncated version of my article "The Form of Mao Zedong's 'Sinification of Marxism,'" *Australian Journal of Chinese Affairs,* no. 9 (January 1983): 17–33.

here, too, those applying to one cannot be mechanically transferred to the other. In studying the laws for directing wars that occur at different historical stages, that differ in nature and that are waged in different places and by different nations, we must fix our attention on the characteristics and development of each, and must oppose a mechanical approach to the problem of war.*

It is evident from this passage that Mao rejected the notion that there can only be laws of war in general. On the contrary, he argues that it is possible and desirable to seek out "laws" describing the characteristics of specific theatres of war.

But what is the relationship between universal laws of history and society and the particular "laws" of Chinese society and the Chinese revolution which Mao was so eager to discover? In the first place, it would seem that universal laws are derived from the many particular "laws" which describe the behaviour of the same phenomenon in different situations. For example, if different forms of class struggle are observed in many different social contexts, the particular "laws" describing those specific instances of class struggle constitute the foundation of a universal law which asserts the existence of class struggle in *all* societies. In the second place, a universal law has a predictive value which asserts the certain existence of the phenomenon described by that law in instances as yet unobserved; the universal law thus draws attention to, and guides analysis of this phenomenon. The function of such a universal law was not, as far as Mao was concerned, to dictate the manner in which that phenomenon would assume concrete form; that could only be disclosed through an empirical investigation whose purpose was to arrive at an understanding of the characteristics of that phenomenon in its specific context. In other words, the particular "law" would be revealed by an empirical investigation informed by knowledge of the relevant universal law. To pursue our example, the universal law of class struggle represented an abstract assertion of the existence of class struggle in all societies (save perhaps the most primitive); knowledge of that universal law had to be mobilised to discover the particular "law" which described the nature of class struggle within Chinese society.

Mao believed that the abstract universal laws of Marxism performed an important function in directing attention to those aspects of society requiring analysis and study. However, such universal laws did *not* by themselves represent Marxism in its entirety. To become a complete ideology, the universal laws of Marxism had to be mobilised

Selected Works of Mao Tse-tung (Peking: Foreign Languages Press, 1967), 1:181–82.

and applied to disclose a society's particular "laws." It was this union of the universal (abstract) laws and the particular (concrete) "laws" which constitute Marxism in its totality. And obviously, such a union of universal and particular could occur only within a specific historical and social context such as the Chinese society during the period of the anti-Japanese war. Consequently, Marxism in the Chinese context consisted of Marxism's universal laws utilised to disclose the particular "laws" describing the nature of Chinese society and the Chinese revolution. Once disclosed, those particular "laws" became for Mao an integral element of Marxism within that historically defined situation. It is in this sense that Mao could call for the Sinification of Marxism.

From this perspective, the Sinification of Marxism was not a question of the elevation of Chinese realities at the expense of Marxism's universality, but the completion of Marxism as an ideological system. Inherent in Mao's Sinification of Marxism is the notion that Marxism as a complete ideological system (rather than just a body of abstract universal laws) is definable only within a concrete historical situation. Thus, although the Sinification of Marxism is, as [Raymond] Wylie claims, a "culturally charged term,"* it does not claim any cultural privilege over Marxism. Within a different cultural or historical context, the universal laws of Marxism would have to be joined with the particular "laws" of that specific situation. Because these particular "laws" would be different from those describing Chinese society, that particular Marxism would differ accordingly. Both, nevertheless, would share a common stock of universal laws.

This view of Marxism led logically to an insistence on the need to pay close attention to the particular characteristics of Chinese society and history. Mao was to return to this point again and again in subsequent writings of the Yan'an period, and he made no attempt to conceal his impatience with those Marxists who were preoccupied with foreign models and history to the exclusion of Chinese history and conditions. He perceived this preoccupation as largely a manifestation of an incorrect interpretation of Marxism, one which regarded the particular "laws" of a largely European form of Marxism as having relevance within the Chinese context. In "Reform Our Study" (1941), Mao isolated three conditions having deleterious effect within the CCP: the study of current conditions was being neglected, as were the study of history and the application of Marxism-Leninism. For Mao,

---

*Raymond Wylie, *The Emergence of Maoism* (Stanford: Stanford University Press, 1980), 52.

these failings were a manifestation of an incorrect interpretation of Marxism. His critique of them was inspired by his own view of Marxism which insisted on the integration of Marxism's universal laws with the particular "laws" describing the regularities characteristic of Chinese society; and that integration was only possible through a detailed investigation and close knowledge of current conditions and Chinese history. . . .

In "On the New Stage" (1938), Mao had asserted that Marxism had to be regarded as a guide to action.* He returned to this theme frequently in the *zhengfeng*² documents, and it represented the major theme of his keynote speech originally entitled "Reform in Learning, the Party and Literature" (1942):

> Our comrades must understand that we do not study Marxism-Leninism because it is pleasing to the eye, or because it has some mystical value. . . . It is only extremely useful. . . . Marx, Lenin, and Stalin have repeatedly said, "Our doctrine is not dogma; it is a guide to action.". . . Theory and practice can be combined only if men of the Chinese Communist Party take the standpoints, concepts, and methods of Marxism-Leninism, apply them to China, and create a theory from conscientious research on the realities of the Chinese revolution and Chinese history.†

For Mao, Sinified Marxism represented the union of Marxism's universal laws and the particular "laws" of Chinese society. How did he perceive this ideology as a "guide to action"? It must be stressed that this ideological system did not contain within it the formulae for automatic and necessarily correct responses to the various political, economic or military contingencies which might arise in the course of revolution. The function of the ideology was to facilitate as accurate an interpretation of the historical context as was possible. This information would allow the revolutionary to take judicious action commensurate with the objective limitations of the situation as outlined by the ideology. The action could only be regarded as appropriate in its conception (rather than as necessarily correct), for there could be no formula for "correct" action implicit in the information provided. Having a clear and, it could be hoped, accurate picture of the historical situation would act as a guide to action by ruling out inappropriate

---

*Schram, *The Political Thought of Mao*, 171.
²zhengfeng: Rectification Movement
†Boyd Compton, trans., *Mao's China: Party Reform Documents, 1942–44* (Seattle: University of Washington Press, 1952), 21–22.

MAO ZEDONG'S "SINIFICATION OF MARXISM"

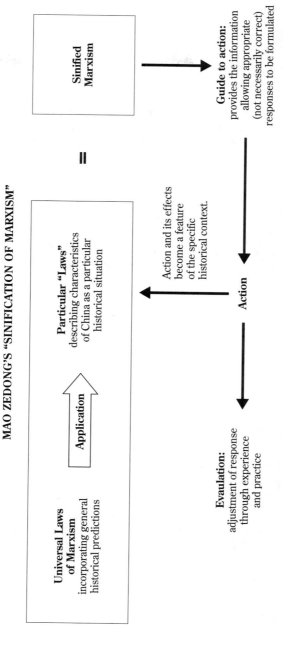

This chart maps the stages of Mao's approach
to solving problems and making Marxism fit China.

responses and presenting certain actions as preferable, or perhaps obvious.

It is in this context that Mao's theory of practice finds relevance. Ideology could only serve as a guide to action by presenting an accurate assessment of the historical situation or process. It was up to the political actor to take full cognizance of the particular "laws" of the situation, to draw the necessary inferences and formulate an appropriate response accordingly. Such a response could not be regarded as "correct" in advance of its implementation, only as appropriate. The only method of ascertaining whether the seemingly appropriate action was correct was by performing the action and evaluating its results. If there was an equivalence between intention and result, then the action and the interpretation upon which it was based were indeed correct; otherwise the disparity between intention and result served to indicate either faulty analysis of the situation, or formulation of seemingly appropriate but incorrect response. Only by thus engaging reality could experience be gained and action refined so that the gap between the seemingly appropriate and the correct response could be minimised.

14

LI ZHISUI

The Emperor of Zhongnanhai
1994

Li Zhisui, Mao's private doctor on and off from the mid-1950s on, published in English this denunciation of the Chairman as evil emperor in 1994. Li depicts Mao as a corrupt king in Zhongnanhai, the leadership compound of the CCP in downtown Beijing. Like Snow's book (see Document 11), Li's has been translated into Chinese and circulates widely (albeit illegally) in China today. It has been criticized by the CCP for demonizing the Chairman and by scholars inside and outside China for its lack of balance (see Document 17). Yet Li paints a vivid picture, and

Li Zhisui, *The Private Life of Chairman Mao*, trans. Tai Hung-chao (New York: Random House, 1994), 272–75, 276–78.

most scholars trust his ability to report what he saw directly. This selection on the Great Leap Forward year of 1958 shows the rarefied atmosphere in which Mao traveled by that time—shielded from unpleasant realities by his staff and essentially duped by their efforts to please him. This picture helps us understand how Mao could have come to think that the unrealistic agricultural policies and backyard steel furnaces of the Great Leap Forward were working.

On September 10, 1958, Mao set out again, traveling by plane, train, and boat, to see for himself the vast changes taking place in the country. His popular adulation grew at every stop we made.

We flew first to Wuhan. Two of Mao's most enthusiastic admirers—"democratic personage" and Guomindang defector Zhang Zhizhong and Anhui's first party secretary Zeng Xisheng—visited him there. Mao thrilled Zhang Zhizhong by inviting him to come along on his inspection tour, and Zhang obliged by showering Mao with flattery. "The condition of the country is excellent indeed," he said to Mao. "The weather is favorable, the nation is at peace, and the people feel secure."

Zeng Xisheng, too, was courting Mao's favor. He wanted the Chairman to visit Anhui province. Zhang Zhizhong, a native of Anhui himself, joined Zeng in encouraging the visit. Mao agreed. We took a boat down the Yangtze to the city of Anqing, just on the border of Anhui, where first party secretary Zeng Xisheng escorted our party by car to Anhui's capital, Hefei. There, we witnessed new miracles. "Backyard steel furnaces" were the local specialty.

I saw the first such furnace—a makeshift brick and mortar affair, four or five meters high—in the courtyard of the offices of the Anhui provincial party committee. The fire was going full-blast, and inside were all sorts of household implements made of steel—pots, pans, doorknobs, and shovels—being melted down to produce what Zeng assured Mao was also steel. Zeng Xisheng picked up a hot nugget from the ground, plucked from the furnace only moments before, to show Mao the fruit of the mill, and nearby were samples of finished steel, indisputable evidence of the success of the backyard steel furnace. Mao had called upon the country to overtake Great Britain in steel production within fifteen years, by using methods that were quick and economical. Even now, I do not know where the idea of the backyard steel furnaces originated. But the logic was always clear: Why spend millions of dollars building modern steel plants when steel could be produced for almost nothing in courtyards and fields? The "indigenous," or "backyard," steel furnace was the result.

I was astounded. The furnace was taking basic household implements and transforming them into nuggets called steel, melting down knives into ingots that could be used to make other knives. I had no idea whether the ingots were of good-quality steel, but it did seem ridiculous to melt steel to produce steel, to destroy knives to make knives. The backyard steel furnaces were everywhere in Anhui, all producing the same rough-looking ingots.

Toward the end of the visit, Zhang Zhizhong proposed that Mao ride through the streets in an open car so the citizens of Hefei could see their great leader. In the summer of 1949, Mao had entered Beijing in an open jeep and the citizens lined the streets to welcome their liberation. In September 1956, during a visit by Indonesian president Sukarno, Mao had ridden in an open cavalcade. But he rarely appeared so openly before the masses. The Chairman's provincial visits were almost always secret, and security was tight. When he visited factories, his exchanges with workers were carefully controlled. Mao's face-to-face meetings were ordinarily confined to high-ranking party elite or leaders of the "democratic" parties. His twice-yearly appearances on the top of Tiananmen were not really exceptions. The crowds in the square were carefully chosen. The risk of appearing publicly before the masses was not only to Mao's security. The Chairman did not want to be accused of fostering his own cult of personality.

Mao believed that the masses needed a great leader and that the chance to see him could have an inspirational, potentially transformative, effect. But he needed the illusion that the demand for his leadership came spontaneously from the masses themselves. He would not be guilty of having actively promoted his own cult of personality. "Democratic personage" Zhang Zhizhong, sensitive to Mao's dilemma, was well suited to push Mao into the limelight. "You seem very concerned about the development of a personality cult," Zhang said to Mao.

Zhang argued, though, that Mao was the Lenin, not the Stalin, of China. Mao, like Lenin, had led the Communist party and the Chinese people to revolutionary victory, living on to lead in the construction of socialism, too. Unlike Lenin, who had died only eight years after the success of revolution, Mao would bless the people of China with his leadership for another thirty or forty years, they hoped. The difference between Mao and Stalin was that Stalin had promoted his own cult of personality. Mao had not. Mao, said Zhang, had a democratic style of leadership that stressed the "mass line" and avoided arbitrariness and dictatorship. "How can our country have a personality cult?" he wondered. "Progress is so fast, and the improvement in the life of the people so great that the masses spontaneously pour out their sincere, passionate feelings for you. Our people truly love their great leader. This is not a personality cult." Mao loved Zhang's flattery. The two were a perfect pair. The Chairman agreed to show himself to the citizens of Hefei.

On September 19, 1958, over 300,000 people lined the streets of Hefei hoping for a glimpse of Mao. He rode slowly through the city in an open car, waving impassively to the throngs, basking in their show of affection. I suspect that the crowds in Hefei were no more spontaneous than those in Tiananmen. The gaily colored clothes, the garlands of flowers around their necks, the bouquets they held aloft as the motorcade passed by, the singing, the dancing, the slogans they shouted—"Long Live Chairman Mao," "Long Live the People's Communes," "Long Live the Great Leap Forward"—suggested that Zeng Xisheng had left little to chance. These crowds had also been carefully chosen, directed by the Anhui bureau of public security. But the crowds were no less enthusiastic, no less sincere in their adulation, for having been carefully chosen. At the sight of their Chairman, they went wild with delight. . . .

. . . Mao's plan for the Great Leap Forward was grandiose, utopian—to catch up with Great Britain in fifteen years, to transform agricultural production, using people's communes to walk the road from socialism to communism, from poverty to abundance. Mao was accustomed to sycophancy and flattery. He had been pushing the top-level party and government leaders to embrace his grandiose schemes. Wanting to please Mao, fearing for their own political futures if they did not, the top-level officials put pressure on the lower ones, and lower-level cadres complied both by working the peasants relentlessly and by reporting what their superiors wanted to hear. Impossible, fantastical claims were being made. Claims of per-*mu* grain production went from 10,000 to 20,000 to 30,000 pounds.

Psychologists of mass behavior might have an explanation for what went wrong in China in the late summer of 1958. China was struck with a mass hysteria fed by Mao, who then fell victim himself. We returned to Beijing in time for the October first celebrations.[1] Mao

---

[1]October 1 is National Day in China, commemorating the founding of the People's Republic in 1949.

began believing the slogans, casting caution to the winds. Mini–steel mills were being set up even in Zhongnanhai, and at night the whole compound was a sea of red light. The idea had originated with the Central Bureau of Guards, but Mao did not oppose them, and soon everyone was stoking the fires—cadres, clerks, secretaries, doctors, nurses, and me. The rare voices of caution were being stilled. Everyone was hurrying to jump on the utopian bandwagon. Liu Shaoqi, Deng Xiaoping, Zhou Enlai, and Chen Yi,[2] men who might once have reined the Chairman in, were speaking with a single voice, and that voice was Mao's. What those men really thought, we never will know. Everyone was caught in the grip of this utopian hysteria.

Immediately after the October first celebrations, we set out again by train, heading south. The scene along the railroad tracks was incredible. Harvest time was approaching, and the crops were thriving. The fields were crowded with peasants at work, and they were all women and young girls dressed in reds and greens, gray-haired old men, or teenagers. All the able-bodied males, the real farmers of China, had been taken out of agricultural production to tend the backyard steel furnaces.

The backyard furnaces had transformed the rural landscape. They were everywhere, and we could see peasant men in a constant frenzy of activity, transporting fuel and raw materials, keeping the fires stoked. At night, the furnaces dotted the landscape as far as the eye could see, their fires lighting the skies.

Every commune we visited provided testimony to the abundance of the upcoming harvest. The statistics, for both grain and steel production, were astounding. "Good-news reporting stations" were being set up in communal dining halls, each station competing with nearby brigades and communes to report—red flags waving, gongs and drums sounding—the highest, most extravagant figures.

Mao's earlier skepticism had vanished. Common sense escaped him. He acted as though he believed the outrageous figures for agricultural production. The excitement was contagious. I was infected, too. Naturally, I could not help but wonder how rural China could be so quickly transformed. But I was seeing that transformation with my own eyes. I allowed myself only occasional, fleeting doubts.

One evening on the train, Lin Ke tried to set me straight. Chatting with Lin Ke and Wang Jingxian, looking out at the fires from the back-

---

[2] These were all senior leaders of the CCP.

yard furnaces that stretched all the way to the horizon, I shared the puzzlement I had been feeling, wondering out loud how the furnaces had appeared so suddenly and how the production figures could be so high.

What we were seeing from our windows, Lin Ke said, was staged, a huge multi-act nationwide Chinese opera performed especially for Mao. The party secretaries had ordered furnaces constructed everywhere along the rail route, stretching out for ten *li* on either side, and the women were dressed so colorfully, in reds and greens, because they had been ordered to dress that way. In Hubei, party secretary Wang Renzhong had ordered the peasants to remove rice plants from faraway fields and transplant them along Mao's route, to give the impression of a wildly abundant crop. The rice was planted so closely together that electric fans had to be set up around the fields to circulate air in order to prevent the plants from rotting. All of China was a stage, all the people performers in an extravaganza for Mao.

The production figures were false, Lin Ke said. No soil could produce twenty or thirty thousand pounds per *mu*. And what was coming out of the backyard steel furnaces was useless. The finished steel I had seen in Anhui that Zeng Xisheng claimed had been produced by the backyard steel furnace was fake, delivered there from a huge, modern factory.

"This isn't what the newspapers are saying," I protested.

The newspapers, too, were filled with falsehoods, Lin Ke insisted, printing only what they had been told. "They would not dare tell the public what was really happening," Lin said.

I was astonished. The *People's Daily* was our source of truth, the most authoritative of all the country's newspapers. If the *People's Daily* was printing falsehoods, which one would tell the truth?

15

RAE YANG

At the Center of the Storm
1997

The Red Guard student groups were at the heart of the Cultural Revolution. Mao paraded them in Tiananmen Square and they roamed with virtual impunity around the country in 1966 and 1967. On the one hand, the Red Guards were utterly idealistic in their desire to serve and follow Chairman Mao. On the other hand, this radical idealism gave vent to the petty resentments of students and frequently led to violent deaths. Rae Yang's recent memoir of her life as a Red Guard demonstrates both results. At first she found the Cultural Revolution thrilling. She created dazibao, *or "big character posters"—big sheets of paper denouncing anyone or anything the Red Guards considered "counterrevolutionary." Her targets, however, were merely high school teachers she didn't like, not the national political figures criticized by Mao. She was transfixed when she caught a glimpse of Chairman Mao at Tiananmen Square. Later, when her Red Guard troop traveled to Guangzhou to "make revolution," they ended up beating a deranged man to death. What began with pure ideals ended with sordid death. The question to consider here is, How much of the complex ideas in Mao's writings did Rae Yang and her fellow Red Guards understand?*

From May to December 1966, the first seven months of the Cultural Revolution left me with experiences I will never forget. Yet I forgot things almost overnight in that period. So many things were happening around me. The situation was changing so fast. I was too excited, too jubilant, too busy, too exhausted, too confused, too uncomfortable. . . . The forgotten things, however, did not all go away. Later some of them sneaked back into my memory, causing me unspeakable pain and shame. So I would say that those seven months were the most terrible in my life. Yet they were also the most

Rae Yang, *Spider Eaters: A Memoir* (Berkeley: University of California Press, 1997), 115–18, 122–23, 136–38.

wonderful! I had never felt so good about myself before, nor have I ever since.

In the beginning, the Cultural Revolution exhilarated me because suddenly I felt that I was allowed to think with my own head and say what was on my mind. In the past, the teachers at 101[1] had worked hard to make us intelligent, using the most difficult questions in mathematics, geometry, chemistry, and physics to challenge us. But the mental abilities we gained, we were not supposed to apply elsewhere. For instance, we were not allowed to question the teachers' conclusions. Students who did so would be criticized as "disrespectful and conceited," even if their opinions made perfect sense. Worse still was to disagree with the leaders. Leaders at various levels represented the Communist Party. Disagreeing with them could be interpreted as being against the Party, a crime punishable by labor reform, imprisonment, even death.

Thus the teachers created a contradiction. On the one hand, they wanted us to be smart, rational, and analytical. On the other hand, they forced us to be stupid, to be "the teachers' little lambs" and "the Party's obedient tools." By so doing, I think, they planted a sick tree; the bitter fruit would soon fall into their own mouths.

When the Cultural Revolution broke out in late May 1966, I felt like the legendary monkey Sun Wukong,[2] freed from the dungeon that had held him under a huge mountain for five hundred years. It was Chairman Mao who set us free by allowing us to rebel against authorities. As a student, the first authority I wanted to rebel against was Teacher Lin, our homeroom teacher—in Chinese, *banzhuren.* As *banzhuren,* she was in charge of our class. A big part of her duty was to make sure that we behaved and thought correctly....

Now the time had come for the underdogs to speak up, to seek justice! Immediately I took up a brush pen, dipped it in black ink and wrote a long *dazibao* (criticism in big characters). Using some of the rhetorical devices Teacher Lin had taught us, I accused her of lacking proletarian feelings toward her students, of treating them as her enemies, of being high-handed, and suppressing different opinions. When I finished and showed it to my classmates, they supported me by signing their names to it. Next, we took the *dazibao* to Teacher Lin's home

[1] *101:* an elite high school in Beijing attached to Beijing University and generally reserved for the children of high party officials or famous scholars or artists

[2] *Sun Wukong:* the lead character in the classical and popular Chinese novel *Journey to the West* (also translated in an abridged version as *Monkey*). He is a naughty and powerful character and was a great favorite of Mao.

nearby and pasted it on the wall of her bedroom for her to read carefully day and night. This, of course, was not personal revenge. It was answering Chairman Mao's call to combat the revisionist educational line. If in the meantime it caused Teacher Lin a few sleepless nights, so be it! This revolution was meant to "touch the soul" of people, an unpopular teacher in particular.

Teacher Lin, although she was not a good teacher in my opinion, was not yet the worst. Teacher Qian was even worse. He was the political teacher who had implemented the Exposing Third Layer of Thoughts campaign.[3] In the past many students believed that he could read people's minds. Now a *dazibao* by a student gave us a clue as to how he acquired this eerie ability. Something I would not have guessed in a thousand years! He had been reading students' diaries in class breaks, while we were doing physical exercise on the sports ground. The student who wrote the *dazibao* felt sick one day and returned to his classroom earlier than expected. There he had actually seen Qian sneak a diary from a student's desk and read it. The student kept his silence until the Cultural Revolution, for Qian was his *banzhuren.*

So this was Qian's so-called "political and thought work"! What could it teach us but dishonesty and hypocrisy? Such a "glorious" example the school had set for us, and in the past we had revered him so much! Thinking of the nightmare he gave me, I was outraged. "Take up a pen, use it as a gun." I wrote another *dazibao* to denounce Teacher Qian.

Within a few days *dazibao* were popping up everywhere like bamboo shoots after a spring rain, written by students, teachers, administrators, workers, and librarians. Secrets dark and dirty were exposed. Every day we made shocking discoveries. The sacred halo around the teachers' heads that dated back two thousand five hundred years to the time of Confucius disappeared. Now teachers must drop their pretentious airs and learn a few things from their students. Parents would be taught by their kids instead of vice versa, as Chairman Mao pointed out. Government officials would have to wash their ears to listen to the ordinary people. Heaven and earth were turned upside down. The rebellious monkey with enormous power had gotten out. A revolution was underway. . . .

---

[3] *Exposing Third Layer of Thoughts campaign:* an earlier ideological remolding campaign in which Rae Yang and her classmates had participated

On August 18, 1966, I saw Chairman Mao for the first time. The night before, we set off from 101 on foot a little after midnight and arrived at Tiananmen Square before daybreak. In the dark we waited anxiously. Will Chairman Mao come? was the question in everybody's mind. Under a starry sky, we sang.

"Lifting our heads we see the stars of Beidou [the Big Dipper], lowering our heads we are longing for Mao Zedong, longing for Mao Zedong. . . ."

We poured our emotions into the song. Chairman Mao who loved the people would surely hear it, for it came from the bottom of our hearts.

Perhaps he did. At five o'clock, before sunrise, like a miracle he walked out of Tiananmen onto the square and shook hands with people around him. The square turned into a jubilant ocean. Everybody was shouting "Long live Chairman Mao!" Around me girls were crying; boys were crying too. With hot tears streaming down my face, I could not see Chairman Mao clearly. He had ascended the rostrum. He was too high, or rather, the stands for Red Guard representatives were too low.

Earnestly we chanted: "We-want-to-see-Chair-man-Mao!" He heard us! He walked over to the corner of Tiananmen and waved at us. Now I could see him clearly. He was wearing a green army uniform and a red armband, just like all of us. My blood was boiling inside me. I jumped and shouted and cried in unison with a million people in the square. At that moment, I forgot myself; all barriers that existed between me and others broke down. I felt like a drop of water that finally joined the mighty raging ocean. I would never be lonely again.

[Later in the fall of 1966, Rae Yang and her Red Guard troop traveled south to Guanzhou to spread their revolution. Early in their stay, the following incident occurred.]

On that night, two female Red Guards who were senior students did not come back until after nine o'clock. We were beginning to worry about them. Then we saw them return with a "captive," who was a big, stout man in his thirties. They explained to us why they had "arrested" this man.

In the afternoon the two Red Guards got lost in the city. Because of the directions this man gave them, they ended up in an abandoned cathedral in the suburbs. In twilight the two young women wandered about the ruin, trying to figure out what went wrong and how to get back to the city. Around them the weeds were tall and the trees were casting long shadows. The wind rustled and insects chirped. Suddenly they heard a commotion behind them. It turned out that a group of local people had seized a man.

It was the same man who had given them the wrong directions; then he followed them all the way to the cathedral. The female Red Guards did not notice him, but the local people, whose revolutionary vigilance had been heightened, became suspicious. They knew that rape had been committed on this site.

Hearing this, I was shocked. Rape! In my mind, it was a crime almost as bad as murder. So we interrogated him. What he said about his name, age, and profession has escaped me completely. We must have inquired into his family background and class status too. Probably he did not belong to the Five Red Categories (workers, poor and lower-middle peasants, revolutionary cadres, revolutionary servicemen, revolutionary martyrs), or else what happened that night might not have happened. In my memory even his face is fuzzy, like a picture out of focus. The only thing I remember clearly is the pair of white cotton shorts he had on that night.

To our angry question of why he had tricked our two comrades into the deserted cathedral, he could not give a satisfactory explanation. That convinced us that he had harbored evil intentions toward our class sisters. We closed in on him. Hands on hips. Fingers pointed at the tip of his nose. Some were already unbuckling their belts. Our questions became sharp.

"So do you hate Red Guards? Tell us the truth! Or else we'll smash your dog head!"

"Yes. I hate the Red Guards."

"Then do you hate the Cultural Revolution too? Do you want to sabotage the Cultural Revolution?"

"Yes. Yes. I hate . . . I want to sabotage . . ."

"Are you a class enemy?"

"Yes. I am a class enemy."

"Are you a Nationalist agent?"

"Yes. I'm an agent. I came from Taiwan."

"Do you hope the Nationalists come back?"

"Yes. I do . . ."

"Do you have guns?"

"Oh yes. I have guns. I have grenades too. I even have a machine gun."

"And a transmitter-receiver to contact Taiwan?"

"Sure. I have a transmitter-receiver."

"Where did you hide these?"

"I buried them in my backyard. You come with me. I'll take you there. You can dig them out."

As the interrogation went on, the man confessed that he had committed all the crimes we could think of. The words that dropped out of his mouth turned into facts in our minds. And these "facts" fueled our hatred toward him. He was no longer a suspect. He had become a criminal, a real class enemy. We started to beat him.

The next thing he did was a real shock to all of us. In a shower of fists, kicks, curses, and thrashes, he suddenly straightened up and pulled his white cotton shorts down. He had no underwear on. So there was his thing, his penis. Large and black. It stuck out from a clump of black hair. To me it seemed erect, nodding its head at all of us.

I couldn't help staring at it. I was dumbfounded. I was embarrassed. I was furious. My hands were cold and my cheeks were on fire. For a few seconds none of us moved. We were petrified. Then the dike burst. Torrents of water rushed out. All the female Red Guards ran out of the classroom. We stayed in the corridor. The male Red Guards charged forward. On their way they picked up long bamboo sticks to hit him.

We all hated him! I could not tell who hated him more. The female Red Guards hated him because he had insulted all of us. The male Red Guards hated him too, because he was a scum of their sex. By exposing himself, he had exposed all of them. They were stripped. They were shamed. This time they beat him hard. No mercy on him. He did not deserve it. He was a bad egg!

The sticks fell like rain. In a few minutes, the man dropped to the ground. The sticks stood in midair. Then someone pulled his shorts back up. After that we streamed back into the classroom. We looked. He did not move. He did not breathe. This man was dead!

CENTRAL COMMITTEE OF THE CHINESE COMMUNIST PARTY

Some Questions on Party History

June 1981

After Mao's death in 1976, there was a period of political transition. By 1979 the new leadership under Deng Xiaoping had consolidated, and it turned its attention to righting the wrongs it had seen in the Cultural Revolution. This left the party with a delicate task: how to acknowledge Mao's errors in the Cultural Revolution without discrediting the entire CCP. The resolution presented here was passed by the Central Committee on June 27, 1981. Like its predecessor, the first resolution on party history passed at the Seventh Party Congress in Yan'an in 1945, this resolution sought to lay to rest unresolved issues and to buttress the current leadership. It was decidedly less successful than the 1945 version in achieving this goal.

We can see in this short extract that in 1981 the CCP wanted to stress the "collective wisdom" nature of "Mao Zedong Thought," along with the contributions of several other party leaders, named in the first paragraph. In addition, the resolution lays the blame for the Cultural Revolution on Mao but tries to separate Mao the man from Mao the ideological lifeblood of the party. The chief logic used is that because of the collaborative nature of "Mao Zedong Thought," with so many contributing to it, the failings of one man, even the figurehead, should not discredit the system.

[The text begins with a two-page summary of the achievements of party rule from 1956 to 1966.]

All the successes in these 10 years were achieved under the collective leadership of the Central Committee of the Party headed by Comrade Mao Zedong. Likewise, responsibility for the errors committed in the work of this period rested with the same collective leadership.

Translation selected from *Beijing Review,* 6 July 1981, 10–39.

Although Comrade Mao Zedong must be held chiefly responsible, we cannot lay the blame on him alone for all those errors. During this period, his theoretical and practical mistakes concerning class struggle in a socialist society became increasingly serious, his personal arbitrariness gradually undermined democratic centralism in Party life and the personality cult grew graver and graver. The Central Committee of the Party failed to rectify these mistakes in good time. Careerists like Lin Biao, Jiang Qing and Kang Sheng, harboring ulterior motives, made use of these errors and inflated them. This led to the inauguration of the "cultural revolution.". . .

Chief responsibility for the grave "Left" error of the "cultural revolution," an error comprehensive in magnitude and protracted in duration, does indeed lie with Comrade Mao Zedong. But after all it was the error of a great proletarian revolutionary. Comrade Mao Zedong paid constant attention to overcoming shortcomings in the life of the Party and state. In his later years, however, far from making a correct analysis of many problems, he confused right and wrong and the people with the enemy during the "cultural revolution." While making serious mistakes, he repeatedly urged the whole Party to study the works of Marx, Engels and Lenin conscientiously and imagined that his theory and practice were Marxist and that they were essential for the consolidation of the dictatorship of the proletariat. Herein lies his tragedy. . . .

Comrade Mao Zedong's prestige reached a peak and he began to get arrogant at the very time when the Party was confronted with the new task of shifting the focus of its work to socialist construction, a task for which the utmost caution was required. He gradually divorced himself from practice and from the masses, acted more and more arbitrarily and subjectively, and increasingly put himself above the Central Committee of the Party. The result was a steady weakening and even undermining of the principle of collective leadership and democratic centralism in the political life of the Party and the country. This state of affairs took shape only gradually and the Central Committee of the Party should be held partly responsible. From the Marxist viewpoint, this complex phenomenon was the product of given historical conditions. Blaming this on only one person or on only a handful of people will not provide a deep lesson for the whole Party or enable it to find practical ways to change the situation. . . .

Comrade Mao Zedong was a great Marxist and a great proletarian revolutionary, strategist and theorist. It is true that he made gross mistakes during the "cultural revolution," but, if we judge his activities as a whole, his contributions to the Chinese revolution far outweigh his mistakes. His merits are primary and his errors secondary. He rendered indelible meritorious service in founding and building up our Party and the Chinese People's Liberation Army, in winning victory for the cause of liberation of the Chinese people, in founding the People's Republic of China and in advancing our socialist cause. He made major contributions to the liberation of the oppressed nations of the world and to the progress of mankind.

The Chinese Communists, with Comrade Mao Zedong as their chief representative, made a theoretical synthesis of China's unique experience in its protracted revolution in accordance with the basic principles of Marxism-Leninism. This synthesis constituted a scientific system of guidelines befitting China's conditions, and it is this synthesis which is Mao Zedong Thought, the product of the integration of the universal principles of Marxism-Leninism with the concrete practice of the Chinese revolution. Making revolution in a large Eastern semi-colonial, semi-feudal country is bound to meet with many special, complicated problems, which cannot be solved by reciting the general principles of Marxism-Leninism or by copying foreign experience in every detail. The erroneous tendency of making Marxism a dogma and deifying Comintern resolutions and the experience of the Soviet Union prevailed in the international communist movement and in our Party mainly in the late 1920s and early 1930s, and this tendency pushed the Chinese revolution to the brink of total failure. It was in the course of combating this wrong tendency and making a profound summary of our historical experience in this respect that Mao Zedong Thought took shape and developed. It was systematized and extended in a variety of fields and reached maturity in the latter part of the Agrarian Revolutionary War and the War of Resistance Against Japan, and it was further developed during the War of Liberation and after the founding of the People's Republic of China. Mao Zedong Thought is Marxism-Leninism applied and developed in China; it constitutes a correct theory, a body of correct principles and a summary of the experiences that have been confirmed in the practice of the Chinese revolution, a crystallization of the collective wisdom of the Chinese Communist Party. Many outstanding leaders of our Party made important contributions to the formation and development of Mao Zedong Thought, and they are synthesized in the scientific works of Comrade Mao Zedong. . . .

Mao Zedong Thought is the valuable spiritual asset of our Party. It will be our guide to action for a long time to come. The Party leaders and the large group of cadres nurtured by Marxism-Leninism and Mao Zedong Thought were the backbone forces in winning great victories for our cause; they are and will remain our treasured mainstay in the cause of socialist modernization. While many of Comrade Mao Zedong's important works were written during the periods of new-democratic revolution and of socialist transformation, we must still constantly study them. This is not only because one cannot cut the past off from the present and failure to understand the past will hamper our understanding of present-day problems, but also because many of the basic theories, principles and scientific approaches set forth in these works are of universal significance and provide us with invaluable guidance now and will continue to do so in the future. Therefore, we must continue to uphold Mao Zedong Thought, study it in earnest and apply its stand, viewpoint, and method in studying the new situation and solving the new problems arising in the course of practice.

17

JEFFREY WASSERSTROM

Mao Matters

1996

Jeffrey Wasserstrom is a historian of Republican China and popular culture. He brings a broader prospective to this review of recent scholarship on Mao than a Mao specialist might. His review is useful because it considers two of the most important books on Mao from the 1990s—Li Zhisui's immensely popular The Private Life of Chairman Mao *(see Document 14) and the challenging postmodern analysis of Mao's political impact by David Apter and Tony Saich in* Revolutionary Discourse in Mao's Republic. *Wasserstrom gives us a sense of the major trend in academic Mao studies today—the shift from studying Mao as either isolated "great man" or symbol of the revolution to studying how and why hundreds of millions of Chinese believed so strongly in him.*

Jeffrey Wasserstrom, "Mao Masters: A Review Essay," *China Review International*, vol. 3, no. 1 (Spring 1996): 1–21.

The two books under review here[1] are obviously of very different kinds—so different, in fact, that some readers may find it odd to find them paired in a review essay. David Apter and Tony Saich are academically trained political scientists who have joined forces to create an often insightful but sometimes difficult-to-follow scholarly study based on the collection and analysis of a variety of source materials, ranging from famous writings by Mao to interviews with survivors of the crucial Yan'an period in the history of the Chinese Communist Party (CCP), and this study makes use of theories and methodologies associated with such fields as anthropology and literary criticism. The recently deceased Li Zhisui, on the other hand, was trained as a physician rather than an academic, and his book is a straightforward, accessible, and deeply personal narrative based almost exclusively on the author's memory of his own encounters with Mao and conversations with members of the Chairman's inner circle.

It should also be noted that each book focuses on a different time and place: Yan'an during the early 1940s in the first case, and Beijing between 1954 (the year Li began serving as Mao's doctor) and 1976 (the year the Chairman died) in the second. Even though these books—which for convenience I shall refer to below as *Mao's Republic* and *Private Life*—are by different kinds of authors, take different forms, and deal with different periods, there are two reasons why it makes sense to place them side by side. First, each in its own way is among the most important contributions to date to what might loosely be called "Mao studies." Second, each directs our attention to one of the two main, diverging directions in which people attempting to come to terms with the Chairman's life and legacy are currently being pulled.

This is because one of the themes that is stressed in *Mao's Republic* is that the man once referred to as the "Great Helmsman" needs to be understood as a multidimensional and extremely complex figure. Apter and Saich's theoretically sophisticated analysis of the rhetorical dimensions of Yan'an politics leaves us with a picture of Mao that is nuanced and shaded. At some points, the authors remind us that Mao tended to view certain ends as justifying even the most brutal of means, but in other places they insist that we see this same man as a prophet with an unusual talent for giving voice to collective dreams and aspirations. In still other instances, they stress Mao's significance

---

[1]David E. Apter and Tony Saich, *Revolutionary Discourse in Mao's Republic* (Cambridge: Harvard University Press, 1994); Li Zhisui, *The Private Life of Chairman Mao: The Memoirs of Mao's Personal Physician Dr. Li Zhisui,* trans. Tai Hung-chao (New York: Random House, 1994).

as both the central subject in and a skilled creator of powerful mythic tales about the heroic redemption of lost patrimonies—tales that would retain their potency long after the People's Republic of China (PRC) was founded in 1949.

By contrast, *Private Life* presents us with an essentially mono-chromatic image of Mao. According to Li Zhisui, if we strip away all of the mythical images that have surrounded his famous (or infamous) patient's life and theories, the man we are left with is nothing more than a tyrant. The Mao that Li describes is a man who was driven above all else by an unbridled lust for absolute power, an extreme paranoia that made him doubt the loyalty of even his most sycophantic allies, and an unquenchable desire to satisfy a variety of hedonistic urges. Official propaganda may have presented the Great Helmsman as infinitely compassionate, but according to *Private Life,* the Chairman was actually an unfeeling dictator who never showed the slightest concern for the misery suffered by others as a result of his policies.

[Wasserstrom reviews earlier Mao studies briefly and then turns to representative works published in the early reform period following Mao's death.]

One of the earliest and most impressive products of this optimistic period was *Mao Tse-tung in the Scales of History,* a collection of essays that appeared in 1977. Dick Wilson, then the editor of the *China Quarterly,* followed a simple plan in putting together this volume: he invited prominent scholars who had previously written pieces on Mao to contribute new essays that focused on specific aspects of the leader's personality and accomplishments. The result was an appealingly diverse and often illuminating work; it contained chapters with such simple titles as "The Soldier" (by Jacques Guillermaz) and "The Chinese" (by Wang Gungwu). Wilson aptly described this collection as a "provisional" assessment of a figure who remained so complex and enigmatic that no one person could be expected to write a "just epitaph."* Throughout the decade or so that followed its publication, the volume stood out as one of the most ambitious and effective efforts by Mao specialists to reveal the man behind the myths. It was greeted by many as an unusually successful effort to bring together in one place all the separate "Maos" that needed to concern us. . . .

---

*Dick Wilson, *Mao Tse-tung in the Scales of History* (Cambridge: Cambridge University Press, 1977), viii.

... Many contemporary readers of the almost twenty-year-old *Mao Tse-tung in the Scales of History* will react to it in one of two very different ways.* Some will wonder why so many important "Maos" were left out of that book, and ask why chapters with such titles as "The Icon," "The Commodity," "The God," and "The Contested Symbol" were not included. In addition, critics may ask why a sharper distinction was not made between the very different "Maos" of different eras. They may even wonder, as I have, whether we might do well in the future to follow the lead suggested by the literature on figures as diverse as Karl Marx and Elvis Presley, and start to differentiate between a more attractive "earlier" or "young" Mao and a less appealing "later" or "old" Mao. ...

MULTIPLE MAOS

I want to argue here that Apter and Saich's book offers one of the strongest and most important cases to date for a plethora of different, though obviously interrelated and overlapping, Maos. ...

Apter and Saich distinguish between these various Maos in several different ways. For example, they speak at times of the need to remember that there was both a "hard" and a "soft" Mao at Yan'an. The former was someone who would do anything to secure and maintain authority. He was, in addition, a loyal member of a Leninist organization whose other top leaders tended to be just as ruthless as he was in the pursuit of power. The "soft" Mao, on the other hand, was a religious figure of sorts whom Apter and Saich portray as having had an almost magical gift for weaving together stories of personal and national loss and redemption into inspiring master narratives—narratives that helped to bind together and lend cohesion to what was in other ways a very fragmented and factionalized Yan'an community. The authors of *Mao's Republic* also stress the need to remember that the Chairman presented himself to this community in various guises, some of which combined the "hard" and "soft" sides of his persona. For example, at times he cultivated the image of himself as a wanderer in the wilderness searching for philosophical truths and honing his skills as a warrior, while on other occasions he and his allies pro-

*Good general overviews of recent trends in Chinese and Western treatments of Mao are provided in Brantly Womack, "Mao Zedong Thoughts," *The China Quarterly*, no. 137 (March 1994): 159–67; and Thomas Scharping, "The Man, the Myth, the Message—New Trends in Mao Literature from China," *The China Quarterly*, no. 137 (March 1994): 168–79.

moted the idea that he was an armed prophet who was equally at home writing sacred texts and leading the faithful into battle. . . .

THE MONSTROUS MAO

Li Zhisui's biases and basic feelings concerning Mao are spelled out at the very beginning of *Private Life*. In the Preface, the physician notes that he once "revered" his famous patient (p. xix) but then came to view him as a despicable creature, a "dedicated philanderer" whose only concerns were to satisfy sexual urges and maintain "total power" (p. xx). . . . This theme of imperial influence is so prominent in *Private Life* that it seems safe to speculate that, had a new edition of *Mao Tsetung in the Scales of History* been commissioned before the doctor's death and had Li Zhisui been asked to contribute a chapter, he might well have chosen to call his essay "The Emperor."

One would guess from the Foreword to *Private Life,* on the other hand, that Andrew Nathan might find "The Dictator" a more appropriate title for such a chapter. This is because, in introducing Li's memoir, Nathan moves beyond Chinese imperial metaphors to place Mao in a rogues' gallery that includes everyone from Caligula to Hitler (as well as Stalin, of course). What unites these tyrants, he suggests, is that they all experienced and were warped by "the deranging effects of absolute power" and ended up descending "into a shadow world, where great visions become father to great crimes" (pp. vii and xiv). . . .

A number of Chinese dissidents have also made much use of imperial and dynastic metaphors in their harsh critiques of autocratic Maoist rule, though in doing so they approach the issue from a somewhat different standpoint and clearly have quite different motivations compared to Western commentators.* What all of these various texts have in common is that they encourage us to think of a single historical Mao. They imply or explicitly state that the various Mao myths created in the PRC should be dismissed as nothing more than a delusionary smoke screen that temporarily hid the monster's true form. This highlights two key differences between *Private Life* and *Mao's Republic*. First, as already noted, Apter and Saich emphasize the need to think of multiple Maos. Second they insist that myths are more than just lies.

*See, e.g., Ruan Ming, *Deng Xiaoping: Chronicle of an Empire* (Boulder, Colo.: Westview Press, 1994), 80, 171, 234, passim.

This reformulation of the problem of mythmaking by Apter and Saich, which draws upon the work of Lévi-Strauss[2] and a variety of other theorists, has several interesting implications for our understanding of Mao. For example, it leads the authors of *Mao's Republic* to take quite seriously the famous interview-based account of Mao's childhood that Edgar Snow presents in *Red Star Over China,* which they note was widely read inside as well as outside China and "persuaded many young people to go to Yan'an" (p. 354 n. 35). Instead of dismissing Snow as a dupe who accepted at face value a largely erroneous account of Mao's early life, they see this text as providing an important window into the narrative and discursive strategies of self-presentation that CCP leaders turned to in their quest to build up a richly endowed fund of symbolic capital. Snow's text, in their eyes, "helped Mao to become a surrogate figure for the China to become," reinforced the idea that he was someone who was "undeterred by any obstacle to revolutionary learning," and, most importantly, served both to humanize Mao and make him "larger than life" (p. 90)....

THE VALUE OF THE TWO WORKS

After my criticism of both books for various failings, many may be tempted not to read either of them, but in fact each has a good deal to offer students of modern China. Mao remains such an important figure that even flawed efforts to understand him are worth looking at carefully, providing there is some kind of payoff. In the case of Li Zhisui's memoir, the most rewarding feature is the wealth of detailed information it provides about a wide variety of little-known people and places associated with Mao's inner circle. Skeptical readers (like myself) may in many cases end up wondering just how accurate a description of a specific locale or event really is—not so much because we doubt the doctor's integrity but rather because we wonder about the ability to remember things so clearly after such a long passage of time. Even skeptical readers, however, are likely to come away from *Private Life* convinced that they know more than they did before about a variety of aspects of PRC society that are usually kept hidden from view....

[2] *Lévi-Strauss:* Claude Lévi-Strauss, a founding theorist of structuralist anthropology who has looked in particular at unconscious patterns of behavior in social groups. Many historians have found his theories useful in explaining human behavior.

Apter and Saich provide a much needed countervailing force to the many current works that seek to focus our attention exclusively on a single, monstrous Mao. Whether or not we give credence to the most appalling information that Li Zhisui presents to us in his memoir, there should be no question now that one Mao worth keeping in mind at all times is the man who became corrupted by power and capable of great callousness and cruelty. What Apter and Saich remind us of so effectively, however, is that there are other Maos to remember as well, including the rebel who was able to inspire a great deal of devotion, first among a band of followers in a remote part of China and later among a much broader segment of the Chinese population. Not only does one need to come to terms with the despot, but one must also come to terms with the visionary author responsible for powerful texts that drew attention so effectively to the humiliations that the nation had suffered at the hands of foreign oppressors and the peasants at the hands of landlords, and who in some cases even dealt eloquently with the abuses that women had suffered at the hands of husbands, fathers, lineage elders, and mothers-in-law. With a revolutionary leader who has been deified in as many ways as Mao has, it is certainly important to highlight his failings. But Mao is too important and intriguing a figure to reduce once again to a caricature. Those of us seeking to understand the confusing trajectories of the Chinese Revolution need to learn to think and talk in new ways about a multiplicity of contradictory Maos, ranging from the inspirational to the profoundly disturbing, and Apter and Saich have done us a valuable service by giving us a strong push in that direction.

18

GEREMIE BARMÉ

Shades of Mao

1990s

While the Chinese Communist party tries to limit Mao's aura and intellectuals use him to push their reform agendas, the ordinary people of China also have space in their hearts—and in their temples—for Chairman Mao. Geremie Barmé, the doyen of China pop and unofficial politics, opens the window to the devotional uses of Mao, as well as the irreverent, with two examples from his book Shades of Mao. *The first selection, by Xin Yuan, is an assessment from the Hong Kong press of Mao's role as a virtual deity in China's enduring popular religious traditions. The second selection is a punning rhyme that reflects Mao's meaning to today's working poor in China.*

A PLACE IN THE PANTHEON: MAO AND FOLK RELIGION BY XIN YUAN

(Published under a pen name, the Beijing scholar Wang Yi has written on such diverse subjects as traditional Chinese gardens and elements of folk religion in the political culture of the Cultural Revolution. This article appeared in the Hong Kong press at the end of 1992.)

From late last year [1991], China has experienced a craze that has involved the re-deification of Mao Zedong. It started in the South and has spread to the North. People have combined Mao's image with gold cash inscribed with the words "May This Attract Wealth"* or images of the eight hexagrams, and placed them in prominent places. Drivers throughout the country have Mao's picture hanging from their rear-view mirrors and claim that Mao can prevent car accidents. The cassette tape *The Red Sun: Odes to Mao Zedong Sung to a New*

---

*In Chinese, *zhaocai jinbao*.

Xin Yuan, "A Place in the Pantheon: Mao and Folk Religion," and "Musical Chairman," both from Geremie R. Barmé, *Shades of Mao: The Posthumous Cult of the Great Leader* (Armonk, N.Y.: M. E. Sharpe, 1996), 195–200, 283–84.

Beat has been a national best-seller. Mainlanders have variously called this the "Red Sun Phenomenon" or the "Mao Becomes a God Phenomenon." It has also given rise to numerous interpretations among political and cultural analysts.

Political conservatives are trying to dragoon this MaoCraze into the service of their efforts to "oppose peaceful evolution."* Deng Liqun has remarked "with the unprecedented international wave of revisionist thought coupled with the tide of Bourgeois Liberalism in China, we have indeed seen 'a miasmal mist once more rising.'"† But Deng has nothing to say on the subject of why the masses are now treating Mao Zedong like Zhao Gong or the Kitchen God.‡

Intellectuals, on the other hand, see the MaoCraze as evidence that elements of the Cultural Revolution still hold sway and that there's been no rational attempt to understand the long-term damage wrought by that period on the people of China. But such views are all superficial and simplistic. No one has tried to discuss the question in terms of the psychology of folk religion. Therefore, it is obvious that further analysis of the phenomenon is necessary.

The present Mao cult is different from the past in that it constitutes a popular deification of Mao, not a politically orchestrated one. People now seek the protection of the Mao-God when they build houses, engage in business, and drive vehicles. Old ladies place images of Mao over their stoves and in niches built for statues of the Buddha and burn incense to him morning and night. Traditional folk religion provides the real basis for the present Red Sun Craze.

In Chinese culture, the power of the gods is always reliant upon the authority of the ruler. As early as the *Zuozhuan,* in the Record of the Fourteenth Year of Duke Xiang, we find the unequivocal statement: "The ruler is the host of the spirits and the hope of the people."§ Politics and religion formed a mutually cooperative whole or, as [the late-Qing politician and military leader] Zeng Guofan put it, "The way of

---

*"Peaceful evolution" *(helping yanbian)* was officially regarded by the Chinese authorities as being the greatest threat to the communist system. It was supposedly a Western strategy that relied on peaceful rather than violent means—cultural, political and economic—to undermine communism and eventually replace it with a Western-style, free-market democratic government.

†See Deng Liqun, "Permanently On Heat," in *Shades of Mao.*

‡Zhao Gong (Zhao Xuantan, or *Zhao Gong yuanshuai),* the God of Wealth. The Kitchen God *(Zao jun, Zaoshen* or *Zaowang),* the spirit who rules over the hearth, was said to report back to Heaven every Chinese New Year's Eve.

§The *Zuozhuan* is a Confucian historical text of considerable antiquity. For this quotation, see James Legge, *The Chinese Classics (The Chu'un Ts'ew with The Tso Chuen),* p. 466, col. 2, and p. 462 for the Chinese original.

the kings rules in this world; the way of the gods in the other world." Both ways witnessed a plethora of rulers, however, with dynasties rising and falling in the human world and, in the other world, rulers like the Jade Emperor, Maitreya Buddha, and so on, gaining ascendancy at one time or another. The only thing that did not change was the immutable link between politics and religion.

With the communist takeover in 1949, popular religion in China underwent the most violent change in its history. First, in the 1950s, there was a movement to wipe out superstition, which was followed in the 1960s by the call to "eliminate the Four Olds"* and the suppression of virtually all forms of religious activity in the country. The effects were particularly devastating as both movements took place in tandem with the creation of grass-roots Party cells and nationwide Thought Reform. In traditional society, at the county level and lower, political life was ruled by popular clan bodies that also had responsibility for other activities including religious observances. The post-1949 organization of society, however, saw this traditional arrangement uprooted and the monopoly rule of Party committees at every level. Folk religion was deprived entirely of the social and organizational basis for its activities. Nonetheless, habits and practices that have weathered changes over the millennia and provided spiritual succor for people for so long are not so easily obliterated. Frustrated in its traditional form, it is only natural that popular religious sentiment would find new ways to express itself. In post-1949 China, the only sanctified form it could take was in worshipping the Red Sun, Mao Zedong.

The legacy of this intermingling of political and religious life is that the people tend to view divine providence and spiritual power in political terms. . . . Harsh rulers were treated with awe and commemorated in special temples with religious observances by later generations. Because of this venerable tradition Mao's actual sentiment for the people, or his munificence, or even his tyranny that was expressed so succinctly in his line that "for the 800 million Chinese, struggling is a way of life," is not really a major issue.[†] With the consolidation and expansion of his power it was inevitable that he become deified.

*The Four Olds (sijiu) were: old ideas, old culture, old customs, and old habits, the elimination of which was formalized in the Party's 16 Articles on the Cultural Revolution promulgated in 1966.
†This Mao quote was published in a *People's Daily* editorial marking the tenth anniversary of the Cultural Revolution.

Mao's deification was synchronous with his political apotheosis. According to reports in the *Beijing Evening News,* Mao badges made an appearance in and around Yan'an as early as 1945. After 1949, Mao's transmogrification[1] continued apace. . . .

Faith in the omnipresence of nonworldly power was reinforced during the Cultural Revolution. When everything else — all belief systems and cultural norms — was swept away and overthrown, Mao Zedong became the supreme and all-powerful super god, the "Sun that never sets." Mao was invested with a type of power equal, if not superior, to all other religious systems, expressed in such beliefs that he was the Sun, "sustainer of all things," a being who "turned the universe red." Because he was both omnipotent and omnipresent, people felt they could invest themselves with an "ever victorious" power through quasi-religious practices not dissimilar to shamanistic ritual and self-flagellation. They therefore paid homage to his image, sang Mao quotation songs, chanted his sayings, performed the Loyalty Dance, "struggled against self-interest and repudiated revisionism,"* and so on.

Faith in the power of the Red Sun in the Cultural Revolution was very much like ancient shamanistic belief. Both held that the power of the spirit could exorcise evil. In the past, people thought they were surrounded by malevolent forces that had to be subdued or expunged. Similarly, in the Cultural Revolution, there was a general belief that the world was full of evil subsumed under such rubrics as Imperialism and Revisionism, the Five Black Categories, as well as the grab-all expression Cow Demons and Snake Spirits.[†] People lived in constant fear that there could be "a restoration of capitalism," or that they would "have to suffer the bitterness of the past again," or that "millions would die" because of a disastrous counterrevolution. Since the Red Sun was a "Spiritual Atom Bomb" that could dispel all those evils, there is little wonder that the level of popular adoration and worship was so hysterical. The creation of a Red Sea (the ubiquitous displays

[1]*transmogrification:* grotesque or humorous change
*The Loyalty Dance *(zhongzi wu)* was a clumsy choreographic group dance designed to add rhythm to the adulation of Mao. To "struggle against self-interest and repudiate revisionism" *(dousi pixiu)* was a popular mantra that summed up the avowed aims of the Cultural Revolution.
†The Five Black Categories *(hei wulei)* were: landlords, rich peasants, counterrevolutionaries, bad elements, and rightists. Cow Demons and Snake Spirits *(niugui sheshen)* was a classical Chinese expression reinterpreted for the denunciation of people in the early stages of the Cultural Revolution.

of Mao's portrait, his quotations, slogans, and images that represented
devotion to him) was a direct result of the "sweeping away of all Cow
Demons and Snake Spirits" and "the rebellion against Class Enemies"
that had seen the exorcising of evil in the first place. More recently,
Deng Liqun's attempts to use the new MaoCraze as a weapon to repel
the "miasmal mist once more rising" is little more than a continuation
of ancient shamanistic practice.

... Traditional deities live on and this is why we see people
throughout the country, in particular in the countryside, erecting
temples to the God of Wealth, Door Gods, Guan Gong, Boddhisattvas,
the King of Death, and other ancient icons to cure illness, for the
begetting of male children, for help in making money, finding the
right marriage partner, and for scholastic achievement.

The speed with which temples are being restored or built is compa-
rable to the rate at which they were closed and destroyed in the 1950s
and 1960s. According to the television documentary, *A Record of Modern Superstitions: Incense Burning,* broadcast on Beijing TV on 9 February 1990, more than a million people travel to the Southern Peak* to
burn incense each year and spend some 100 million yuan on incense
alone. The *Guangming Daily* has also reported that in recent years
many shamans have appeared in Fang County, Hubei Province. Some
of these are state cadres or retired cadres. Similar reports abound.
Things are more controlled in the cities where years of centralized
education have meant that primitive beliefs have to find new forms for
expression. Because Mao has been the only all-powerful figure for so
long, he was the obvious choice for popular adulation during the
recent religious revival in China. He has become the idol to which the
revived worship of the God of Wealth, Guan Gong, Guanyin Bod-
dhisattva, and other gods is married.

It would seem farcical that Mao, a man who led the assault on capitalism during his lifetime, should in death be put on a par with the
God of Wealth and inscribed with traditional imagery. But the misprision[2] and distortion of gods, their reinvention and reinterpretation, is a
central element of popular religious activity. As was said long ago: "In
a temple that has stood for five generations you can find all manner of
strange things." The [Song dynasty literatus] Ouyang Xiu noted nearly
a thousand years ago that people often misunderstand the spirits they

---

*The Southern Peak *(Nanyue),* is Hengshan in Hunan Province, one of China's Five
Sacred Mountains which feature in popular religious belief.
[2]*misprision:* act of contempt against a superior

worship when he wrote: "Of all distortions in the world those that one finds in a temple are the most extreme."

MUSICAL CHAIRMAN

The floating population, deracinated rural workers and beggars, *mangliu* in Chinese, became an increasingly major social problem as the economic Reforms continued in the 1980s and 1990s. Urban dwellers often spoke of the masses of roving peasants (tens to hundreds of millions depending on what sources you accepted) as being a major threat to social stability and future prosperity. Some *mangliu,* however, believed that it was from their ranks that a new strongman, someone perhaps with the stature of Mao Zedong, would eventually appear to rule the nation.

Mao himself had an early career as a *mangliu* of sorts, details of which are recorded in a book by his companion at the time, Siao-yu.* In the 1990s China's floating population armed itself with the invincible weapon of Mao Thought, or as a popular rhyming saying put it:

Beijing kao zhongyang,
Shanghai kao laoxiang,
Guangzhou kao Xianggang,
Mangliuzi kaode shi Mao Zedong sixiang.

北京靠中央，
上海靠老鄉，
廣州靠香港，
盲流子靠的是毛澤東思想。

Beijing relies on the Center,
Shanghai on its connections,[†]
Guangzhou leans on Hong Kong,
The drifting population lives by Mao Zedong Thought.[‡]

---

[*]Siao-yu, *Mao Tse-tung and I Were Beggars. A Personal Memoir of the Early Years of Chairman Mao.*

[†]Beijing relies on the power of Party Central to protect it and prosper; Shanghai on all the officials in Beijing of Shanghai provenance (the so-called "Shanghai Gang": Jiang Zemin, Zhu Rongji, Huang Ju, and so on).

[‡]In "Sailing the Seas Depends on the Helmsman" *(Dahai hangxing kao duoshou),* the unofficial anthem of the Cultural Revolution, there is a line that goes: "The Revolutionary Masses rely on Mao Zedong Thought" *(geming qunzhong kaode shi Mao Zedong sixiang).*

A China Chronology (1893–1976)

1893 Mao born to a farming family in Hunan province.

1895 China defeated by Japan in the Sino-Japanese War.

1900 Boxer Rebellion and counterattack by foreign powers.

1905 Qing dynasty ends the civil service exams.

1911 Republican revolution; fall of the Qing dynasty.

1912 General Yuan Shikai replaces Sun Yat-sen as president of the republic.

1913 Sun Yat-sen founds the Guomindang (GMD), or Nationalist party.

1915–
1925 New Culture Movement.

1919 May Fourth Movement in Beijing opposes the Versailles treaty.

1921 Official founding of the Chinese Communist party (CCP) in Shanghai; Mao Zedong is one of the founding members.

1923 CCP and GMD cooperate in the first united front; Mao then works in the GMD Propaganda Department and the Peasant Training Institute.

1925 Sun Yat-sen dies; Chiang Kai-shek eventually takes over the GMD.

1926 Northern Expedition under GMD leadership starts out from Guangzhou in southern China to reunify the country. Mao returns to Hunan to work in the countryside.

1927 Mao writes his "Report on the Peasant Movement in Hunan." Chiang Kai-shek turns against the CCP and in April massacres CCP activists.

GMD forms a new national government and moves the capital of the Republic of China to Nanjing.

1930 Changsha uprising, led by Mao, fails; Mao moves to develop rural soviets.

1931 Japanese begin to occupy northeast China and will declare Manchukuo a separate country the next year.

Formal establishment of the Jiangxi soviet; Mao elected chairman of the soviet.

1931–
1934 GMD national government launches five "encirclement campaigns" to destroy the Communist party and Jiangxi soviet; CCP survives the first four.

1934 Communists flee the Jiangxi soviet and set off on the Long March.

1935 Mao gains a central leadership position in the CCP at the Zunyi Conference during the Long March.

1936 Communists make their new capital at Yan'an, in the northwest province of Shaanxi.

1936–
1947 Yan'an period, during which Mao consolidates his supreme position and develops policies that lead to CCP victory in 1949.

1937 Japan invades China, beginning World War II in Asia.

1942–
1944 Yan'an Rectification Movement promotes Mao's ideas and leadership.

1945 Japan formally surrenders to the Allies on September 9, ending World War II.

1945–
1949 Chinese civil war between the CCP and GMD.

1949 CCP declares a new national government, the People's Republic of China (PRC), with Mao as its head.

1950 **February** China and the Soviet Union sign the Treaty of Friendship, Alliance, and Mutual Assistance.

October Chinese forces enter Korea, joining the Korean War.

1952 Land reform completed in most areas of China.

1955 First Five-Year Plan (1953–57) formally adopted to organize China's planned economy.

Nationwide mass campaign to criticize two intellectuals, Hu Shi and Hu Feng.

1956 Khrushchev denounces Stalin in the USSR.

Mao calls for public criticism of the CCP in the Hundred Flowers Campaign, but the response is muted.

CCP holds its Eighth Party Congress in Beijing; celebrates successes of the PRC.

1957 **February** Mao delivers his speech "On the Correct Handling of Contradictions among the People" to boost the Hundred Flowers Campaign.

May   Hundred Flowers Campaign blooms, but with biting criticism of the CCP.

June   Anti-Rightist Campaign attacks those who spoke up in the Hundred Flowers Campaign; Mao's "Contradictions" speech is published in a highly edited form.

1958   CCP adopts Mao's Great Leap Forward plan.

August   Mao's talks at Beidaihe popularize collectivization of agriculture in the people's communes.

1959   Uprising in Tibet against Chinese rule is suppressed by the People's Liberation Army (PLA).

April   Liu Shaoqi succeeds Mao as state chairman (Mao remains as party chairman).

August   Peng Dehuai criticizes the Great Leap Forward and is purged, showing that Mao can no longer be criticized even by his senior colleagues.

1960   Soviet Union withdraws all experts from China.

Famine deepens in China.

1961   CCP begins economic and political reforms to undo the damage of the Great Leap Forward.

1964   China explodes its atomic bomb.

1966   Cultural Revolution begins as an attack on Beijing party intellectuals but quickly spreads to the purge of senior party leaders, including, by 1967, Liu Shaoqi.

Mao writes a big-character poster, "Bombard the Headquarters," to encourage Red Guards to attack "the four olds" and "to rebel is justified"; Red Guard terror begins.

1969   Mao declares the "victory" (that is, end) of the Cultural Revolution and supports General Lin Biao as his new successor; radical policies continue.

1971 July   U.S. secretary of state Henry Kissinger secretly visits Beijing.

September   Lin Biao dies in a plane crash while trying to escape Mao's secret police; he is formally denounced.

October   China joins the United Nations, leading to the expulsion of Taiwan.

1972   U.S. president Richard Nixon visits China.

1976 January   Zhou Enlai, the highest ranking moderate in the CCP, dies.

September   Mao Zedong dies.

Questions for Consideration

1. How would you sum up Mao Zedong's life? Try making a list of dichotomies: Mao as hero vs. Mao as demon, Mao as state founder vs. Mao as voice of the people, Mao as thinker vs. Mao as actor, or Mao as historical figure vs. Mao as living icon. What other contrasts can you find?

2. Consider the different objects of Mao's attention in the three periods covered in our selections: social movements in the 1920s, state power and nationalism in the 1940s, and problems of administration and development in the 1950s and 1960s. Why did Mao's focus shift? What continuities do you find in Mao's writings over these years?

3. In what ways do the concrete policy suggestions and ways of looking at the world suggested in Mao's major writings before 1949 address the issues of imperialism and how to deal with the West — issues that confronted China so forcefully by 1900?

4. What experiences informed Mao's approach to rural revolution? Compare the picture Mao gave Snow (see Document 11) with other accounts of Mao's early life.

5. Why did Mao take the oppression of women and youths seriously? How did their liberation fit into his model of revolution? What became of Mao's "feminism"? Did the CCP follow his lead on women's and youth liberation over the years? Did Mao himself return to this theme in his later writings?

6. Why were the ideals for China outlined by Mao in "On New Democracy" (see Document 2) attractive to China's students and urban middle class in the 1940s?

7. Who were Mao's competitors for top leadership in the CCP in the 1940s, and how did his Yan'an writings (see Documents 2–4) answer their challenge? How did these writings function in the 1942–44 Rectification Movement?

8. How does Mao's view on revolutionary leadership (see Document 4) relate to his philosophical method, as explained in Document 13?

9. What issues confronted the ruling CCP in 1956? How did Mao try to address them in "On the Correct Handling of Contradictions among the People" (Document 7)? Why was Mao out of synch with his senior colleagues in the CCP?

10. How do Mao's Beidaihe talks of 1958 (see Document 8) compare with his Yan'an talks (see Documents 2–4)? Look at the contextual readings, such as Li Zhisui in Document 14 and Stuart Schram in Document 12, as you consider what contributed to these differences.

11. Why is it so difficult to separate Mao from the CCP today? Consider, for example, the party resolution of 1981 in Document 16 and popular views in the 1990s in Document 18.

12. How does the Mao cult, especially in the Cultural Revolution (see Documents 10 and 15) compare and contrast with other notable leadership cults of the twentieth century, such as Stalin's, Hitler's, or Mussolini's?

13. Land reform, or "land to the tiller," was a key issue for developmental states in the twentieth century. How did CCP policy and practice change from the 1940s to the 1960s to the 1980s?

14. Developmental states need to find a way to link an elite that can function in an international environment defined by Western science, legal norms, and commercial practices with a majority agrarian population that often holds radically different attitudes, values, and practices that are contrary to those international norms. How did Mao and the CCP try to bridge this gap?

15. Developmental states must find a way to achieve security—both international respect and domestic order. What were Mao's answers to these fundamental state questions?

Selected Bibliography

This bibliography gives a taste of the scholarship on Mao and his context.

MOVIES AND DRAMA

The images of films (many now available on video) and modern plays are an effective way to present the history of Mao's times and to give a sense of how various Chinese experienced Mao's revolutions. The movie *Huozhe* (To Live) by Zhang Yimo is a vivid account of a commoner's life through these years. It is readily available on video (with subtitles). Chen Kaige's *Farewell My Concubine* provides a parallel history from the perspective of the Chinese intellectual and artistic elite. *Small Well Lane,* a play written by Li Longyun and translated by Hong Jiang and Timothy Cheek (Ann Arbor: University of Michigan Press, 2002), is the compelling story of how people in a small Beijing neighborhood experienced Mao's revolutions from the 1940s to the 1980s.

BIBLIOGRAPHIES AND GUIDES

The best bibliography for those new to China studies is Charles Hayford, *China* (Santa Barbara, Calif.: Clio Press, 1997). There are several other fine bibliographies, such as the *Bibliography of Asian Studies,* available at research and college libraries.

The only English index of topics and names in Mao's works is John Bryan Starr and Nancy Anne Dyer, *Post-Liberation Works of Mao Zedong: A Bibliography and Index* (Berkeley: Center for Chinese Studies, University of California, 1979). However, the indexes in the comprehensive series of Mao's works in English by Schram and by Kau and Leung (see "Mao's Writings") are also useful.

Handy historical dictionaries with short entries on names, terms, and events in China's revolutions include the following:

He, Henry Yuhuai, *Dictionary of the Political Thought of the People's Republic of China* (Armonk, N.Y.: M. E. Sharpe, 2001).

Leung, Edwin Pak-wah, ed., *Historical Dictionary of Revolutionary China, 1839–1976* (Westport, Conn.: Greenwood Press, 1992).

Schoppa, R. Keith, *The Columbia Guide to Modern Chinese History* (New York: Columbia University Press, 2000).

Sullivan, Lawrence R., with Nancy Hearst, eds., *Historical Dictionary of the People's Republic of China: 1949–1997* (Lanham, Md.: Scarecrow Press, 1997).

TEXTBOOKS

Fairbank, John King, and Merle Goldman, *China: A New History* (Cambridge: Harvard University Press, 1998).

Lieberthal, Kenneth, *Governing China: From Revolution through Reform* (New York: W. W. Norton, 1995).

Saich, Tony, *Governance and Politics of China* (London and New York: Palgrave, 2001).

Spence, Jonathan, *The Search for Modern China,* 2nd ed. (New York: W. W. Norton, 2000).

MAO'S WRITINGS

The standard edition from China is *Selected Works.* There are now major scholarly editions of all periods of Mao's writings in English, which also include guides to the Chinese sources and interpretive issues.

Kau, Michael Y. M., and John K. Leung, eds., *The Writings of Mao Zedong, 1949–1976,* 2 vols. (Armonk, N.Y.: M. E. Sharpe, 1986, 1992).

MacFarquhar, Roderick, Timothy Cheek, and Eugene Wu, eds., *The Secret Speeches of Chairman Mao: From the Hundred Flowers to the Great Leap Forward* (Cambridge: Harvard Contemporary China Series, 1989).

Schram, Stuart, *The Political Thought of Mao Tse-tung,* rev. ed. (New York: Praeger, 1969).

Schram, Stuart, *Mao Tse-tung Unrehearsed: Talks and Letters 1956–1971* (Harmondsworth: Penguin, 1974).

Schram, Stuart R., and Nancy J. Hodes, eds., *Mao's Road to Power: Revolutionary Writings, 1912–1949* (Armonk, N.Y.: M. E. Sharpe, 1992–).

Selected Works of Mao Tse-tung (Peking: Foreign Languages Press, vols. 1–4, 1975; vol. 5, 1977). Available on-line at <http://www.marx2mao. org/Mao/Index.html>.

BIOGRAPHIES AND STUDIES OF MAO

There are numerous studies of Mao, but these are among the best. Of the three fine short biographies (Breslin, Davis, and Spence), Spence's is the most engaging. Schram's classic study, *Mao Tse-tung,* still repays reading. There are also a number of useful specialized studies. This section ends with some of the more thoughtful scholarly essays that assess these and other studies and put them in the context of scholarly opinion.

Breslin, Shaun, *Mao: Profiles in Power* (London: Longman, 1998).
Davin, Delia, *Mao Zedong* (Phoenix Mill: Sutton Publishing, 1997).
Dirlik, Arif, Paul Healy, and Nick Knight, *Critical Perspectives on Mao Zedong's Thought* (Atlantic Highlands, N.J.: Humanities Press, 1997).
Martin, Helmut, *Cult & Canon: The Origins and Development of State Maoism* (Armonk, N.Y.: M. E. Sharpe, 1982).
Schram, Stuart, *Mao Tse-tung*, rev. ed. (Harmondsworth: Penguin, 1967).
Schram, Stuart, *The Thought of Mao Tse-tung* (Cambridge: Cambridge University Press, 1989).
Spence, Jonathan, *Mao Zedong* (New York: Viking Penguin, 1999).
Starr, John Bryan, *Continuing the Revolution: The Political Thought of Mao* (Princeton: Princeton University Press, 1979).
Wakeman, Frederic, Jr., *History and Will: Philosophical Perspectives on Mao Tse-tung's Thought* (Berkeley: University of California Press, 1973).
Womack, Brantly, *The Foundations of Mao Tse-tung's Political Thought* (Honolulu: University of Hawaii Press, 1982).

Knight, Nick, "Mao and History: Who Judges and How?" *Australian Journal of Chinese Affairs,* no. 13 (January 1985): 121–36.
Scharping, Thomas, "The Man, the Myth, the Message—New Trends in Mao-Literature from China," *The China Quarterly,* no. 137 (1994): 168–79.
Schram, Stuart, "Mao Zedong a Hundred Years On: The Legacy of a Ruler," *The China Quarterly,* no. 137 (1994): 125–43.
Wasserstrom, Jeffrey N., "Mao Matters: A Review Essay," *China Review International,* vol. 3, no. 1 (1996): 1–21.
Womack, Brantly, "Mao Zedong Thoughts," *The China Quarterly,* no. 137 (1994): 159–67.
Womack, Brantly, "Mao before Maoism," *The Chinese Journal,* no. 46 (July 2001): 95–117.

CHINA'S REVOLUTIONS AND MAO

Long-Term Perspectives

Mao's contributions and faults can most fully be appreciated with an awareness of some long-term perspectives in Chinese history, as well as a sense of how Americans report on China. These are some challenging studies.

Jespersen, T. Christopher, *American Images of China: 1931–1949* (Stanford: Stanford University Press, 1996).

Levinson, Joseph, *Confucian China and Its Modern Fate* (Berkeley: University of California Press, 1968).

MacKinnon, Stephen, and Oris Friesen, *China Reporting: An Oral History of American Journalism in the 1930s and 1940s* (Berkeley: University of California Press, 1987).

Pussey, James, *China and Charles Darwin* (Cambridge: Harvard Council on East Asian Studies, 1983).

Schwartz, Benjamin I., *In Search of Wealth and Power: Yen Fu and the West* (Cambridge: Harvard University Press, 1964).

Wong, R. Bin, *China Transformed: Historical Change and the Limits of European Experience* (Ithaca: Cornell University Press, 1997).

Chinese Communist Party History

These fine studies and documentary collections give a sense of when and why Mao was in synch and out of synch with the Communist party (if not the broader Chinese population).

Guillermaz, Jacques, *A History of the Chinese Communist Party 1922–49* (New York: Random House, 1972).

Hartford, Kathleen, and Steven M. Goldstein, *Single Sparks: China's Rural Revolutions* (Armonk, N.Y.: M. E. Sharpe, 1989).

Hunt, Michael H., *The Genesis of Chinese Communist Foreign Policy* (New York: Columbia University Press, 1996).

Lampton, David M., *Same Bed Different Dreams: Managing U.S.-China Relations* (Berkeley: University of California Press, 2001).

Roy, Denny, *China's Foreign Relations* (Lanham, Md.: Rowman & Littlefield, 1998).

Saich, Tony, *The Rise to Power of the Chinese Communist Party: Documents and Analysis* (Armonk, N.Y.: M. E. Sharpe, 1996).

Teiwes, Frederick C., *Politics and Purges in China: Rectification and the Decline of Party Norms, 1950–1965,* 2nd ed. (Armonk, N.Y.: M. E. Sharpe, 1993).

1920s–1930s

Dirlik, Arif, *Anarchism in the Chinese Revolution* (Berkeley: University of California Press, 1991).

Jui, Li, *The Early Revolutionary Activities of Comrade Mao Tse-tung* (White Plains, N.Y.: M. E. Sharpe, 1977).

Saich, Tony, and Hans J. van de Ven, eds., *New Perspectives on the Chinese Communist Revolution* (Armonk, N.Y.: M. E. Sharpe, 1995).

Stranahan, Patricia, *Underground: The Shanghai Communist Party and the Politics of Survival, 1927–1937* (Lanham, Md.: Rowman & Littlefield, 1998).

van de Ven, Hans J., *From Friend to Comrade: The Chinese Communist Party, 1920–1927* (Berkeley: University of California Press, 1991).

Yang, Benjamin, *From Revolution to Politics: Chinese Communists on the Long March* (Boulder, Colo.: Westview Press, 1990).

1940s

Apter, David E., and Tony Saich, *Revolutionary Discourse in Mao's Republic* (Cambridge: Harvard University Press, 1994).

Dai Qing, *Wang Shiwei and "Wild Lilies": Rectification and Purges in the Chinese Communist Party, 1942–1944* (Armonk, N.Y.: M. E. Sharpe, 1994).

Goldman, Merle, *Literary Dissent in Communist China* (Cambridge: Harvard University Press, 1967).

Levine, Steven I., *Anvil of Victory: The Communist Revolution in Manchuria, 1945–1948* (New York: Columbia University Press, 1987).

Pepper, Suzanne, *Civil War in China: The Political Struggle, 1945–49* (Berkeley: University of California Press, 1978).

Selden, Mark, *China in Revolution: The Yenan Way Revisited* (Armonk, N.Y.: M. E. Sharpe, 1995).

Watson, Andrew, *Mao Zedong and the Political Economy of the Border Region* (Cambridge: Cambridge University Press, 1980).

Wylie, Raymond F., *The Emergence of Maoism: Mao Tse-tung, Ch'en Po-ta, and the Search for Chinese Theory, 1935–1945* (Stanford: Stanford University Press, 1980).

People's Republic of China

Barmé, Geremie R., *Shades of Mao: The Posthumous Cult of the Great Leader* (Armonk, N.Y.: M. E. Sharpe, 1996).

Chan, Anita, Richard Madsen, and Jonathan Unger, *Chen Village under Mao and Deng,* updated ed. (Berkeley: University of California Press, 1992).

Cheek, Timothy, and Tony Saich, eds., *New Perspectives on State Socialism in China* (Armonk, N.Y.: M. E. Sharpe, 1997).

Davies, Gloria, ed., *Voicing Concerns: Contemporary Chinese Critical Inquiry* (Lanham, Md.: Rowman & Littlefield, 2001).

Landsberger, Stefan, *Chinese Propaganda Posters: From Revolution to Modernization* (Armonk, N.Y.: M. E. Sharpe, 1995).

MacFarquhar, Roderick, *The Origins of the Cultural Revolution,* vols. 1–3 (New York: Columbia University Press, 1974–97).

Meisner, Maurice, *Mao's China and After* (New York: Free Press, 1986).

Schoenhals, Michael, ed., *China's Cultural Revolution, 1966–1969: Not a Dinner Party* (Armonk, N.Y.: M. E. Sharpe, 1996).

Schrift, Melissa, *Biography of a Chairman Mao Badge: The Creation and Mass Consumption of a Personality Cult* (New Brunswick, N.J.: Rutgers University Press, 2001).

Yan Jiaqi and Gao Gao, *Turbulent Decade: A History of the Cultural Revolution,* trans. and ed. D. W. Y. Kwok (Honolulu: University of Hawaii Press, 1996).

Acknowledgments

Geremie R. Barmé. "Shades of Mao." From *Shades of Mao: The Posthumous Cult of the Great Leader.* Copyright © 1996 by Geremie R. Barmé. Reprinted by permission of M. E. Sharpe, Inc., Armonk, NY 10504.

Jack Belden. "Land and Revolution." From *China Shakes the World* by Jack Belden. Copyright © 1949 by Jack Belden. Reprinted by permission.

Michael Bullock and Jerome Ch'en. "Snow." From *Mao and the Chinese Revolution,* translated and edited by Michael Bullock and Jerome Ch'en. Oxford University Press, London, 1965. Reprinted by permission.

Central Committee on the Chinese Communist Party. "Some Questions on Party History, June 1981." Translation from *Beijing Review,* July 6, 1981. Foreign Language Bureau, Beijing Review Publishing Company.

Boyd Compton. "Resolution of the Central Committee of the Chinese Communist Party on Methods of Leadership, June 1, 1943." From *Mao's China: Party Reform Documents 1942–1944,* edited and translated by Boyd Compton. Copyright © 1952 by Boyd Compton. Reprinted by permission of the University of Washington Press.

Nick Knight. "Mao Zedong's 'Sinification of Marxism.'" From *Marxism in Asia,* edited by Colin Mackerras and Nick Knight. Copyright © 1985 by Colin Mackerras and Nick Knight. Reprinted with the permission of St. Martin's Press.

Li Zhisui. "The Emperor of Zhongnanhai, 1994." From *The Private Life of Chairman Mao,* translated and edited by Tai Hung-chao. Copyright © 1994 by Tai Hung-chao. Reprinted with permission of Random House, Inc.

Roderick MacFarquhar, Timothy Cheek, and Eugene Wu. "Talks at the Beidaihe Conference, August 1958." Excerpts from *The Secret Speeches of Chairman Mao: From the Hundred Flowers to the Great Leap Forward,* translated and edited by Roderick MacFarquhar, Timothy Cheek, and Eugene Wu. Copyright © 1989 by the Harvard University Asia Center. Reprinted by permission.

Mao Zedong. "On the Correct Handling of Contradictions among the People, June 1957." Translated from *Selected Works of Mao Tse-tung.* Foreign Language Press, 1977. "Bombarded the Headquarters." (New China News Agency, August 4, 1967). Translated from *Quotations from Chairman Mao Tse-tung,* Foreign Language Press, 1968.

Bonnie S. McDougall. "Talks at the Yan'an Conference on Literature and Art: A Translation of the 1943 Text with Commentary." Copyright © 1980 by the Center for Chinese Studies, The University of Michigan. Reprinted with permission.

243

Rae Yang. "At the Center of the Storm." From *Spider Eaters: A Memoir.* Copyright © 1997 The Regents of the University of California. Reprinted by permission of the University of California Press.

Michael Schoenhals. Excerpt from *China's Cultural Revolution 1966–1969: Not a Dinner Party.* Reprinted by permission of M. E. Sharpe, Inc., Armonk, NY 10504.

Stuart R. Schram and Nancy J. Hodes. "Report on the Peasant Movement in Hunan, February 1927." From *Mao's Road to Power: Revolutionary Writings, 1912–1949: Volume II: National Revolution and Social Revolution, December 1920–June 1927,* translated and edited by Stuart R. Schram and Nancy J. Hodes. Copyright © 1994. Reprinted by permission from M. E. Sharpe, Inc., Armonk, NY 10504.

Stuart R. Schram and Nancy J. Hodes. "On New Democracy, January 15, 1940." From *Mao's Road to Power: Revolutionary Writings, 1912–1949: Volume VII, 1940–1941,* translated and edited by Stuart R. Schram and Nancy J. Hodes. Reprinted by permission from M. E. Sharpe, Inc., Armonk, NY 10504.

Stuart R. Schram. "The Chinese People Have Stood Up, September 1949," "American Imperialism Is Closely Surrounded by the Peoples of the World, 1964." From *The Political Thought of Mao Tse-tung,* Second Edition, translated and edited by Stuart R. Schram. Copyright © 1969 Praeger Publishers, a division of Greenwood Publishing Group. Reprinted by permission.

Stuart R. Schram. "Just a Few Words (Talk at the Central Work Conference), October 25, 1966," "The Struggle on Two Fronts, 1967." From *Mao Tse-tung Unrehearsed: Talks and Letters 1956–1971,* translated by Stuart R. Schram. © 1967 Penguin Books Ltd. Reprinted by permission.

Edgar Snow. "Interview with Mao." From *Red Star Over China* by Edgar Snow. Copyright © 1968 by Edgar Snow. Used by permission of Grove/Atlantic, Inc.

Jeffrey Wasserstrom. "Mao Matters." From *China Review International,* vol. 3, no. 1 (Spring 1996). Copyright © 1996 University of Hawaii Press. Reprinted with permission.

Index

245